MY MELANCHOLY BABY

Michael G. Garber

My Melancholy Baby

THE FIRST BALLADS OF THE GREAT AMERICAN SONGBOOK, 1902–1913

Michael G. Garber

University Press of Mississippi / Jackson

The University Press of Mississippi is the scholarly publishing agency of
the Mississippi Institutions of Higher Learning: Alcorn State University,
Delta State University, Jackson State University, Mississippi State University,
Mississippi University for Women, Mississippi Valley State University,
University of Mississippi, and University of Southern Mississippi.

www.upress.state.ms.us

Designed by Peter D. Halverson

The University Press of Mississippi is a member of
the Association of University Presses.

First printing 2021

∞

Library of Congress Control Number: 2021938307

Hardback ISBN 978-1-4968-3429-4
Trade paperback ISBN 978-1-4968-3430-0
Epub single ISBN 978-1-4968-3431-7
Epub institutional ISBN 978-1-4968-3432-4
PDF single ISBN 978-1-4968-3433-1
PDF institutional ISBN 978-1-4968-3428-7

British Library Cataloging-in-Publication Data available

Dedicated to
Amey Acheson Geier Garber and John Michael Garber (my parents)
and Dr. John Diamond
and Susan Joyce Carpenter

CONTENTS

CHAPTER SEVEN
"Some of These Days"
115

CHAPTER EIGHT
"The Sweetheart of Sigma Chi" and the Power of a Subculture
The Strange History of the American Waltz, Part Five
148

CHAPTER NINE
"My Melancholy Baby"
155

CHAPTER TEN
"When I Lost You" and the Muse of Friendship
The Strange History of the American Waltz, Part Six
197

CHAPTER ELEVEN
"You Made Me Love You"
216

CHAPTER TWELVE
Conclusion: Authors and Torch Songs
255

APPENDIX
A Summary of the Development of the Personal, Intimate, and Internal
260

ACKNOWLEDGMENTS

Along with my dedicatees, acknowledgments to Susan Burghardt Diamond; Peter C. Muir; Larry Starr; Howard Pollack; Jan-Piet Knijff; Ivan Hunter; Joanne Vun; Brendan Blendall; John Spitzer; Ben Sears; Brad Connor; Anna Wheeler Gentry; George Ferencz; William Everett; Paul Laird; Rick Altman (Charles F. Altman); Paul Charosh; John Graziano; Jonas Westover; Miles Kreuger; Eric Davis; Amy Asch; Robert Kimball; Edward Berlin; Thomas Riis; Debra Caplan; Katherine Hollander; Alisa Sniderman; Claire Solomon; Alexandra Ripp; Julius Novick; David A. Jasen; Tony Haggert; Lloyd Ecker; Sue Ecker; Mark Cantor; John Spitzer; David Troy; Ann Jennifer Mastrogiovanni; Jeanne Graves; Rick De Croix; Edwin M. Bradley; Jeanine Basinger; Erinna Delaney and her family, in Ireland; Vivian and Yvonne Robbins, of Buxton, Canada; Noah Phelps and Bill Fleming, of Sigma Chi.

My siblings—Katherine, Amey, John, Elizabeth—and their partners and spouses.

All the older adults who have sung these songs with me or consented to be interviewed.

All the friends and relatives who have talked and sung their way through this material with me.

All who played or sang with the Diamond Jubilators jazz band.

My students in *Great Broadway Songwriters* at Purchase College in 2009.

The anonymous peer reviewers and the editors of my article on "Some of These Days"; my unpublished article on torch songs and crooning; and this book.

Attendees for my papers presented at the Song Stage Screen conferences in 2009 and 2014.

Librarians and staff of (among others) the New York Public Library for the Performing Arts; the Museum of the City of New York; the Library of Congress, including Wayne Shirley, Karen Moses (who found Watson's original lyric for "My Melancholy Baby"), David Sager, Mark Horowitz, James Wintle, and Harrison Behl; the Shubert Archive, including Maryann Chach; the American Music Center at the University of Colorado at Boulder; and State University of New York, Purchase College.

. . . it took a village!

A NOTE TO THE READER

In this book, I look at history, analyze music and lyrics, interpret recordings, and explore how a set of songs are used in plays, movies, and literature. Each chapter is organized, more or less, in this sequence: first, history; then analysis; then recordings; finally, plays/movies/literature.

I am interdisciplinary, writing for several audiences and going into a lot of detail. Please feel free to skip around, following your own interests. If you are more intrigued by history, focus on those parts. If you like song analysis, dwell on those sections. If you want a companion for listening to recordings, jump to that section of the chapter. If you like narrative analysis, linger on each final subsection. In the introduction, I may cover things you already know (if you are an aficionado of old songs)—if so, just speed ahead to the next subsection.

There is a summary of part of my discussion in the Appendix at the end.

Above all: Enjoy!

PREFACE

I fell in love with old popular songs when I was twelve. They had been in my ears all my life, but I had never paid any particular attention to them. My parents and four older siblings had already well worn the vinyl grooves of Peggy Lee's *Jump for Joy*, Frank Sinatra's *Come Dance with Me*, and the soundtrack of *The Music Man*; therefore, I surmise that I must have heard these songs in the womb. My mother lulled me to sleep with "Can't Help Lovin' That Man of Mine" and "I've Got My Love to Keep Me Warm." Nevertheless, my tastes remained unfocused, because around my ears swirled folk, soul, British Invasion, classical, and international ethnic musics. Then, one autumn, my eldest sister took me to a screening of Fred Astaire and Ginger Rogers's *Swing Time*, and another sister extracted from a moving box our old copy of *Ella Fitzgerald Sings the Harold Arlen Songbook*. The result: I became a lifetime aficionado of Broadway, Hollywood, and jazz songs.

During my first year of enthusiasm, I was enraptured by the driving rhythm songs, the sparkling charm songs, and the witty comedy songs. The slow love songs bored me. I had not had the kind of music-listening experience Gregory F. Pickering described in his psychological study of this repertoire: "I found myself feeling inside myself. It was as if the world had receded somewhat and I was 'me-here-inside.' I felt inside in the sense, yes, of separate and alone, but also in the sense of a delicious kind of homecoming."[1] Then, in my thirteenth summer, one afternoon with headphones on, I listened to "My Funny Valentine" sung by Ella Fitzgerald. For the first time, I understood these ballads carry a sense of inner life—and help us feel our own inner life.

Since that afternoon, I have appreciated that the ballads—the slow, serious songs—are the core. Rhythm songs may be the swaying hips and striding legs. Charm songs may be the playful mind. Comedy songs may be the witty tongue. But love songs are the tenderly enfolding arms, the heart and soul of this tradition. Thus, this book is about personal ballads.

TERMINOLOGY

One of the oddities of this repertoire is that it has no widely agreed-upon name. At the time of its flourishing it was simply considered *the* popular music by the mainstream media. The terms people have used since the 1970s tend to be either too limited or a bit presumptuous. "Songs of Tin Pan Alley, Broadway and Hollywood" tries to encompass it all but leaves out the crucial worlds of jazz and blues—and the country-western field that often shared repertoire with the others.[2] Just after 1900, "Tin Pan Alley" became an umbrella term for the popular music publishing industry. Nevertheless, the label really should include those who, in the 1880s and 1890s, pioneered new, aggressive practices in the music printing business—that first generation whom critics generally ignore in favor of the second- through fourth-generation Alley songwriters.[3] Not all songs from Broadway and Hollywood would fit into the category we are talking about.[4] "Jazz standards" also presents problems.[5] Many songs have been enduringly popular without having been much performed by jazz artists—for instance, "When I Lost You," the focus of chapter 10. Also, many jazz standards are instrumental pieces. Further, each style of jazz has its own repertoire, although those often overlap.[6]

"The Golden Age of American Popular Song," "the Great American Song-book," "classic American popular song" (and its short form, "classic pop"), "popular standards," "Songs of the Golden Era"—all these assume a kind of primacy for the Tin Pan Alley songs of circa 1920 to 1950.[7] In my heart I agree with that evaluation—that is the reason I am writing this book. Nevertheless, my more rational self realizes that other people might apply these terms to other repertoires with weighty arguments to back up their opinions. Indeed, even as a die-hard Tin Pan Alley lover, I often think the best musical genre is the one that I happen to be listening to at any one moment. African, Indian, Aboriginal Australian, European, American, classical or popular, country-western, operetta, rock and roll, soul, folk, protest—whatever I hear, it often seems like it is "classic," "great," or of a "golden age." Therefore, I employ these terms for convenience, without necessarily advocating for their continued use.

I will often use the terms *ballad* and *love song* and *torch song*. Writers and musicians are not consistent in how they define and bandy about such terms. For me, when discussing the classic pop genre, a *ballad* is defined, primarily, by its slow tempo and, secondarily, by an underlying seriousness to its lyric.[8] However, part of the strength of this genre is that songs elude categorization and labels evade definition. This is a result of the freedom—the promise of freedom—contained in jazz and other American popular music genres. It is that very fluidity in American pop that is one of my main topics.

Some writers equate *ballads* with *love songs*—but *love song* is more logically delimited by a lyric about romantic love and, therefore, could be of any speed or playfulness.[9] In parallel, many of the most famous ballads do not concern romantic love, such as "Over the Rainbow" (1939) and "White Christmas" (1942). I spotlight the development of the *love ballad*. Among the many qualities that can be found in love ballads, I focus here on three: the personal ("I and you"); the intimate ("I and you are close emotionally or physically"); and the internal ("there is a landscape of feeling inside me").

Around 1927, the term *torch song* developed (stemming from slang that figures love as a flame). The inconsistency in applying this label is extreme. Many writers define such songs as ballads about unrequited love.[10] Yet, the more cautious qualify this by saying "typically," "generally," or "usually"—wisely, for the works put in this category rarely fall into such strict limits.[11] In the chapters that follow, I will draw on but also challenge that narrow definition until, in my conclusion, the result will be a fresh perspective. In the meanwhile, I will let songwriters Al Dubin and Harry Warren, interviewed in 1933, supply me with a working definition. They state that torch lyrics are suffused with "a longing for something you haven't got," with an accompanying "melody that matches the sentiment" which "is extremely plaintive" (sad, sorrowful, mournful) and "fairly dramatic."[12] As was noted almost from the start, many songs can be sung *as* a torch song—or not.[13] Again, their capacity to be interpreted in different ways is part of their magic—and part of the story I will unfold.

COLLECTIVITY VERSUS THE "GREAT MAN"

While still young, I absorbed Alec Wilder's seminal analysis and appreciation, *American Popular Songs*.[14] I accepted Wilder's opinions, and I sought out the songs he praised and explored the output of the composers he deemed the "great innovators." Eventually, my youthful "great man/great song" view of the popular standards was disrupted by two experiences.

First, I began to go into nursing homes and sing with the residents. I discovered that when I am holding their hands, gazing in their eyes, and trying to encourage them to sing, at that moment "Let Me Call You Sweetheart" has more value than the most sophisticated Broadway song. In this context, I had to evaluate a completely different repertoire of "great songs" from the ones celebrated in the ballad-with-a-beat albums I had memorized (such as Sinatra's *Come Dance with Me*), the nightclubs I haunted, and the critical histories over which I pored. In the nightclub, the great Cole Porter ballad is "I've Got You Under My Skin." In the nursing home, the great Cole Porter ballad is "True Love." Part of a song's value is how useful it is within a specific context.

Second, I came to this realization: tens of thousands of everyday Tin Pan Alley songs were necessary for the creation of hundreds of songs that transcended triteness. Reynold Wolf reported in 1913 that Irving Berlin "turns out an average of three songs a week. . . . By a process of elimination about one in ten is finally published."[15] Of those published, only a few became hits. Of those that became hits, only a few endured in active repertoire. Run-of-the-mill songs—whether half-successful or unsuccessful, merely slightly imbalanced or downright lame—undergird the great ones.[16]

My vision does not only include the lesser works of each master. I also see that Berlin and the other elite writers did not only stand on the shoulders of the giants of music *before* them; they also stood on the shoulders of the crowd of their contemporaries *around* them. The presence of the jostling crowd filled them all with enthusiasm: their creativity exploded in a chain reaction.

SCOPE, CORPUS, SOURCES, AND METHODOLOGY

An odd kink in the winding history of copyright law kept luring me on: songs copyrighted or printed through 1922 had fallen into the public domain in the United States.[17] These songs now belong to the *public*—to you, me, and future generations, to do with as we will. The public domain status of early Tin Pan Alley works has enabled university libraries to post online digitized sheet music of many of the songs I required for this study—and of further songs that supplied additional context. (It also means I can print the extracts in this book without any extensive waiting period and costs for permission from copyright holders.)

After determining to explore the early twentieth-century repertoire, I had to decide which specific songs to study. To choose my corpus, I spent several years surveying recordings and discographies, histories and critical literature, sheet music and songbooks, stage and movie musicals, old newspapers and new websites, and my own and other people's memory banks. I finally settled on a list of about ten songs from 1902 through 1913 that prefigure the great ballads of the ensuing years, emerging from the era's flood of popular music. Rather than being flotsam, washed away by currents of time, these ballads proved to be sturdy, solid foundations for much of what has come since. In this book, I tell the story of how these songs were created and then re-created again and again throughout more than a century, until they rank as among the most familiar of standards in many fields of popular music.

I started with a group of songs discussed by Wilder and Philip Furia—and, to a lesser extent, James R. Morris and Max Morath.[18] Then I looked at other hits of the naughts and early teens that were revived in key eras and realized that there were a few songs that no critical evaluator mentioned, but that were important to the history of the early enduring Golden Age ballads—such as "I Wonder Who's Kissing Her Now."

The songs I write about have full, rich lives. To do justice to even one, I could spend decades thoroughly studying every recording and news article. I did what I felt I reasonably could, and the result opens a fresh vision on a wellspring of American art that has been famous and celebrated, and yet, paradoxically, also neglected and undervalued.

I present a historical narrative of the creation and dispersion of these songs alongside critical analysis, interpretation, and valuation. My approach is teleological: I favor the perspective not of the time when the works were first presented, but of posterity. We now know what they could not know in 1910 or 1930: that there would come a day when the personal, vernacular ballad of the United States would be celebrated in almost every slice of its society, as well as internationally. These are the first such songs that endured in popularity. Therefore, mine is a history of the victors—but one that seeks to complicate and deepen the usual tale of their success.

There was already a wealth of wonderful secondary literature on each of these songs. Scholars and critics preceding me functioned as chief inspirations and motivators. A base was supplied by reference books and secondary literature. But I also went through all the newspaper articles about these songs that I could find, gathered from an electronic resource, the ProQuest Historical Newspapers databases.[19] This methodical survey supplied much fresh material never before covered in conventional histories. I combed my personal archive of recordings, the product of forty years of collecting. During my research, wonderful electronic resources multiplied even as I gazed: Freegal, YouTube, iTunes, and others. Crucial were trips to the Library of Congress to look at copyright cards, sift through sheet music archives, and listen to recordings—as well the librarians' replies to my emails: it was thrilling when I received news of the discovery of a lyric neglected for a hundred years.

My approach is an idiosyncratic mixture. I present historical research, critical analysis, and creative interpretations of these songs. I draw on my background in dramatic analysis, acting, and visual analysis learned from cinema studies. I often ask: how does the song link to images in my mind and in the minds of others?

Further, I am fascinated with psychology, philosophy, and response. Reception theory teaches us to be attentive to how listeners encounter songs—and experience and interpret them, investing them with meaning. Thereby, songs become woven into the fabric of individual lives and of society as a whole. I look for evidence of this process in the journalistic record, in literature, recordings, film, and plays, and in my own memories and the autobiographical accounts of others.

The song-gazers emboldened me to offer my own critical readings of these songs. Some are musicological.[20] Some emphasize literary elements.[21] Some seek to analyze the interaction of words and music, the melopoetics.[22] I emulate all these approaches.

My understanding of the early twentieth-century repertoire draws on many experts. I lean on the work of discographers, before whose careful work I bow.[23] I also depend on those who created lists of popular hits of the past, such as Joel Whitburn (for recordings) and Edward Foote Gardner (for overall popularity).[24]

I am often caught between aesthetic ideals ("Is this a great song?") and pragmatic experience ("Is this a useful song?"). I find partial reconciliation by seeking the potential for greatness in every song. We can dig deeply into any song, trying to feel more subtly its gesture, drama, emotion, and atmosphere. I hold a special fondness for the creative writers of the essays about American narrative songs in *The Rose and the Briar*—they inspired me to let my imagination run freely.[25] The result: some of my own rather wild interpretive excursions.

Saturating this book are insights drawn from the writings of my longtime mentor, Dr. John Diamond, psychiatrist, philosopher, and pioneer of the holistic approach to the arts. Although I have tried to cite his specific works, there are bound to be lapses, for Diamond's work is ingrained in me, manifesting in ways I no longer even notice.[26] Seeing Dr. Diamond help married couples by having them sing "Always" to each other made me realize how important these songs are . . . and how powerful . . . and how useful. My conversations with him about popular songs and related matters, over a period of thirty years, have influenced my viewpoint, spurred my thinking, and raised many questions—some of which I have tried to answer in this survey.

Underlying all is my own experience of singing these songs. This I do almost constantly, performing with a Dixieland jazz band, making music with residents of nursing homes, and moving through daily life. I am a shower singer—and more: a kitchen, bedroom, living room, pool, garden, forest, sidewalk, parking lot, stairwell, elevator, and automobile singer.

There are two major goals when interpreting a song—and these impulses can cooperate or clash. One is musical: for each melody, I hear it as a vehicle for ragging, jazzing, swinging, bopping, or rocking. Another is dramatic: to enter a world of specific emotion. Like all singers (and many instrumentalists), each time I draw breath to make music, I discover anew the protagonist of the song's story. The characters live in a particular time and place. They are surrounded and framed, as on the stage or screen, within a particular mise-en-scène. These song-protagonists have a lifetime full of emotions and attitudes, vibrate in response to a vivid world around them, are locked into relationships with others, intent on goals both immediate and long-range . . . intent, ultimately, on giving love.

PERIODIZATION AND REPERTOIRE

The beginning point for my survey was easy to find: enduring personal songs in a jazzy vein do not start until the early years of the twentieth century. Once they do commence, however, they continue in one tradition through many decades. Therefore: when to end? By 1913 many of the basic elements of the classic American popular ballad were set in place by this study's group of songs. World War I was about to start and shift the scene considerably, with war topics bringing a brief pause in the flow of enduring love ballads.

The innovative ballads of the twentieth century's early years were often revived. In tracing these reincarnations, I focus on particular eras. These key periods fascinate me and supply my framework as I contemplate the steady stream of renditions of the earliest torch songs. First is the period from 1925 through 1934, when the electronic microphone came to the fore. Using it, pioneer crooning singers established their fame, igniting so much of what we love in jazz and pop singing, and, along the way, reviving many songs of the past.

The big bands of the subsequent decade, 1935 through 1945, also depended on older songs for much of their repertoire. The band singers firmly entrenched the crooner style and integrated it with the dance rhythms of the swing orchestras. This trend overlapped with the first flourishing of the Hollywood nostalgia musicals, which offered banquets of old tunes. Both the big bands and Americana movie musicals redefined ditties from earlier years as intimate songs suitable for the microphone.

In the mid-1940s, many singers graduated from the big bands and took up solo careers that, yet again, pushed to the fore a certain group of vintage torch songs. In the 1950s, these singers cultivated the format of the long-playing album, which crystallized the idea of a cream-of-the-crop repertoire. This consisted largely of post-1923 songs, usually ones that have since been analyzed favorably by music analysts (such as Alec Wilder, Allen Forte, et al.) and literary critics (like Philip Furia). The high standards these songs attain make it meaningful that an elite group of precursor songs hold their own in that repertoire.

In the 1950s and 1960s came the group I like to call the transition generation. These singers could convincingly swerve from genre to genre, like Bobby Darin. They joined their big-band predecessors in defining early songs as capable of being punched over in the ballad-with-a-beat mode. Then they also added folk, rhythm and blues, and country-western styles to the interpretive options for Tin Pan Alley songs.

My main veins are: In jazz, I rarely venture past the early jazz and swing eras. For singers, I range from the vaudeville generation (Al Jolson, Sophie Tucker, Bessie Smith) through the first rock and roll generation (Elvis Presley, Ray Charles, Brenda Lee). Nevertheless, I focus mainly in the middle: on the crooners who matured during the big band era, such as Frank Sinatra, Ella Fitzgerald, Judy Garland, and Nat King Cole.

Some tunes were widely adopted in only one of my key eras, and therefore I will merely glance at them in passing during the following discussion. For example, "Cuddle Up a Little Closer" (1908) was featured prominently in Hollywood nostalgia musicals, convincingly crooned by Mary Martin in *The Birth of the Blues* (1941) and Betty Grable in both *Coney Island* (1943) and *Four Jills in a Jeep* (1944). Nevertheless, it is otherwise rarely heard in the repertoires of the pioneer crooners, big bands, long-playing ballad-with-a-beat albums, or transition-to-rock singers.

A number of other treasured songs will not enter my tale—or, if so, only peripherally. Some are personal statements, but not sufficiently about love, such as "Nobody" (1905). Supporting my judgment of whether or not a piece is a personal love song lies in my empirical experience: when I walk around the block, if I can sing a song loudly without getting embarrassed, then it is not very personal. If I feel awkward singing a lyric so that my neighbors can hear, then I know it is has the confessional touch that marks a truly intimate love ballad—that "personal point of view" that Wilder noted.[27]

Why has the value of this core group of early songs been half-hidden? One reason is that people take them for granted. The fact they continue in the repertoire may be noted once, but then not given a second thought. Further, they have been under-criticized—mentioned (if at all) more as stepping-stones and less as satisfying achievements in themselves. Yet, they have tremendous use-value, some of it still untapped. They have been performed in a wide range of ways—and their past adaptability indicates that they may, in the future, be rendered in even more styles and yield to ever deeper interpretations.

This book studies the foundational texts of a *repertoire*—a word that derives from the Latin for *to get*. Therefore, a repertoire is a warehouse where you put things so you can get them again.[28] But the word root also means *to beget*—to give birth to—in this case, to give birth to again. This interpretation offers a more profound view of repertoire: the performer, whether female or male, is like a mother, who delivers the song as it is reborn. It is that sense of rebirth, of fresh vision, that the following study seeks to convey—and to inspire in the reader.

MY MELANCHOLY BABY

Chapter One

THE WORLD OF THE
GREAT AMERICAN SONGBOOK

his book is for those who love "Georgia on My Mind" (1930), or "At Last" (1941), or "Fly Me to the Moon" (1954) and want to know where such beautiful songs come from—what their musical ancestors are. These love songs, or ballads, or torch songs, as they are variously called, sprang from the worlds of Broadway, Hollywood, and the sheet music publishing business, called Tin Pan Alley, during the first half of the twentieth century. We still value them for their craft, versatility, and depth. How did this style of ballad originate? It is a tale that startles even experts, a saga of intrigue and surprise, of buying and stealing and giving, of grieving and loving.

My adventure of discovery started with a request for help: my friends, the Dixieland jazz musicians, were booked into a venue where they could not play any songs that were still in copyright.[1] They had to use tunes in the public domain. This meant, in the United States in 2003, works published before 1923. As far as instrumental numbers, this limitation presented no problem—there were plenty of early ragtime, jazz, and blues pieces to choose from. But the singer needed a love song. Usually she sang ballads dating from the Golden Age of American Popular Song, the mid-twenties through the fifties, from "It Had to Be You" (1924) through "When Sunny Gets Blue" (1956). What in the public domain could match those standards?

The classic American popular ballad really starts in 1924 with a sudden flood of enduring standards. As well as "It Had to Be You," the year produced "I'll See You in My Dreams," "The One I Love Belongs to Somebody Else," "What'll I Do," "All Alone," "Lazy," "Somebody Loves Me," "The Man I Love," "Oh, Lady Be Good," "Tea for Two," "I Want to Be Happy," "How Come You Do Me Like You Do," "Mandy, Make Up Your Mind," "Everybody Loves My Baby," "Jealous," "June Night," "My Blue Heaven," as well as operetta ballads that became jazz favorites, "Indian Love Call" and "Golden Days."[2] Following that gush of 1924, wonderful songs flowed forth: "As Time Goes By" (1931), "Try a Little Tenderness" (1933), "I Only Have Eyes for You" (1934), "Over the Rainbow" (1939), "Blueberry Hill"

3

(1940), and "White Christmas" (1942). The tradition continued through decades, producing favorites that bypassed the currents of the rock era, such as "Till There Was You" (1957), "Moon River" (1961), "What a Wonderful World" (1968), and "Send in the Clowns" (1973).

Since most of the great ballads came after 1923, however, they were in copyright, and my friends were in a predicament.[3] Their panic led me to create a list of public domain love and torch ballads for the singer to choose from. Eventually they settled on "You Made Me Love You" (1913), which worked out well.

The jazz band's practical problem set into motion a train of thought in my head. What creations of the 1910s can occupy an equal place with the great works of the second quarter of the century? I realized that there is a specific group of compositions from the years 1902 through 1913 that pioneered that new style, paving the way for the later masterpieces. These pioneer works stayed in the repertoire of singers and instrumentalists, being revived again and again through the decades. Here is the short list:

1902: "Bill Bailey, Won't You Please Come Home?"
1905: "Kiss Me Again"
1909: "I Wonder Who's Kissing Her Now"
1910: "Let Me Call You Sweetheart"
1910: "Some of These Days"
1911: "My Melancholy Baby"
1912: "When I Lost You"
1913: "You Made Me Love You"

These love-themed songs crystallized the styles of their era in a way that proved long-lasting. I shall call them *my focus songs* or *my corpus*. Aficionados will immediately ask: Why "Bill Bailey"? It is not a ballad. Nevertheless, as I shall reveal, elements of it contributed to the development of the classic pop ballad. (In fact, all my focus songs have been labeled as ballads—even "Bill Bailey," albeit less frequently than the others.)[4] In addition, I identified a handful of numbers, important enough to my discussion to merit sidenotes, although of less enduring appeal, versatility, or influence, such as "I Love You Truly" (1906), "The Sweetheart of Sigma Chi" (1911), and (jumping ahead a bit to 1916, but, as I shall reveal, for a good reason) "I'm Sorry I Made You Cry." Yet another few dozen tunes also weave in and out of my tale to a more limited extent.

Such classics could not have been written without a foundation of tens of thousands of other songs, now forgotten. Over time, singers, instrumentalists, and other artistes found that my core group was especially useful. Each contributed to the final result: the Golden Age ballad. Each led to what Philip Furia describes as that "perfect 'voice' for wittily turned lyrics that balance nonchalance and sophistication, slang and elegance," that earthy, romantic, "thoroughly American rainbow-chaser."[5] Each of these landmark works added a piece to the creation of that fresh "voice," that protagonist of the classic American popular ballad.

During my research, I found that hundreds of renditions of my core song-set are available on YouTube or through iTunes, Freegal, or Amazon. They would hardly seem to need championing—yet they do. Nowadays, high-profile stars rarely feature them.[6] Those who do cover them usually offer a limited vision of the song. Indeed, interpretations are often perfunctory. Overall, mainstream artists largely ignore the pre-1924 repertoire.

Musicians and fans who do know these early songs tend to be unaware how old they are. Those familiar with "My Melancholy Baby" usually do not realize it was copyrighted in 1911. They think of it as a product of later decades—and associate it with Gene Austin in the twenties, Benny Goodman in the thirties, Frank Sinatra in the forties, or Barbra Streisand in the sixties. "Wow! I didn't realize it was that old," I heard again and again as I told people about my research—which is one sign of how such songs proved to be ahead of their time.

I soon discovered that even the most perceptive critics wrote little of substance about these pioneer ballads. Analysts enthuse about some of them, true, but fleetingly—as it were, merely in passing on the way to the meaty songs of later years. Even historians discuss them only briefly. All around, people celebrate the Great American Songbook, but we exist in a state of ignorance about its germination. I set out to tell in detail the fascinating biographies of these ballads and to analyze the songs in depth. The wonderful work of previous scholars and analysts lay scattered, and I had to synthesize them and fit the pieces together, as well as delve into previously untapped sources. I had to explore the geography of Tin Pan Alley.

TIN PAN ALLEY

In the first decades of the 1900s, the music industry made its money by selling sheet music.[7] Each printed song was arranged for piano and voice, in a key convenient for amateur players and singers. The covers were graced with art suitable for home decoration (often with a little inset square for a photo of one of the many performers who were using the song). On the flip side of the covers and often on the margins as well, the publishers crammed spare space with advertisements for other pieces put out by the same company.[8] The New York portion of this sheet music industry centered on Broadway. At the turn of the twentieth century it clustered around 28th Street, where it began to be called Tin Pan Alley. Over the ensuing decades, it slowly migrated uptown,

Figure 1.1. "My Melancholy Baby" (1912). Publisher Theron C. Bennett lists offices in four cities, with specific addresses for the main ones: Denver and New York. The cover features a pair of fancy indoor plants, as might decorate an upscale living room. In the frame-in-the-frame is a photograph of one of several performers who featured the song: handsome Fred Watson, looking cocky—brought into the home along with the sheet music. Photo courtesy of the Lilly Library, Indiana University.

until by the late 1930s it mainly roosted at 49th Street in the Brill Building. By extension, the term Tin Pan Alley came to be used to mean the entire commercial songwriting business, whether of New York or Chicago or Los Angeles or points in between.

At first, sheet music was king. Beyond a few experiments, there was no radio, no television, no sound movies—and recordings were just beginning to rise to the fore. There were no industry associations who could extract fees from the theatres and restaurants that used the songs, as there would later be, when the American Society for Composers, Authors and Publishers (ASCAP) began to take the matter to court. Performers were viewed by publishers as a necessary evil: their renditions served as advertisements, but the stars often had to be bribed to include a song. The staffs of the music houses demonstrated the tunes to performers in the office by day and, after sunset, traveled all night around town to plug the songs. Depending on the era, these song pluggers would go from saloon, to theatre dressing room, to bandstand, to recording studio, to radio station.

The songwriters rarely got much profit from their creations. It was the publishers who invested thousands of dollars to make a ditty available to the public. If the gamble paid off, it was the publishers who got the profits. To get a song known to many people in the 1910s took intensive work, many contacts in the entertainment industry, and large amounts of money invested in staff, overhead, cover art, printing costs, the aforementioned bribes, and various musical arrangements for all kinds of amateur and professional performers. They could not depend on advertising alone. In 1916 publisher Louis Bernstein tried a concerted newspaper campaign; it failed. In 1920 L. Wolfe Gilbert got the Woolworth store chain to promote his house's song "Afghanistan"—again, a flop. Bernstein proclaimed, "songs must be heard by the people who buy them."[9] Therefore, song pluggers continued to go out and visit the performers to persuade them to put the company's products in their repertoire books. Eventually, the pluggers invaded the recording studios in the guise of "artists and repertory" men, to control (or, at least, try to control) what songs got on disc.

Tin Pan Alley helped promote the musical scores of Broadway and the songs of Hollywood, but they were not in the business of filling theatre seats: their profits always came from sheet music sales. At the peak of the business, around 1910, printed copies of a song could sell in the four or five millions and bring wealth to the brash Tin Pan Alley entrepreneurs who publicized and sold each aspiring hit to the public. The Alley developed a song style that saturated the musical landscape, permeating the great American middle-class household from coast to coast, and bleeding into every other genre of music.

THE COMPLICATED AUTHORSHIP OF CLASSIC POPULAR SONGS

In mapping the history of the enduring Tin Pan Alley ballads, I found I was exploring uncharted terrain—partly because most writings on classic American popular song focus on a few great artists, ignoring the thousands of others who contributed to the style. Take, for instance, Alec Wilder: in his influential musical analysis, *American Popular Song: The Great Innovators, 1900–1950*, he dwells for half the book on only six composers: Jerome Kern, Irving Berlin, George Gershwin, Richard Rodgers, Cole Porter, and Harold Arlen.[10] In his introduction to Wilder's book, James T. Maher articulates this view clearly: "Innovation . . . followed the metabolic rise and fall of the creative output of individual song writers."[11] Therefore, Wilder followed "the strands of the separate careers of those composers who have contributed most" to the "musical distinctions of the American popular song."[12] Writing years later, Allen Forte focuses on the exact same half-dozen songwriters in over 60 percent of his tome, *The American Popular Ballad of the Golden Era, 1924–1950*.[13] The lyricists who set words to the melodies of those six composers are the focus for Philip Furia, who lingers for almost 80 percent of *The Poets of Tin Pan Alley* on only ten wordsmiths.[14] These critics reveal deep beauties in what they examine—but stick to a narrow corpus. Judging by such studies, the invention of the classic American popular song style would seem the accomplishment of a few handfuls of geniuses.

My exploration of these earliest classic ballads songs, however, opens our sight to unexpected vistas. Yes, the great artists are represented here—in particular, Irving Berlin. In addition, however, there are other important figures—surprising ones. Many of the early innovators were uncredited at the time and are now so obscure that we can only barely identify them. Further, all these songs were changed after publication—revised, pared down, added to—sometimes by the authors themselves, often by the publishers, and always by the performers, who adapted them freely. The singers, arrangers, and instrumentalists became, over the course of time, uncredited co-authors of the songs. Performers made alterations that became part of the tradition surrounding the song—indeed, that, for most practical purposes, became part of the song itself.

Innovation in classic American popular song was social, collective, communal. The contributions of uncredited songwriters and arrangers before publication or for re-publication—and of performers after publication—all those factors point to this valuable addition to our understanding. I will be presenting evidence of this throughout the following pages.

There are other aspects of this phenomenon. First, songwriters wrote under the influence of the competition, encouragement, and inspiration offered by others. This is sometimes manifested in the spurring on of friends. In one famous instance, E. Ray Goetz prodded Irving Berlin into writing "When I Lost You," a tale I will tell more fully in a later chapter.

Second, songs also tended to be published in cycles. Thus "I'm Always Chasing Rainbows" (1918) is followed by "I'm Forever Blowing Bubbles" (1919), "Castle of Dreams" (1919), and "I'm Always Watching Clouds Roll By" (1920). The traits of successful works were repeated in new pieces and, through this process, became established as conventions. Because the Tin Pan Alley style consolidated (or, harsher critics might say, ossified), for generations songwriters could continue to lean on these innovations-turned-cliché. Therefore, it is not surprising to find, more than ten years after "I'm Always Chasing Rainbows" and "I'm Forever Blowing Bubbles," a derivative song like "I'm a Dreamer That's Chasing Bubbles" (1929). For decades, writers could lean on the generic patterns established by previous creators.

Third, Tin Pan Alley songwriters like to quote other songs, whether music or words—or, often, both together. Irving Berlin does this in "Alexander's Ragtime Band" (1911)—probably the most famous example. His lyric reads, "the Swanee River played in ragtime," while the music quotes Stephen Foster's "Way Down Upon the Swanee River" (or, in its proper title, "Old Folks at Home," 1851). As in this instance, when a Tin Pan Alley song self-consciously quotes a preexisting tune, usually the lyric makes some reference to the older piece.

In all these ways, therefore, the creativity of a Tin Pan Alley writer was enmeshed in a social system: quoting older melodies and lyrics; following the patterns set by previous songs; contributing to a song cycle; responding to peer pressure; and using material from unacknowledged contributors. Then would come the publisher's arrangers, and finally the singers and instrumentalists and dancers and *their* arrangers, all of whom introduced elements that might become widespread. The Great American Songbook is a product of collective genius.

Indeed, inspired by the trends in thinking of the turn of the twenty-first century, I have come to see innovation as a process of give-and-take within a large group of people. Thus, I write a kind of "it takes a village" approach to the history of the Great American Songbook. In this, I join many writers who detail or theorize how innovation is a group process, a social process.[15] Such dynamics have been sketched for ancient philosophic movements, and detailed histories seem to prove the point, whether about eighteenth-century English intellectuals, 52nd Street jazz musicians between the wars, 1960s Hollywood filmmakers, or 1970s American comedians.[16] Yet, this approach has never been applied to Tin Pan Alley.

Because it is usual for performers to transform Tin Pan Alley songs, one cannot fully assess the value of these pieces without taking into account the performance tradition. They are inextricably bound to the kind of practice Anne Dhu McLucas defines as "oral tradition in music."[17] These are "those aspects . . . that are passed down by humans teaching one another the art form," in contrast to the impersonal nature of notated music.[18] In McLucas's view, this oral process can be effected "in person or by means of recordings, radio, television, or other non-written means."[19] True, the songs exist as literate phenomena, spread through printed sheet music. In addition, however, they also exist as oral (and aural) phenomena, passed from lip to ear. They are learned through both methods, which is part of their value and importance.

The Tin Pan Alley tradition supplies further evidence in favor of McLucas's argument that "the importance of oral tradition in relation to the written in American music has given that music its particular stamp, its freshness and vitality, and its ability to capture the attention of musicians and audiences worldwide."[20] As Max Morath puts it, in the making of popular standards there grew an "inherently collaborative relationship between songwriter and performer" that "invited . . . innovation."[21] Stephen Banfield agrees: he examines "Bill" (1927) and posits that "the nuances . . . as well as the reflexive colloquialism" within the song are "an invitation to performer-freedom."[22] Through their accumulated traditions the performers act as additional authors, influencing the creation of the songs, passing them on orally, and influencing the form in which their music and lyrics are preserved.

The songs beckon the performer to take liberties. Will Friedwald hints at the crucial issue when he claims that "the classic American song is the most flexible form of music. . . . One can interpret . . . all [such] pop songs . . . in any tempo, in any time signature, in any style."[23] The result is a quality that caused these songs to attain a status as world-class works of art. McLucas puts it bluntly: "the power of American music exists chiefly in its oral traditions."[24] McLucas and others demonstrate how true this is for blues or folk music traditions; here, I will demonstrate that this is also true for classic pop.

Tin Pan Alley songs often seem to come into their own only over time. This is a part of the consequence, in this genre, of the collective nature of creation. Early arrangements of "I've Got a Crush on You" (1930) or "Blue Moon" (1934) scarcely seem like the same song that we now know and love. It might take dozens of performers, each refashioning the piece, over the course of a decade or more, before the song emerges in its most familiar range of tempos, phrasings, and character. Therefore, unlike most of my predecessors, I analyze not just the sheet music but also recorded performances from radio, television, movies, theatre, the studio, and the internet.

THE PERSONAL SONG

The collective nature of Tin Pan Alley creativity is as true for rhythm songs, such as Irving Berlin's "Alexander's Ragtime Band," as it is for ballads, such as his "When I Lost You." Nevertheless, there is a special element in many ballads: they are personal, intimate, and internal. These traits are either lacking or not as apparent in other types of songs. The saga I unfold reveals how our society learned to fuse this introspection and intimacy with the brash, extroverted, wise-cracking American character.

Each age may have its own songs about love and inner emotions, but the personal love song is especially central to the repertoire of the Great American Songbook. Between 1900 and 1920, all the traditions from earlier ages—of courtly love, amorous yearning, and witty deflation of romance—were translated into the idiom of American popular song. The song with an American melody and a colloquial love lyric crystallized shortly after the turn of the twentieth century.[25] These songs feature everyday language, true rhymes, strong melodies that are either syncopated or conducive to being syncopated, and deep emotions treated either sentimentally or flippantly or (miraculously) both ways at once. The musical scores flirtatiously beckon the performer to jazz it up, to swing. The lyrics speak in conversational English, and their sentiments are personal. Look at the examples I mentioned in my first paragraph. "In dreams I see," exclaims the protagonist of "Georgia on My Mind." "I looked," the protagonist of "At Last" remembers ecstatically . . . and not just "I looked" but "I looked at *you*." Not just a general command to "Fly Me to the Moon," but an intimate entreaty: "darling, kiss me." The folk ballads of an older tradition often tell a narrative story about "him" and "her," one that might cover days, years, or decades of action.[26] In contrast, Tin Pan Alley redefined what we call a ballad—as a scene in the here and now, in which "you and I" might inhabit the central space.

Lyricist Dorothy Fields spoke for them all: "I'm always looking for a new way to say 'I love you' . . . for the boy. . . . soul wracked with emotions he can't express."[27] These intimate confessions bring the singer and listener closer and closer. Therefore, in retrospect, the kind of microphone-friendly singing that arose after 1925 (and that we now take for granted) seems like an inevitable development. Rudy Vallee was one of the first artists to master microphone singing and, from 1929 on, was one of radio's most successful purveyors of the personal love song. One newlywed fan wrote about Vallee: "Hubby and I just sit and hold each other while he is on the air. . . . We just look into each others eyes while he is singing."[28] The promotion of such tender closeness was one of the basic tasks of these ballads.

Two terms arose in the late 1920s for this newly intimate, personal mode: crooning and torch song, propagated by the crooner and the torch singer. Gene Austin was one of the pioneer crooners, and he mined the value of pioneer ballads of the teens, helping establish "My Melancholy Baby" and "The Sweetheart of Sigma Chi," both published in 1912, as standards of the late 1920s. In retrospect, such ballads of the 1910s might be seen as defining a new genre: the torch song. They prefigured the developments of the 1920s and, indeed, set the pattern for the next forty years.

THE TORCH SONG—WHAT IS IT?

The saga of the torch song starts with a white singer—a thin wisp of a man, an opium addict—hushing the noisy, drinking, smoking crowd of a nightclub with a song. The year could be anytime in the teens or twenties, and his name is Tommy Lyman. Nobody remembers him today, but back then he was called "the saloon singer's singer."[29] Bricktop, the legendary African American nightclub hostess and singer, idolized him. Writing seventy years later, she remembered Lyman, leaning against the bar, "his eyes heavy-lidded, his long, tapering fingers resting on the edge"—and "he'd sing sooo quietly."[30] Lyman used to drop by the nightclub where Bricktop worked early in her career, and through the ensuing decades she never lost a chance to hear him: "There was no song he sang better than 'Melancholy Baby,' and we wouldn't let him quit until he'd done it. The way he sang it was unforgettable. Maybe it was because he was such a melancholy man himself."[31] In 1927 Walter Winchell reported to the American public that Lyman had dubbed a new genre in popular music: the singer announced, as his next number, "My famous torch song, 'Come to Me, My Melancholy Baby.'"[32] The torch song, as a new category of ballad, was born.

In that same article about Broadway slang, Winchell further informs the readers of *Vanity Fair* that "a 'flame' is a fellow's sweetheart." Perhaps this flame of love is a burning torch, for when he "'carries the torch' . . . his steady has quit him for another or he is lonesome for her." The torch burns when apart from the beloved. The columnist reports that "'sing a torch song' is commonly used in Broadway late-places, as a request for a ballad in commemoration of the lonesome state."[33] Thus, loneliness was the first emotion attached to the torch genre—as previously discussed, unrequited love was later listed as the main ingredient. Harold Arlen, composer of "Stormy Weather," is regarded as one of the greatest torch song writers (indeed, perhaps the very greatest), and he defined a torch song as "a sentimental ballad of unrequited love."[34] Arlen is echoed by singer (and composer of the classic torch song "Born to Be Blue") Mel Tormé, who described torch songs as "the ones about lost or unrequited love."[35] These commentators offer the narrowest definition of the term.

"My Melancholy Baby" was published in 1912. Therefore, Tommy Lyman applied the newly coined term of "torch song" to an old warhorse.[36] Apparently, the singer had the brilliance to see that "My Melancholy Baby" fit into a fresh, modern vision of age-old romantic suffering, adapted to American vernacular culture and manifested in this up-to-date slang phrase. Carrying the torch for someone who is distant geographically or emotionally was now potentially a central experience in life. By extension, and inadvertently, Lyman redefined a slew of decade-old songs that had translated heartache into the urbane, colloquial verbal and musical languages of the ragtime and early jazz eras.

Figure 1.2. Melancholy, mesmerizing Tommy Lyman was the first person to use the phrase *torch song* (1927) and one of the first to be labeled *torch singer* (1929). Photos of him, as on this 1946 sheet music cover, are rare. Photo from author's collection.

Winchell's article, however, reveals a contradiction. The first piece labeled as a torch song, "My Melancholy Baby," does not fit the description by Winchell. As I shall later explore further, the protagonist of this song is not longing for his sweetheart nor has he lost her.[37] She is in the room with him. Bricktop's implication—that the protagonist of this song is melancholy—is not necessarily true. It is his *sweetheart* who is sad, not him. It is the singer's beloved who is beset with a melancholy that is never explained. The singer's role is to help cure her of her sadness. He is loving, tender, and optimistic: "Every cloud must have a silver lining," he reassures her. While this is definitely a personal song, it is not a lament for unrequited love, loss, or loneliness. It is a gentle song of comforting.

Since "My Melancholy Baby" is apparently the first piece dubbed "torch song," we must grant that the genre is not necessarily about unrequited, absent, or lost love. Right at its beginning, "torch song" illustrates a truth about the nature of a genre label: it can connote various attributes. From the early 1930s into the twenty-first century, songs of happy, fulfilled love such as "Always" (1925) and "Violets for Your Furs" (1941) have frequently been included in the torch genre.[38] In my informal survey of songs labeled "torch," 69 percent expressed negative emotions but, in contrast, 31 percent were positive depictions of love relationships.[39] Judging by such a corpus, the torch repertoire is more fully defined as being about romantic love in general (98 percent). Another prevalent factor is that the torch song is told from a first-person point of view (93 percent). To an extent, the phrase "torch song" can function as a synecdoche, capturing in a nutshell the whole tendency in the Tin Pan Alley tradition toward personal expression, whether of sadness or happiness.[40] In such a frame, "torch song" serves as a shorthand for the "I" point of view in American popular song.

Before Lyman propagated the term "torch song," what was this type of song called? The term "love ballad" was common at least as far back as the 1870s, before Tin Pan Alley hit its stride.[41] The terms "rag ballad" and "syncopated ballad" began to be used around 1913.[42] Irving Berlin claimed he had "accomplished a number of things which were thought impossible," including having "established the syncopated ballad."[43] Later, the term for these became rhythmic ballad, often shortened to rhythm ballad.[44] Throughout the eras of ragtime, jazz, swing, and bop, there was an ever-increasing blurring of lines between rhythmic songs and ballads. Due to his limited vantage point in 1913, Berlin overestimated his role in establishing the rhythm ballad genre. Nevertheless, Berlin was one of the first to emphasize publicly that "syncopation . . . alone can catch the sorrow—the pathos—of humanity. That note in ragtime is almost unexplainable—I call it the 'wail' of the syncopated melody."[45] The alchemy of American music lies, in part, in this mixture of dance-inspiring syncopations and the personal emotions (the "wail") of ballads.

Mezz Mezzrow, the jazz clarinetist, wrote about the start of his career in the early 1920s and categorized "My Melancholy Baby" with an older term, "tearjerker,"[46] along with "The Curse of an Aching Heart," "My Gal Sal," and "Ace in the Hole," because these songs made the prostitutes weep. Another common name for the tearjerker was "sob ballad." This latter term slowly faded from use in the 1930s, as it became increasingly associated with 1890s sentimental "story songs"—third-person narratives like "The Little Lost Child."

In 1925, a few years before the term "torch song" was born, Irving Berlin used "sob ballad" to describe his waltzes of the 1920s: "What'll I Do," "All Alone," and "Remember." Berlin was scornfully denying that his "sob ballads" were proof that he was engaged to heiress Ellin Mackay: "The idea is ridiculous that because a man writes sob ballads he is writing about his own experiences."[47] The creation of songs was, to Berlin and his Tin Pan Alley colleagues, not an emotional outlet, but their profession: they claimed that you do not necessarily have to be sad to issue forth a sad song. Their protestations raised the complicated issue of the relationship of life to art.

Contradicting Berlin, Hollywood repeatedly insisted that the apparent anguish of the torch song performer or writer was real, not pretend. Through their depictions, these moviemakers helped further define the torch song genre. The earliest movie musicals, from 1927 onward, create a correlation between professional singers and the song they sing, in "weepies" such as *My Man* (1928), wherein Fanny Brice suffers enough to warrant singing her trademark, the title song. *Honky-Tonk* (1930) has Sophie Tucker protecting her daughter at all costs, affirming "I'm Doing What I'm Doing for Love." In *Applause* (1930), burlesque queen Helen Morgan financially supports her younger lover, singing "What Wouldn't I Do for That Man," while, in split screen, he is revealed kissing another troupe member. Over on Broadway, Irving Berlin parodied this correspondence of singer and song in "Torch Song," in the 1932 *Face the Music*. In Berlin's musical satire, Jean Sargent played "a lady of the evening," who had deliberately sought to find a "faithless lover" to seduce and abandon her, leaving her to a life of prostitution—but all "for the sake of Art," so that she would be qualified to sing a torch song.

Despite this convention being dissected under Irving Berlin's scalpel, Hollywood kept repeating that sad songs came from sad singers, to the point of cliché. In *Torch Singer* (1933), Claudette Colbert expresses the woes of the fallen woman by singing "It's a Long, Dark Night" and "Give Me Liberty or Give Me Love" in nightclubs, before she can tearfully reunite with her abandoned child (see figure 1.3). In *Gold Diggers of 1933*, Dick Powell is made to assert "I've Got to Sing a Torch Song": because he is feeling sad, he cannot sing a glad song.[48] In *Torch Song* (1953), Joan Crawford (or, rather, the dubbed voice of India Adams) intones several torchy songs, each revealing a separate part of her mystique. Her blind piano accompanist has been obsessed with her since before his wartime impairment, remembering her singing "Tenderly." But she is, as she later sings, a "Two-Faced Woman": her hard-as-nails exterior hides her tenderness—until, of course, the hero helps her soft side reemerge. Without her realizing it, the torch songs they perform together perfectly describe her power over him: "You Won't Forget Me" (he cannot forget her) and "Follow Me" (he does).

In Hollywood's pseudo-biographies of quintessential torch singers, they must be revealed as suffering as much as the protagonists of their songs: Fanny Brice (*Rose of Washington Square*, 1939; *Funny Girl*, 1968), Lillian Roth (*I'll Cry Tomorrow*, 1955), Helen Morgan (*The Helen Morgan Story*, 1957), and Billie Holiday (*Lady Sings the Blues*, 1972)—for all of them, in Hollywood's

Figure 1.3. Claudette Colbert glamorizes the image of the *Torch Singer* in a 1933 tearjerker. As Mimi (née Sally), she intones "Give Me Liberty or Give Me Love" in a fancy nightclub, leaning against a baby grand.

scenarios, private heartbreak and public performance material must become one.[49] While this is partly romantic fiction, it illustrates an important point. At their best, torch singers make us feel they are singing about themselves—and torch songs become convincing as sincere confessions. This is a personal mode of expression.

CROONING AND INTIMACY IN POPULAR CULTURE

The terms "torch singer" and "crooner" spread widely at the same time, in the late 1920s, and singers like Bing Crosby, Helen Morgan, and Ruth Etting found themselves placed in both categories.[50] The electronic microphone became common in 1925, and crooners quickly exploited its potential with a fresh style. Their light vocal production contrasted with both the hard-sell tactics of earlier vaudeville greats and the power and fullness of the classical singing tradition. Pioneers among the new "soft-songsters" included Vaughn De Leath, known as "the original radio girl"; Rudy Vallee, initially famous for amplifying his voice with a megaphone; and Bing Crosby, who said "I'm not a singer; I'm a phraser," emphasizing his lack of vocal power and classical technique.[51]

Figure 1.4. Matronly Vaughn De Leath, "the original radio girl," caresses and croons into the microphone. Records and radio allowed her to portray a wide range of 1920s song-protagonists, from mother in "Louisiana Lullaby" to torch-bearing lover in "Are You Lonesome Tonight."

Admittedly, crooning and torch singing were not quite the same. Sophie Tucker developed her vocal prowess in the acoustic period and never significantly altered her style to adjust to the microphone, yet in this new era she was dubbed a "torch mamma."[52] Ethel Merman was characterized early on as a torch singer—yet she thrived in unamplified Broadway theatres and, as a result, her technique is now considered the epitome of loud "belting."[53]

Nevertheless, even before the electronic microphone and amplification took over starting in 1925, some singers were already working toward a fresh, clear, light style. Like pioneer crooner Ethel Waters, they could boast that they "never had that loud approach" cultivated by their professional rivals.[54] This trend seems to have manifested in all areas of show business. They came from the Broadway stage (like Fred Astaire), dance bands of the Southwest (like Willard Robison), Tin Pan Alley song plugging (like Gene Austin), and Chicago nightclubs (like Ruth Etting). Their intimate styles developed in an acoustic era. When the electric microphone began to be used for commercial recordings, in 1925, they were poised to take full advantage of it. Their greatest successes would be tied to the triumph of the electric microphone. Soon they all would be disseminating not only the new crooning technique, but also the new torch genre.

Crooning fits into broader aspects of twentieth-century culture. It was fore-shadowed by a series of social situations where people were drawn in more closely to each other. The 1910s saw the flourishing of a series of intimate formats: cabaret, small-scale musical comedies, the telephone, and amateur radio. Meanwhile, African Americans transformed the *blues ballads* (like "Frankie and Johnny") into the *blues* proper, and choral spirituals became hushed solos.

Americans borrowed the term *cabaret* from France, and this kind of intimate venue—for food, drinks, singers, bands, and dancing—flourished in the United States from 1912 onward.[55] In the early teens, in all kinds of saloons and nightclubs—increasingly called cabarets—performers like Bricktop were learning "the trick of saloon singing—you weren't trying to get the whole audience, just one table after another as you went along."[56] Singers were not belting out to the whole room, but close to individuals at each table, standing near, bending over, sitting next to them.

In France, operetta downscaled itself to suit theatres of only 200 to 900 seats, with enormous success, from *Son p'tit frère* (1907) through *Phi-Phi* (1918) and on into the 1920s.[57] (Out of that same culture would come "Mon Homme" [1920], discussed later, which would become one of the most-rendered torch songs in the English-speaking world as "My Man.") Seemingly, the movement toward intimate communication was international.

On Broadway, musical comedy also lost weight, producing a famous series of successful musicals at the 299-seat Princess Theatre from 1915 to 1918. Most of these featured the work of composer Jerome Kern, just achieving artistic maturity, and one featured an early version of his torch song "Bill" (1918). Other pivotal shows were born at Broadway's 780-seat Vanderbilt Theatre, such as *Oh, Look!* (also from 1918, with another introspective ballad of long-lasting appeal, "I'm Always Chasing Rainbows"), as well as the major international success of 1919, *Irene*.[58] These small-scale theatres and their streamlined productions reduced the size of sets, cast, and orchestra and, most importantly for our discussion, brought the performers into a more intimate relationship with their audiences.

The telephone was increasingly prominent, linking people thousands of miles apart—and, at the same time, paradoxically breaking through the usual comfortable conversational distance of three or four feet by drawing people to within inches of the receiver. In 1899 ragtime was associated with the new technology, via "Hello, My Baby," in which the verse sets up a very modern scenario: the protagonist has never met his sweetie except over the telephone. In 1911 an even more suggestive scenario was painted in "Harry Von Tilzer's Great Telephone Song" (as the cover proclaimed) "All Alone," in which the heroine's pa and ma have gone out and she insists over the phone that her lover come over for "lots of kissing."[59] The telephone was soon depicted as a medium for love talk, even a device of seduction.

The first transcontinental phone call was celebrated in *Ziegfeld Follies of 1915* with "Hello, Frisco." This long-remembered hit was always done as a medium-tempo charm song, with lively, patter-like "answer" phrases to make it into a conversational duet. Yet, despite its sprightliness, the lyric does reveal the scenario that encouraged the new intimacy of love ballads: "When I close my eyes, you seem so near."

Nearly thirty years later, *Hello, Frisco, Hello* (1943) became the title for a lush, nostalgic Technicolor movie musical. In the show-within-the-film, the bouncy 1915 song is used as a frame to introduce the newly composed love ballad "You'll Never Know," which Alice Faye murmurs into a telephone receiver. This mise-en-scène might be based on the real-life 1924 Broadway staging of Irving Berlin's "All Alone"—a different song from Von Tilzer's—when Grace Moore and Oscar Shaw stood on opposite ends of a darkened stage, illuminated by lights in the mouthpieces of the phones they held, lamenting how they are "waiting for a ring" on the telephone from their beloved.[60] Such stagings embody the concurrent advent of the telephone and newly intimate American popular ballads.

R. Murray Schafer points out that with the advent of the telephone, radio, and phonograph, "sound was no longer tied to its original point in space."[61] This is a manifestation of what Schafer calls schizophonia, "the splitting of sounds from their original context."[62] With the telephone, people got used to confiding, even when hundreds of miles apart, as if lip-to-ear. We can add this paradoxical distant closeness to the long list of what Ithiel de Sola Pool describes as the "inherently dual effects" of the telephone.[63] Thus, the telephone can be viewed as an important symbol of the paradoxes of modern intimacy.

In 1929, Tommy Lyman was among the first to be dubbed a "torch singer," in relation to this revealing anecdote: every night, Hollywood star Marie Prevost phoned him at his New York club to have him sing to her over the wires.[64] (Probably among his telephoned croonings was "My Melancholy Baby," now established as his theme song.) Perhaps Lyman, too, was privy to the oxymoronic far-nearness of telephone romance.

The amateur crystal set vogue of the 1910s led, in the 1920s, to the establishment of the radio with speakers, featuring commercial broadcasting. With this development, Berlin's "All Alone" helped usher in an era of radio plugging for new tunes. John McCormack recorded Berlin's tune in December 1924, and, when he came to sing for his very first broadcast on January 2, 1925, he squeezed "All Alone" into the final two minutes of the program.[65] The "plug" worked: the song went on to sell a million copies of sheet music, as well as more than a million records, in seven different renditions ranging from McCormack's classical-based rendering to the jazzy one by Abe Lyman's California Orchestra.[66] While radio would continue to welcome McCormack and other classical singers, the singing style most idiomatic to the new medium was that "discovered" by the crooners—conversational, mellow, confessional, low in pitch, and low-key in mood.[67] Resonating on one's home crystal set, these intimate vibrations cast a magic spell.

Some African American genres were also becoming, if not more intimate, then certainly more personal. The 1890s had seen the flourishing of blues ballads, which were usually story-songs: for example, "Frankie and Johnny were lovers" until he cheats on her and she shoots him. Over the next twenty years, the form and harmonies of the blues ballads got tweaked, transforming into what is now considered the standard blues: twelve measures of a set harmonic structure, underpinning three lines of lyrics, with gaps at the end of each line. Meanwhile, the lyrics became personal, changing from the third-person narratives like "Frankie and Johnny" to first-person emotional laments, as in "The St. Louis Blues" (1914): "I hate to see the evenin' sun go down / Because my baby's done left this town."

The old blues ballads had expressed the go-getter character of the emerging American personality by breathlessly sprinting ahead at the end of the second phrase, rushing into the concluding third line of the stanza. By contrast, at this same point the "blues proper" pauses, taking a moment for introspection.[68] Thus, a new personal quality was also reflected in the evolving music of the blues. These innovations corresponded to a tidal wave of fresh popularity for this African American tradition. In 1912 several blues publications, including "The Memphis Blues," a landmark hit, opened the faucet, and, subsequently, 1916 and 1919 witnessed surges of printed blues.[69]

Meanwhile, the African American classical composer Henry Burleigh was issuing a series of arrangements of traditional spirituals, transforming them from choral pieces into vehicles suitable for solo voice recitals. In the fall of 1916, the "runaway popularity" of one of these arrangements crystallized this new trend.[70] As Wayne Shirley documents: "It was 'Deep River' that made it thinkable for spirituals to appear on a mainstream vocal recital—rapt singer standing in front of piano, attentive accompanist playing from the notes."[71] Soon the image of that "rapt singer standing in front of a piano" would translate from classical to popular music, from the concert singers to the nightclub singers (see figure 1.3). No longer only a communal expression, spirituals now might also be private meditations; meanwhile, both blues and Tin Pan Alley songs were also taking on the mood of internal soul-searching.

During these same years, the United States became increasingly aware of psychoanalysis. Sigmund Freud visited America in September 1909, just as the early torch song "I Wonder Who's Kissing Her Now" was peaking in popularity. Within a year, newspapers were helping Americans view human nature as a thing of "repression," "psychoneuroses," and "latent" desires.[72] Articles pictured ordinary people as creatures with "inmost thoughts" that lie "underneath the shell," in "the deepest recesses and darkest corners of the mind"—in the "unconscious personality."[73] The tug of war described in these articles, between "a number of personalities" that leave "the patient literally at war with himself," is paralleled in those same years by the powerful contradictory emotions of the protagonists of innovative popular ballads discussed in the upcoming chapters, such as "Some of These Days" and "You Made Me Love You."

EXTROVERSION AND INTROVERSION

The introspective early blues and torch songs are exceptional, because, in general, American popular songs of the turn of the twentieth century can be broadly described as brash and extroverted. In the early 1920s, Jerome Kern described "both the typical Yankee" and the typical Irving Berlin tune: they shared "humor, originality, pace and popularity; both were wide-awake, and both sometimes a little loud."[74] These are wonderful qualities, but introspective traits are missing from the list. Berlin's 1911 landmark, "Alexander's Ragtime Band," supplies an example of boisterous virtues, as do hits by his contemporaries such as "Take Me Out to the Ballgame" (1908), "Waiting for the Robert E. Lee" (1912), or "By the Beautiful Sea" (1914). Such songs seem to be almost entirely centrifugal—their emotional energy radiates outward. By the mid-1920s, however, many more songs exhibit a sense that there is a person inside. Without losing their American spunk, the songs become more centripetal, their affective energy moving toward the song-protagonist's inner landscape.

The protagonists exhibit this new interiority in two particular ways. They confess the pull-and-tug of mixed emotions: "I'm happy, I'm sad" declare, in effect, the protagonists of "It Had to Be You" (1924), "Sometimes I'm Happy" (1925), and "It All Depends on You" (1927). Also, they reveal a secret inner life of dreams, wishes, and desires that is at once abstract yet filled with concrete, sensual images: "I'll See You in My Dreams" (1924) with your arms that hold, lips that touch, eyes that shine. Even jazz becomes interiorized. No longer do the protagonists merely proclaim that exciting music sets them dancing—instead, they declare that it pounds "through my brain," as Ira Gershwin describes it in his lyric for "Fascinating Rhythm."

Increasingly from 1924 onward, into this extroverted world of American popular song creeps the spirit of introspection. The ballads in particular become increasingly bittersweet, conjuring a kind of twilight enchantment. These traits suffuse the lyrics, as the protagonists ruminate about "Star Dust" (1929) in their "Solitude" (1934). This indigo spell suffuses the music, too, particularly through the use of blue notes, the play between major and minor, and harmonies influenced by French classical music of the Impressionist school.

Then there are aspects of the melopoetics—the way the words and music fit together and inflect each other—creating complex dynamics between happiness and melancholy. These factors interweave so subtly that often you cannot put your finger on how the mood is created. The very first popular songs that enduringly combined this twilight atmosphere with the jazzy, wide-awake alertness of twentieth-century America are those covered in this book.

It is hard to imagine what zeitgeist could unite Freud, in Austria, and the African American creators of the first blues in towns in the American South.[75] There are, however, parallels between the two movements. Blues songs were described as a way to cure "the blues," which was often equated during this period with the medical diagnosis of neurasthenia.[76] Freudian dream analysis, too, was presented as a way to "shake off the blues feeling."[77] Authorities of the time declared that the "most promising fields" for psychoanalysis included "neurasthenia . . . and melancholy."[78] The talking cure from Vienna and the singing cure from the American South—when these two impulses migrated to American cities from different directions were their overlapping goals a coincidence? Perhaps these modalities, vastly different in many ways, were somehow responding to the same societal needs and opportunities of modern life.

Equally, there seems minimal connection between Freud and Tin Pan Alley. These songwriters strove for what lyricist E. Y. Harburg called "a kind of rainbow world"—seemingly far removed from the ambience of psychoanalysis.[79] Yet, by 1924 we can feel that Freudianism now underpins the world in which Tin Pan Alley exists—although, admittedly, before 1924 there are scarcely any songs that have that brooding atmosphere. Yet, even while Freud's concepts are slowly creeping into general consciousness, some of the songs in my corpus also begin tentatively to form an inner landscape of conflicting emotion and soliloquy. Such simultaneous shifts in art and thought can emerge from the same changes in society—and feed into each other.

During the same era, rhythm songs, charm songs, and comedy songs were also proliferating and transforming—a process that produced gems that still glitter for audiences today. Nevertheless, part of my argument is that we need to pay careful attention to the ballads. They have special importance because the development of these ballads was one of many strands toward contemplation, personal expression, and intimacy in the early decades of the twentieth century. Further, they are also important because of their relationship to the lullaby.

CROONING AND THE LULLABY

Before *croon* was applied to microphone vocalizing, it was preceded by a long period when its most frequent connotation was of a mother singing a lullaby. *Croon* has a convoluted history—it is one of those words that reversed in meaning over time. It started out in the 1500s meaning a loud sound—cattle's mooing, the clamor of church bells, and the wailing lament of women mourning at a funeral.[80] Between the 1810s and 1870s, it slowly came to mean another type of sound associated with women—the mother's singing of a lullaby, a connotation it held into the early 1920s and after. Newspapers demonstrate this, with their frequent references to "the wonderful babe the mother rocks and croons to sleep at her breast," perhaps while "Mother Nature croons the earth to rest."[81] An advertisement for a recording of "Lullaby" promises that "the cello's melody croons the mother's song while the piano carries you glidingly into the land o' dreams"; and a play titled *Lullaby* drags its heroine through the gutter, but, "throughout," each time she thinks of her long-lost son, "she croons her lullaby."[82] Crooning was what mothers did.

Rhetoric often linked the act of crooning to a web of associations, leading from the stereotype of the African American "mammy" (who clasps her master's daughter and "croons lovingly") through, by association, Southern music (the Dixie Jubilee Singers offer "soft Southern croons by a mixed quartet") and thence to the blues and jazz.[83] In 1926 the Club Alabam' claimed that when the comely, white Jean Starr, "queen of jazz singers," "croons . . . her Down-south blues," she "stops the show."[84] This trail of connotations leads from the lullaby to blues to jazz to nightclub crooning.

Many at the time felt that lullabies laid the foundation for an individual's love of music throughout life. In 1919 the National Child Welfare Association proclaimed in an exhibit, in its associated book, and (through book reviews of the latter) in newspapers that "the time to begin to teach a child to appreciate music is when the mother croons her first lullaby to her babe."[85] They continue, "this must be true or the maternal instinct would not find such universal expression in this way," positing that infant-directed music-making is basic human behavior.[86] The association quotes composer Charles Gounod, best known in that era for his opera *Faust*: "My mother always sang while she was nursing me and I can faithfully say I took my first music lessons unconsciously."[87] Similarly, in 1913 a newspaper piece appeared with Irving Berlin's byline, in which the songwriter discusses how, as the article title puts it, "Song and Sorrow Are Playmates." He claims that the dynamic tension between sadness and happiness features in his own "When I Lost You" and originates in the "sweet, sad song of the cradle" that "convinced the first song-loving audience the world has known—and carried baby to the realms of slumber-land."[88] Seemingly, Berlin believed in the primacy of the lullaby and traced the qualities of his own songs back to that wellspring.

There are two contemporaneous reasons, therefore, for emphasizing the connection between lullabies and the evolution of the classic American popular ballad. First is the belief, by some at the time, that the lullaby was foundational, to music in general and, according to Berlin, to popular song in particular. Further, as electronic microphones became increasingly emblematic of pop music in the 1920s, there was a perception, to an extent, that the crooning of lullabies by parents was somehow linked to the crooning of popular songs by performers.

Crooners were sometimes associated with motherly qualities. Allison Mc-Cracken describes how two of the most prominent female crooners relate to the archetype of the mother. Vaughn de Leath, perhaps the first radio crooner, projected the image of the "soothing," "desexualized 'friend' suggesting a crooning mammy figure giving comfort"[89] (see figure 1.4). Similarly, Kate Smith also "exemplified this motherly persona."[90] Female crooners could project maternality.

Even male crooners could fulfill this maternal role. Gene Austin, one of the pioneer microphone singers, contrasted his style with that of his showbiz predecessors, stating that "I knew I could never sing as loud or perhaps as good as Mister [Al] Jolson, so since he was always talkin' about how his mammy used to croon to him, I just croon like his mammy."[91] Austin is joking, of course—but, as Freud outlined, humor addresses unconscious truths. Fans of Rudy Vallee viewed him in a wide range of ways, from love-god to pal to rival, but one function of his music has been less commented upon than others: to lull to sleep. As one fan wrote, "all I need to do when my baby is crying is turn on your program and she is soon asleep."[92] Thus, even male crooning might function as a lullaby.[93]

In the early 1930s, the idea of a "crooner" became centered on three male singers—Vallee, Crosby, and Russ Columbo—and the term became gendered, primarily denoting men.[94] As the 1930s Swing Era progressed, many big bands toured with a pair of singers, male and female, who were known respectively as "crooner and canary," although both sexes used the microphone techniques of crooning. Meanwhile, the image of "torch singer" became centered on the female persona (as in figure 1.3). By then, although male singers were said to sing torch songs, sometimes very torchily, they were practically never referred to as "torch singers." By the turn of the twenty-first century, those gendered distinctions had become rigid. Nevertheless, these two innovations of 1920s popular vocalizing were widespread, not confined by race, religion, or class—and not by gender. Many of the pioneers of crooning were women, and Lyman was among the first to be dubbed a torch singer.

Crosby came to embody the motherly-fatherly crooner persona, as his image formed and developed through dozens of Hollywood movie musicals. The star was often depicted as having a lullaby-like soothing power in his voice, hinting at the link between microphone crooning and lullaby crooning. Scenes where he lullabies or comforts children by singing to them occur in *Pennies from Heaven* (1936), *East Side of Heaven* (1939), *Blue Skies* (1946), *Here Comes the Groom* (1951), and *High Society* (1956).[95] Crosby delivers sleepy-time songs to adults, too, in *Going My Way* (1944) and *White Christmas* (1954).[96] Further, his dulcet tones quiet a pet bear in *We're Not Dressing* (1934) and settle down the horses in *Rhythm on the Range* (1936). Through these many scenes, the most enduringly famous of the early crooners became associated with the calming influence exemplified by lullabying.

From 1939 onward, Bing Crosby sang early torch songs to children in movie musicals, boosting again the popularity of those vintage works. In *The Star Maker* (1939), a young girl is riddled with stage fright when auditioning for him, so he relaxes her by singing "I Wonder Who's Kissing Her Now." In *If I Had My Way* (1940), he bonds with his young ward, Gloria Jean, by crooning to her the 1913 title song. In *The Birth of the Blues* (1941), he cradles his sweetheart's young relative—a literal "melancholy baby"—as he lullabies her with "My Melancholy Baby" (see figures 1.5, 1.6, 1.7). Through his crooning, Crosby redefined some of the early torch songs, imbuing them with the comforting qualities of the lullaby.

The importance of the lullaby may lie deep in human nature. This possibility adds importance to the early twentieth-century perception of the link between the era's popular song and the crooning of the lullaby. John Diamond writes that "all music flows from the mother" and, from that point of view, "the essence of music is the lullaby."[97] For Diamond, as for the National Child Welfare Association in 1919, the foundation of music lies in the maternal instinct. Diamond goes further, to posit that the "life history of music" is traced in the path from the "lullaby to love song"—love songs convert the lullaby into a form appropriate to adult social life and relationships between love partners.[98] Eric Lott analyzes Bob Dylan's "Lonesome Day Blues," a song touching on loss of both sweetheart and mother; and Lott, too, draws a link between the lullaby and romantic woes:

> The mother is the pre-linguistic source of all music, her heartbeat the first rhythm we hear, her hum among the first melodies; losing her in the process of individuation is our first loss, the first lost object to be introjected as part of the ego's melancholia and one template for our later relationships.[99]

For such writers there is no hard-edged line, in the unconscious, between the mother-infant love relationship and the adult romantic love relationship.

Perhaps, therefore, the importance of love songs is to remind us of the lullaby. Admittedly, early standard ballads usually come across as unhappy or sad and, as well, are sometimes presented as fast, raucous, raunchy, or even

Figure 1.5. Another setting for the torch song: as soothing influence and lullaby. Bing Crosby croons "I Wonder Who's Kissing Her Now" to help Marilyn McKay through her audition in *The Star Maker* (1939).

Figure 1.6. Crosby cheers up Gloria Jean by reviving the 1913 title song in *If I Had My Way* (1940).

Figure 1.7. Crosby lulls six-year-old Carolyn Lee with "My Melancholy Baby" in *The Birth of the Blues* (1941).

vindictive. Nevertheless, in Diamond's view, "every song" is "a potential love song."[100] Within any song lies a lullaby-like, heart-to-heart ballad, given the right tempo, phrasing, focus, mood, and intent—all of these being elements that the performer may change as they like in the popular music culture of the golden age of American popular song.

The link between the torch song and the lullaby is deeply embedded in my own life. By the time I was six or so, my mother was including in her lullabies, for me and my siblings, "Can't Help Lovin' That Man of Mine" (1927) and "I've Got My Love to Keep Me Warm" (1937). The former has long been placed in the torch category, while the latter uses imagery associated with the genre: a flame in the heart that burns ever higher. Both ballads are prime examples of the interiorized, emotionally complex, personal Tin Pan Alley song.

The generation of torch singers and crooners born between 1902 and 1913 might almost literally have cut their eyeteeth on my focus songs: Bing Crosby, Rudy Vallee, Russ Columbo, Helen Morgan, Mildred Bailey, Lee Wiley, the Boswell Sisters, the Mills Brothers, Ivie Anderson, Ethel Merman, Maxine Sullivan, Mary Martin, Buddy Clark, Helen Ward, Frankie Laine, and Billy Eckstine—all were born during these years. The big hit when Crosby and Bailey were born in early 1903 was "Bill Bailey, Won't You Please Come Home." Maxine Sullivan might well have heard "Some of These Days" while still in the womb in late 1910, and she grew up to sing it on film. The 1909 hit "I Wonder Who's Kissing Her Now" was still a favorite in vaudeville when Buddy Clark was born in 1912—and decades later Clark was humming that melody into a microphone for the movie musical *I Wonder Who's Kissing Her Now*.[101]

These people were born alongside the songs that they would someday revive into new fame, and these songs in turn helped make them famous. By a trick of historical timing, the new electronic media of recordings, radio, movies, and television transported their voices and images across the nation and, eventually, the world . . . and through time: their recordings and films outlived their bodies. Thereby, this generation—of singers and of songs—became touchstones of global culture.

PROMINENCE THEN AND NOW

The gestalt of the primal lullaby–love song connection, the shaping of personas for a generation of electronic-era stars, and, through them, the transporting of Yankee cultural seeds abroad: all of these are factors that argue for the importance of the classic American popular ballad. In addition, love songs were usually given a top ranking both as works of art and as money-makers. Ian Whitcomb concludes that, for Tin Pan Alley, "the staple survival food was the ballad."[102] Too, these are the compositions most praised by critical analysts, and therefore it is not surprising to find Allen Forte devoting an entire musicological tome exclusively to *The American Popular Ballad of the Golden Era*. The high value placed on ballads supplies part of the raison d'être for the following study: Which are the earliest of the enduring, jazzy yet poignant personal ballads—and what are their stories?

In the eyes of the most acclaimed singers, too, the ballads held a special status. Sinatra, the ultimate icon of the Great American Songbook, in his 1965 television special says that "probably the most satisfaction I get—or any singer gets, for that matter—is singing a well-written ballad."[103] When he sat down in the mid-1990s with his daughter Tina to select his favorite tracks from the 450 that he had recorded for the Reprise label, he chose twenty ballads—most of them very torchy.[104] Such love songs were always the most central part of Sinatra's output.

The first torch songs created that alchemy of the twentieth century: vernacular American lyrics and music, combined with the personal statement about love (or life). We take this treasure for granted, but it took work to develop it. We are still in the era that started then. These songs were admired and performed in the rock and roll era, which acted as the foundation for today's popular music. Many of the pioneers who established the sounds of rock embraced such Tin Pan Alley songs. Elvis Presley had a hit with the 1928 "Are You Lonesome Tonight"; Little Richard with the 1926 "Baby Face"; James Brown with 1931's "Prisoner of Love." Etta James put a permanent imprint on 1941's "At Last"; Bob Dylan recorded the 1934 "Blue Moon"; and Janis Joplin liked to feature 1935's "Little Girl Blue." In more recent decades, rock-era icons have recorded uncounted albums either partially or exclusively in tribute to classic pop: from Ringo Starr (1969) through to Lady Gaga (2014) and beyond, with the most prominent instances probably being two series: Linda Ronstadt (1983–1986); and Rod Stewart (2002–2010).

Rock-era stars recorded old Tin Pan Alley ballads—but, further, the same artists triumphed with new songs that became landmarks of rock and roll songwriting and are in much the same category. Consider these personal vernacular songs about love: "I Want You, I Need You, I Love You" (Presley), "I Don't Know What You've Got But It's Got Me" (Little Richard), "Lost Someone" (James Brown), "Don't Cry, Baby" (Etta James), "Just Like a Woman" (Bob Dylan), "Piece of My Heart" (Janis Joplin). These were hits, touchstones, and style-setters. Before we could have any of these—and all that has followed them—the torch songs of the early twentieth century first had to set the mold. When I started writing this book, I defined torch songs for a colleague, and he said, "Oh, you mean just about every song Adele has ever written!" Although for a while it seemed that popular music divided in 1955, in retrospect we can see that Tin Pan Alley, while perhaps not being "roots music" in the sense of low-profile or rural, nevertheless constitutes one of the roots of the rock era.

DESCRIBING AND VALUING TIN PAN ALLEY SONGS

As its critics claim, Tin Pan Alley songs can sometimes be trite, maudlin, phony, and artificial.[105] In them there is a strong tendency toward the idealization of love. The centuries-old tradition of courtly love—which makes the object of desire into a perfect being, an angel, in the mold of the Virgin Mary or Sir Lancelot—found a warm welcome in Tin Pan Alley.[106] The titles proclaim "You're a Heavenly Thing" (1936). This image of an immaculate lover, chaste and spotless, sometimes merges with an infantilization of the love object—she (or he) is a pure, untouched "baby." "Pretty Baby" (1916) and "Baby Face" (1926) are topped by "Angel" (1945), and all are trumped by "Angel Child" (1921).

In 1955, S. I. Hayakawa, critiquing the trajectory of romance sketched in these songs, wrote: "an enormous amount of unrealistic idealization" results "inevitably in disappointment, disenchantment, frustration, and, most importantly, self-pity," and finally takes pathological refuge in a "retreat into a symbolic world" (such as with the protagonist who decides to take as his sweetheart a "Paper Doll"—a 1942 hit first copyrighted in 1915).[107] He contrasts those attitudes with the outlook of the blues, which is more realistic and resilient. In a blues lyric, "the object of love is . . . looked at fairly realistically," with "the physical basis of love" being "more candidly acknowledged" and the duties being "those of living up to one's obligations as a mate."[108] Yet, as we shall see, the lines between the blues and popular song are not solid; there is space for going back and forth. Hayakawa's article is full of contradictions (not the least of which is that several songs he praises are not blues at all).[109] Nevertheless, any balanced assessment of Tin Pan Alley songs must acknowledge the oft-mentioned fact that they often present a sappy, sugary, cutesy façade.

There are many factors, however, that counteract the shortcomings of classic pop style. The lyrics are usually conversational, and this trait keeps them tied to the everyday. They frequently employ slang, which can sometimes undercut the sentimentality. The words and music engage in a dance that is usually well coordinated and often playful and witty. They are frequently self-conscious about their own conventionality, subtly calling into question—even making fun of—their own idealized picture of romance. They can be a complex mixture of tongue-in-cheek and straight-faced, of cool and warm.

Elements I have already discussed prove also to be factors that mitigate these songs' sentimentality. Tin Pan Alley compositions tacitly give freedom to the performers to inflect each song with individuality and spontaneity. The flexibility in Tin Pan Alley products not only was understood from the musical and cultural context but also was written into the sheet music in subtle ways—ways that we will examine again and again in the upcoming chapters. One consequence of this factor is that, although I write about torch songs and other love ballads as slow, serious songs distinct from other subgenres such as rhythm songs, charm songs, comedy songs, and so forth, there are really no clear-cut dividing lines. In this musical culture, fast may be done slow and slow may be done fast. Even more germane to the present discussion: in this tradition, serious songs may be approached playfully and playful songs seriously. (Instances will abound in the discussions that follow. For example, below I will analyze Sinatra's infusion of the sprightly "Ida [Sweet as Apple Cider]" with ardor.)

Are Tin Pan Alley songs corny? Sometimes yes, sometimes no—but, with the tradition's implicit permission, performers may mock or bypass, or inject or emphasize, or transcend the corniness seemingly inherent in any particular song. As part of this legacy of ambiguity, performers (even songwriters themselves) may render the songs with almost any attitude, from sincerity through irony. Everyone in showbiz knew you could mess with a song in any way you could get the audience to accept.

Further, the depictions of love in the personal ballads might cut deeply into the psyche. Beneath the conventions of love and loss in the torch song, all the cutesy idolization and infantilization of the beloved, perhaps lies a deeper truth: every relationship in life may be seen as a metaphor for the primary relationship, of mother and baby.

SONG STYLE

The short refrains of Tin Pan Alley songs are, as Gerald Mast puts it, "compact exercises in musical logic."[110] At the start, in the 1890s and early twentieth century, many had brief eight-measure or sixteen-measure choruses. When compared to the classic songs of the 1920s, early sixteen-measure refrains sometimes seem over before they have really got going—and despite the fact that many of them proved to be enduringly popular. Perhaps because such short refrains felt insubstantial, the average chorus length grew, eventually settling on thirty-two measures as the standard. That is the length of the refrains of favorites like "Take Me Out to the Ball Game" and "White Christmas." There is sometimes an extension of those thirty-two bars, as with the familiar second ending of "Over the Rainbow," or a doubling of the measures to sixty-four bars, as with "I've Got My Love to Keep Me Warm." Nevertheless, overall, these songs stay, as Ian Whitcomb describes them, "neat and tight."[111]

Yet they are not too short. Their thirty-two measures are big enough to bear emotional weight. They are long enough to have drama—to have a clear beginning, middle, and end. As singer Julius LaRosa appreciated (and, of course, tried to do himself), Sinatra "was able to turn a thirty-two bar song into a three-act play."[112] Thus, the actual length is less important than a more elusive factor: the sense of eventfulness in the song. Jerome Kern can write satisfying refrains of sixteen measures, like "Bill," or of thirty-two bars, like "They Didn't Believe Me" (1914). The two compositions have much the same "weight" and seem equally melody-filled and dramatic. The secret lies in a combination of tune, rhythmic textures, harmonies, and (in terms of the words) rhyme, logic, and dramatic action—and the overall interaction between these elements.

These songs are usually divided into clear segments. The Tin Pan Alley refrain is most often thirty-two measures long and structured into four parts—therefore, each part is eight bars long. The sections repeat—often with some slight variation, but in such a way that they are easy to learn. Until 1924 the most common form was a binary form, in two halves, wherein the initial melody repeats at the mid-point: ABAB or ABAC. "Fly Me to the Moon" is basically ABAB, and "Take Me Out to the Ball Game" and "White Christmas" are in the ABAC shape.[113]

From 1924 onward, the most common form is AABA, as with "Over the Rainbow," "Georgia on My Mind," and "At Last." By contrast, in the era of the pioneer torch songs, AABA was relatively rare; none of the songs featured in this book have that structure. Most of these early ballads are either ABAC or close variations thereof.

Almost all my focus songs have another trait that was already a strong convention. Peter van der Merwe describes how such songs create "a sort of limerick effect towards the end, whereby the final cadence is preceded by a short repeated rhythm."[114] The music and lyrics work together, melopoetically, to create this effect, for "often, as in the limerick itself," the rhythmic quickening is "reinforced by an actual verbal rhyme."[115] They deliver a quick one-two punch in a pair of penultimate lines. Here is my own whimsical example:

> A song that is from Tin Pan Alley,
> When it gets near its end will not dally.
> They throw in a couplet,
> But not a sextuplet,
> To prove they will not shilly-shally.

This way of ending can be very effective in performance. In comedy songs, the quickening can create a final laugh. In torch songs, the penultimate couplet can be used for sentimental effect, as the singer holds for a momentary allargando, lingering on the climactic thoughts.

At the start of the twentieth century, the verses (i.e., the introductory sections) were often the main part of the song—as they had been in most folk songs and would be again in many rock-era songs.[116] Writers tended to take a bit more leeway in varying the length and structure of verses, compared to refrains.[117] Usually, during this period there were two verse stanzas, each one followed by the refrain. In the 1910s, songwriters such as George M. Cohan and Irving Berlin confessed that finding the second set of lyrics to fit the verse melody was their "bugbear," for their "interest cools, and . . . eager to go to work on a new idea" they procrastinate, until they are forced to yield to "the demands of the professional singer."[118]

Berlin must have been relieved as verses to songs became less and less important during the first decades of the twentieth century. The performance histories of my corpus songs display evidence of a trend: singers on vaudeville and Broadway stages found that two verse stanzas helped them put a song over, but the formats of recording, radio, and sound movies slowly transformed this situation.

As the 1920s turned into the 1930s, verses started to be omitted from recordings and radio performances—and, eventually, even from many song sheets, such as with the big torch hits of 1933, "Stormy Weather" and "Smoke Gets in Your Eyes." By the end of the 1930s, hearing the verse in a performance, whether instrumental or vocal, became the exception rather than the rule.[119] Thus, over the course of the early twentieth century, the "weight" of the song shifted from verse to refrain, and this put new demands on the refrain to deliver a strong emotional impact.

Tin Pan Alley songs are built to be memorized and sung. The compact structures aid in this, as do repeated verbal and musical elements. Within each song, there is what Raymond Knapp describes as "a strong feeling of periodicity," using the same material over and over, with "the repetition of key phrases."[120] Knapp points out that the title phrase is often "a kind of built in 'jingle.'"[121] The title words (plus the melodic motif they are set to) act as a basic building block, governing, as Banfield puts it, "the melopoetic structure of a whole song."[122]

The songwriters themselves often emphasize the importance of the title phrase. Johnny Mercer said that an appealing title was "half the battle won," and Sammy Cahn called it a "sort of trigger" which he could then "follow wherever it leads."[123] Lyricists often supplied this title phrase as the initial kernel of the song, which would then inspire the composer to create the tune.[124] Whether created before or after the melody, those title words were key.

Lyrics became increasingly conversational, veering away from the highfalutin poeticisms of past song texts. In the era of the pioneer torch songs, the rhymes were a mixture of true and false. Lyricists might match "home" with a perfect rhyme like "roam"—or they might pair it with an off-rhyme, creating an assonance with "alone." By 1934 veteran Alley writers like Irving Berlin had stopped using imperfect rhymes, saying "I don't rhyme *m* with *n* anymore.... I look at the old things and blush with shame," because of their naïve vocabulary.[125] Yet, despite this change of style, the pioneer torch songs I write about continued to hold their own in the more sophisticated thirties.

Songwriters also grew more adept at matching the emphasis of the words to that of the music. In the mature Tin Pan Alley style, the accents of the syllables usually match the accent of the music.[126] They avoided leaning hard on unimportant words in the phrase, such as "the" or "too." More and more, also, the style dictated that the match of tune and words should be syllabic—one note matching one syllable. If there did happen to be more than one note to a syllable, it usually was at the end of a phrase where it did not ruin the colloquial flow. All these conversational traits intensified the personal mode of the germinating torch song genre. The songs became like the confessions of a friend sitting down and telling you their problems in ordinary, everyday speech—but sung instead.

LACK OF ORIGINALITY IN TIN PAN ALLEY

Tin Pan Alley cared little for originality and was always more concerned with the pragmatic questions "Does it work?" and "Will it make a profit?" In 1905, in the first issue of show business bible *Variety*, the lyricist Will D. Cobb reported that his hits "Good-Bye Dolly Gray" (1900) and "Good-Bye Little Girl" (1904) were "ridiculed" because of their "sameness."[127] This was most deliberate, Cobb declares: "I put that 'sameness' in the second song because I wanted a sameness in the money I received."[128] In 1916 Irving Berlin stated: "There is no such thing as a new melody. . . . all of them have been traced back to some other melody. Our work is to connect the old phrases in a new way, so that they sound like a new tune."[129] Original melodies were not possible and not important, Berlin claimed, and "the real originality in song writing consists in the construction of the song rather than in the actual melodic base."[130] Indeed, the songwriter declared, putting a song together is "like reassembling furniture."[131] Bert Williams, stage star and composer of hit songs such as "Nobody," referred similarly to the creative process behind his melodies: "The tunes to popular songs are mostly made up of standard parts, like a motor car. As a machinist assembles a motor car then, I assembled the tunes."[132] In the early 1920s, bandleader Paul Whiteman voiced the same sentiments almost prescriptively: "More than half the modern art of composing a popular song comes in knowing what to steal and how to adapt it."[133] Music publisher Edward Marks reported that "L. Wolfe Gilbert, once our professional manager, and the author of many a hit lyric, once said that a melody, to be successful, must be reminiscent."[134] Marks goes on to matter-of-factly note, with a kind of pragmatism that is almost shocking, that "if a song writer is ethical, he will not cop a tune within three years of its publication."[135] Therefore, clearly, it was perfectly moral to reuse somebody else's tune, as long as the older tune had already had its chance on the marketplace for a few years. For many early twentieth-century songwriters, the creative models were stealing, adapting, recombining, assembly. To a certain extent, therefore, the concept of authorship is a problematic frame on which to hang the study of the origins of this genre—and, so far, most scholars have used it as their main organizing principle and critical lens.

I shall now present a preliminary example of Tin Pan Alley song theft and performance tradition. This will also serve to illustrate a type of song that *almost* fits my criteria for a ballad, but not quite. Its history will prepare us for the upcoming chapters, placing in perspective the strange stories surrounding my corpus.

In 1900, for a Broadway show, John Stromberg and Edgar Smith wrote "Ma Blushin' Rosie (Ma Posie Sweet)," which was a hit.[136] In 1903 Eddie Munson and Eddie Leonard published "Ida (Sweet as Apple Cider)," which was also a hit. The two lyrics paint the same scenario: nighttime, a man serenading his sweetheart, praising her, and urging her to a rendezvous. The persona is shared and conventional: a love-besotted African American male. (The fact that the protagonist is Black is indicated in the verses of both lyrics—and in the dialect Smith uses throughout in "Rosie," so stereotyped that I prefer to call it "blackface dialect" to distinguish it from any of the real world's Black dialects.) The meters are the same (two-four). Both refrains feature the overall melodic structure of ABAB'. All of those are traits shared by many songs of the era.

Beyond such general similarities, "Ida" also appears to be closely modeled on "Ma Blushin' Rosie" in its details. The initial melopoetic kernels are similar: the first half-phrase is the beloved's two-syllable name, set to an ascending whole step (*f* up to *g*). This is followed by the second-half phrase, ending with a rhyme for the lady's moniker (in the case of "Ida," a charmingly false rhyme, "cider")—all of which spans the interval of a fourth. The phrasing and note values of "Ida" mostly follow those of "Rosie" (see musical examples 1.1 and 1.2).

The later song does make some minor alterations. Notably, "Ida" includes a pair of skipping sixteenth-notes at refrain measures 2 and 10, and some changes in three bars of the final section (which makes the second B section almost deserve the marking C, as a new strain). Both songs share the same schema for the internal and end rhymes throughout the first two stanzas: aab cdb. Perhaps most telling are the parallels in the second sections, where the two lyrics are clearly equivalent: "Come out heah in de moonlight" and "Come out in the silv'ry moonlight." In both instances, these words are accompanied by whole steps and accidentals in the melodic line, and, in the following phrase, a similar descending whole step (from *d* down to *c*, although with the notes for "sweet lub" in "Rosie" being an octave higher than those for "whisper" in "Ida").

Example 1.1. "Ma Blushin' Rosie (Ma Posie Sweet)," refrain, melody line.

The two works clearly resemble each other, but the reason can never be proved. Did one imitate another—and, if so, purposefully or unconsciously? "Rosie" was the first in print and in hit status, yet it is possible "Ida" had been written earlier.[137] Were both pieces modeled after a third, now forgotten, model? If the authors of these songs were unknown, and folklorists had collected these

Example 1.2. "Ida (Sweet as Apple Cider)," refrain, melody line.

examples, they would undoubtedly be viewed as representatives of a single folk song family, especially since the two songs originate in the same region (the United States) and culture (show business). Such resemblances between songs during this era place in perspective the liberal borrowings (or stealings) illustrated in the chapters to come.

It is remarkable that the public embraced both "Ma Blushin' Rosie" and "Ida." They were hits when first introduced, and their popularity was sustained for decades by major stars and numerous movies. Throughout the 1940s, Al Jolson kept "Ma Blushin' Rosie" alive on radio, record, and screen (in 1946's *The Jolson Story*). "Ida" stayed in the repertoire of its writer, Eddie Leonard, till his death at age seventy in 1941. Another star, Eddie Cantor, whose wife was named Ida, took it up and often featured it prominently on his broadcasts. "Ida" entered the jazz (particularly Dixieland) repertoire, thanks to hit records by Red Nichols (1927) and Glen Miller (1941).

Judging by iTunes and YouTube, performances of "Rosie" are fewer than those of "Ida": the latter has proved more useful to performers and the vast public. "Ida" conjures an extra fascination that "Rosie" does not quite attain. This added sparkle gleams from tiny facets of both the music and the words: the initial motif being sequenced upward in the fifth measure, short rests at the end of lines, shorter half-phrases in the second part, the lack of blackface dialect in the lyrics, teasing off-rhymes and inner rhymes, mini-climaxes. The second at bat outscored the first at the plate.

Leonard got around to recording "Ida" for his guest appearance in the Bing Crosby movie *If I Had My Way*. Leonard illustrates how much latitude the performer has in this tradition to define the song in a manner distinct from the printed text. Leonard's rendition of his signature song reveals that he probably originated a performance-tradition melodic elaboration that is heard in a majority of recordings: descending and ascending figures at the end of certain phrases, commonly added to refrain measures 3–4, 19–20, and 23–24

Example 1.3. Eddie Leonard's variation on "Ida (Sweet as Apple Cider)," refrain, melody line.

Example 1.4. Common variant on "Ida," mm. 1-8.

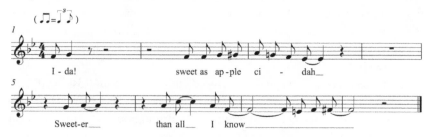

(see example 1.4). These added notes make the piece skip along, increasing the soft-shoe feeling that is hinted at in the printed score. One of the credited authors of the printed song has himself redefined its melody through a purely orally transmitted variation. This demonstrates how compelling is the dynamic between composing and performing in this American popular music tradition.

Could I analyze "Ida" as a love ballad—perhaps even a torch ballad? It certainly is a personal song—"you and I"—and it is in the vernacular, both musically and verbally. Maybe, but it lacks the aspects that I am ferreting out. For one, it has very little sense of intimacy. After all, the protagonist is trying to lure his beloved out to meet with him, therefore she must be at some physical distance from him. More importantly, though, "Ida" conveys only a minimal *emotional* intimacy. Indeed, the protagonist does not communicate much inner life.

"Ida" generates little heat or deeper resonances—nor does it seem to try to. The mood of the lyric is playful—marked by that goofy off-rhyme of "Ida" and "cider." The melody seems designed for the kind of light and easy soft-shoe dance that Leonard does so beautifully in *If I Had My Way*, helped by those skipping notes in the second measure.

Songs like "Ida," wonderful and enduring as they are, find only passing mention in my survey. Despite the fact I love them, I will sadly neglect such charmers as "Oh, You Beautiful Doll" (1911) and that irresistible "moon" trilogy, "Shine On, Harvest Moon" (1908), "By the Light of the Silvery Moon" (1909), and "Moonlight Bay" (1912). Nor can I discuss the lively hits that helped spread the new musical gospel of American rhythm, such as "Alexander's Ragtime Band," "Waiting for the Robert E. Lee," or "Ballin' the Jack" (1913). Among ballads, some simply did not contain enough substance for later decades of crooners and became primarily useful in nostalgic contexts, such as "You Tell Me Your Dream" (1900), "Sweet Adeline" (1903), and "Down by the Old Mill Stream" (1910). Appealing as they are, these items do not aim for the intimacy, the substance, and the hint of an internal life that marked the primary mode of the classic American popular ballad.

Nevertheless, all of those sentimental barbershop favorites, soft-shoe numbers, or rhythm songs can be performed in a way that brings out any potential intimacy, interiority, and emotional poignancy. Sinatra (while with the Tommy Dorsey Orchestra) was recorded on a 1941 radio show transcription, singing "Ida." Taken at a lively tempo, the tune swings. Yet the singer manages to turn the piece into a strongly romantic plea. In Sinatra's hands, the song's friskiness is transformed into something quite sexy. The crooner suffuses the whole with a creamy tone quality, and he changes and adds a few words. Also—perhaps most crucially—he avoids the playful added notes common to the performance tradition. Instead, he creates subtle alternative melodic decorations, connecting phrases—and bending notes, such as on "know," "low," and "without." He builds toward the climax, substituting for "oh" the more fervent "please." Then he does incorporate a performance-tradition touch as he slides up from "honey, do" to a slightly impassioned "Ida-a," thereby segueing dramatically into the final section, leaning a bit into the concluding high notes. Overall, through skill and will, he injects some emotional heat into this lover's wooing. Sinatra was very intent on doing this, stating that "even when the words didn't mean much—and most of them don't," he aimed "to sing them in such a way that they seemed to."[138] With such an approach, a performer can transform any song into a torch song. It takes some doing to delve a bit deeper—but is worth the effort, for these songs are many-sided.

In this book, I will trace the performance traditions for the earliest enduring ballads of the Golden Age as they are documented through recordings. These supply a generous sample of variants. Nevertheless, beyond those audio snapshots lie many undocumented professional and amateur renditions of these songs, with innumerable further variations.

For example: as I am leaving the nursing home, I stop to sing with the lady on the couch near the entrance. She merrily chirps along with the radio, making up her own adaptation of "Some of These Days" on the spur of the moment: "One of these days, I'll be lonely / One of these days, you're gonna miss me." Her spontaneous variations on the original lyric demonstrate the folk song process in action. With group singing, too, a song often takes on a life of its own, sometimes straying far from the printed version. Most of these variants will remain forever lost to posterity. Renditions that do happen to be recorded must be viewed as merely the tip of the iceberg.

Scott Yanow asks about the swing-era crooners who tried performing rock-era material in the late 1960s: "How many more decades could they sing the same old Cole Porter and Gershwin warhorses?"[139] Given a healing touch, there was a lot more life in those bruised old warhorses than met the eye—and a whole herd of other old horses where they came from, ready to come out and play, if the singers only had the support system for finding them. To push the metaphor a bit, these are my goals in the study that follows: exploring the herd, reviving the old nag, and looking in its eyes for the window to its soul. I seek to accomplish this by unlocking the story of a song's creation, its performance and reception history, and examining anew the musical, dramatic, and emotional potentialities within it.

Through my reexamination of these early ballads I aspire to polish the somewhat tarnished image of these seminal works—and, hopefully, intrigue performers and listeners enough to get them to search through Tin Pan Alley more extensively. Admittedly, in the 1910s, the Alley's tin pans were still in the middle of brewing their full alchemic magic. Therefore, I do not promise that you will find gold—but you might find silver.

Put together, these songs reveal a spectacular kaleidoscopic history. The people are fascinating—the names on the sheet music (composers, lyricists, arrangers, publishers, and performers) and many, many more—all with a nation bustling around them. This is an American story.

These sagas are entertaining in and of themselves, full of strong passions, glamorous high life and gritty low life, odd accidents of fate, comedy and tragedy. But they also reveal more: the creation of a work of art and its spread throughout the culture is a mixture of complex events, combining mysterious, miraculous processes inside the artist, and an intricate web of social processes—collaborating, competing, stealing, borrowing, giving, sometimes ignoring and sometimes exploiting the marketplace. Their stories offer fresh insight into the nature of human creativity.

Chapter Two

"BILL BAILEY, WON'T YOU PLEASE COME HOME?"

"*B*ill Bailey, Won't You Please Come Home?," a 1902 hit composed by Hughie Cannon, is the first enduring song that presents central elements of the torch genre. In all such pieces the music is jazzy and the lyric is vernacular, and in "Bill Bailey," as in others of its type, the scenario is that the beloved has left or is just leaving. As a result, the protagonist says, "I'm alone and blue" or "I'm about to be alone and blue." Then follows one of several potential further responses: "I hope you get hurt as much as you hurt me," "I want to find someone new," or the simple supplication, as in Cannon's song, "Come home."

"Bill Bailey" firmly sits on the foundation of its introductory verse, which is a precursor of the then-developing blues idiom—one of several such harbingers during this era. The verse is much less often performed than the refrain (although, thanks to its championing by Pearl Bailey, the intro did receive a thorough airing in the mid-twentieth century), yet its place in early blues culture supplies one crucial link between the torch and blues traditions.

"Bill Bailey" is rarely done purely as a love ballad. Nevertheless, it foreshadowed a long series of torch numbers, including "Some of These Days" (explored in chapter 7), as well as standards that issued forth soon thereafter, such as "I Ain't Got Nobody" (1914) and "After You've Gone" (1918). By 1919 this same mold produced one of the core songs of the torch repertoire, "Baby, Won't You Please Come Home?"—which echoes in form and lyric its 1902 forerunner. All of these served as progenitors of decades of jazz-friendly pieces that depict related scenes of abandonment, reacted to with vengefulness, with loneliness, or with a beseeching for reconciliation: "Someday, Sweetheart" (1919); "Who's Sorry Now" (1923); two songs of the 1920s pleading "Daddy, Won't You Please Come Home"; "Goody-Goody" (1936); "Hurry Home" (1938); "'Round Midnight" (1944); "Cry Me a River" (1953); "I Wanna Be Around" (1959); "May I Come In" (1963) . . . the list goes on. As it turned out, Bill and his missus became the trunk of a large family tree.

Cannon's ditty also became a staple of popular culture. As one sign of this status, it is probably the most parodied song discussed in this book. Through the decades, the folk—sports fans, athletes, labor union members, journalists, voters, politicians, and banquet speakers—wrote their own words for the song, adapting it to almost any occasion.

When it appeared in 1902, Cannon's song was one example of an already established genre: songs with blackface dialect and a lot of capacity for rhythmic oomph. The genre had flourished in the American minstrel format, from its inception in the 1840s onward. In the mid-1890s, a fresh wave, often incorporating the new style of ragtime music, swept the popular music scene. This vogue crystallized with a hit of the 1895–96 theatrical season, "The Bully," in which the established bully of the town roams around, including to a dance, to hunt down his new rival—and eventually finds and kills him. This African American folk song was printed in six different versions, all adaptations by white men. Star singer May Irwin, a hefty, assertive white comedienne, popularized it as "May Irwin's Bully Song."[1] That success sparked a trend, and for the next ten years and more, music publishers issued many of these blackface dialect songs.[2] They were commonly called "coon songs." The word "coon" as a designation for people of color comes from the dark-faced "raccoon"—an insult, because a raccoon can be a scavenging nuisance, but nevertheless some victims of the label remembered that the animal also often outsmarts its opponents.

The music publishers Howley and Haviland—soon to be joined by their star songwriter, Paul Dresser—were among the most important promoters of the coon genre, issuing a long series of such pieces. (Frederick Haviland was a Quaker and probably the canny partner, because, later, when he left, the firm quickly went bankrupt, while his own new firm stayed in business for decades. Patrick Howley was a bright, friendly chap with a physical disability. Paul Dresser [the brother of famed novelist Theodore Dreiser] was a comedian on stage and a melodramatic sentimentalist in his songwriting—and a good-hearted patsy in either capacity, from all reports.)[3] African American writers created many of the firm's products in this line, such as "No Coons Allowed" (1897) and "The Luckiest Coon in Town" (1899). Today, the mere titles are offensive. Nevertheless, as is implied by "No Coons Allowed," these lyrics have the potential to be as complex a metaphor as the raccoon, presenting a double-edged message, partaking both of oppression and resistance.

THE CREATION OF THE SONG

In 1900 Howley, Haviland and Dresser began to tap the talents of a friendly circle of five white minstrel show performers. The publishing house first discovered this bonanza through the success of Hughie Cannon and John Queen's 1901 comedy song, "Just Because She Made Them Goo-Goo Eyes"—a catchy tune with a lyric about a blackface minstrel performer, undone by a flirtatious woman in the audience, quickly losing both his job and her affection. As with "Bill Bailey," the introductory verse of "Goo-Goo Eyes" can be analyzed, as demonstrated by Peter C. Muir, as one kind of "proto-blues."[4] These were precursors of the blues—in this case, similar to the enduring standard "Frankie and Johnny." In the final tally, the firm ended up publishing ten songs that prefigured the blues culture of the rest of the twentieth century, many of which have a verse of the "Frankie and Johnny" type. The most enduring of their songs with proto-blues verses, appropriately, is the centerpiece: the fifth in that sequence, Cannon's "Bill Bailey, Won't You Please Come Home?"

Cannon was part of a group, and his most famous song, "Bill Bailey, Won't You Please Come Home?" is also part of a group, a cycle of songs linked in various ways. The dramatic situations, character names, verbal phrases, and musical harmonies of these songs often echo each other. Together they form a protracted dance of rejection and pleading, back and forth, man to woman, woman to man. These songwriters—Cannon especially—conveyed their sagas of loss in blunt terms and with a straightforward, down-to-earth tone. The protagonists are spirited even in dejection, needy but resilient, humorous, and filled with gumption.

Cannon straddled the line between folk songster and commercial musician, as Muir details, "applying the process" of folk variation to Tin Pan Alley hits, "working creatively in this field."[5] Indeed, Muir claims, "he must be regarded as the first composer to base his songwriting career . . . around the commercialization of blues culture," anticipating W. C. Handy, acclaimed as the Father of the Blues, "by well over a decade."[6] Cannon died young. In 1912 he was only thirty-five years old, penniless and alcoholic, when his divorce became final on June 17—and he died that same day, in a charity ward hospital in Ohio.[7]

Cannon's early life saw him bouncing around the nation with his mother, an actress. She divorced his father (an actor-writer), took the young Hughie touring, settled down in Pennsylvania for a stretch with a second husband, then divorced him, too, but stayed in town where she married yet again. She and her third husband managed theatres and put on shows. By the 1890s, Cannon was already alcoholic—he had been "pickled" since age sixteen, he claimed—and had probably hit the road himself as a minstrel performer, pianist, and songwriter.[8] (He was also supposed to be a fine soft-shoe dancer.) Ten years after his death, his chums Frank and Bert Leighton wrote that "Hughie's songs, which netted publishers tens of thousands, were sold by him in barrooms where he played the piano for a living"—in one instance for "a round of drinks for the house and a suit of clothes."[9] It is fitting, then, that his most famous song, "Bill

Bailey, Won't You Please Come Home?," became, as the 1950s turned into the 1960s, the quintessential nightclub song.

Cannon and the Leighton brothers were part of an intertwining social fabric of performers who are credited with almost half of the early significant proto-blues songs.[10] The others, according to the Leightons, were legendary ragtime pioneer Ben Harney; Walter Wilson (whom the Leightons call Gutter Wilson); and John Queen (Johnny to the Leightons). The brothers claimed that this group brought, in "sterilized versions" and "strongly censored form," to the "sanctity of a good American Methodist home" the "pathetic lamentations of the unfortunates of the underworld . . . Negro outcasts . . . cowboy, miner and gambler."[11] Among such songs the Leightons confidently place the refrain of "Bill Bailey," which, they state, "came to being in the soul of some dusky light o' love, dwelling . . . far beyond the world" of the white parlor piano and its middle-class customers of sheet music.

From some contemporary perspectives, Cannon and his circle might be seen as the typical white men stealing, for money and glory, the music of Black people. On the basis of a closer examination, however, Muir posits that "Cannon was not merely a transcriber of other people's folk material, but a folk artist who with each song reworked material of the 'Frankie' song family afresh."[12] Cannon's hit songs did not, in the end, help him rise above the conditions of poverty, no more than did the compositions of the even more forgotten African Americans who were creating the blues ballad (and blues proper) songs of the time.

Although Cannon uses blackface dialect throughout "Bill Bailey," "there is," as Muir puts it, "little sense of denigration in Cannon's work, and in this he was part of a wider cultural trend that, from about 1902, treated coon songs not as vehicles for racist attitudes, but merely as ragtime songs using black dialect."[13] "Bill Bailey" might be seen as part of a group of blackface dialect songs that, like "Good Morning, Carrie" (1901), have been viewed in retrospect as part of an attempt by songwriters to reform the coon song genre, moving away from violence and crime and toward celebrations of music and dance and the exploration of love relationships.[14]

The first hit song about Bill Bailey and his lady love was "Ain't Dat a Shame?" copyrighted on June 3, 1901, with authorship credited to John Queen (lyrics) and Walter Wilson (music), and, of course, published by Howley, Haviland and Dresser. Bert Leighton also claimed authorship of "Ain't Dat a Shame."[15] This confusion of authorship may relate to the fact, presented by Muir, that "Shame" can be viewed as just one of many variations on a folk song that had already been set in print in a 1898 Boston publication, "Take Me Back, Babe," credited to T. Barrett McMahon.[16] The texts and the authorship credits overlap to a great extent—and this fact testifies to the communal roots of these innovative works.

As with so many songs of the time, Wilson's sixteen-measure refrain melody seems to be over before it has gotten into gear. Nevertheless, "Ain't Dat a Shame?" ignited the Bill Bailey saga. By July 1901, Edward Foote Gardner estimates, "Shame" was achieving wide success, starting to be mentioned in the news, and its popularity peaked in November.

Cannon wrote "Bill Bailey, Won't You Please Come Home?" as his "answer song" to Queen and Wilson, making his chorus a relatively expansive thirty-two measures. This greater refrain length allows for more musical, verbal, and dramatic development.

Example 2.1. "Bill Bailey, Won't You Please Come Home?," verse and refrain, piano-vocal score.

big gang hang-ing 'round; And to dat crowd
I see you no more?" Bill winked his eye,

She yelled out loud:
As he heard her cry:

fz

REFRAIN

Won't you come home, Bill Bai - ley, won't you come

mp-f *ff*

home? She moans de whole day

long;　　　　　　　　　　I'll　do　de

cook - ing,　dar - ling,　I'll　pay　de　rent;

I　knows　I've　done　you　wrong;

—　　　　　　　'Mem - ber　dat　rain - y　eve　dat

The success of "Ain't Dat a Shame" set Cannon and his chums on a spree, writing follow-up songs about Bill Bailey, with five songs from this crowd, stretching from 1901 through 1908. All five have verses that are variations of the "Frankie and Johnny" type of blues ballad—in phrasing, sometimes in melody and harmony, and in the use of the "done me wrong" verbal motif. Other song-writers jumped on the bandwagon, too, with songs less related to the original series musically, but still using the name Bill Bailey. There were also, in these years, many closely similar songs about other Black lovers, such as "Hannah, Won't You Open That Door" (the protagonist here being Bill Johnson, perhaps an allusion to the vaudevillian-songwriter Billy Johnson who contributed to Haviland's "Bill Bailey" series) and "Alexander, Don't You Love Your Baby No More?," both of them 1904 hits by Harry Von Tilzer and Andrew Sterling. There is little difference between the "Bill Bailey" songs and others by Cannon and his circle that do not mention Bill at all: "You Needn't Come Home" (1901), "Fare Thee, Honey, Fare Thee Well" (1901), "Alec Busby, Don't Go Away" (1903), and "Ain't Dat Too Bad" (1905). For some reason, however, audiences seemed attracted to Bill Bailey himself. Here is a summary of his saga in song:

1) "Ain't Dat a Shame" (1901) (John Queen/Walter Wilson)—When Bill first appears, he is storming out into the freezing night. He gets wet in the rain, and hungry, and tries to come back. But Mrs. Bailey locks the door and (seemingly, at any rate) entertains another man.[17]

2) "Bill Bailey, Won't You Please Come Home?" (1902) (Hughie Cannon)—It is now summer, and Mrs. Bailey wants Bill back and loudly tells the neighbors about it. In the second verse, Bill comes back with an automobile, footman, and diamond; but all he does is wink his eye when she pleads for him to come back.

3) "I Wonder Why Bill Bailey Don't Come Home" (1902) (Frank Fogerty/Matt C. Woodward/William Jerome)—Her Uncle Ephram dies and leaves Mrs. Bailey lots of money. Nevertheless, Bill still does not come home, and she cannot figure out why.

4) "Since Bill Bailey Came Back Home" (1902) (Billy Johnson/Seymour Furth)—To avoid the winter cold, Bill comes back, and Mrs. Bailey welcomes him with open arms (and open purse strings).

5) "Won't You Kindly Hum Old 'Home Sweet Home' to Me?" (1903) (Hughie Cannon)—Bill's friend, Eli Crosby, is locked out by his lady love, who accuses him of having been out carousing with Bill.[18]

6) "He Done Me Wrong (The Death of Bill Bailey)" (1904) (Hughie Cannon)—Bill dies of cholera, and Mrs. Bailey laments his loss (but acknowledges that, at times, "he done her wrong").

7) "Bill, You Done Me Wrong" (1908) (Bert Leighton/Frank Leighton)—This song is a close variation of Cannon's 1904 "He Done Me Wrong," in which, yet again, the wrong-doing Bill is mourned by his widow after his death.

"Ain't Dat a Shame" enjoyed some afterlife, reissued in folios and sheet music, being recorded into the thirties. The other Bill Bailey episodes lay neglected. Some published songs are even more obscure than the ones listed above: "Bill Bailey's Spree" (Charles E. Bain, copyrighted in Chicago by Success Music in 1906); and "Bill Bailey's Application" (Edna Hooker Day; copyrighted, yet again, by Haviland in 1910). The last Bill Bailey hit song came in 1915: "When Old Bill Bailey Plays the Ukulele" (Charles McCarron/Nat Vincent). On the sheet music cover, an aged Uncle Tom–like Bailey sits under the moon, seemingly going Hawaiian as he strums his ukulele. In 1923, in "Oh! Sister, Ain't That Hot!" (Harry White/Will Donaldson), Bill Bailey turns up as a "struttin' fool," making the Black women sigh as he praises the dance band "full of pep" when they play the "lovin' blues." Despite these other glimpses of Bill's life, Cannon's song is the one by which posterity remembers Bailey.

There ensued intermittent speculation about a real-life person and incident behind the song's Bill Bailey and his leaving home. Many men carried the name, for example the St. Louis baseball pitcher, addressed in 1908 by a fan (a tenor) with the famous song; and the African American entertainer of the Bailey and Cowan vaudeville team.[19] There was also a white banjo-playing Bill Bailey in vaudeville in the early twentieth century; he might be the same person who later moved to Japan, was a prisoner of the Japanese during World War II, and, when released, immediately opened a bar and boarding house in a Singapore mansion that became an institution of both tourist and local life for decades.[20] Despite the first portion of the song being prominently posted—music and lyrics—on the wall of his saloon, this Bill Bailey affirmed he was "never going home."[21] And he never did: he died in Singapore at age eighty.

There were other contenders. Writing in 1931, James J. Geller propagated a myth that Cannon knew an African American William Bailey, "lazy, shiftless," in subjugation to his "angry spouse, weary of supporting him," who "finally turned him out."[22] As a result, Cannon wrote an imaginary scenario in which Bill triumphs, because, Geller claims, Cannon felt "women must be subjugated, come what may."[23] Geller claims that John Queen introduced the song in a show called *Town Topics* in Newburgh, New York, and that "Ain't Dat a Shame" followed after, but Geller does not seem to know (and certainly offers no explanation why) "Shame" was copyrighted and popularized a year earlier than "Bill Bailey."

In another story, set in Jackson, Michigan, in Diedrich's Saloon, Cannon supposedly serenaded a real Bill Bailey who hung around drinking rather than going home—but that was probably in Cannon's post-songwriting years, well after Wilson, Queen, and Cannon had created their songs.[24] This Bill Bailey's wife was interviewed decades later: she had resented the song, she admitted, and eventually divorced her Bill ("He was my sweetheart, but he was everybody else's too").[25] Nevertheless, the pair remained friendly, and by the time she reached the age of one hundred, in 1976, both Bill and the sting of his not coming home had long passed.

Perhaps Bill Bailey was a folk hero—once real, but soon passed into mythology, like Frankie and Johnny, or Casey Jones, or Stackolee. Muir suspects so, because Bill appears in a "Frankie and Johnny"–type folk tune collected by Dorothy Scarborough and published in 1925, "I Went to the Hop-Joint" ("hop" being alcohol or drugs), in which Bailey saunters in on the action in a manner similar to the folk-hero in "The Bully Song." Muir speculates that perhaps "this was the kind of folk song that was the direct inspiration for Cannon and his colleagues."[26] Or perhaps the folk simply adopted Bailey as their own, as they were adopting so many show-business products of the time. Indeed, almost immediately, "Bill Bailey, Won't You Please Come Home" took on a kind of folk culture–like pervasiveness, enmeshed in American life.

THE SONG SPREADS

In 1902, the year the song was published, future Broadway star Ethel Shutta, five years old, won a contest at Madison Square Garden by cakewalking and singing "Bill Bailey."[27] In November of that year, in Washington, DC, *Lilliputians in Fairyland*, a production played by 150 children, included Cannon's hit, sung by little Joseph Dierken in blackface as the Wizard of the Nile.[28] The song was, of course, not just part of juvenile life. Mamie Munroe was singing it at Kleinbaum's saloon in Chicago on December 18 when an irate, recently fired former employee, Joe Kane, threw a glass of beer at her, starting a fight the riot squad had to stop.[29] In January 1903, President and Mrs. Teddy Roosevelt heard it played as a march by the Marine Band at their first state reception of the season.[30]

The song was transformed into a work song: in September 1903, a whimsical Chicago journalist reported conspiring with "the man who gets paid for whistling 'Won't You Come Home, Bill Bailey' around my home during house-cleaning time, while he keeps time to the music with a mop," who aids and abets him in quietly disposing of unwanted houseware like tricky patent coffee pots and stew pans.[31]

One day in March 1904, on West 46th Street in Manhattan, a battle of music raged: the Salvation Army band played "The Holy City," vying with Italian organ grinders, who trumped them with "Bill Bailey."[32] This backstreet competition serves as a symbol of the era's conflict between religious culture and secular popularism. A cop eventually broke up the ruction, but not before the whole block got involved in the contest and both sides had collected a lot of money.

Around 1909, future country music legend Jimmie Rodgers, age twelve, won an amateur contest by performing "Bill Bailey" in Mississippi.[33] Thus, the song offered a training ground for performers whose fields ranged from hillbilly to Broadway. It saturated American society, from neighborhood sidewalks to kiddie shows to saloons to the White House.

The ditty crossed the Atlantic as well, and became well-rooted in British culture. By 1905 George Bernard Shaw, writing a parodic one-act titled *Passion, Poison and Petrification* for a charity benefit, resolves his absurdist plot by having the angels welcome one of the protagonists to heaven by singing "Bill Bailey" to usher him through the golden gates.[34] The following year, in the children's novel *The Railway Children*, Edith Nesbit paints this tongue-in-cheek picture of working-class folk music, vintage 1906: "The peace of the evening was not broken by the notes of the sedge-warblers or by the voice of the woman in the barge, singing her baby to sleep. It was a sad song she sang. Something about Bill Bailey and how she wanted him to come home."[35] Too bad the barge-woman's husband, himself named Bill, did not come home more quickly, because the barge catches fire and the eponymous young heroes have to save the day. Although written tongue-in-cheek, this passage may demonstrate how quickly popular songs, including this torch song forerunner, entered into the folk lullaby repertoire. In their contrasting stories, Shaw and Nesbit (who shared a wry humor and a fervent belief in socialism) seem to look somewhat askance at "Bill Bailey," but nevertheless include the song as a cultural touchstone that needs no further explanation—and this within only a few years of its creation.

By 1926, however, when Shaw finally published his one-act *Passion, Poison and Petrification*, he wrote, "As the Bill Bailey song has not proved immortal, any equally appropriate ditty of the moment may be substituted."[36] Nevertheless, it would be a pity to insert any other strain in place of "Bill Bailey," for Cannon's song is unusually appropriate to Shaw's little satire. The number is redolent of both low life and humor, which helps to highlight, by contrast, the absurd highfalutin passions of Shaw's protagonists, the members of a fatal love triangle of husband, wife, and her lover—the last-mentioned is the one who gets poisoned, petrified, and welcomed "home" to heaven by the angelic choir.

Shaw underestimated the lifespan of Cannon's song. In 1927 London air pilots ended their stunt show by landing "home" to the strains of "Bill Bailey, Won't You Please Come Home." Back in the United States, in 1929 it was part of a "smashing arrangement of old hits" by Brusiloff and His Forty Jazzmanians at a movie premiere in the nation's capital.[37] The song was not just jazzed up—it also was being actively recorded in the country music field during this period.[38] Admittedly, for a couple of decades, the song does fade from the big urban media outlets, but it never disappears entirely. For instance, at the start of one of James Cagney's most successful movies, *The Strawberry Blonde* (1941), the gang hanging around on a summer's day sings it, immediately helping establish the movie's era of action, the turn of the century. New sheet music editions came out: two country-oriented editions, from Calumet Music (1937) and Paull-Pioneer (1940), alongside an "Unforgettable Songs of America" edition from Edward Marks (1938).

"Bill Bailey" slowly gathered steam in the mainstream again in the late forties. Jimmy Durante and his longtime performing partner Eddie Jackson are caught on record singing it at Durante's nightclub in 1949—enthusiastically siding, in this battle of the sexes, with poor Mrs. Bailey (here identified as "Isabel"), all done in a rambunctious spirit of comedy. In 1950 they put their rendition onto wax for MGM Records.[39] Rising star Pearl Bailey made it a theme song. (Her tap dancing brother was, in fact, named Bill Bailey.) West Coast singer-pianist Nellie Lutcher recorded it in the same era. Others on the 1950s nightclub circuit were also featuring the song regularly. Beatrice Kay, lively and raucous, split her act between regular pop and jocular renditions of turn-of-the-twentieth-century favorites, and her sets always included "Bill Bailey."[40] In 1955 former big-band crooner Karen Chandler was among the first singers to be reviewed by *Variety* as performing the number in Las Vegas, at the New Frontier.[41] Roberta Sherwood, a Florida-based white jazz singer of the 1950s, was caught a year later by *Variety* delivering Cannon's tune in the same Las Vegas venue. In the description of how Sherwood delivered her crying-in-your-beer repertoire, *Variety*, typically, coined a new term as the reporter opined that "she lends simple, unaffected dramatics to standard torchants," because "the earthy quality to her voice feeds realism to her lyrics."[42]

Interestingly, both Lutcher and Pearl Bailey recorded the blues ballad–like verse, perhaps unwittingly creating a bridge to the African American heritage shared by themselves and the song. Nevertheless, in the same era, other forums saw the original bluesy verse being replaced. Indicating the continued currency of "Bill Bailey" in the country field, in 1952 Paull-Pioneer reissued its 1940 version. Meanwhile, Hill and Range Songs issued an arrangement by country star Wade Ray with a new, completely different verse. (Mrs. Bailey now has another first name: Bessie.) On his recording, Ray inflects this somewhat conventional intro with a country-blues quality. Yet another alternative verse—one drained of the folk-derived vitality of the original—appears in a 1962 folio; it was promulgated in a couple of recordings, including the well-distributed Reader's Digest *Gaslight Era* box set. In the 1960s, Nancy Wilson featured a freshly invented verse—this one entirely in the sophisticated nightclub mode—in her extended dramatization of the song.

At mid-century, "Bill Bailey, Won't You Please Come Home?" was lifted to new heights of visibility by the surge of popularity of Dixieland jazz—often in a very clichéd form, but usually fun nevertheless. In 1952, in the Childs Paramount restaurant at Broadway and 43rd Street, celebrities swarmed to listen to the resident Dixieland band, featuring a singing waiter whose special solo spot was "Bill Bailey."[43] The newspapers reported big-band-trained singers like Sinatra, Rosemary Clooney, and Georgia Gibbs gathering to hear this fashionable musical nostalgia. By 1961 Gibbs was using "Bill Bailey" in her own nightclub act—but, by then, so were "lots of girls."[44] Also by then, Cannon's classic had become "President Kennedy's favorite song," reporters informed the American public—an Oval Office connection that faintly echoes the tune's performance at the 1903 Roosevelt White House reception; the song had come full circle.[45] Ted Kennedy liked the piece, too, and harmonized it with a college friend at a party in 1960.[46] Alpha males are seemingly drawn to the jolly melody and the lyric's comic depiction of abject womanhood.

By 1962 "Bill Bailey" was being dubbed "the national anthem" of Las Vegas, and "its rhythms come out of lounges with the insistence of an earache."[47] Along with "When the Saints Go Marching In," it was almost a requirement for all club acts. Appropriately enough, when the Broadway songwriting team of Kander and Ebb had to create the title song for the 1966 musical *Cabaret*, a number that would capture the essence of nightclub life, composer Kander echoed, probably unwittingly, the initial musical motif of "Bill Bailey." Kander and Ebb's paraphrase, in turn, itself became a hit song and cultural touchstone—its possible relationship to "Bill Bailey" going largely unnoticed.[48]

"Bill Bailey" also thrived via two related musical vogues of the long-playing album era. The rage for recordings of honky-tonk piano—old popular songs in a ragtime style, often on deliberately jangly "doctored" pianos—spread throughout the fifties. From at least 1950, "Bill Bailey" was a staple of this repertoire.[49] Quickly taking root and thriving in this atmosphere of Dixieland and honky-tonk nostalgia, the sing-along format premiered on LP in 1956.[50] By 1958 Mitch Miller dominated the field in a series of best-selling albums, one of which was the 1960 *Memories*, featuring "Bill Bailey."

Perhaps two factors helped tip the scales to make "Bill Bailey" one of the pivotal songs of the era. First, Louis Armstrong performed it (and, probably not coincidentally, "When the Saints") in the 1959 biopic *The Five Pennies*, starring Danny Kaye as trumpeter Red Nichols. In the fall of 1959, the soundtrack album was a best-seller.

Second, live recordings became popular. Soon it seemed like every singing star had to have a live album—often at Carnegie Hall or the Copacabana nightclub, two contrasting venues that illustrate the span of cultural cache that popular songs had during this period. Many of these live acts featured "Bill Bailey": Sam Cooke, Connie Francis, Trini Lopez, Matt Monro, Gloria Lynne, Nancy Wilson, Sarah Vaughan . . . even that seminal folk group, the Weavers, performed it at Carnegie Hall. Soon, it seemed, you were just not *with it* if you did not do "Bill Bailey" in your live performances.

Bobby Darin helped further revive the piece. In February 1960, that budding singer of jazz standards recorded his third album—this time, not with a big band as previously, but with a small combo.[51] They had seemingly wrapped everything up when they started fooling around with "Bill Bailey." Combo leader Bobby Scott reported, "It was an afterthought."[52] Yet, they should have guessed it would be a success, because Darin had already hit big with another Armstrong specialty number, "Mack the Knife." Darin's single of "Bill Bailey" soared to *Billboard*'s Top Twenty by May and stayed on the chart for eleven weeks. Della Reese also made the song her own, with a single that brushed 1961's Hot 100 chart in April.[53]

By 1963 Cannon's song was ripe for parody. In January, singing comedian Allan Sherman's second hit album, *My Son, the Celebrity*, charted with his parody, "Won't You Come Home, Disraeli"—which, one observer opined, "only helped to make" the original "more popular than ever."[54] By that year so many people were singing "Bill Bailey" that Ella Fitzgerald created her own swing-comedy mixture, wherein she might imitate up to six other singers, Armstrong, Reese, Pearl Bailey . . . like a party of all the performers who did (and some who did not do) the song. A live version of her arrangement, released as a single, charted for three weeks in April 1963, and rose to seventy-five on the Hot 100. Thus, in the 1960s the song was thriving on many levels: as jazz nostalgia (Dixieland and, in Britain, trad jazz); as sing-along and honky-tonk nostalgia; as entertainment showmanship (duet renditions on television abounded, such as by Durante and Fitzgerald, Pearl Bailey and Carol Channing, Darin and Bob Hope); in many kinds of vocal styles (rock and roll by Brenda Lee; soul by Aretha Franklin); and through a spread of parodies, professional and amateur.

In 1902 "Bill Bailey" had been a hot number in the tough saloons where you might get hit by a beer glass as you sang it. By 1965, as a symbol of that lost world, it could be turned into nostalgia-kitsch: in the alcohol-free Western saloon at Disneyland you could hear "the tough proprietress Slue Foot Sue" belting it out.[55] By 1971 "Bill Bailey" could be brushed aside as part of the world of "the plastic Las Vegas lounge group."[56] In 1981 Lynne Thigpen brought "authority, passion," and "sass" to her rendition in the stage revue *Tintypes*, but Mark Taper, favorably evaluating her performance, confessed, "I thought I never wanted to hear 'Won't You Come Home, Bill Bailey' again."[57] To many, the song had become a cliché.

Through the 1980s and 1990s, barbershop quartet singers and Dixieland musicians kept "Bill Bailey" alive—until, by the turn of the new century, it was reevaluated, with fresh ears, by new fans. By 1996 cabaret legend Julie Wilson was including it in her sets. Audiences of the 1990s swing-dance-and-lounge-music revival rediscovered Darin, too, leading to the 2004 biopic *Beyond the Sea*, which features "Bill Bailey." Pianist-singer (and sometime matinee idol) Harry Connick Jr., in a 2007 tribute to his native New Orleans, tackles it: an instrumental refrain with Connick's economical piano punctuation, followed by his vocal and then by the band strutting in the hard-edged, percussive, and slightly cool style so typical of contemporary swing.

ANALYSIS

As mentioned, the verse of "Bill Bailey" is a proto-blues in many ways similar to the famous "Frankie and Johnny": it offers variants on a series of chords that are almost like the later standard blues harmonic sequence, with (like the blues) a twelve-bar structure made up of three phrases. Unlike the later blues, however, the third phrase is rushed into—this phrasing entails what musicologists call a "hypermetric shift."[58] That dash into the third phrase can create a galvanizing effect: the melody-and-words unexpectedly, enthusiastically gallop ahead, seeming to exemplify American bustle-and-go. Peter van der Merwe points out that this type of song structure is a folk variation of old British pieces such as "Frog Went a-Courtin'."[59] (I first encountered "Frog" in music class in second grade. Little did I realize, as I sat there wondering why I was singing about the courtship rituals of frogs—rather risqué, it seemed—that I was being educated in the roots of American blues.) The lyric of the verses is in third-person: she did this, he did that. As outlined in the preceding chapter, this is very characteristic of the impersonal nature of many popular songs at the time.

The refrain is a quintessential Tin Pan Alley song of the era: ABAC form, thirty-two bars. The penultimate couplet ("I know I'm to blame / Ain't dat a shame") creates the limerick effect van der Merwe describes—in fact, he uses "Bill Bailey" as his main example. It also quotes the title of the preceding song in the series, "Ain't Dat a Shame."[60] The lyric of the refrain is mostly spoken personally by Mrs. Bailey, except for one brief return to the third-person mode: "she moans the whole day long." As I shall detail soon, in later decades this is sometimes changed to the first person, "I moan the whole day long," fitting Tin Pan Alley's general drift toward personalization.

Alec Wilder opines that the refrain's first four measures have a "natural" quality.[61] The cakewalk-friendly lift of this opening rhythm is repeated ten times.[62] (This adaptability to the high-stepping cakewalk dance was probably congenial to performers: recall five-year-old Ethel Shutta winning her amateur contest.) For Wilder, however, this phrase's spontaneous energy is spoiled by what he hears as the "contrived" quality of the end of the first two sections: "lo-ong" and "wro-ong."[63] In these instances, as was typical, the melisma (the seeming mismatch of one syllable stretched out over two notes) occurs at the *end* of a phrase. Wilder claims that he had never heard "Bill Bailey" before he wrote his book (surprising, and implying that he was neither a nightclubber nor a record buyer in the early 1960s). If Wilder had witnessed the song in action, then perhaps here, as often in his book, he would have remarked that performance tradition had wrestled with this "problem" in the song and discovered two options: either a condensing (omit the melisma) or an expanding (lengthen the melisma). Indeed, the printed notes might be seen as a signal, giving singers permission to stretch these words further into more elaborate melismas. Among those I examined, just under a quarter of singers who render "Bill Bailey" add even more notes at this point in the refrain, making "long" even more long; "lo-o-o-ong." Exploring the other option, and perhaps to avoid the "contrived" quality Wilder objects to, more than half of singers drop the melismas altogether at some point in their rendition and often throughout.[64]

The lyric is in the interrogatory mode, focusing much of the time on questions: "Won't you come home?" "'Member that rainy eve?" "Ain't dat a shame?" Just as most of us inflect our voices to a higher pitch to ask a question, so Mrs. Bailey does, too: the musical kernel of the song is a series of ascending figures, in groups of three, four, or five notes. Each section builds to a climactic high: first D, then E, then F. This progression helps to give the refrain's melody a dramatic arc.

The final payoff is that little intensifying word *"please"*—"Won't you *please* come home?" As Stephen Banfield points out, a song's title phrase usually supplies a key to understanding "the melopoetic structure of a whole song."[65] "Bill Bailey, Won't You Please Come Home?" offers a perfect example, and it pursues what Banfield calls the "refrain" type of strategy in ending with the title phrase: it "build[s] . . . towards a melopoetic point of arrival."[66] Admittedly, the lyrics of the opening phrase and closing phrase are almost the same—in fact, people often refer to the song by its first line rather than its last. Nevertheless, the thing that has changed for the protagonist by the end of the song is the increased

ardor of her pleading, displayed in that one yearning *"please."* Despite this climactic mutation, however, many singers seem to feel that "Bill Bailey" needs
yet something more, to resolve fully. Therefore, six out of ten artists extend the
song in a tag that helps to bring the song to further resolution.[67]

Mrs. Bailey formulates her lament as a series of questions, but with a pes-
simistic twist, perhaps indicating her doubts that she will get what she wants:
her all-important central plea is not "Will you come home?" but rather the
negative "Won't you come home?"—seeming to lay her open for an answer of
"No" rather than "Yes." The emotional climate of the song shifts if the phrase
is altered to more affirmative "I want you home, Bill Bailey, I want you home."
By contrast with that more assertive option, Mrs. Bailey seems in a fatalistic,
depressive position.

As with many American favorites, however, the melancholy words of "Bill
Bailey" conflict with the resilient music. The American 1805 classic, "Listen to
the Mockingbird," supplies an early example: the melody is "like the laughter of a
little girl at play" (as Abraham Lincoln said of this, his favorite song), yet the lyric
tells of death and grief.[68] This dynamic manifests, too, in important later songs,
such as "Some of These Days" (the focus of chapter 7), "I Ain't Got Nobody," and
"After You've Gone"—one of several qualities shared among these songs. Some
notable later pieces also feature this contradiction: the 1923 "Swinging Down the
Lane" pairs lamenting words for an absent love to a jaunty tune; standards such
as "All of Me" (1930) and "Don't Get Around Much Anymore" (1942), as Ted Gioia
writes, can feature "world-weary words" that "seem at odds" with "merry-making
music.[69]" In "Stormy Weather" (1933), as John Diamond once expounded in my
presence, the triumphant, upwardly ascending opening gesture seemingly jars
with the moaning lyric.[70] "Bill Bailey" forecasts this phenomenon.

Mrs. Bailey sings, "I drove you out, with nothin' but a fine-tooth comb": the
fine-tooth comb yields a certain fascination. Along with Bill himself, the comb
is the emblem of the song. For instance, when the sixties nightclub duo Sandler
and Young did a lengthy parody of "Bill Bailey," taking the story around the
world to seven countries and back through the centuries to the era of Bach,
the one element they retained in these many musical skits was the fine-tooth
comb. The most obvious meaning of the comb is that it is next to nothing: not
a quarter, not a dime, not a nickel, not even a penny—just a comb . . . and, at
that, as Sandler and Young say, such a "little," "puny," "teeny-weeny" comb. Philip
Furia has suggested that the clichéd, theatricalized African American would
be assumed to have very thick hair, in tight kinks: a fine-tooth comb would
be useless in the Afro hairdo of such a Bill Bailey.[71] But a novel about World
War I reveals another meaning that today most American audiences would,
thankfully, miss: a fine-tooth comb is a tool for getting off lice.[72] Through this
one gift, loaded with irony, Mrs. Bailey implies that, without her, Bill is going

Figure 2.1. On the original sheet music cover for "Bill Bailey, Won't You Please Come Home?" (1902), Mrs. Bailey and Bill share similarly shaped eyes, eyebrows, cheeks, noses, lips, chins, and ears. *Bill Bailey, Won't You Please Come Home?*, Charles H. Templeton Sr., Templeton Sheet Music Collection, Manuscripts Division, Special Collections Department, Mississippi State University Libraries.

to end up in the flophouse with the lice-ridden. At the same time, she seemed to assume that he was going to come back—perhaps she gave him the comb because she does not want him dragging lice back into the house. The implied image of Bill, combing to filter out the cooties, is both sad and funny.

The fine-tooth comb is mentioned in the climactic phrase. "Tooth" rides on the highest note, a wailing, bluesy flatted seventh. This juxtaposition—verbal humor mated to the one musical phrase that might make the refrain poignant—irresistibly tilts the piece toward the comic mode.

Combining these factors results in a song critics aptly describe in performance as "rousing," "rowdy," and a "playful, kick-up-your-heels" number that spices up an act.[73] Nevertheless, in some of the earliest recordings, artists (such as the African American–abroad Pete Hampton or the prolific Bob Roberts) adopt a soft, almost plaintive tone. This is partly a matter of tempo; for instance, Roberts sings at a moderate speed (quarter note = c. 85). By contrast, many later performers of the song, such as Pearl Bailey (quarter note = c. 140), charge through the song.

There's a wonderfully theatrical scenario implied in the chorus of this song—both comedic and dramatic. (I vividly remember, about 2010, two high school students in the South Bronx who regularly acted it out in a colleague's music class, with bended knee pleading, laughter rippling through the room, especially at "I threw you out.") The song manages to create sympathy for Mrs. Bailey and imbue Bill with a certain fascination. The original sheet music cover pictures the pair, displaying two of the era's conventional stereotypes for African Americans: the "mammy" (hefty, broad-featured, with a bandana around her head) and the "Zip Coon" or "buck" (teasing grin, sporting a dapper hat at a jaunty angle).

Closely examining the illustration yields a surprise: they have almost exactly the same face. Female stage mammy figures were often played by males in drag, so perhaps the resemblance of man and woman here reflects that era's common performance practice: it could be one actor, in different getups. Perhaps it is due to laziness on the part of the illustrator.[74] Seen today, the effect is almost eerie, conjuring up the doppelgänger of folk tales. Male and female, yin and yang, the one who leaves and the one who gets left, are the same. Janus, the ancient Roman god of endings and beginnings, was also pictured with two faces; an analogous image is somehow appropriate to discover, here, with a song that draws on the past but also heralds the beginning of a new era.

INTERPRETING THE RECORDINGS

Singers, in approaching the repertoire covered in this book, take more liberties with the "Bill Bailey" lyrics than with any other. This perhaps reflects the fact that the piece is not often taken seriously as ballad material. Yet it eventually came to be performed as a torch song, thereby showing its connection to and possible influence on the torch tradition. To bring the number closer to the torch genre, certain variations are required. First, singers often flatten the main melodic motif: they ignore the ascending gesture and commence the refrain with a series of little pushes: repeating, lingeringly, on the third-degree of the scale, at times sliding with subtle variation down to the flatted blue third. The freedom allowed by this tradition gives the singers leeway to change the lifting impulse of a cakewalk dance into a torchy, assertive shove—or a cooing, intimate murmur.

Example 2.2. "Bill Bailey," a common variant by singers of the refrain's first phrase.

A second torch tactic is to imbue the song with some sincerity. This is not so easy to do, because of the joyous lift of the music, the lyric's buoyantly bouncing "b" sounds, the specificity of the name "Bill Bailey," and the ever-comic "fine tooth comb." Whether singing the lyric in first-person or third-person mode, men tend to render "Bill Bailey" in a quick tempo and to treat the dramatic situation with tongue in cheek. Sam Cooke offers something of an exception: he truly seems to be offering Bailey a bit of serious matrimonial advice: "And I know, I know that it's a shame, Bill, / But maybe you're the blame, Bill." Cooke does not try to make the number a torch song, but he does approach it with at least a soupçon of dramatic seriousness.[75]

More than most, Nellie Lutcher, in her early-1950s recording, is conveying a story—albeit in her own idiosyncratic style: quirky phrasing and buoyant piano. She sets up the saga with the verse; in the refrain, she uses the third-person "she moans," but later sometimes speak-sings in the role of Mrs. Bailey, elaborating on the lyric: "I'll . . . give you a substantial allowance. 'Cause I *know*," breaking into a falsetto squeal, "I *know* I did you wrong. . . . I can't help it, Minnie, I'm an honest woman. Maybe wrong, but very honest." Playful, yes (she giggles at the end of the first refrain), but somehow she seems in earnest as she exclaims, "I need you madly, William!" (Her relatively slow, loping speed also helps; quarter note = 110.)

Sometimes the achievement of the torch ambience involves not just dramatic seriousness, but also intensity. Della Reese was pivotal in consolidating this element as part of the "Bill Bailey" tradition. Reese does have the typical late-fifties sardonic edge to all her singing, and she does distance herself from the pleading sentiment by keeping it in the third person, but, despite these factors, she infuses "Bill Bailey" with a gospel-like fervor.

Despite the achievements of Lutcher and Reese in their approaches to "Bill Bailey," the ultimate step in torching the number is to make the lyric first-person: not "she moans" but "I moan." This only works as a personalizing device if done by a female, because emotional sincerity in the crooner tradition almost always depends upon the singer taking on the character of the protagonist. Therefore, a woman can make the song more personal if they change "she" to "I"—and more than 80 percent of female singers choose to do so.

Men sometimes sing the lyric in the first person, taking on the persona of Mrs. Bailey—about one in four, with Trini Lopez offering a typical example.[76] The effect, however, is to make the song less personal, rather than more.[77] Men may convey the "Bill Bailey" lyric in the first person but only because they do not approach the emotions of Mrs. Bailey seriously. In the popular singer tradition, as it developed in the 1920s and 1930s, a man usually cannot sing with sincere emotion in the voice of a woman. Conceivably, a man might substitute "sweet mama," "my baby," or some such phrase for the words "Bill Bailey"—but no male performer does. In fact, the only variation that adopts anything similar to that strategy is a print version: the Leighton brothers' 1922 article, wherein they claim that Cannon did not write the song but only took it from some anonymous African American—"Bill Bailey" there becomes "dear daddy." No recording artist seems to have ever applied this idea to a performance (although future generations may change this situation).

Singers soon combined the gospel-tinged approach of Reese with the first-person mode: her emphatic tradition was continued by Gloria Lynne and

Aretha Franklin, but both of them sing "I moan." In contrast to their fervor, Marian Montgomery stays cool throughout. Sticking to the personal torch mode, she sounds like a swinging 1960s bachelorette phoning Bill from her urban apartment, addressing him with confidence and a sly wit, using the charming indirection, "some somebody has been doin' Bill wrong, now." Nancy Wilson, in an elaborate version—called "Saga of Bill Bailey," with a captivating new special material verse, both comic and tragic—combines the two modes: she starts off as the cool urbanite and builds through three refrains (which, after the first, only seem to glance at the original melody) into a gospel-tinged finale.

The final technique in torching "Bill Bailey" is to slow down the tempo. Many recordings—particularly the New Orleans revival renditions—move at a relaxed lope that, like the earliest recordings, lends the tune a certain dewy charm. In her "Saga of Bill Bailey," Wilson, too, travels through the song at a slowly loping speed (quarter note = c. 85), maintaining this even as the rendition builds in volume and force.

Nevertheless, only two recordings really take the tempo down to ballad speed and supply an intimate focus—and then only for half the track (they both speed up to the usual lively tempo for the second half). Those two wire-walking risk-takers are Patsy Cline and Ann-Margret (quarter note = 78 and 88, respectively). These women do an exquisite job—each quite differently—in making Mrs. Bailey's plaint quite tender and loving—indeed, very persuasive. Both deliver the torch-like melodic variant, focusing on both the minor and major third-degree of the scale.

Cline, with a bare-bones choral part going "oo-oo" in the background, slides her notes around sensuously; inserts a quiet, throaty moan, "aaah"; and, at the end of the first refrain, wistfully delivers the lyric's emotional climax with a delicately downward gliding *please* . . . and, then, as the guitar picks up the tempo, her next note, an upward swooping "ye . . . eah," catapults the listener into a lively second refrain, concluded by a half-tempo, high-kicking tag. Cline's arrangement influenced Michael Bublé, on his first, poorly distributed 2001 album.[78] While using his own slick, delicately sensual tone throughout, he matches Cline in her tempo changes and in many other details of her performance (but not, of course, in her first-person "I moan" lyric).

Ann-Margret's 1964 partly-ballad rendition is one of the many duet versions of the era, this time with spoken responses and trumpet playing by pop-Dixieland star Al Hirt. In her slow, seductive first chorus, the singer lets her breath play on the microphone. In the middle of the first stanza she voices a little intake of breath ("I moan," gasp, "the whole night lo-ong"), a kind of reverse sigh. She then twice returns to this device, making it a very intimate punctuation. Hirt (as Bill) speaks dialogue between each of the actress' sung phrases, giving her something to bounce off of dramatically, which spurs her acting chops and leads to some detailed moments of emotional subtlety. She admits she turned him out with only a fine-tooth comb, and he replies "That sure wasn't much equipment, was it?"—she goes "Oh!" not expecting him to take that hard-line attitude. Then she recovers, continuing "Well, I know," tongue click, "I know I'm to bla-ame." As with Cline, she (and Hirt) then proceed to do a fast refrain; but both women leave behind a strong impression of what "Bill Bailey, Won't You Please Come Home?" can be when delivered in a slow, intimate, personal manner—as a torch song.

A final consideration in the "Bill Bailey" performance tradition is the issue of assertiveness. In the original, the lyrics make Mrs. Bailey downtrodden, abject, humble, pleading (although this, as previously stated, is potentially belied by the music's force and thrust), and most renditions stay with that scenario. I found, however, that, among both female and male singers, one out of seven performers shifts the blame for the separation onto Bill.

As the decades move from 1900 toward the mid-century, lyrics of loss sometimes can become more self-assertive. Evidence is seen in a string of hit songs that increase in vengefulness. In "Who's Sorry Now" (1923), lyricists Bert Kalmar and Harry Ruby have their protagonist exult in the fact that now the former beloved "must pay." The same year, in "I Cried for You," wordsmith Arthur Freed's protagonist sounds quite content that the erstwhile lover must now "cry over me." The series of vindictiveness continues with "Goody-Goody" (1936), "Cry, Baby, Cry" (1938), and onward. Sob songs, weakly pleading in 1918, can, twenty years later, become full of spunk. This was one option in twentieth-century emotional life, and a sign of this increased assertiveness perhaps lies in that slice of singers who tend to foist the blame on Bill, rather than on his wife, and to relish asserting his guilt.

Tommy Butler (of the Billy Barnes Revue) and Matt Monro, both offering avuncular advice to Mr. Bailey, emphasize that Bill is to blame. Ella Fitzgerald and Sam Cooke (who seems to follow Fitzgerald in this and some other telling details) both hedge around the issue by saying that "maybe" he is to blame—soft-soaping him. Nancy Wilson, cleverly, starts out saying that she is to blame, but later sneaks in a slight element of doubt ("They say I threw you out . . . Who says I done you wrong?"). By the end, perhaps under the force of her passion ("I want that man's arms around me . . . till it hurts!"), and with his continued withholding of himself, she starts to accuse him: "You stole my fine-tooth comb . . . Shame, shame!" Finally, after three intense refrains, she has completely turned the responsibility around: "I know it's you who's to blame." The saga that Wilson chants parallels one historical side-trail in the history of the torch song, which transforms the mood of abjection to that of defiance. (Nevertheless, Wilson still wants Bill to come home.)

Even more accusatory is Roberta Sherwood, in her 1959 recording (which probably reflects how she had been performing the song for years). Shouting with church-like fervor, she has no doubts that "I ain't to blame!" He threw her out; he done her wrong; and therefore: "You wash the dishes. I'll get all that back rent! . . . Bring some money!" In nightclubs in 1968, Rhetta Hughes, who "performs like a girl who's really in charge," reportedly took Mrs. Bailey's assertiveness training to the final degree, singing "Don't You Come Home, Bill Bailey!"[79] The incipient feminism of the late twentieth century finally clearly comes forward.

MOVIES AND LITERATURE

Film and literature reveal other deep sides to "Bill Bailey." An independent film, *I'll Take You There* (1999), places the song very firmly within a torch-bearing scenario. The first shot is a bird's-eye view of the protagonist, Bill Baylor (Reg Rogers), and his wife, Rose (Lara Harris), in bed, as she sings "Bill Bailey" to him, both playfully and intimately. "I miss you all day long," she breathes and chuckles, before whispering the customary extended tag ending.

After Rose deserts Bill in favor of his best friend, the song continues to haunt the soundtrack (as it does, presumably, Bill's thoughts), showing up in a wide range of versions. At one point, a new group of friends—Bernice (Ally Sheedy, as his potential new love interest), her grandmother, and the latter's

Figure 2.2. *I'll Take You There* (1999). In the first shot, Rose (Lara Harris) nuzzles her husband Bill Baylor (Reg Rogers), using "Bill Bailey" as her love song. After she leaves him, Cannon's classic will symbolize the torch he carries for her.

elderly beau—try to perform it for him (on piano, tuba, violin, and vocals). When he asks them not to, the grandmother regales him with a close variant on the Geller origin myth about the forlorn vaudevillian, Bill Bailey, and his friend Hughie who gave him money for a hotel room and who "wrote him a song, promising that his wife would come back to him." Baylor clings to that same kind of hope and, in desperation, pursues his wife, managing to separate her from her new flame ("I miss Bill," she confesses), before realizing that his affections have shifted to Bernice. Until Baylor's ultimate emotional renewal, however, the 1902 tune takes on, for him, the same role that is usually filled by its more obviously torchy, cry-in-your-beer successors.

"Bill Bailey" more usually symbolizes the place of the patriarch in the domestic circle of spouses and children. With action taking place at the turn of the twentieth century, *Papa's Delicate Condition* (1963) draws on both the saloon-culture connotations of the song and its potentially more poignant emotional resonances. Cannon's hit is the favorite tune of the hard-drinking, impulsive Jack Griffith (Jackie Gleason as the eponymous "Papa"), and he renders it at several moments when his decisions become risky. Jack's church organist wife, Amberlyn (Glynis Johns), prefers more refined music and more sober behavior. After their painful separation, when he comes to the doorstep, reformed but shy, she plays "Bill Bailey" on the piano as a kind of mating call that draws him back inside to her and their two daughters. Their chauffeur, Walter, declares to the cook, Ellie, "Looks like Bill Bailey finally made it home!" The broken circle is repaired, as the whole family sings, "Bill Bailey, won't you please *stay* home!"

As mentioned before, in the 1959 biopic of jazz trumpeter Red Nichols, *The Five Pennies*, the inclusion of both "When the Saints Go Marching In" and "Bill Bailey" seems to have consolidated the place of the two numbers in the nightclub repertoire. The whole movie is built around the conflict between Nichols's "home" in music, particularly Chicago-style jazz, and his "home" with his family and all its accompanying responsibilities.

Three encounters with Louis Armstrong are pivots in the life of Nichols (Danny Kaye). Krin Grabbard sees this relationship as exemplifying the role of Black jazz musicians in Hollywood stories: interaction with the iconic jazz master helps establish Nichols's virility, particularly on his first date with his future wife.[80] Two further scenes with Armstrong serve to illustrate Nichols's attempt to link family and music, including a babysitting segment when father, daughter, and Armstrong perform a vocal trio at a nightclub. At the movie's conclusion, Armstrong and "Bill Bailey" reappear in a musical finale wherein Nichols is able to have both family and music.

When Nichols neglects his child, she contracts polio—a condition that takes longer than a decade of daily attention from her father to overcome even partially. In the end, she is able again to stand, walk, and, in the final sequence,

Figures 2.3 and 2.4. Renditions of "Bill Bailey, Won't You Please Come Home?" bookend *Papa's Delicate Condition* (1963). For railroad employee Jack (Jackie Gleason), the masculine place of work is replaced by the feminine domestic sphere, the flask of alcohol offered to the workers by the reconciliation bouquet offered to his wife (Glynis Johns).

dance. Through this circumstance, Nichols, like Bailey, is called back home, back to the domestic circle. When Armstrong first sings "Bill Bailey, Won't You Please Come Home?" the connection between song and Nichols's fate may not be apparent, but, when the song is reprised in the climactic resolution, the meaning falls more clearly into place. Nichols regains his "lip" and resurrects his musical career, thanks to the prodding of both wife and daughter. At his comeback performance, Armstrong appears as a surprise guest, and together he and Nichols reprise "Bill Bailey" (see figure 2.5). The two meanings now coexist: Nichols is able to be both "home" with his family and "home" in his music.

Figure 2.5. *The Five Pennies* (1959). At the end, Red Nichols (Danny Kaye) is finally "home" in both the world of jazz and his nuclear family, surrounded by daughter, wife, and jazz great Louis Armstrong (center) who reprises "Bill Bailey, Won't You Please Come Home?"

In a 2003 novel, Edgardo Vega Yunqué utilizes *The Five Pennies* as one seminal element in the backstory of his detailed (634-page) saga of American life as the 1980s turn to the 1990s, entitled *No Matter How Much You Promise to Cook or Pay the Rent You Blew It Cauze Bill Bailey Ain't Never Coming Home Again.*[81] The protagonist (jazz pianist Billy) was taken to see the Nichols biopic as a child and then later had his own brief encounter with Armstrong. In part, his story parallels Hollywood's version of Nichols's life in *The Five Pennies.* Due to wartime violence, the pianist loses both his emotional health and the full use of his hand—and thus loses his music. Later, his one attempt at domesticity ends with his leaving home, wife, and daughters. His disrupted relationship with his grown-up daughters is one main focus of the action, including when one, his co-protagonist Vidamía, tries to spur his return to playing jazz.

Throughout the novel, "Bill Bailey" represents the entire jazz tradition—a "home" this late twentieth-century hero may not be able to go back to, just as he may not fully reconcile with his daughters. In the end, he briefly returns to music-making before dying. After his death, Vidamía listens to a performance by her boyfriend Winn and her half-sister Cookie, "singing in her smoky voice," as they launch into "Bill Bailey, Won't You Please Come Home?" She is filled with yearning, "wishing with all her might that her father had not left them," yet knowing that the song represents "a useless plea." The final page of the epic meditates on the meaning of Cannon's song as applied to their lives:

Bill Bailey was never coming home again, and the prospect of life without him made her ache. She smiled painfully and even though she knew the entire matter was a rationalization, she felt as if Billy had come home. He had left the horror of his sorrow and stepped out into life, with all its disappointments and pain, to do what he loved and play jazz again. She had helped him accomplish this, and in return he'd filled her with enormous confidence in herself.[82]

As with Nesbit and Shaw at the turn of the last century, in this century film and literature writers continue to include "Bill Bailey, Won't You Please Come Home?" in their stories, thereby tapping into certain deep emotional resonances: what a man means to his household in our society; what it means to "come home"; and what it means to reach out to someone who has wandered from their home and beckon him/her back to that place of fulfillment, safety, and comfort.

Chapter Three

"I'M SORRY I MADE YOU CRY" AND "JAZZ HANDLING"

The Strange History of the American Waltz, Part One

*C*an a torch song be a waltz? Lyricist Al Dubin raised this question in a 1934 interview. He immediately mentions one of his own waltz hits, but is ambivalent about it: "'Dancing with Tears in My Eyes' is a torch lyric, but a real torch song is not a waltz."[1] In contrast, Edward Jablonksi answered in the positive almost thirty years later, affirming that "many" torch songs "are written in the once wicked and vivacious three-quarter time of the waltz."[2] The vivacious waltz mutated into a defining expression, as Jablonski put it, of "the Everyman of the American landscape, alternately sad, wistful, reflective—and alone."[3] That was part of the process of Americanizing the waltz—turning it introspective.

But the trajectory circles back on itself, for then the American waltz turned vivacious again—by ceasing to be a waltz! During the 1910s, performers began to alter waltzes into duple meters. They transformed three-four meter into two-four, or four-four, or cut time. This change enabled listeners to march, or two-step, or fox trot to melodies that were originally conceived of as waltzes. By rewriting these rhythms, the arrangers and singers became collective innovators of popular standards.

This process can be seen as marking a radical change in the American waltz tradition. The essence of American-ness in music is sometimes symbolized as a *one-two-three-four* beat where the emphasis is placed on *two* and *four*—the offbeats—rather than on the customary strong beats of *one* and *three*.[4] Duke Ellington liked to demonstrate this offbeat in his concerts, and the 1999 Broadway revue *Swing!* celebrates it in a song called "Two and Four."[5] It is easiest to manifest this offbeat when there are an even number of beats. Therefore, by converting three-four into four-four, performers paved the way for the melodies of the waltz to become more Americanized. By doing so, they also asserted their right to redefine compositions, becoming, in effect, co-creators of a new identity for a song.

The waltz was first associated with the German-speaking countries of Europe and had become Anglicized by the 1870s. By the turn of the twentieth century Americans, too, were masters of creating exuberant waltzes—the type that Alec Wilder has praised as the "back-porch waltz."[6] In the United States, sports lovers still enthusiastically take a seventh-inning stretch to one example, a quintessential piece of Americana, "Take Me Out to the Ballgame." That 1908 hit song lent its title to a 1949 hit movie musical—a practice that Hollywood loved. Numerous cinema successes were titled after extroverted waltzes: "Sweet Rosie O'Grady" (1896; film, 1943), "In the Good Old Summertime" (1902; film, 1949); "Meet Me in St. Louis, Louis" (1904; film, 1944), "The Daughter of Rosie O'Grady" (1918; film, 1950). Alternately, films featured them, as with "The Band Played On" (1895; in *The Strawberry Blonde*, 1941), "On a Sunday Afternoon" (1902; in *Atlantic City*, 1944), "Forty-Five Minutes from Broadway" (1904; in *Yankee Doodle Dandy*, 1941), and "Nellie Kelly, I Love You" (1922; in *Little Nelly Kelly*, 1940). These songs typified what Jerome Kern described as those "typical Yankee" "wide awake," "loud," extroverted traits.[7]

In this era, Americans could also write moodier waltzes, yet the most popular among those remained impersonal. An atmosphere of melancholy pervades the refrains of "After the Ball" (1892) and "Toyland" (1903), but the words are generalized statements. Some are third-person narratives—these became known as the "tearjerkers" or "sob ballads" of the Gay Nineties—such as "In the Baggage Coach Ahead" (1896) or "A Bird in a Gilded Cage" (1900). None of these darker enduring waltz hits were mated with truly personal lyrics.

The waltzes with personal lyrics that eventually did emerge are often either heartbroken plaints of loss or besotted pleadings for love—sometimes both. In 1959 Ira Gershwin spoke about such longings in a volume of whimsical commentaries on his own song lyrics. Although he was not writing about waltzes, his thoughts are relevant to these early triple-meter torch songs. Gershwin named two prominent categories: the *importunate male* and the *importunate female*.[8] Gershwin had regaled the public with many duple-meter examples, from which he anthologizes "Someone to Watch Over Me," "I've Got a Crush on You," "Embraceable You," and "I Can't Get Started." Such torch-song protagonists are pleading for love: *importunate* comes from *to importune*, in its sense of *to repeatedly request or persistently plead* for love.[9] Many of the earliest of the enduring America classic ballads that feature these importunate protagonists are waltzes—but ones that proved themselves susceptible to jazz treatment.

In the new century, enduring waltz ballads with personal lyrics and tender melodies were created that developed a tradition of being performed both as waltzes and as fox trots: "Kiss Me Again" (1905), "I Wonder Who's Kissing Her Now" (1909), "Let Me Call You Sweetheart" (1910), and "When I Lost You" (1912). Each work is a link in a saga of arrangers and performers engaging in a process of re-composition, by rendering these three-four compositions in duple meter. These waltzes are transition pieces. They can be ponderous; the public's ear has been regaled with many dragging or saccharine performances. Or they can be highfalutin or at least overly serious about themselves. They can also be entrancing—luxurious, tender or, particularly when done in four-four meter, sparkling and jolly.

These four waltz ballads were immediately successful and influential. Eventually, as the decades went by, they also became influential by being converted into duple meter. Yet, they were not the first tunes to be transformed in this way. Other waltzes were even more pivotal in the saga of how waltzes became fox trots, and understanding the history of these later songs is essential to understanding the trajectory of the four focus waltzes.

The earliest of these pioneers was probably a highly sentimental ditty of 1916, "I'm Sorry I Made You Cry," written by Nick J. Clesi in New Orleans, just as that city witnessed the transformation of ragtime into jazz. The song was published three years after the period covered in the present study and thus violates the periodization. Nevertheless, we must first trace the history of Clesi's 1916 tune to be able to understand what happened to the waltz ballads of 1905 through 1912—and how performers collectively rewrote them as jazzy rhythm ballads.

WHEN THE WALTZ BECAME A JAZZ FOX TROT

Decades later, Clesi, songwriter and real estate agent, would spin an anecdote about the origins of his title "I'm Sorry I Made You Cry": his young son uttered this phrase after destroying a rose that his little sister had picked for their mother.[10] By March 1916, O. M. Samuel reported from New Orleans that "local songs by local writers have superseded the imported [New York] brand."[11] He listed "I'm Sorry I Made You Cry" among four outstanding local hits.[12] Sam Rosenbaum printed Clesi's tune through his local Triangle Music company.[13] Presumably to peddle the song, Rosenbaum traveled to New York in September.[14] By August 1917, piano rolls of the piece were selling out in Los Angeles.[15] By the end of 1917, the publisher opened an office in Chicago.[16] In March 1918, the Feist publishing company bought up Rosenbaum's song catalog, reportedly solely to obtain the flourishing "I'm Sorry I Made You Cry."[17] With Feist's powerful show business engines pushing the number, in 1918 sheet music and record sales boomed, from May to November.

With "I'm Sorry I Made You Cry," Clesi wrote a standard ABAC thirty-two measure refrain. At the start of the chorus, he creates a conversational match of words and music. In the next two stanzas, Clesi crafts effective word patterns using an alliterative pair (forgive, forget) and a list (word, smile, kiss). At the end of each section, the music reaches for mini-climaxes. Finally, in the C segment, the penultimate phrase ascends to the tune's highest note, on the word "sigh," achieving a melodic intensity not quite matched by the lyric.

Example 3.1. "I'm Sorry I Made You Cry," refrain, melody line.

In the end, the song feels overstrained. Nevertheless, in this composition Clesi clearly presents singers with an opportunity to milk sentiment from each lingering fermata. Samuel had early on dubbed it "a Charles K. Harris sort of ballad," referring back to the man who had made Tin Pan Alley history with his tear-jerking million-selling waltz of 1892, "After the Ball."[18] "I'm Sorry" combines the fresh, personal point of view of the new century with an old-fashioned sentimentality that harks back to fin de siècle waltzes.

From the outset, "I'm Sorry I Made You Cry" was hailed for the way its lyric applied to ordinary emotional life. A 1917 commentator on the song noted, "There are few persons who, at some time in their lives, have not been responsible for tears shed by those they love best."[19] He judged that this widespread emotional relevance overcame "Sorry" being such a "simple little piece."

The ballad's slenderness, however, was soon perceived to hold another virtue. In June 1918, a *Billboard* columnist noted that Clesi's tune was "so simple . . . that it admits of both serious and 'jazz' handling."[20] Jazz musicians of the era seem to have welcomed this opportunity: taking its skeletal melody and fleshing it out—and transforming it from a triple-meter ballad into a duple meter dance tune.[21] Near the end of February 1918, Earl Fuller's Jazz Band set it on disc—even before the big record companies got around to having their full-bodied tenors wax their "straight" versions. Fuller would eventually record the tune four times. His arrangement wheels and whines in hard-swinging early jazz fashion, offering breaks to the clarinet at the end of each section, with the trombone sliding the band back in. Before summer, Ford Dabney's Band had also recorded it, and so had Wilbur Sweatman's Original Jazz Band in a medley with the even more strongly enduring "Darktown Strutters' Ball."[22]

These jazz renderings of "I'm Sorry I Made You Cry" recreate the number as a lively swinger in duple meter. What seemingly starts as a performance practice quickly shows up in the tune's print history. Soon, novice bands did not need to improvise a jazzed-up "I'm Sorry": they could buy it. In the late spring, Feist copyrighted "I'm Sorry I Made You Cry" in an edition as a "jazz fox-trot."[23] The arranger was Frank Henri Klickman—a composer, usually Chicago-based, of rags, waltzes, sentimental songs, Hawaiian novelties, almost anything (whom we shall meet again). This print edition offers the earliest indication yet found of a waltz being issued in a duple meter fox trot transformation. *Billboard* advises tersely, "In writing to publisher performers should state which version they desire."[24]

Many decades later, Sophie Tucker performed "I'm Sorry I Made You Cry" on a faux-live album called *Cabaret Days*. She renders the song first as a slow waltz and then in a lively duple meter. In her spoken introduction, she claims, "I introduced this next song in 1915, as a ballad, and this was the first time any singer went into a fast tempo, which later became the style used by all the bands." (Smugly, cockily, she adds, "And I'm very proud of myself.") Tucker's claim of being "the first" is questionable. Nevertheless, as with the 1918 journalistic coverage, copyright notice, advertisements, and jazz band recordings, Tucker links "Sorry" with a seemingly new practice. Tucker says "fast tempo," but what she and her accompanying band are really doing is not merely quickening the speed but also converting the time signature into a duple meter and inflecting the song with a jazzy style.

In the aftermath of World War I, doughboys paraded to this waltz-transformed-into-march. In 1919 the lyric was used as a message to German villagers who had befriended their occupiers, especially the small children who "cried. . . . toddling and wailing beside the columns of men."[25] The soldiers had grown fond of the townsfolk, too, and "those who marched out of Weihlen, with the band playing 'I'm Sorry I Made You Cry,' were not cheerful, for a moment, even though they were starting home."[26] It was not only Yankee military power that World War I spread across Europe, but also American popular songs and their implicit freedom to be altered by the performers.

"I'm Sorry I Made You Cry" also continued to be delivered in its original three-four meter, for instance by Alice Faye near the start of the 1938 movie musical *Rose of Washington Square*. Faye's voice throbs, but she also smiles, tilting her head back proudly, and picks up the coins that the audience throws to her. She little knows that fate intends *her* to be the one made to cry, when she falls in love with an imperfect, adventuring conman. In 1946 Frank Sinatra sang "I'm Sorry" as a very slow waltz—so slow it almost loses its waltz momentum—in a hushed, beautifully controlled rendition. He and his arranger Axel Stordahl make that climactic high note, on "sigh," float into the ether and disappear. These steady collaborators go a long way toward making the ballad convincing, but this slight song has trouble bearing the sag of that much dewy intensity.

Faye and Sinatra, notwithstanding, what Tucker does with "I'm Sorry I Made You Cry" became a standard practice, both for that tune and many others: shifting mid-performance into a faster tempo and, in general, translating a song into a new meter—and, in particular, jazzing up waltzes by playing them in four-four time. Thus, when "Sorry" was re-popularized in 1937, in Thomas "Fats" Waller's rambunctious rendition, it was as a duple meter swing tune.

Chicago jazz musicians, New Orleans revivalists, and British trad bands also perform "I'm Sorry" in a lively four-four, from Eddie Condon (in 1928, with a fine jazzy, crooning-style vocal) through Red Nichols (1932), Mugsy Spanier (1945), Louis Nelson (1988), and so on. Cliff Edwards (the twenties' Ukulele Ike, later famous as the voice of Disney's Jiminy Cricket) also did it in four-four in 1956 with a Dixieland combo. He sells the lyric with both out-of-tempo mockery (in the verse) and swinging sincerity (in the refrain).

A few converted the melody to four-four but with a slow ballad tempo. In 1940 Art Hallman delivered a fine band-crooner refrain, with Mart Kenney's top-ranking Canadian dance orchestra. (Afterward, the band breaks into fast tempo for a fevered trumpet solo.) In 1957 Roberta Sherwood walked a tight-rope, with only a rhythm section and at a draggy tempo, just barely sustaining the momentum, until it all pays off in her full-voiced ending. She perhaps inspired Connie Francis's 1958 duple-meter ballad single, which was perhaps most successful of all. Clesi's ancient hit again soared into the Top Ten, on the wings of Francis's plaintive, floating drawl inflected with a rock and roll style.

Except perhaps by courtesy of that late-fifties revival, "I'm Sorry I Made You Cry" was never among the most famous songs—yet it retained a kind of presence among the folk. In the twenties and thirties, cartoonist W. E. Hill represented Great War veterans whistling it in the bathtub and "big hard-boiled guys" weeping as they sang it.[27] Tough guys seemed to find in the song a kind of sentimental release from guilt. In Denver in 1934, a thief seized a woman, drove her out of the city, and, when he found she had only sixty cents in her purse, punched her. She began to cry, so he crooned to her "I'm Sorry I Made You Cry." She stopped crying, and, "pleased with the soothing effect of his sing-ing, the kidnapper kept it up for two hours, then released her to walk home."[28] This bizarre incident hints at the contradictory internal qualities implied in the lyric of "Sorry"—wild ("I've wandered in life's gay whirl," the verse confesses), yet penitent.

When the Denver kidnapper fell to crooning, he perhaps had in mind the microphone singers who had been filling the airwaves, maybe not with "I'm Sorry I Made You Cry," but with later songs that painted the same scenario with their lyrics yet did so usually in a duple meter. As crooning and torch songs came into vogue, the protagonists of two enduring songs proclaimed that, though they knew they made their beloved cry, they were so sorry: "(What Can I Say) After I Say I'm Sorry" (1926; revived twice, in 1940 and the mid-1950s); and "Forgive Me" (a hit for Gene Austin in 1927; also revived twice—by Eddie Fisher in 1952 and Al Martino in 1965). The height of the crooner era witnessed "I Apologize" (a success for Crosby in 1931, and charting again in 1951 for both Billy Eckstine and Tony Martin) and the penitent "Have You Ever Been Lonely" (1933; which entered the country repertoire via Ernest Tubb's hit in 1949, a status reinforced by Jim Reeves and Patsy Cline in 1962). Sinatra's "swooner" period was framed by his charting of the apology-filled pleadings of 1944's "I Couldn't Sleep a Wink Last Night" and 1950's "Sorry." For all of these, "I'm Sorry I Made You Cry" is the most notable forerunner.

"You Always Hurt the One You Love" (1944) returned to the old-fashioned feeling and three-four time signature of "I'm Sorry I Made You Cry"; yet the Mills Brothers' hit recording of "You Always Hurt" followed the tradition set by

Clesi's old tune—the brothers do the first refrain in waltz meter, and then pick up the tempo and change to duple meter for the rest of the track. Rendering "You Always Hurt the One Your Love" in four-four time became the rule rather than the exception, in the many performances that struck gold over the ensuing decades—including successful recordings by Clarence "Frogman" Henry, Pat Boone, and Connie Francis that brought it into the rock and roll era—and that reveal the lingering influence of "I'm Sorry" and its performance tradition.

Just prior to "I'm Sorry I Made You Cry," a handful of other enduring waltzes emerged in the first decades of the twentieth century—also with torchy lyrics that are filled with loss or longing or imploring; also performed, at least at times, in duple meter; and also influencing later songs. The history of "I'm Sorry" has set the stage for understanding their stories. Having done so, I will now backtrack to resume my chronological sequence. Each saga illustrates how the creation and re-creation of ballads involved not just the credited authors, but also other songwriters, performers, arrangers, and publishers. Each offers an individual silhouette of song history. Yet, along with the history of "I'm Sorry," these vignettes also cohere as one chronicle—a tale of how performers transformed early waltz ballads.

Chapter Four

"KISS ME AGAIN" AND THE WISDOM OF WITMARK

The Strange History of the American Waltz, Part Two

*V*ictor Herbert was the most famous composer of American musicals in the early twentieth century, a distinguished German-Irish cellist and conductor. He was fond of showing off his fecund creativity in extended musical numbers, such as variations on "Rock-a-bye Baby" in *Babes in Toyland* (1903) and "Game of Love," from *Sweethearts* (1913), in which the lyrics introduce five different ways to court a girl, each with its own separate melody. For *Mlle. Modiste* (1905), he and lyricist Henry Blossom wrote a showcase for the female star, "If I Were on the Stage," in which the sprightly verses set up three different refrains.

The heroine is a dressmaker (then called a *modiste*) who sings "If I Were on the Stage" as she dreams of being a theatre star in dramatic parts: first, a simple country maid, all "tra la la"; second, a majestic queen; and, in the final portrayal, "a strong romantic role / emotional and full of soul," for which she would sing "a dreamy, sensuous waltz / . . . Kiss me again." As performed by the operetta's star, prima donna Fritzi Scheff, this routine made a sensation and cemented her enduring fame.

"If I Were on the Stage" was published, along with the rest of the score, but had only moderate sales. The piece's publisher, Julius Witmark, realized that the "Kiss Me Again" refrain needed to be separated from the rest of the routine, so he pushed Herbert and Blossom to create another verse to introduce the song.[1] They delivered, and the new packaging worked. "Kiss Me Again" went on to sell over a million copies of sheet music and be often revived on stage, screen, radio, and record.[2] This ballad became so ubiquitous over the next few decades that, as cartoonist W. E. Hill jokingly claimed, it was nearly "America's unofficial national anthem."[3]

The structure of the "Kiss Me Again" refrain is closely akin to the era's standard ABAC—except that it concludes with an additional D section, which extends the song by ten measures. In performance, this coda-like conclusion is often omitted altogether or held back to be used as a climactic second ending. The refrain starts out at its lowest extreme, on B (in the original key of F major), undulating with a mostly simple step-wise motion.

Example 4.1. "Kiss Me Again," the "pop" verse and the refrain, melody line.

In the first two phrases (the first four measures), Herbert steals a fleeting passage from the impressionistic piano piece "Córdoba" (1898), by his Spanish contemporary Isaac Albéniz.[4] This unacknowledged theft in perhaps Herbert's most famous song is a surprise, because he was (and is) so strongly viewed as a pioneer of American music, a model of integrity, one of the greats. The practice of borrowing melodies from classical instrumental compositions for serious popular love ballads, however, would soon develop as a strong tradition, with "I'm Always Chasing Rainbows" (1918) and "My Castle of Dreams" (1919), both based on Chopin, and "Avalon" (1920) based on Puccini—and on and on. Here, Albéniz's melody describes a beautiful, languorous arch. It is a harbinger of the arching melodies that would follow to swell out the standard repertoire, but usually in duple meter and spread out over more measures, such as with "Star Dust" (1929), "Little White Lies" (1930), "Blue Moon" (1934), "Over the Rainbow" (1939), and "Blueberry Hill" (1940).

4.2 Motif from Isaac Albéniz, *Córdoba, Chants d'Espagne.*

Melody only

From that opening kernel, Herbert unfolds a very different development from Albéniz. In Herbert's B section, the melody builds up to an F, before subsiding for a repeat of the A section. This again builds upward, to an E—then further to a G as the C segment begins. The ensuing wide-ranging intervals (drops of a ninth, jumps of a sixth) contrast with the final section's repeated notes (and words) that again build the song upward, ending on a high G held for more than four measures. This final section accentuates the wide range of the melody, an octave and a fifth—a wonderful showcase for the trained classical singer.

"Kiss Me Again" has primarily dwelt in the realm of the operatic singer—and, later, of the easy listening maestros—but such was its fame that it inevitably did receive some attention from the nightclub set. Sinatra paid homage to it twice on record, in 1943 on V-Disc, and later in the studio, on December 19, 1944. (This was the same date at which he recorded Gershwin's great *importunate male*

Figure 4.1. A 1905 operetta standard is carried over into the crooning repertoire: in the mid-1940s, Frank Sinatra is featured on records and sheet music of "Kiss Me Again." Photo from author's collection.

lyric, "Embraceable You," as well as the quintessential torch numbers "When Your Lover Has Gone" and "She's Funny That Way." Indeed, the Columbia label issued Sinatra's rendition of "Kiss Me Again" backed by "My Melancholy Baby," the first song called a torch song. Perhaps this intimates that the singer and the label viewed "Kiss Me Again" in the same category as these *echt* torch songs, despite its operetta pedigree.) In both, Sinatra omits the concluding D section, streamlining the tune into the standard ABAC format. The crooner is in fresher voice on the V-Disc; in the studio, he sounds a bit strained at the lower and upper reaches of the tune, and he also avoids the drops of a ninth (which he had assayed easily in 1943), using repeated notes instead. Nevertheless, overall, on both he delivers a fine-grained lyricism with a final tender bending of "aga-ain" that might well have set the bobbysoxers screaming.

In 1947 Frankie Laine, in his youthful jazz vein, converts Herbert's waltz to slow duple meter, conjuring a moody nocturnal scene of romantic drama. In 1960 the Mary Kaye Trio, pioneers of the Las Vegas all-night show, jump and jive through "Kiss Me Again" in a lively four-four meter: "Lay those big, bad chops on me—kiss me again." These popular singers alter and add words—and drop many of the high notes down an octave to make the song even more conversational.

The performances by Laine and Sinatra remind us how similar "Kiss Me Again" is to many of the intimate songs that came afterward. It is the first enduring American ballad to accomplish certain tricks that later songs mastered even further. Writing in 1905, Herbert and Blossom weave the soft, dark, romantic spell of the night with a heady atmosphere rarely found before the torch-and-crooner era, when it came to dominate pieces such as "Deep Night" (1929) or "Stars Fell on Alabama" (1934).

Blossom's refrain lyric divides into two. First he describes the nocturnal scene; the overall effect is as "dreamy" as the original verse describes it. In the second half, Blossom turns to the personal ("safe in your arms"), manages to keep the lyric just barely within the bounds of the colloquial ("far from alarms / daylight shall come but in vain")—no small accomplishment in 1905—and then becomes remarkably sexy, or "sensuous," as the stage verse had put it ("Tenderly pressed, / Close to your breast, / Kiss me! / Kiss me again!"). The concluding coda-like D section repeats this romantic plea several times, achieving a swooning climax rare for the era.

Blossom's rhetoric contrasts with the texts of other waltz hits that Herbert composed during this period. Herbert's highly chromatic "Ask Her While the Band Is Playing" (1909; lyric by Glen MacDonough) and his sweeping "Sweethearts" (1913; lyric by Robert B. Smith) have impersonal words. Further, his previous lyricists, MacDonough and Smith, create twisted passages such as "while the cello, sweet and mellow, aids the winsome maid to woo" and "such joys in life as love imparts are all of them yours"—the opposite of vernacular. Blossom wrote a rollicking back porch waltz with Herbert for The Red Mill (1906), "The Streets of New York," that avoids such convoluted syntax, but he focuses his lyric on description, with "the maids of Manhattan for mine" being as personal as it gets. By comparison, "Kiss Me Again" presents an opportunity for direct, conversational expression that is notable for its time and genre.

Blossom creates a rhetoric so steamy for 1905 that both versions frame the scenario to make it more distant, less immediate. "If I Were on the Stage" contextualizes "Kiss Me Again" as make-believe. The titular modiste is not actually outdoors in the night with her lover embracing. This "dreamy sensuous waltz" is part of an audition—just play-acting. As with all shows-within-the-show, however, this musical monologue may not merely present a theatrical pose— it may express an underlying truth about the heroine. Through the song she flaunts her capacity for romantic passion.

Blossom's substitute verse for the pop sheet music edition uses a different distancing device—it makes the sensual nocturnal encounter an event of long ago: "How often I think of the past! / Could it be you forget?" This strategy diffuses the taboo sexual implications of the picture painted in the refrain. In doing so, however, it also foreshadows many later torch songs about lost love. It lent the song what Mezz Mezzrow called a "tearjerker" quality for at least one prostitute whom he encountered while gigging, circa 1920, in Burnham, Illinois—she "always asked for . . . 'Kiss Me Again' and began to rain in the face like a professional mourner every time she heard it."[5] Interpreted as part of a tale of abandonment, the remembered moment of tenderness becomes all the more poignant.

Blossom's lyric is sufficiently unspecific, however, that it may refer to a recent nighttime tryst. It is used with this meaning in the 1931 *Kiss Me Again*, Hollywood's second adaptation of *Mlle. Modiste*. Here, the dressmaker's assistant, Fifi (Bernice Claire), and the nobly born soldier, Paul (Walter Pidgeon), are still in the first, fine, careless rapture of their class-shattering romance. On an oversized lawn chair, they are nestled together. They start with a kiss, then she sings the popular verse to him. Here, remembering past lovemaking is not regretful but rather a kind of foreplay, a prelude to doing it again. At the end of the C segment (they omit the D section), he joins her singing—and they do indeed "kiss again."

The title song is reprised three times. Convinced by Paul's proud father to sacrifice her romance, Fifi pretends to mock their love song, playing it on the piano and laughing ("Isn't it silly?"), until Paul is forced to leave. After he walks out Fifi continues, sadly, sobbing, breaking down before the final word. The context thus transforms the piece into the tearjerker that Mezz Mezzrow remembered it being for the prostitute who begged to hear it.

Later, Fifi has changed her name to Madame Bellini (thereby eluding Paul's search for her) and become a famous singer. On foreign duty, Paul hears her sing "Kiss Me Again" over the radio; but the set gets accidentally broken before he can hear the announcement with her new name. The episode symbolizes the triumph of radio: "Kiss Me Again" was, in truth, frequently broadcast. In the plot, a song that was once sung while physically close is now altered into a

Figure 4.2. *Kiss Me Again* (1931). The title song works its magic for the young lovers (Bernice Claire and Walter Pidgeon), cuddling throughout their rendition and lip-to-lip here at the song's conclusion. (The original color version of this movie adaptation of *Mlle. Modiste* is lost.)

song sung while physically distant—a poignant instance of R. Murray Schafer's schizophonia.

Near the end of the movie, at Paul's homecoming party after fighting abroad, Fifi, now an idolized star, sings the entirety of "If I Were on the Stage." She climaxes with the "Kiss Me Again" passage, at last with the climactic D section supplying an intensification of its message. The song acts as a signal revealing the heroine's truest self, amidst role-playing. Pidgeon rushes backstage to claim her love—and, by defying his father, gains the old man's consent. As the crowd cheers, the lovers . . . kiss again. The film manages to present "Kiss Me Again" in all four of its guises: intimate cuddling ballad; regretful sob ballad; microphone number; and prima donna showpiece.

"Kiss Me Again" was the first enduring twentieth-century American operetta waltz—a harbinger of many to come, most obviously Herbert's own final hit, "A Kiss in the Dark" (1922). Many more instances would parade an impassioned lyricism alongside the pop market's more intimately scaled waltz hits: "Will You Remember" (1917), "Deep in My Heart, Dear" (1924), "Huguette Waltz" (1925), "Love Me Tonight" (1925), "Pagan Love Song" (1929), "The Touch of Your Hand" (1933), and "Love Me Forever" (1935). The young Oscar Hammerstein II sustained his success partly on such operetta waltzes as "The Desert Song" (1926), "You Are Love" (1927), "One Kiss" (1928), and "When I Grow Too Old to Dream" (1935).

Romantic imperatives such as "Kiss Me Again" would become a staple of the Great American Songbook, perhaps especially in duple meter ballads. Dean

Martin, for one, built much of his early career on the offspring of Blossom's lyric. In hit recordings, he pleaded "Love Me, Love Me" (1953), "Kiss" (1954), "kiss me sweet" ("Innamorata," 1956), and (in extensions of the same romantic notion) "sway with me" ("Sway," 1954) and "let's fly" ("Volare," 1958). In ensuing years, he continued in this vein with "Call Me Darling," "Love Me, My Love," "Be an Angel," et cetera. Duets on his later television variety show often drew on seminal examples: the concise "Cuddle Up a Little Closer" (1908) with Lainie Kazan; the playful "Put Your Arms around Me, Honey" (1910) with Janet Leigh; and "Let Me Call You Sweetheart" (1910), with Kate Smith—about which more to come. At century's end, humanity sent one of these importunate waltz ballads up to the moon—"Fly Me to the Moon" was on the Apollo 13 spacecraft—but not as a waltz: rather, in a rendition by Frank Sinatra with Count Basie and his Orchestra, in a swinging duple meter. Meanwhile, as an independent pop song, "Kiss Me Again" continued living a double life—as a mourning for lost love and as an importunate pleading for love in the present moment.

Chapter Five

"I WONDER WHO'S KISSING HER NOW" AND WORK-FOR-HIRE

The Strange History of the American Waltz, Part Three

"I Wonder Who's Kissing Her Now" embodies many Gemini-like ambiguities. First, it is a waltz that, since 1937, a third of the time is not performed as a waltz. Second, the lyric is by the prolific pair of Will M. Hough (pronounced "huff") and Frank R. Adams, but how these two collaborated and who deserves credit for what is unknown. Third, the melody was credited to the famous performer-songwriter Joseph E. Howard but was actually composed by Harold Orlob. Fourth, it was introduced in the Chicago-based musical *The Prince of To-Night* (opened March 1909), one entry in a famous theatre series produced by Mort Singer, many with Hough-Adams-Howard scores. But sheet music of it was also issued as part of the score by the same team for a later show, *The Goddess of Liberty* (opened August 1909). Finally, in 1947 it rose again to popularity—especially in not just one but *two* recordings by Perry Como, and no source can distinguish which Como disc was more successful in stores, in jukeboxes, and on the radio!

Chicago was the center of the universe in the 1910s, or so it might have seemed to the young talents who swarmed there. Hough and Adams met at the University of Chicago, where they created a series of musicals for student productions. Singer gave them a chance at the big time in 1905, and through 1910 they delivered for him a series of hit musical comedies. Harold Orlob, from Utah, arrived in Chicago by late 1908, hired to contribute anonymously to the scores Howard had been churning out in collaboration with Adams and Hough.[1] For his first assignment, *The Prince of To-Night*, Orlob composed a waltz melody that became a hit and a standard. As a work-for-hire, the melody belonged to Howard, and the publisher Charles K. Harris issued it as a Howard creation.

By September 1909, Orlob had negotiated a soupçon of front-cover credit for another Singer-Hough-Adams-Howard success, *The Flirting Princess*—"special musical numbers by Harold Orlob"—and credit for his compositions on the inside cover of the sheet music.[2] Orlob went on to a modest career, sporadically writing scores for Broadway musical comedies into the late twenties. Perhaps more significantly, he was a founding member and longtime officer of ASCAP. In 1948, in one of the most famous legal cases of Tin Pan Alley legend, Orlob sued Howard to get credit for his authorship of "I Wonder Who's Kissing Her Now."

Joseph E. Howard, born in 1878, five years older than Orlob, was an early starter. He had been publishing songs since 1895 and by 1909 had paid his dues in what was already a long career in show business. Among his credits were two versions of the folk song "Looking for a Bully" which (as mentioned in chapter 2) was one progenitor of the blues.[3] Howard's biggest hit, co-credited with his stage partner (and later wife) Ida Emerson, was the telephone song (mentioned in chapter 1) "Hello, My Baby"—a standard and an exemplar of ragtime era songwriting.

Howard was not known for observing the niceties of intellectual property laws. His 1904 hit "Goodbye, My Lady Love" combined motifs not only from his own "Hello, My Baby" but also from an instrumental hit of 1901 by William Myddleton, "Down South."[4] Vaudeville historian Anthony Slide reports that whatever song Howard performed—no matter how old—was always his "latest success," which helped contribute to "the opinion of many in vaudeville that Howard should have been dubbed the 'opportunist of song.'"[5] Howard kept performing until the last instant—he died onstage in 1961 while taking a bow—and he copyrighted and published songs until the end. Among those hundreds of compositions, perhaps most were children of his own muse, but in light of his free-and-easy attitude toward creation and credit it is hard to know how many.

The Prince of To-Night opened in March 1909, and "I Wonder Who's Kissing Her Now" was introduced by the hero, played by Harry Woodruff. In May, the show went on tour, and the number started its rise to success.[6] In July the Victor record company issued a medley of the show's tunes, prominently featuring the vocal ensemble giving "I Wonder" a lively whirl. The publisher bragged in early October that the piece was "sweeping the country like wild fire."[7] He adds that "while this is an operatic number"—by which Harris probably meant a musical theatre song—"it has been taken up throughout the country, and it is selling like a popular song."[8] Indeed, it quickly sold three million copies of sheet music, and undoubtedly more as the decades rolled by.[9] In January 1910, both Henry Burr and Manuel Romain proved in the recording studios that the song responded to a big-voiced, quasi-operatic approach. At the same time, Billy Murray gave it the pop treatment through his resonant and slightly sardonic style.

Meanwhile, Howard had made a foray into producing, sinking his money into a New York production of *The Goddess of Liberty* (another Singer-Hough-Adams show from Chicago) and failing. It ran less than four weeks

Figure 5.1. "I Wonder Who's Kissing Her Now," already a hit, was shoehorned into the post-Broadway tour of the musical *The Goddess of Liberty*. On the sheet music cover, the modern woman has set aside the traditional torch of liberty in favor of a new one, the transgressive cigarette, cockily busting conservative gender roles of her era. Photo courtesy the Sheet Music Collection (Collection PASC 147-M), Library Special Collections, Charles E. Young Research Library, UCLA.

on Broadway in early 1910. Stepping into the lead male role, he took it on tour and interpolated "I Wonder Who's Kissing Her Now" into the production. The Harris staff bragged that by then it was "probably the greatest production hit known in years, and still selling big"—and they put out a new edition of the song—the same content (seemingly printed using the same plates as before) but now with a cover for *The Goddess of Liberty*. "I Wonder" is tagged on, almost as an afterthought, at the end on the list of available selections.

As late as October 1910, various vaudeville singers were still delivering it, or parodying it. By December 1910, it is reported in Christmas pantomimes in London. Although its first popularity inevitably faded, Sime Silverman could still describe it even as late as November 1911, as "the most popular selection among ivory ticklers for 'variations'" (though whether those variations included performing it in duple meter is unknown).[10]

Meanwhile, in 1911 Orlob had come out of the closet with his authorship, at least to industry insiders, when *Variety* announced that he was "the chap who wrote 'I Wonder Who's Kissing You Now,' which he sold to Joe Howard."[11] This did not immediately spoil the relationship of the two men. Although they subsequently operated in slightly separate spheres, decades later they co-wrote (and Howard published under his own imprint) the 1937 "There's Nothing Like a Good Old Song."

Throughout his lengthy performing career, Joe Howard included "I Wonder Who's Kissing Her Now" in the repertoire of himself and his various troupe members—in vaudeville (which he went back to in 1914), short films (1928), and nightclubs (1936)—on phonorecords (1936) and radio (1939). When Hollywood used the title from one of the best-remembered Hough-Adams-Howard shows for an early talkie, *The Time, the Place and the Girl* (1929), the only vintage song used was "I Wonder." The song was by then one of the "melodies of long ago" that contrasted with the hot jazz of the day, to be performed by ensembles like the Old Timer's Orchestra.[12]

In 1935 Cliff Edwards appeared on screen in *Red Salute* as a secondary character, assisting the screwball romance of the leads, Barbara Stanwyck and Robert Young. For his one vocal solo, Edwards chose "I Wonder Who's Kissing Her Now": "I looked over an album collection of three hundred old tunes, and decided on that one."[13] Result: "a reissue of the famous old song and new glory for its composer" as the movie screened across the States in early 1936. (Edwards, aw-shucks-ing, declared: "I'm glad it's going to do somebody else some good besides myself.") Indeed, Howard hit the mainstream again that same year, with fresh recordings and a long run at the Gay Nineties club in New York. Perhaps riding the same snowballing momentum, in 1936 "I Wonder" also enjoyed a major revival in England.[14]

The time came to renew the copyright on "I Wonder Who's Kissing Her Now." Unfortunately, the trio of Hough-Adams-Howard had drifted apart. Hough and Adams assigned their renewed rights to the Jerry Vogel publishers, while Howard assigned his to the Edward Marks company. Meanwhile the widow of Charles K. Harris, the original publisher, claimed her rights, too. Result: more than six years of court cases, starting in the fall of 1938 and not ending until the winter of 1944. (The end decree was that the two new publishers had equal rights to the song—and that the songwriters and initial publisher should divide the money from both later editions.)[15]

One of the key arrangements of "I Wonder Who's Kissing Her Now" would eventually prove to be Ted Weems's 1939 waxing in a duple-meter arrangement. The events leading to Weems's adaptation unfolded over two years. First, in March 1937, Tommy Dorsey had a landmark hit record with a swinging duple-meter arrangement of the 1929 waltz "Marie"—a pivotal event in the history of the American waltz. (Dorsey's record of "Marie" became a model and a touchstone—so important to the history of transforming waltzes into duple meter that I will fleetingly allude to it again, in chapters 6 and 8, and discuss it in more depth in chapter 10.) On Dorsey's disk, Jack Leonard crooned a straightforward rendition of the ballad, while the band filled in with punchy rhythmic interjections. Seemingly in response to the renewed success of "Marie," in April, Marks announced a new arrangement of "I Wonder," featuring the old favorite both as a waltz and fox trot.[16] Throughout 1938, Dorsey kept reviving old hits using the "Marie" pattern (with "Who" and "Yearning"). Probably because of this, by May 1938 Howard was convinced that "the best way to bring back old tunes is to swing 'em."[17] His idea of swing was the sweet band of Horace Heidt, who in 1938 recorded a fox trot arrangement of "I Wonder."

Howard was about to become even more prominent in a new venue: entrepreneur Billy Rose opened his 1890s-themed basement nightclub, the Diamond Horseshoe, in New York, which did top business for thirteen years. Rose often prominently featured Howard singing "I Wonder Who's Kissing Her Now."[18] Furthermore, starting in August 1939, cinema audiences could partake of Bing Crosby rendering "I Wonder Who's Kissing Her Now" in *The Star Maker*, as a waltz in a period setting. Finally comes Weems's October 1939 rendition for Decca (Crosby's label) featuring the young Perry Como (a Crosby soundalike) plus a trio of bandsmen interjecting rhythmic phrases à la Dorsey's "Marie." But the disc made no splash—at least, not till seven years later.

In 1942 Allan Jones sang "I Wonder Who's Kissing Her Now" in the low-budget movie *Moonlight in Havana*, and Ted Lewis and his band rendered it on screen in 1943, in another B-musical, the loosely biographical *Is Everybody Happy?* In 1944 the high courts finally decided who had the legal privilege to renew copyrights and how profits afterward were to be split.[19] "I Wonder" was the test case, but the ruling applied universally. Perhaps not coincidentally, 1944 also saw a rise in the number of old songs revived into major hit status: from one to three a year, the numbers increased to ten to fifteen.[20] Waltzes of the past like "Meet Me in St. Louis, Louis" (1904) and "Too-Ra Loo-Ra Loo-Ral (An Irish Lullaby)" (1914) suddenly became major money-earners again.

At the same time, Hollywood found new delight and profit in fictionalized show-business biopics, especially of songwriters.

Thus, by 1945 the stage was set for a Joe E. Howard movie biography, to be called *Hello, My Baby*. The Harry Fox Agency untangled the rights to various Howard compositions and negotiated deals with his four ex-wives.[21] A year later the film was in production, now titled *I Wonder Who's Kissing Her Now*, and crooner Buddy Clark was commuting by airplane weekly from his New York radio show to Hollywood to lay down the vocal tracks to which film star Mark Stevens would eventually lip synch.[22]

Through the fall of 1946 and winter of 1947, the music industry geared up for "a revival via the movie route" for "I Wonder Who's Kissing Her Now."[23] Already, Ted Weems had been the beneficiary of one of the most odd and dramatic song revivals: in early 1947, a North Carolina disc jockey stumbled across his 1933 Decca disc of "Heartaches" and "played it every day for a week"—by the seventh day, "record dealers in the South were suddenly swamped with requests for the record."[24] The Decca label sifted through its Weems back catalog—a number of titles having the added benefit of Perry Como on vocals—and, with the Howard biopic coming out, seized on the Weems-Como "I Wonder" as their next reissue to ride this fresh momentum.

Como was now a solo star at RCA Victor, with a string of oldies revivals already to his credit, so that company competed with a new Como waxing of "I Wonder Who's Kissing Her Now," but this time in a slow waltz treatment more suited to his current balladeer mode. Thus, Como was set to be his own worst competitor, via two startlingly distinct renditions: bouncy duple meter and sluggish triple meter.

At the end of June 1947, Twentieth Century-Fox premiered *I Wonder Who's Kissing Her Now*, starring June Haver and Mark Stevens (as Howard). The movie went on to be a major money-maker, working its way through the big cities, continuing until the fall of 1948 when small-town audiences also delighted in it.[25] By Christmas 1947, the movie and the revival of its title song also landed in England in a big way.

By the start of August, the whole machinery of 1947 song hit production was behind "I Wonder Who's Kissing Her Now." Sheet music sales of "I Wonder" were booming (with new editions from both Vogel and Marks). There were twenty recordings available for phonographs and jukeboxes, and thirteen radio transcription versions.[26] *Variety* and *Billboard* were filled with evidence of the heavy play "I Wonder" was getting on jukeboxes, but the agents reporting seemingly did not distinguish between the two Como discs. *Variety* decided to give credit to the new pressing on Victor, while *Billboard* opted for the Decca reissue—and, in its end-of-year summaries, simply lumped the two together.[27]

All this hoopla got Orlob riled up, and he finally took Howard to court to prove his authorship of the "I Wonder Who's Kissing Her Now" melody.[28] He did not seek damages, nor seemingly any future profits, just credit.[29] This may not seem like much, but "I Wonder Who's Kissing Her Now" was Howard's theme song, the title and credits music for his radio and television shows, the subtitle of his autobiography, the name of his movie biography—it was his self-declared "master song."[30] To surrender all credit for it would have been a major blow. In the end, Howard (and both publishers) agreed that he would share equal credit with Orlob for the creation. Indeed, many performers had received co-credit for doing much less plugging than Howard had, ceaselessly keeping the song alive for forty years.

The 1947 revival of "I Wonder Who's Kissing Her Now" gave it a new cachet—it was now both a beloved oldie and a fresh hit, both a slow dreamy ballad and a romping rhythm song. It enjoyed these double statuses for three more decades. Youth-market singers of the 1950s rocked it: in the United States, Doug Franklin and Connie Freed; and, in England, Russ Hamilton and Emile Ford. Meanwhile, by contrast, records of minstrel shows and sing-alongs reinforced its nostalgia value. A series of charting albums and singles from 1964 through 1977 kept it current during tumultuous changes in music and society.

"I Wonder Who's Kissing Her Now" is a very ordinary song for its time in many ways. Perhaps this is why no recent critic has singled it out for discussion. Its quality lies in the melopoetic fit of the refrain's words and music and, most of all, the overall concept behind the lyric. As with so many hits and enduring standards, the core idea can be applied generally: who has not sat around wondering what has happened to people they used to know?

The verse sounds like many from that era, with just enough melodic interest to sustain it but not so much it will overshadow the chorus. The refrain runs in the common ruts: an ABAC structure with a final short couplet in the penultimate lines, creating the limerick pattern, before the final repetition of the opening words, the title phase, now set to a fresh snatch of melody. The range is a modest octave and a third (smaller than the octave and a fifth of "Kiss Me Again," but the same as "I'm Sorry I Made You Cry").

The initial motif starts dramatically, with an ascent, through one passing tone, to the octave. Then the first phrase concludes by softly undulating. The overall effect is innocuous, yet pensive. Each phrase ends with a long note, used by arrangers and performers as an opportunity for planned or spontaneous interjections or call-and-response patterns.

The predominant, simple quarter-note rhythm continues into the B section, but subsequently changes: now the longer notes and descending motifs create the sighing that the lyric mentions. Reaching up to a high note and then

Example 5.1. "I Wonder Who's Kissing Her Now," verse and refrain, melody line.

descending chromatically, the melody implies intense emotion and pain: "telling lies." After a repetition of the main strain, Orlob creates a climax, ascending to the two highest notes in the tune (again, similarly to the later "I'm Sorry I Made You Cry").

In the verse, Hough and Adams paint a universe in which promiscuity is taken for granted—that of men and, more radically, of women. This gently melancholy cynicism is not untypical of Hough and Adams. (Another of their enduring songs, "The Waning Honeymoon" [1906], is about how spouses become disillusioned and marriages deteriorate.)[31] The verse has a strong "you"—"my boy"—or perhaps a "you all"—meaning "all you men," but it has no "I." Its generalities can be spewed forth by either a man or, perhaps more pointedly, by a woman. As with "Bill Bailey" and "Kiss Me Again," the authors use the verse to distance us from the potent emotions of the chorus.

By contrast, the refrain has a strong "I" but no "you"—only a "her." The shift is jarring, and the chorus encourages a retroactive reinterpretation of the verse: what had seemed like a rather pedantic lecture might have been self-admonishment. Taken on its own—as it most often is—the refrain can easily apply to a specific single heartache, rather than to what the verse implies are memories of numerous sexual conquests or of a randomly chosen single lover from a history of many.

The protagonist is engaged in the act of imagining—the refrain takes place in his head. The sensual details—of kissing, sighing, gazing, drinking wine, sweet-talking—are heady. The degree of emotional, sexual intimacy is open to interpretation, both between the singer and this woman in the past, and between her and her current beau. With the verse, the refrain lyric is ambiguous enough—without the verse, it takes on even more possible connotations. What is this protagonist's situation, his uppermost emotion? The possibilities range widely: longing, lonely, wistful . . . rueful, regretful, repentant . . . depressive, insignificant, castrated . . . altruistic, worried, protective, benevolent . . . prideful, competitive, bragging . . . angry, jealous, envious . . . masochistic, compulsive, self-punishing, . . . voyeuristic, kinky, obsessed . . . lazy, curious, pensive but content . . . or in the midst of an epiphany: "I love her. Is it too late?" One of the virtues of this song is that the protagonist can easily be imagined as having a mixture of two or more of such conditions. When performed as originally printed, however, as a medium-slow waltz, the music does lean the singer and listener in various directions.

The main strain is dreamy and contemplative, even soothing. The second phrase imitates the first but at lower pitches, lending a downcast, depressive feeling. With the second stanza, the melody starts to ascend—the protagonist is getting excited, emerging at least slightly out of his melancholy stupor. When the singer builds to a high note and then descends chromatically on "telling lies," he seems in emotional pain—although which of the many kinds of pain outlined above is not necessarily clear. The long ascent to the climactic high note gives emphasis to the conjecture "I wonder if she / Ever tells him of me." Clearly, to this speculating male, the question has particular poignancy. But which is important: "Does she still care about me?" or "Am I being humiliated—and to another guy?"

When done as a slow waltz, the danger of the piece is that, instead of conveying pondering, it becomes merely ponderous—heavy, dragging, overly sweet yet bland. Indeed, for many decades I only encountered "I Wonder Who's Kissing Her Now" as a stately piece of period nostalgia—none of the singers who carried the Great American Songbook to me ever made a studio recording of it—not Sinatra, Fitzgerald, Cole, or Peggy Lee. Instead, I was stuck with the high, floating, rather boring tenor of Frank Fontaine. (He sang "I Wonder" on the 1963 album, *Songs That I Sing on the Jackie Gleason Show*, that charted for a full year and was the number one album in the nation in early 1963 for over a month. Fontaine is sweet but stultifying—typifying what made the Beatles in 1964 seem like such a breath of fresh air.) The other option also creates problems: when converted into a jaunty duple meter, the song swings well but sounds emotionally insincere.

The gender politics of the song were clear from the outset in 1909: women, startlingly, were now independent agents. The issue is explicit in the verses, and even in the isolated refrain it is strongly implied. That June, when the ditty was "scoring a tremendous success throughout the country," *Billboard* credited its vogue to "the season of the summer resort girl"—presumably, her fast-and-loose ways made the lyric relevant to fly-by-night romances.[32] In 1910 *Variety* joked that "all divorced men" should "stand up and sing" it. During World War I, the doughboys invented "sexy interpolations into the lyrics," and it "became one of the theme songs in the army."[33] The government admonished show business for planting in soldiers' minds the seeds of suspicion about the fidelity of their women; and the military upper hierarchy tried to have "I Wonder" eliminated from camp life, to no avail.[34] The soldiers loved it, despite or because of its ambiguous suggestiveness. Similarly, during World War II, Radio Tokyo tried to undermine the American and British troops by broadcasting it, suggesting their wives were fooling around back home. But the tactic backfired: soldiers' memories of it were too fond, and hearing it lifted their spirits.[35]

In some potential scenarios, the protagonist of "I Wonder Who's Kissing Her Now" is a cuckold—and the tragedy of a cuckold is that he is always comic. A Max Fleisher sing-along cartoon in 1931, with a cast of felines, drummed home the piece into the listeners' ears, "with the finish showing a tabby kissing her tomcat good-bye and then inviting in a whole retinue of lovers" for a "laugh finish."[36] The song preys on male anxiety.

Or perhaps the song acts therapeutically to alleviate male anxiety—by formulating men's inchoate, unarticulated thoughts. Take, for example, the 1947 biopic *I Wonder Who's Kissing Her Now*. Howard (Mark Stevens) is haunted by a wordless melody through two or three years of struggling up the show-business ladder. Finally his lyricists think of the right title for it—"I Wonder Who's Kissing Her Now"—just after he runs away, disillusioned about women who have deceived or let him down. The girl—now grown to womanhood—who has loved him all along (June Haver) takes over the star role in his abandoned show and makes a hit with the newly completed song. In the end, its spreading popularity lures him back to the theatre for the final clinch.

In the biopic's finale—a meandering, gaudy splurge of spectacle—Haver sings "I Wonder Who's Kissing Her Now" in the guises of two politically and sexually potent women of history, Madame du Barry and Catherine the Great, depicted as insouciant heartbreakers who do not care that men express doubts about their fidelity. The experience of seeing Haver in these guises proves cathartic. Stevens's romantic wounds are healed, perhaps because his inner doubts have been expressed and laughed at—through the medium of the newly mature feminine power of his old friend.

"I Wonder Who's Kissing Her Now" never found what would seem its natural dramatic setting: a lonely guy, alone in his room singing to an old photo, or at a bar late at night confessing to a couple of friends. Perhaps the closest is when Allan Jones sings it in *Moonlight in Havana*. His character has one foot in show business and one in baseball, with a woman representing each career. He is in love with the performer, but the baseball-loving lass is the one who is assisting him, giving a lift in her car. As he sings "I Wonder," he is simultaneously self-mocking and sincere. The combination makes her laugh and, seemingly, become reconciled to losing him.

The Prince of To-Night, the song's original showcase, had its impecunious, college-boy hero being coached by a wise old man into a one-night fortune. This allows him one Cinderella-like ball with the object of his desire, who has said he must be rich to woo her.[37] The heroine is, presumably, urbane and modern enough to be pragmatic about the role of money in a capitalist romance.

The next show to feature "I Wonder Who's Kissing Her Now," *The Goddess of Liberty*, had an image on the sheet music covers that exemplified the New Woman. The outdated torch of liberty is cast aside for its modern equivalent, a cigarette (a symbol of women's equal rights during this era), which the woman brazenly, smugly lights (see figure 5.1). In the plot, this New Woman is an heiress obsessed with sports; and the nobly born British hero (again, impecunious) must try to match her athleticism to seal the advantageous alliance. (The original lead actor had to quit because the role was proving too strenuous.)[38] In the end, though, he falls for a lass whose forte is fanciful make-believe. (He thinks she is poor, but she turns out to be rich.) These contrasting heroines both have strong quirks; each embodies an element of the "liberty" of the New Woman, either the physicality of the athlete or the imagination of the artist.

The dreamy, soothing aspect of Orlob's tune lent itself to the delivery of generations of post-1920s crooners, and two of the foundational ones sang "I Wonder Who's Kissing Her Now" on screen. In 1935's *Red Salute*, the puckish Cliff Edwards drives a camper through the American landscape, on the cross-country journey typical of screwball comedy. He tenderly provides mood music for the sparring potential lovers in the trailer: Barbara Stanwyck (who is romantically interested in a Communist activist far away, partly in defiance of her conservative father) and Robert Young (who is helping her to get back to her lover and meanwhile becoming besotted). The lyric's doubts about the fidelity of a sweetheart far away, plus the romanticism of the waltz melody, suffuse the soundtrack. Meanwhile, the act of imagining being in someone else's shoes and the mood of introspection are captured in a series of pensive close-ups that display the glances of the potential lovers, into space and at each other. Unformed, ineffable emotions fill the air, setting the stage for their ultimate romantic union.

In *The Star Maker*, Bing Crosby has a knack with children which leads to his nationwide business of creating kid acts for vaudeville. One little girl refuses to sing at her audition, so Crosby tries to prime the pump by rendering "I Wonder" himself (see figure 1.5). After a false start, he starts from the top, and then is framed in close-up for half the refrain. His blue-eyed good looks and smooth, finely tuned baritone combine to create a matinee idol moment. Image and sound meld together to make "I Wonder" into a wooing rather than a lamenting. After he concludes, it cuts to a newspaper item showing that he has hired the little girl. As with Allan Jones and Cliff Edwards, Crosby proves effective: he uses the vocalizing to achieve his emotional and dramaturgical goals. Yet, the inner drama of the song itself is scarcely exploited.

In 1945 *Variety* reported "I Wonder Who's Kissing Her Now" was ranked as "the number one torch song in Tin Pan Alley" by Billy Rose (himself no slouch at writing exemplary torch lyrics, such as "More Than You Know" and "When a Woman Loves a Man").[39] Around the same time, journalist Bill Halligan claimed that "the greatest line" that applies to "the world of torch carriers I have met on my travels" is "I wonder if she / Ever tells him of me," the song's penultimate phrase.[40] In 1956 *Variety* said that the ribbon for "champ torch song" was a tie between "I Wonder" and "My Melancholy Baby." "I Wonder" was prominent among specifically male torch songs, and its dynamics potentially could be threatening to the male dominance manifested so often in Hollywood stories and in society. This may be why the dramatic situations in which it was placed seem to avoid the issues the lyric raises—a backhanded tribute to its power.

The recordings that most richly capture the song's potential are diverse. The hushed, restrained loveliness of the piece is brought out in a slew of renditions during its late forties vogue—starting with Jerry Cooper and Jean Sablon, bested in sales by Como, followed by Tony Alamo and Tony Martin. But the most believable is (surprisingly) by Danny Kaye, a reminder what a fine ballad singer the comedian could be. As well as nicely controlled light vocal production and subtle detail—such as a quiet, inventive melisma on "lies"—Kaye's underdog persona fits the song. His air of uncertainty tips the advantage toward him. He sounds like a loser, unlike the other crooners.

Frank Sinatra, captured on radio's *Your Hit Parade* when "I Wonder Who's Kissing Her Now" was at its 1947 peak, offers a unique take. He sings with a smile in his voice, sounding like he is genuinely glad for her: he wishes her well, knowing she's happy with someone new. It is completely unconvincing as a lament, but he does sound like he *is* wondering. (But was his smile actually caused by remembering a wicked parody of "I Wonder" that he had performed on radio two years earlier? During it, he rolls his "r"s and widens his vibrato grotesquely to sound old-fashioned, while Bing Crosby and Judy Garland ham their way through corny old comedy routines between each of his stanzas.)

Many of the up-tempo duple-meter arrangements sound like parodies, starting with the 1939 Ted Weems–Perry Como track. Even wittier is Ray Noble's hit 1947 record. On it, Snooky Lanson and the Sportsmen trade phrases, including a unique, saucy couplet that follows "I wonder who's buying the wine": "I wonder if they / Get to first base that way."

Taking a different tack, Billy Butterfield and his band demonstrate the tune makes a fine, swinging instrumental. Dean Martin (from a broadcast) and Joe Williams show it can fit into the ballad-with-a-beat groove, albeit by jettisoning the depression implicit in the original and opting for buoyancy instead. The Dutch trad jazz group, the Freetime Old Dixie Jassband, roll it along nicely at an easy medium tempo. A quartet of New Orleans veterans led by trombonist Louis Nelson keep "I Wonder" as a loping waltz—but prove it can still be jazz in triple meter, through their subtle hesitations, slurs, and ellipses.

The young Ray Charles in 1951, singing and on piano, sounds almost more like Nat King Cole than did Cole himself, at least vocally. Charles is not exactly convincing, but offers a nice sustained version with a late-night mood, in a gently swinging duple meter. He also is the only one who addresses the song to "you," in an original tag: "Pretty baby, how I wonder, / I wonder who's kissing you now." This small-label release was obscure at the time. Nevertheless, because of his status as an idolized foundational rock artist, Charles's arrangement (along with the "pretty baby" tag), although not rock at all, is now standard among younger artists internationally, such as the Russian Uros Perich, the Portuguese Salvador Sobral, and the Brazilian Lúcio Ricardo.

Perhaps most interesting is the trajectory "I Wonder" made in the era following the advent of rock and roll. The youth market renderings, from 1958 on, are all in duple meter, in both America and England: Doug Franklin, Russ Hamilton, Emile Ford, and Connie Freed (for whom a new duple-meter sheet music edition was issued, as "I Wonder Who's Kissing <u>Him</u> Now"—for the first time changed in print for a female singer). Bobby Darin stretched his song-reviving muscles for the last time in 1964 with a modestly charting, slow, duple-meter single refrain. The arrangement is Nashville Sound, replete with chorus that does not quite spoil the whole thing. Darin adopts a bluesy country drawl, with a remarkably detailed use of nasality, slurs, rasp, and sob. It is a put-on—but for once the image is vivid of the bereft guy in the bar, after a few too many drinks, with the jukebox playing in the background, oozing out his thoughts.

At the end of 1967, Marilyn Michaels poured the song into a new mold with another modestly charting single (in the Easy Listening category), as, in a rare instance, "I Wonder Who's Kissing Him Now." Unusually for a rendition that is not nostalgia-based, she includes the verse (cut down to half-size), done out of tempo over a doctored piano. She then supplies what the published version lacks—a transition from the generalizations of the intro to the personal state-ment of the chorus, via an economical linking phrase: "I mean." In the refrain, female choral interjections (renditions in the 1960s had a hard time avoiding the ever-ubiquitous chorus) create a tip-off that the song is not being taken seriously, with sighing effects and a sexy repetition of "lips." Yet, backed by a duple-meter arrangement lightly touched with a go-go, semi-Twist rhythm, Michaels creates a convincing persona: the liberated, urbane single woman. She could be the ex-girlfriend of Darin's "I Wonder" protagonist, reciprocating his speculations—or cousin to Marian Montgomery in her contemporaneous "Bill Bailey."

The lines "I wonder who's buying the wine / For lips that I used to call mine" have always been slightly problematic. The sentence is the least conversational in the refrain, plus it implies a certain level of both masculine imperative and sophisticated adult dissolution. The British added a more innocent option, "I wonder if she's got a boy / The girl who once filled me with joy," which goes to the other extreme and threatens to be jejune. It sounds particularly right, however, in the mouth of 1950s English teen idol Russ Hamilton, with his cheeky, innocent persona. For the 1960 Connie Freed edition, the publisher Marks altered it to "I wonder who's holding him tight / Like I used to do every night"—a fine option that performers never took up. From the Chordettes in 1954 onward, the few women who "Miss Him Now" (including Marilyn Mi-chaels) simply change it to "sharing the wine."

A more obscure source offers one of the best renditions of "I Wonder"—the rocker John Randolph Marr, on an eclectic self-titled album of 1970, on which this one old standard seems to clinch his idiosyncrasy.[41] He perhaps owes some-thing to Darin's interpretation—they could be hanging out at the same bar—but his intimate, gentle rasp is all his own and captures the contemplative mood of the song beautifully. Further, Marr's arrangement is much more spare than Darin's—with one of the best instrumental interludes for the tune—and is in the original triple meter. The concept is Marr's own.

Marr recorded for the Warner Brothers label, on an imprint run by a more renowned eccentric, Harry Nilsson.[42] When Nilsson sealed his own idio-syncrasy in 1973 with a whole album of standards, he imitated Marr in his arrangement of "I Wonder Who's Kissing Her Now"—in meter, tempo, overall concept, and even elements of phrasing such as starting particular lines with "and" or "oh." In addition, Nilsson converts "teaching" to "showing," as had Marilyn Michaels. Nilsson, in turn, was seemingly copied by later artists, for they use the same Marr-Nilsson-Michaels concepts and details: George Hamilton IV (a modestly charting 1977 country single), Anne Murray, and Deborah Robertson (the latter two, like Michaels, wondering about "Him Now"). Along with that of Ray Charles, theirs has become another chain of influence in how "I Wonder" is performed.

One of the notable aspects of Hough and Adams's original lyric is the conversational ellipses of the second, third, and penultimate lines: they drop the "I" (and its pick-up note) and simply launch off with "Wonder who's . . ." and "Wonder if . . ." Performers have usually added at least one and most often all three missing "I"s—and, in this as in the conversion to duple meter, the publishers have been influenced by performance tradition. The Jerry Vogel company added two "I"s to their 1947 edition, although the Edward Marks company did not, conservatively sticking with the slightly more slangy 1909 original.

Vogel also alters a note in refrain measure ten. (It is debatable which choice is the more sophisticated. As originally composed, measures nine and ten are predictable. Nevertheless, schematically, they cleverly condense the first eight refrain measures into two bars.) Yet, when the previously conservative Marks company put out their 1960 edition, they not only printed it in four-four, but also adopted Vogel's measure ten alteration, added even more "I"s, and also changed two notes in the penultimate bar to match how many performers rendered it (see musical example 5.3). All of these shifts redefine the text and demonstrate the print and performance traditions in interaction.

Example 5.2. "I Wonder Who's Kissing Her Now," variation of refrain mm. 9-10, 1947 Vogel edition.

Example 5.3. "I Wonder Who's Kissing <u>Him</u> Now," variation of refrain mm. 28-31, 1960 Marks edition.

Hough and Adams spun a concept in "I Wonder Who's Kissing Her Now" that would become so standard in Tin Pan Alley hits that it is startling to realize that it was, in 1909, fresh and new: obsessive wondering about the fate of the lost beloved. Hits such as "I Wonder If You Still Care for Me" (1921), "I Wonder Who's Dancing with You Tonight" (1924), and "I Wonder Where My Baby Is Tonight" (1926), and many more dwell on the issue.[43] The interrogations are seemingly endless—"Do You Ever Think of Me?" (1921) or "Are You Lonesome Tonight?" (1926)—and endlessly revived (the latter most famously by Elvis Presley). In the 1926 waltz hit "Charmaine," songwriters Erno Rapee and Lew Pollack follow the pattern of "I Wonder" to a tee: they repeat "I wonder . . . I wonder . . . I wonder" right up to the climactic high notes of the limerick-couplet at the end, wondering if Charmaine ever thinks about her torch-bearing lover, too—just as Hough and Adams's protagonist wondered if "she ever tells him of me." The mine staked out by Hough, Adams, and Orlob kept producing gold for many decades.

Chapter Six

"LET ME CALL YOU SWEETHEART" AND COMPETITION-AS-MUSE

The Strange History of the American Waltz, Part Four

*I*n the early twenty-first century, "Let Me Call You Sweetheart (I'm in Love with You)" continues to fill a special place in American culture, part of Valentine's Day courtship, bride-and-groom dances, and anniversary rituals.[1] It was a sheet-music success as much as, and maybe more than, a vaudeville-record-radio hit. One estimate is that it sold six million copies of sheet music in its first forty-five years, vying for the greatest sales record of any Tin Pan Alley song.[2] Thus, the piece floats between the worlds of professional performance and what used to be called the "community sing."

In 1935 the US Congress adjourned for the summer by singing "Let Me Call You Sweetheart" together.[3] At least this was one agenda item they could all agree upon. In 1943 the city of Indianapolis sponsored Let's Sing Week and insisted that the core repertoire include "Let Me"—the only personal love song considered to be absolutely essential to any sing-along event.[4]

My own history with the piece reflects this: I never heard a recording until years after I had learned the song aurally during sing-alongs. Its power was proved to me forever in 1999, when dining with friends in a restaurant, depressed over institutional red tape stopping our volunteer music work. A couple, about forty years old, hearing us try out snippets of various songs, requested a serenade—and came up with "Let Me" at the exact same instant we did, too. That moment of synchronicity with a pair of sweethearts over "Let Me" revived our enthusiasm and determination to keep on singing for others.

The song is simple, in both melody and lyrics. The refrain's second line, the subtitle, brings the lyric close to a pure love statement: "I'm in love with you." Admittedly, the remainder of the lyric is a pleading for reciprocation, painting a picture of love not yet fulfilled. Still, the "lovelight" is already "glowing" in the eyes of the beloved—this, combined with the singer's innocence and tenderness, strongly implies that the love will be (indeed, perhaps already is) reciprocated.

Example 6.1. "Let Me Call You Sweetheart," verse and refrain, melody line.

Yet, the song's origins are enwrapped in mercantilism and sibling rivalry. Starting in 1907, twenty-nine-year-old Beth Slater Whitson, a Tennessee poet whose work appeared often in the *Metropolitan* magazine, and Leo Friedman, an Illinois popular composer, joined up writing songs that Friedman would publish in Chicago under his own imprint. In 1909 they hit the jackpot with "Meet Me Tonight in Dreamland." Friedman promoted it sufficiently to get the major Chicago firm of Will Rossiter to buy it outright—for a modest fee and no royalties—and Will plugged it into a multi-million sheet music seller with the help of his right-hand man and protégé, his younger brother Harold. Whitson and Friedman never got more than the small initial fee. Soon, however, the Rossiter brothers argued, and Harold walked out.[5] He opened up his own music publishing company in the office right next door to his brother. Writers for two of Will's biggest hits took their wares to Harold and, this time, got royalties—but also got blacklisted by Will. One of those songwriters was Shelton Brooks, the subject of the next chapter, and the other was the team of Whitson and Friedman.

Whitson and Friedman clearly pattern "Let Me Call You Sweetheart" on their earlier "Meet Me Tonight in Dreamland." In waltz time, both songs entreat the beloved to the "let me" or "meet me." The first verse for "Let Me" focuses on dreams, conjuring up "Meet Me" and, indeed, seeming to be inevitably leading to the earlier song. Both refrains have ABAC structures, in which the third stanza mentions "the lovelight" in "eyes so blue" or "so true," which the sweetheart is entreated to keep "shining" or "glowing."

In the first run of popularity, "Meet Me Tonight in Dreamland" was as successful as "Let Me Call You Sweetheart," and both became strong standards. But in the long run "Let Me" has proved the more often revived and widely used. The two writers were just a little bit more canny on their second try. "Meet Me" deals with fantasy, "Let Me" with reality. The tune of "Meet Me" is more floating, but that of "Let Me" is both more distilled and more emphatic. The ending of "Meet Me" is more complex, but that of "Let Me" more savvy, exactly repeating the opening words, which are the title and subtitle.

As with "Meet Me Tonight in Dreamland," Friedman himself was the first to publish "Let Me Call You Sweetheart," in early April 1910, and he nurtured it to popularity. By mid-December the song was riding high, and Whitson and Friedman handed it over to Harold Rossiter on a percentage basis.[6] Angered, Will Rossiter swore to drive brother Harold out of business and ran snide ads—"Men Originate; Monkeys Imitate"—but to little avail.[7] Through the autumn of 1911, Harold's publication proved to be, as performers Cook and Stevens reported, "the biggest encore-getter ever used" and, for the Empire State Quartette, "getting bigger every performance."[8] Ironically, what has been called "perhaps the ultimate American love ballad" reveals a new wrinkle in collective innovation: the muse of revenge—in this case, on Will Rossiter, by Whitson and Friedman at his injustice, and by Harold as part of an internecine feud.[9]

When the copyright renewal was due in the mid-1930s, "Let Me Call You Sweetheart" endured some of the same travails as "I Wonder Who's Kissing Her Now," though with a swifter resolution. Friedman's mother, as his heir, sold her rights to Shapiro, Bernstein, while Whitson's heirs assigned theirs to Paull-Pioneer. By 1939 the contestants had reached an agreement, and sheet music was subsequently issued only by Shapiro, Bernstein. In the process, "Sweetheart" was publicly "recognized as one of the most valuable copyrights among old-time tunes."[10]

Some of the pioneer crooners featured "Let Me Call You Sweetheart." Just as radio first gripped America and electrical recording became common, this waltz was revived into popularity. It started quietly enough, with the Columbia record label's house orchestra issuing a disc in the spring of 1924 and a couple of radio singers featuring the old tune. In October 1924, Harold Rossiter issued an arrangement by Ferde Grofé. The issuing of this new print edition was synchronized with a record release from the Victor label of an inventive rendering by the International Novelty Orchestra, with a solid vocal by tenor Lewis James.[11] Sales began to rise again for the evergreen favorite. Composer Friedman was able to see his biggest success once more reported as "a hit from coast to coast" and one of the "big sellers" through 1925 and 1926, before intestinal trouble brought about his death, leaving only his mother to survive him.[12]

Friedman lived long enough possibly to have heard "Let Me" jazzed up, in duple meter, when in 1925 the Columbia label issued a true-blue New Orleans arrangement by the Halfway House Dance Orchestra, a Louisiana hotel band run by Albert Brunies. That same year, Art Gillham, "the Whispering Pianist," was broadcasting the ballad in his quiet, half-spoken manner, a harbinger of the crooner revolution just getting underway.[13] Also from the mid-twenties onward, the country music field was embracing the song, with pioneer Riley Puckett waxing a particularly fascinating 1927 rendition in which he includes a verse that is entirely original—music and lyrics—and not entirely comprehensible, what with his bluesy rendering, rural accent, and the early recording technology.

When the crooner era was full-blown, seminal electrical mic stars continued to linger on "Let Me Call You Sweetheart," in some of the most satisfying renditions. In 1931, on disc and in a film short, Ruth Etting sang both verse and chorus. So did Dick Robertson in 1932, straddling crooning and country with his version backed by sliding guitar. In 1934, when Bing Crosby was lured to the Decca label by his manager Jack Kapp, "Let Me" was among the first songs he waxed. The very slow arrangement is prevented from dragging by his lush timbre, flexible phrasing, and intimate, subtle melismas. Kate Smith, taking it equally slowly, with celeste filigree behind her, is just saved from ponderousness by her warmth and restraint. Quietly insistent, she seems actually to be singing to a specific individual. Decades later, Smith duetted on "Let Me" with Dean Martin on his television series—and her smiling, tender, intent focus on her partner becomes, delightfully, visual as well as aural.

"Let Me Call You Sweetheart" can conjure images of a man on his knees in the family parlor, or a woman on a moonlit bench with her fellow, each pleading his or her case. It has never received such an embodiment on stage or screen, however. Usually, in stage and film musicals, it is utilized without emphasis, as part of the sonic wallpaper of the American soundscape, as when, in 1943, both Betty Grable (in *Coney Island*) and Gene Kelly (in *Thousands Cheer*) danced on screen to instrumental renditions.

From the mid-1920s onward, about one in five performances are either entirely or partially in duple meter. Among the most interesting is Ethel Merman in a Max Fleisher short film of 1932 that alternates animated comedy with Merman leading a follow-the-bouncing-ball sing-along routine. Her final refrain in duple meter is a bluesy non sequitur, sung over a cartoon, as a comic contrast to the preceding straight waltz choruses.

In 1947 Tommy Dorsey finally got around to giving "Let Me Call You Sweetheart" the "Marie" treatment. On this disc, Stuart Foster holds back most of the oil in his voice while displaying his smoothly modulated breath control. Meanwhile, the band members do their jivey choral interjections about the "glow-worming, slow-burning" lovelight. The whole is lightly swinging, perfectly punctuated, and beautifully restrained.

In the 1950s, Patti Page presented her velvet-voiced if slightly smug version, starting as a waltz, transitioning to a swinging duple meter, and ending with a slow-down big finish. In 1965, on a charting album, Arthur Prysock gave the piece the classic ballad-with-a-beat treatment. Such renditions represent the place "Let Me Call You Sweetheart" holds in the temple of swinging classic pop.

Friedman fills his tune with long, sustained half-notes—and then even longer dotted half-notes that convey the intensity of Whitson's oh-so-direct "I'm in love with you." Translating these into duple meter while keeping the phrases intact is difficult—at least, for performers less flaunting of their breath control than Merman, Foster, Page, and Prysock—and most do not even try. Instead, one tactic is to add complex melismas and slides—or extra notes and words: "I'm so in love, I'm, oh, so in love with you." Another tactic is to break apart the statements into punchy fragments: "Let. Me. Call you. Sweetheart. I'm. In love. With. You." Both tactics are apparent in Dixieland renditions, such as those led by Bob Scobey, Sing Miller, and De De Pierce. They are even more apparent in the rock and roll renditions. These commence with a charting 1962 single by an Italian American miss, Timi Yuro. What she loses in tenderness and keeping sentences whole, she makes up for through an infectious dance beat, a warm urgency, and her successful building to a climax. She *really* wants to be sweethearts—*now*! The rock-era utilizations continued with the young Barry White (1963, backed by the Atlantics) and the mature Fats Domino (1965). Ian Whitcomb reported in 1972 that "Jerry Lee Lewis and blues veteran Furry Lewis both play 'Let Me Call You Sweetheart' whenever they can."[14] Despite its turn-of-the-twentieth-century innocence, "Let Me" proved still to hold allure for legends of a later, more earthy era.

Such hip transformations of "Let Me Call You Sweetheart" highlight its pioneer status. Philip Furia and Michael Lasser dismiss it as one of the "dated barbershop quartet staples" that soon gave way to the "distinctively *modern* song."[15] By contrast, Nicholas E. Tawa praises Friedman's music: the "attractive" "harmonic coloring" in the verse; the tune's "effective contrasts" of shorter and longer notes which create, at times, a "braking . . . slowing down" effect; the refrain's "pleasantly free swing" and its "final move" from low to high to middle "which the listener senses to be absolutely right."[16] However, Tawa also acknowledges that, through 1910, the waltz genre "frequently seems to hark back to European antecedents . . . and to remain cautiously within standardized parameters," with music that "tends to be more conservative," and he makes it clear that "Let Me" is no exception.[17]

Yet Tawa also presents the Whitson-Friedman piece as an exemplar of the turn-of-the-century "newer song of feeling that was more cognizant of contemporary conditions" fit "for a changing society."[18] These "new songs" were filled with "the depiction of the sensations over which the individual had little or no control," such as the ever-haunting dreams and ever-mounting longings Whitson describes in her verses.[19] In the chorus, the steady, plodding long notes on "I love you" are emphatic, driving the point home. The refrain sweeps away the fantasies and airy moonbeams and birdsong of the verses, replacing them with a direct plea. Thus, Whitson and Friedman create a transition within the song itself: the poeticism of the verse changes to a refrain with different qualities—ones I would describe using Tawa's terms, manifesting more of the "realism" of "the actual world."[20]

Another important point emerges from Tawa's survey of these "new songs": only 9 percent of waltz lyrics of that era were both in the first person and gender-neutral.[21] Thus, Whitson was among the vanguard by making her lyric personal throughout and an expression equally valid from a man or a woman. Because "Let Me Call You Sweetheart" explores modern emotional terrain in this flexible manner, it proved easily adaptable to the styles of jazz and crooning and rock and roll.

Besides the alteration to duple meter, there are other performance tradition touches—that never appear in the print tradition—for "Let Me Call You Sweetheart." About one in three singers replace "true" with "blue," a shift found in recordings as early as the 1925 disc by Jimmie Wilson's Catfish String Band. Then, starting at least by 1938, "glowing" is changed to "burning" (an irresistibly alliterative match with "blue") about one time in six. These variations are found especially in group singing and folk-like renditions. The eye color might come from two other hits that celebrate "eyes of blue": the 1910 "Down by the Old Mill Stream" (a success of the same magnitude as "Let Me," but one that never achieved an equal versatility of treatment) and Whitson's own "Meet Me

Tonight in Dreamland." Whitson cannily went from the overly specific "eyes of blue" of "Meet Me" to the more generally applicable "eyes so true" of "Let Me," thereby including the other five-sixths of humanity in the potential scenario.

A brief digression, for a worthy song: Among enduring lyrics from Tin Pan Alley, Beth Whitson's "Let Me Call You Sweetheart" can be considered one of the purest expressions of love. Another long-lasting pure love song from that turn-of-the-century era is also by a female songwriter: "I Love You Truly," by Carrie Jacobs-Bond. First published in 1901 in a set of seven semi-art songs, it was issued as a separate stand-alone number in 1906, became a hit in 1907, was revived to even greater popularity in 1912, and remains in active repertoire. It is, overwhelmingly, a wedding ceremony standard, yet was also crooned by Crosby (at the same session as "Let Me Call You Sweetheart") and others; fox-trotted by Guy Lombardo; and occasionally swung, as in the Dixieland-tinged version by Elisabeth Welch on her final, most personal album.[22] Jacobs-Bond flourished outside of the Tin Pan Alley field. Self-publishing, she produced several widely popular pieces. Two—"I Love You Truly" and "Just Awearyin' for You"—are personal, colloquial, and American, yet in a style slightly apart from the other songs in this book.[23] The odd fate of "I Love You Truly" is that it was written in two-four meter, and yet performers developed a sub-tradition, by at least the early 1930s, of rendering it as a waltz.[24] Later publishers eventually capitulated, printing it as a waltz in some editions.[25]

To the millennial generation, "Let Me Call You Sweetheart" may be most familiar from its rendition by George Hearn, playing the grandfather of two of the child protagonists of *Barney's Great Adventure* (1999). On their small-town farm, Grandma frequently teases her husband, but always with affection and gentleness, and Grandpa banters "I don't want to lose my girlfriend." "We were childhood sweethearts," he explains, which cues his straightforward rendition, in which his eyes gleam with lovelight via well-placed lighting (see figure 6.1). In a nutshell, the song captures their relationship: loving, long established, yet also kept in a state of perpetual courtship. Together, Grandpa and Grandma embody parental nurturance. This is the trait the children must learn to emulate in a symbolic manner, as they seek to keep safe a magic egg through hazardous adventures.

No one has ever classified "Let Me Call You Sweetheart" as a torch song, but torchy images infiltrate its tradition, lurking along the edges. Riley Puckett, in 1927, starts his unique, idiosyncratic lead-in to the refrain with the foreboding words, "Dark and shadows falling, / I'm thinking, dear, of you." This is the same nighttime world of sorrowful reminiscence that Henry Blossom used to frame the equally pleading, equally tender "Kiss Me Again."

In Ruth Etting's 1931 short film *Old Lace*, she offers a young woman advice: do not reject a poor man you love in order to marry a rich man just for

Figures 6.1 and 6.2. *Barney's Great Adventure* (1999). On their farmhouse porch, Grandpa (George Hearn) sings to Grandma (Shirley Douglas): "Let Me Call You Sweetheart." The 1910 hit suits their bantering but tender relationship, displayed in this shot/countershot.

security's sake.[26] Etting herself, it is revealed in a flashback taking place around 1910, had made the wrong choice. The end came at a party; after singing her rich husband's "favorite song" for the guests—"Let Me Call You Sweetheart"—she discovers him ardently kissing another woman. Again, the memory of "Let Me" becomes associated with loss and regret.

In 1969 Furry Lewis brought "Let Me Call You Sweetheart" into the blues tradition. For his middle refrain, he creates new lyrics saturated with the salty darkness and ambivalence of the down-home blues.[27] He ends this portion with, "When I cried 'Have mercy,' / And I cried in vain. / Now, my darlin', / I hate to hear your name." Then he transitions, "But won't you let me call you sweetheart," and launches into the next, more conventional refrain. He has drunk from the cup of bitterness, but he still wants her for his sweetheart.

It is Lewis's version that is referenced in the 1979 film *The Rose*. Bette Midler, as a Janis Joplin–like, tragically ill-fated rock singer, arrives heartbroken and high on drugs at what proves to be her final concert. After a rocking tune, she sways on her feet as she confesses to the audience that the next song is "the first blues I ever heard, by this funny little man named Furry Lewis," adding "I made my mama go and buy the record." (Whoever wrote these lines clearly did not realize that Lewis's record dated only to 1969—improbably making Rose about twenty-five years old, and still dependent on her mother, before she ever heard a blues.) She starts to murmur "Let Me Call You Sweetheart," brokenly, and then collapses. The scene starts the movie—audio only, first during blackness, then over images of her childhood memorabilia—and a shortened version ends the movie (and a differently shortened version appears on the soundtrack album). As life slips away, Rose thinks about her mother, via a song that bridges rock and Tin Pan Alley and the blues—"Let Me Call You Sweetheart."

A PRELIMINARY PHILOSOPHICAL SUMMATION—THE LULLABY AND THE LOVELIGHT

As well as being jazzed up, the waltzes of Tin Pan Alley function at times as lullabies. When singer-songwriter Melissa Manchester chose a special song to soothe her children with, it was neither one of her own compositions nor the hits by others that she had covered. It was "Let Me Call You Sweetheart."[28] Even "I Wonder Who's Kissing Her Now"—with a lyric that would seem to be far from a lullaby—casts its quiet spell on YouTube when sung to an infant, as a grandfather in Ireland croons to his granddaughter (while her father accompanies on the piano) (see figure 6.3).[29]

Through their beseeching messages, these waltzes can also function as torch songs. "Oh, listen to my plea," sings the penitent in the verse of "I'm Sorry I Made You Cry." The protagonists of "Kiss Me Again" and "Let Me Call You Sweetheart," too, are pleading. They all clearly fit under Gershwin's category *importunate*; and the root here is *port*, as in harbor. The primal image would seem to be of a ship pleading for permission to come into port, to anchor, to land in the sheltering arms of the bay. By analogy, the importunate torch singer also longs to come to rest and peace within the safe haven of the lover's embrace. As (hopefully) does "Bill Bailey," they "come home."

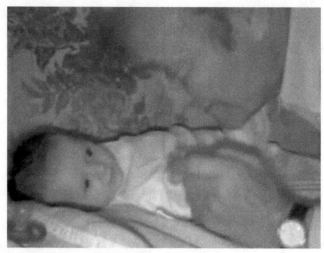

Figure 6.3. In 2007, a grandfather in Ireland lullabies his granddaughter with spontane-ous variants of "I Wonder Who's Kissing Her Now," a 1909 waltz from the United States: "Wonder who's telling her how . . . I wonder who's buying her wine." Photo courtesy of Erinna Delaney.

Within this web of imagery, Henry Blossom's notion in "Kiss Me Again" of being "safe in your arms, far from alarms" takes on a broader, more universal significance. The goal of all humanity is to feel safe; the goal of all philosophy is to transcend alarms.[30] Even the woebegone castoff who ponders "I Wonder Who's Kissing Her Now" can be analyzed as yearning for that lost port of comfort and security. The "lovelight glowing" in the eyes of the "sweetheart" is the beacon, the torch, in the dark that will lead the lover who is lost, through the darkness of the world, into harbor.

Chapter Seven

"SOME OF THESE DAYS"

"Some of These Days" has often been acclaimed as the real breakthrough in twentieth-century popular American songwriting, setting the pattern for the ensuing forty-plus years of the Great American Songbook.[1] It was published in 1910, with words and music by the twenty-four-year-old African Canadian Shelton Brooks. Good fortune brought it to a superb performer: the twenty-three-year-old Jewish and Russian American Sophie Tucker. The match of singer and song was perfect, and she adopted "Some of These Days" as her theme throughout a career of stardom that lasted until just before her death in 1966. Though the song benefited from Tucker's fifty-six years of advocacy, it scarcely needed the extra plugging, for it quickly became a favorite for a wide range of singers and jazz instrumentalists.

Brooks told a wonderful story about writing "Some of These Days." And Tucker told a wonderful story about how he first brought it to her. Too bad that neither story is true.

Among the histories related in this book, the origin of "Some of These Days" seems to represent one of the clearest cases of theft. Shelton Brooks stole his main phrase from an earlier song by a now-obscure songwriter named Frank Williams. Or, to give Brooks the benefit of the doubt, perhaps they both took the motif from the freely circulating oral tradition. The opening melody and words of the two songs—the title phrases—are almost identical. Further, the final gestures also have some similarities: both songwriters repeat the title words, both adding "yes" just before it, both placing this on the same beat of the penultimate measure. Compare them.[2] (See musical examples 7.1 and 7.2.) But otherwise the songs are very different. What role did Frank Williams play in the creation of the enduring standard by Shelton Brooks?

THE SONG'S BEGINNINGS

Frank Williams seems fated to be surrounded by mystery. Did he have a middle initial to his name, and, if so, what was it? Is this the Frank B. Williams who

Example 7.1. "Some o' Dese Days," refrain, melody line.

appeared on Broadway in 1899 as one of a quartet of barbers in the all-Black musical *The Policy Players* (starring Bert Williams and George Walker), and who later, in 1906, had a hit lyric with "Just One Word of Consolation"?[3] Or is this the Frank H. Williams who appeared on Broadway in 1908 as one of a quartet of board members in *Bandanna Land* (also starring Bert Williams and George Walker), and who had a song lyric in that show, "Somewhere"?[4] Are Frank B. and Frank H. the same person? Differing sources further confuse the issue: one lists Frank B. and the other lists Frank H. as the songwriter of "My Dahomian Queen," featured in yet another Williams and Walker show, *In Dahomey* (1903).[5] In another case: *Rufus Rastus* (1906), a show starring Ernest Hogan, also featured song lyrics by, according to one source, Frank H. Williams, while a different source lists just plain old Frank Williams.[6] Because all of these shows featured African American casts and personnel, it is clear that Frank B., Frank H., and just-plain-Frank were Black—whether these names represent several people or just one person. If they were all the same Frank Williams, then a sketchy biography emerges.

Frank Williams was born about 1868. At the age of thirty he was singing as part of a barbershop quartet in one of the earliest Black musical comedies on Broadway. Between 1903 and 1913 he wrote a series of songs, often just as

Example 7.2. "Some of These Days," verse and refrain, piano-vocal score, 1910 Rossiter edition.

13

go a - way,_ Her lit - tle heart with grief 'most broke._ She
cho - ly news,_ He quick-ly came back home a - gain._ But

16

said you know it's true I love you best of all,_ So hon-ey don't you go a -
when he reached the house he found his girl was gone_ So down he rush - es to the

19

way,_ Just as he went_ to go, it grieved the girl - ie so
train_ While it was pull - ing out, he heard his girl - ie shout

22 *rall.* - - - - - - - -

These words he heard her say._
This lov - ing sweet re - frain_

13
You'll miss me hon - ey_____ When you go a -

16
way_____ I feel so lone - ly_____

19
Just for you on - ly_____ For you know

22
hon - ey_____ You've had your way_____

And when you leave me I know 'twill

grieve me You'll miss your lit - tle

ba - - by Yes some of these

days Some of these

D.C. al Fine

the lyricist but sometimes creating both words and music. The peak of his songwriting career was 1906—he was pushing forty years old—when he and composer Tom Lemonier achieved success with "Just One Word of Consolation." This sentimental ballad endured until at least 1936, when Bing Crosby recorded it. When Williams set lyrics to other people's melodies, it tended to be those of Lemonier, Joe Jordan, or J. Leubrie Hill—all part of the Bert Williams and George Walker in-crowd. By 1942 Frank Williams was blind. When he died that year in a Harlem hospital, *Variety* gave him a brief obituary which he seems to rate because of the still-remembered "Just One Word of Consolation."[7]

On January 12, 1905, the Attucks Music publishing company, a rare outlet devoted to (and run by) African American songwriters, sent in the copyright deposit for a song with words and music by one "Frank Williams" called "Some o' Dese Days." Williams may have written the song just as 1904 was reaching its end. The cover image matches the lyric, and both are vaguely evocative of Bert Williams's star persona: the tramp-like blackface underdog. A year later, in January 1906, "Frank Williams" is given main credit as lyricist for a musical show on Broadway, *Rufus Rastus*, which starts to tour in March.[8] Sometime in 1906, an "F. B. Williams" is publishing (words and music both), with a firm in Chicago, the song "The Mid-Winter."[9] Did the *Rufus Rastus* tour somehow result in Williams traveling to Chicago? This is important, because in Chicago then was Shelton Brooks, eighteen years younger than Williams and just breaking into show business.

Shelton Brooks was born in 1886 in Canada. His mother was Native American, his minister father African American.[10] Both, it seems, played the organ—and so did young Shelton, who spent formative years in the thriving African Canadian musical culture of Buxton, Ontario, once a terminus of the underground railroad.[11] At age fifteen, Brooks crossed the river to Detroit—and from there he gravitated to Chicago, but nobody is sure exactly when. By 1908 he was featured as the star comedian by the all-Black Pekin Stock Company, which had begun operating in 1906.[12] That might place Brooks in Chicago when "F. B. Williams" was publishing in that city. Did Brooks hear Williams's "Some o' Dese Days" during those years? Or was the kernel of both men's songs floating around Black show business during this time?[13]

In the heat of summer 1910, on July 6, the William Foster Music Company published Shelton Brooks's "Some of These Days," with music arranged by Will Dorsey, an African American musical director of the Monogram Theatre, who had just set himself up as an arranger.[14] The printer perhaps set the plates just after Independence Day. Two days later, July 8, the Library of Congress received the copyright deposit copies. The mustard-yellow cover has full figure drawings of a white couple: on the left vertical panel stands the man leaving and, on the right, a tearful woman being left behind. (Ironically, on the back cover is an

Figure 7.1. "Some of These Days" (1910). A frame-in-a-frame circumscribes the forsaken woman—but not her glance. The image is genteel, but enigmatic. Photo courtesy of the Lilly Library, Indiana University.

ad for a piece by Joe Jordan, one of the collaborators of Frank B. Williams.) By July 25—a scant nineteen days later—the Library of Congress received a new copy of the song, now reassigned to the Will Rossiter company—but still with the same image on the cover. During those nineteen days, someone at Rossiter had arranged a significantly altered piano accompaniment for the whole song and written a new verse—a fresh melody and somewhat altered lyrics, though still telling a similar story (see musical example 7.2). Soon the Rossiter company would redesign the cover—a woman's face in profile—and issue it again and again, with photos of the many different performers who featured the song (see figure 7.1). Also, in all these 1910 editions from Rossiter, there is a separate page giving an unaccompanied arrangement for "Male or Mixed Quartette" (actually a quintet arrangement with the top line doubled an octave apart).

Competing in vain with the ever-increasing popularity of Brooks's "Some of These Days," Attucks Music continued to keep in print Williams's "Some o' Dese Days." The company had merged with another firm to become Gotham-Attucks and was still engaged in the struggle to survive as a Black publishing house in a white-dominated society. Gotham-Attucks advertised "Some o' Dese Days" on the inside cover of another publication, the 1912 "Everybody Makes Love to Someone, Why Don't You Make Love to Me?"[15] They ascribe to "Some o' Dese Days" the copyright year of 1908—perhaps just an error, or perhaps an attempt to make the song seem newer—and declare: "This Is A Great Song—Try It Over. . . . We say it is a great song[.] We don't ask you to believe it until you play it and then we know you will." There is something gallant and beautiful in Gotham-Attucks's effort to champion a dying cause. Weakened, not powerful enough to take the big white publishers to court, they nevertheless make this determined little gesture to promote Williams's number. But to no avail: stripped of its treasures, a good song has been superseded by a great one.

The Frank Williams "Some o' Dese Days" would stay forgotten for many decades . . . until, one day, Wayne Shirley, a longtime mainstay of the Library of Congress, trying to help in a dispute over the ownership of "Some of These Days," stumbled across the copyright card for the Frank Williams song.[16] Shirley told the sheet music historian James J. Fuld about it, and Fuld included Williams's key phrase in his standard reference work, *The Book of World-Famous Music*—announcing the mystery to the (mostly uninterested) world.[17]

Why the five-year delay between the appearance of Williams's 1905 song and Brooks's 1910 song? Who was transmitting the material shared by the two compositions? We can only speculate. In several of his other works, Brooks does seem to refashion material that was presumably floating around in the Black musical culture. As Peter C. Muir points out, Brooks's "All Night Long" (1912) and "Love-Sick Blues" (1914) both include variants on the "Frankie and Johnny" type of folk-based blues-ballad.[18] (Of course, Hughie Cannon had used this same folk pattern in 1902, for the verse of "Bill Bailey.") The refrain of Brooks's "The Darktown Strutters' Ball" (1917) starts off with a close variation on what would soon become a standard bass line for boogie-woogie (and, later, rock and roll)—a pattern that might already have been in use by late-ragtime and early-jazz pianists.[19] Apparently, Brooks drew from oral culture in these cases; if so, this strengthens the possibility that he did likewise with "Some of These Days."

After "Some of These Days" became a success, Brooks and others told tales about the origins of the song that, in light of the existence of "Some o' Dese Days," must contain some degree of falsehood. Jack Burton relays the fable that Brooks "had been toying for weeks with the melody" but could not get a lyric for it until he was in a Cincinnati restaurant, when he heard a woman lay down the law to her gentleman friend: "Better not walk out on me, man! For some of these days you're gonna miss me, honey."[20] Brooks then supposedly wrote the lyric on the back of a menu and "that night sang the song in his own act."[21] This account is filled with details, so much so that they seem to prove its veracity—but it could not be true, for the same words-and-music kernel had been published five years before Brooks emerged with his version.

By the time he was interviewed by Ian Whitcomb in 1969, Brooks had transferred his moment of inspiration to a sidewalk setting: "One time I heard a woman shout out in the street to her lover—'You gonna be sorry, baby, some of these days!'"[22] Yet another source states that before others took up the piece, "Brooks sang the tune himself at Chicago's Majestic Theater."[23] Because Brooks was an active performer, he undoubtedly was the first person to present to the public his transformation of the material originally mined by Williams.

Sophie Tucker now enters the saga of "Some of These Days." Reminiscing twenty-eight years later, the singer claimed, "It was my colored maid Molly who insisted I see a colored chap who had a song he wanted to show me. I read it over one afternoon and sang it that night."[24] Then, the article implies, Tucker sang it for the summer crowds at White City Park, "in a princess gown, her hair in curls on the top of her head."[25] In her 1945 autobiography, Tucker relates in even more detail how at first she refused to meet with this young, unknown songwriter—and only when her maid (and stage assistant) Mollie Elkins scolded her for having a high-handed attitude would she let in Shelton Brooks.[26] This episode has taken on a remarkable significance: it has been repeated again and again in histories and seems to symbolize the simultaneous closeness and separation of Blacks and whites in American society.[27]

As Tucker expert Lloyd Ecker points out, however, there are several problems with Tucker's story. Ecker has examined the singer's scrapbooks as well as the many manuscript versions of Tucker's autobiography (the earliest is from 1934), and he finds that the story does not appear until the second draft of the biography, when the singer brought in a professional writer to help her with the project. By contrast, Tucker's clippings amply demonstrate her lifelong, unceasing efforts to supply publicity fodder to journalists. It seems unlikely that she would have neglected for twenty-eight years to exploit this colorful story.[28]

Moreover, Tucker was not even in Chicago in the summer of 1910. Here is the chronology. Tucker was playing the western regional circuits from at least June 12, 1910, and she hit the West Coast by June 20.[29] July 2: Just days before

Foster sent in the first copyright copies of "Some of These Days," Tucker is being reviewed by *Variety* in Portland, Oregon.[30] (Their succinct assessment: "hit.") July 25: Rossiter mails in the copyright for their revised version. July 30: *Billboard* announces that "Sophie Tucker will be the first to introduce Rossiter's new coon lament, entitled 'Some of These Days,'" adding "the Texas Steer Quartette with use it later."[31] November 12: Tucker is still on the West Coast, touring the Pantages circuit, wiring *Billboard* that "'Some of These Days' has been so good for her that it now closes her act."[32] Thus, "Some of These Days" is a well-established highlight of her act long before she lands back in Chicago, by December 18.[33]

Everything that Tucker writes confuses 1910 with 1911. In her 1938 interview for the *Chicago Tribune*, she gives 1911 as the year she both met Brooks and sang his song outdoors at the White City pleasure park, wearing that "princess gown." However, there is no contemporaneous evidence she ever played White City—although she did play the other Chicago-area outdoor park, Sans Souci, in June 1911.[34] In her autobiography, Tucker dates her meeting with Brooks from just before she starred in her hit show, *Louisiana Lou*, and that show opened in Chicago in September 1911 (not 1910). But by the end of July 1910, Rossiter is already bragging that it got the song to her—and she boasts of making it a hit at least as early as November of that same year.

This trail of events implies that the real connector between Brooks and Tucker was not personal (not Mollie Elkins, the maid), but professional: it was Rossiter who got the piece to Tucker to plug for his outfit. Rossiter did not stop there, for his sheet music covers herald the many vaudeville performers who spread the song's popularity: Blossom Seeley; Willa Holt Wakefield; Beulah Dallas; the Courtney Sisters; the boy-and-girl team of Knight and Dreyer; George Austin Moore; Mabel Bunyea; and Carl McCullough, who appeared with Tucker on that December 18 vaudeville bill in Chicago. (I wonder who won the right to sing "Some of These Days" that week.) In 1911 recordings were made by Tucker, by Billy Murray with the American Quartet, and by Elise Stevenson. If Brooks can be called the "author" of the number, transforming Williams's earlier effort, then perhaps Rossiter can be called the "author" of its success: the publisher as genius—or at least as Iris, the messenger goddess.

Despite the multitude of performers, ads in the winter of 1911 still identified the song with the star who introduced it, proclaiming that it was "Sophie Tucker Popularizing Will Rossiter's Hit."[35] That February, Tucker preserved for posterity her first interpretation of the song, on an Edison cylinder that is considered a milestone in the path of American music. Hindsight reveals it was a signpost saying, "This is the way we are heading."

It is hard to calculate how often Tucker performed "Some of These Days" during the 1910s. Armond Fields, in his biography of the singer, claims that soon so many others were performing the number that "Sophie's identity with it had all but disappeared. As other new songs became popular, Sophie always sought them out to keep her act fresh."[36] Therefore, as with all the other ephemeral songs of the time, "Some of These Days" "was soon dropped from her repertoire."[37] Nevertheless, jump to November 1920: Tucker plays the Palace Theater in Chicago with her Five Kings of Syncopation (and Mollie Elkins, still featured as a dancer in the act), and alongside the latest hits she is again including "Some of These Days."[38] In December 1920, at least one Chicago-area fan was nostalgically sentimental about Tucker's 1911 performances of the song: a human interest news column in the *Chicago Tribune* headed "In the Wake of the News—Do You Remember 'Way Back When'" continues: "We medical students went to the Kedzie Theater to hear Sophie Tucker sing 'All Alone' and 'Some of These Days'?—P. M. M. of Meekin, Ill."[39] Here, after only nine years, the doctor is already nostalgic for his prewar youth, symbolized by Tucker and her association with "Some of These Days."

Meanwhile, Brooks was becoming more prominent in the Chicago mainstream news. He played at white society functions and was "singing his own song hits" as part of a bill at Ascher's Chateau. It would be surprising if he had not kept "Some of These Days," one of his greatest successes, in his repertoire.[40]

By the summer of 1922, Rossiter was announcing in *Variety* that "the cabaret and dance hall jazzers in the Windy City, of their own accord, have revived" Brooks's song, "playing it from memory," and therefore the publisher planned to "reissue" the piece "in the fall."[41] Rossiter wrote yet another set of lyrics for the verse, redesigned the cover with a large photo of Tucker, boosting her connection to the song, and sent the sheet music to the Library of Congress in order to copyright this new edition, "revised and re-arranged by W. R. Williams and F. Henri Klickman," as the first page declares.[42] W. R. Williams was Rossiter's own pseudonym for himself as a songwriter; Klickman (the arranger of the 1918 "jazz fox-trot" version of "I'm Sorry I Made You Cry") occasionally worked for him.[43] Together they created a fresh setting for "Some of These Days" that brought the piece into the Jazz Age: added syncopations indicate the pointed rhythmic style of the 1920s, and a final instrumental coda echoes the novelty piano style that was flourishing in Chicago at the time (see musical example 7.3).

The manner in which the cover heralds the new edition signals that this reissuing was a special—probably unusual—occurrence: "Will Rossiter's Sensational 'Come-Back' in response to the Public's demand, reissues this old-Time-Favorite." (It is remarkable that a song only twelve years old is already considered "old-time.") "Re-introduced to the American Public by the Great and Only Sophie Tucker. On all the Records. Get your favorite to-day."

Tucker was probably dealt in on this campaign. In 1922 the singer was reformulating her act and, according to Fields, seems to have "reinstated the song

Example 7.3. "Some of These Days," excerpts, 1922 Rossiter edition.

Sample of added syncopations in the refrain:

New piano part for the refrain ending:

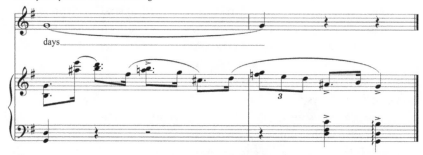

. . . at that time, forming an insoluble bond that lasted for more than forty-five years."[44] By October 2, 1922, the star was in New York, putting over her old hit at the Palace and then "resinging the chorus . . . as any Jewish cantor might sing it."[45] As Tucker flourished throughout the decade, Rossiter reissued his jazzy new arrangement with covers that herald her (and the song's) conquest of the decade's triumphant new media sensations: radio and talking pictures. Meanwhile, in 1923 Brooks was in England with the revue *Dover Street to Dixie*, including "Some of These Days" at a command performance for King George and Queen Mary.[46]

Tucker recorded "Some of These Days" three times in the late twenties. In a November 1926 session, the rambling, squealing sounds of the clarinet of Ted Lewis provide her with a loose-limbed atmosphere. Joel Whitburn calculates that, starting in February 1927, this recording proved very popular.[47] Perhaps because of that, 1927 witnessed a steady stream of recordings, mostly in New York studios. (This resurrection into hit status overlapped with that, discussed elsewhere in this book, of "Let Me Call You Sweetheart," "The Sweetheart of Sigma Chi," and "My Melancholy Baby.") Both Al Jolson and Vernon Dalhart recorded it, but neither waxing was ever released and they now are presumed lost. The "Radio Girl," Vaughn De Leath, rendered it in February. White singer Betty Morgan recorded it in March, backed by a 1922 song that was one of the many "Some of These Days" imitators, "Someday, Sweetheart." In October, Ethel Waters echoed Morgan's pairing by setting down the same two songs. With her deep musical and dramatic intuition, Waters was adjusting her style to the electronic microphone (as well as to a vocal node that she had the surgeons

Figures 7.2, 7.3, and 7.4. *Broadway Melody of 1938.* In one refrain of "Some of These Days," Sophie Tucker demonstrates her theme song's wide emotional range: suffering, smug, self-presentational.

remove in 1930), and her performance is husky and intimate. The Original Indiana Five recorded it twice. And, down in Birmingham, Alabama, regional ragtime pianist George H. Tremer used "Some of These Days" to back up his own "Spirit of '49 Rag."

Before 1927 was out, Tucker again went into the studio and set down yet another rendition: in contrast to her version with Ted Lewis, the arrangement is quite tight. Even more significantly, the song is presented after Tucker's lengthy biographical monologue, delivered in her characteristic sing-speaking mode. Here, the monologue and song are a clear attempt by the singer to make her career into nostalgic myth and entwine her image with "Some of These Days." Tucker delivered her theme song in her movies, too. Her 1929 starring vehicle, *Honky Tonk*, is a lost film, but the soundtrack survives, and we hear her sing

"Some of These Days." The MGM musical *Broadway Melody of 1938* features probably the most often heard Tucker rendition. Her role is as a has-been vaudeville performer who is promoting the career of her young daughter (Judy Garland), and she succeeds in getting both of them recruited for the cast of the finale's hit Broadway premiere. Her impromptu audition: one rousing refrain of "Some of These Days," straight at the camera (see figures 7.2–7.4). It becomes, in part, a message from Tucker to the entertainment industry, as if to say, "If I leave, you're gonna miss me! Show business cannot do without me!"

After 1927 the floodgates stayed open as pioneer artists of many sorts exploit the song. 1929: Louis Armstrong tackles it in the recording studio, resulting in two discs, one with and one without his vocal. 1930: Cab Calloway and his orchestra rip through it at a breakneck tempo, Calloway making phrases into a wail followed by a spurt of words. 1932: Bing Crosby also takes it very fast. For the main vocal, he sidles sideways toward the emotion of the lyric in his typical manner and then follows it with a stream of very impressive scat passages. 1935: Milton Brown, pioneer of Western Swing, sings it. (Brown seems to have opened up this song for many artists who straddled the country tradition and the world of pop music—such as Brenda Lee, who did two versions, a youthful 1959 relaxed rendition and a masterful mature version in 1991, with honky-tonk style accompaniment.)

In 1937 the copyright renewal came up for the song, and Brooks (as the writer) was able to reclaim it. He assigned the publication rights to Jerry Vogel. That music house reverted to Rossiter's 1910 verse and rearranged the music to suit the swing style of the late 1930s—a style that became so standard that this edition stayed in print for decades, using the same plates. In 1937 Vogel put out a deluxe edition—shiny silver cover—featuring large portraits of the most prominent performers associated with the tune: Tucker, Crosby, and Shelton Brooks himself, still going pretty strong after decades of show business fame, including stints on Broadway in the twenties and various radio appearances in the thirties (see figure 7.5).

Brooks, despite his busy career, was only rarely recorded or filmed. Low-budget Black-cast movies made for the limited African American cinema circuits, like *Double Deal* (1939), reveal him as tall, handsome, with a million-dollar smile, a slightly husky voice used with an intimate style, and body language full of subtle syncopation. Luckily, Brooks was captured for posterity playing and singing "Some of These Days" at a promotional concert for ASCAP, in San Francisco, September 24, 1940. Brooks's voice is a bit worn, but full of zest. "Swing it!" he shouts to the orchestra, and, amidst an echo-filled ambience, they do.

Maxine Sullivan rendered "Some of These Days" in a 1942 "soundie" (which functioned like a juke box record, but with a motion picture image to go with it). This is how I first encountered the song, in a little hole-in-the-wall revival

Figure 7.5. Shelton Brooks, about 1950. The Native American/African/Canadian singer-songwriter has the 1937 edition of "Some of These Days" on the music rack, with a glamorous headshot of himself on the cover. Photo courtesy of Susan and Lloyd Ecker, the Sophie Tucker Project.

cinema in Cambridge, Massachusetts, in the 1980s, part of a program of musical shorts. Sullivan is poised and delicately sprung. Her smile is broad yet cool. She swings the song in a subtle manner (such that I could guess, before I knew for sure decades later, that Peggy Lee was influenced by her). Surprisingly, she sings the lyrics to the verse from the 1922 edition. (Somebody at the Soundies company was not up-to-date in their sheet music collection!) Despite the old-fashioned verse, the performance is pure swing era. Meanwhile, the scenario of abandonment that the verse's lyric describes is enacted out by little doll figures of an African American couple, in a squeaky-clean American dream cottage, white picket fence and all. This trite and somewhat tacky imagery contrasts with the tasteful restraint that was Sullivan's trademark.

ANALYSIS

The refrain of "Some of These Days" is built up of short, terse phrases of four or five syllables (of course, matching four or five musical notes) (see musical example 7.2). It is, in Stephen Banfield's term, a "motif song": the initial title phrase sets the pattern for everything that comes after.[48] The little chromatic movement of the opening gesture is hypnotic, attention-grabbing: three pick-up notes move a half-step down and then back up again and finally resolve down a whole step: B-A♯-B-A. This little moan lends itself to the jubilation-lamentation mixture of Sophie Tucker's first rendition as well as to the bluesy traditions that Brooks would tap into later in the 1910s for some of his other songs.

The opening motif is soon repeated—but after that we never hear it again, at least not exactly. What Brooks does, instead, is to sneak it in at different pitch levels. He takes that little chromatic down-and-up movement and uses it in the pick-up phase into the second section and then twice in the fourth section, the last time again resolving down a half-step just as it did at the start of the chorus.

Every phrase ends with a half note or whole note, each tied to a quarter note at the start of the next bar. The song is remarkably consistent: these gaps occur every two measures, giving the refrain a marvelous roominess. (Contrast this with the every-fourth-measure gaps in "Bill Bailey" and "I Wonder Who's Kissing Her Now." The driving, long-held notes in "Some of These Days" are also very different in effect from the every-other-bar gaps in rival refrains of the time, such as "Sweet Adeline," which invites rubato choral response, or "By the Light of the Silvery Moon," which evokes the tripping fill-ins of a soft-shoe dance.) These holes allow the performers to be creative. Singers can stick in exclamations, choral interjections may occur between the soloist's phrases, and accompanists can decorate with filigree or respond with echo phrases. In her later renditions, Tucker likes to have the band play the first statement of the melody, and then she echoes *them*.

The refrain of the song is structured ABCD. This non-repeating internal form is not as rare as previous writers try to make us believe.[49] During this era, customers could buy other big hits, such as "Sunbonnet Sue" (1906), also utilizing ABCD structures.[50] But Brooks uses it more effectively than most, because here it contributes to the portrait of an emotionally scattered protagonist. Through his thirty-two bar refrain, Brooks creates a melody that flows on, never precisely repeating after the first eight measures, yet never straying far from the kernel of the song. The lyric, too, rushes forward like a flooded stream. Together, the music and lyrics create a miniature dramatic monologue. By contrast, Williams's "Some o' Dese Days" is like many sixteen-measure songs of the era—it seems over before it has begun. The difference between the two works is caused by both the greater length and the broader scope of the refrain—and is the same contrast that we saw between Wilson and Queen's "Ain't Dat a Shame" and Hughie Cannon's "Bill Bailey, Won't You Please Come Home?"

In "Some o' Dese Days," Williams uses very thick blackface dialect—writing, of course, in 1905, when blackface conventions were highly popular. By contrast, "Some of These Days" does not use any dialect. It is conversational and colloquial, but still in standard English. This difference between the songs by Williams and Brooks captures in a nutshell the change that was taking place. The style of music and lyrics derived or inspired by African American culture was becoming less associated with the blackface conventions of the nineteenth century—not yet completely, of course, but to a certain limited extent. Brooks or his publishers now felt free to put out a song that was like a "coon song" of the past (indeed, it is specifically like Williams's coon song, "Some o' Dese Days") and yet not use either dialect or cover images that refer to Blacks in any way.[51] The new Black-influenced sound was being integrated into the lives of white people and being accepted as part of their world, of their aesthetics, of their emotional range.

The protagonist of "Some of These Days" imagines the future, predicting the worst. The first two stanzas focus on how the departing lover will miss the protagonist. Then, suddenly, in the third and fourth stanzas, the singer starts to veer wildly between ideas—four mood swings in eight lines of lyrics. In effect, the protagonist says: I miss you; You had your way; You're going to make me grieve; You'll miss me. Indeed, this second half of the song makes little logical sense: accusatory warning swiftly alternates with pathetic pleading. The tenses swing wildly: the present tense suddenly interjects itself ("I feel so lonely") only to be swept away again in the past ("You had your way") and the future ("It will grieve me").

The flow of thought is full of gaps, particularly in the third stanza. Why should "I feel so lonely" be followed by "For . . . you've had your way"? One possible explanation might lie in a sexual interpretation of "having your way": "I feel so lonely and sexually frustrated now, because I was accustomed to giving you your way by having sex with you often, and that gave me an active sex life." Perhaps it is persuasion: as a song written twenty years later puts it, "gee, baby, ain't I good to you"—therefore, stay with me. With either of these scenarios, the singer is nearly incoherent.

Meanwhile, just when we expect the melody to repeat at the song's midpoint, it keeps unfolding in new permutations of the terse opening pattern. The harmony, too, is restless: "it never ceases to move harmonically," as Wilder points out.[52] The composition causes Nicholas E. Tawa to exult: "the avoidance of the home key . . . is extraordinary. . . . Amazingly, the music does not get back to the home key until the last two measures!"[53] This disoriented step-by-step search for "home" adds to the song's emotional impact.

The cover that Rossiter settled on for its main 1910 edition has some remarkable aspects about it (see figure 7.1). Unlike the Foster edition, there is no attempt to illustrate the scenario described in the verses. Instead, there is the enigmatic profile of a woman in a frame-in-the-frame. She is placed just to the right of a window opening, and she turns her head toward the light that glows in dully across the sill. There are hints she is a rural woman: high-piled hair above a low brow, a rather old-fashioned collar, and drab-colored dress. Outside the frame that confines her image, there lies a trio of daisies amidst a vaguely defined green and brown, perhaps windblown thicket. Her face is almost expressionless, yet that turn of her head—toward what? emptiness?—seems to define the dreary vacancy of her life. Yet her head is slightly lifted, her long Grecian nose has a patrician air. A very ambiguous image: Proud? Lonely? Bleak?

The upper edge of this standard 1910 Rossiter cover presents a verbal phrase—in quotation marks—that immediately became part-and-parcel of the song, featured in the first recordings, yet rarely included in the sheet music editions: "You'll miss your little dad-dad-dad-dad-dad Some of these days." This paratextual banner is unusual—such quotations of a lyric on the cover are customarily from the text printed inside. The 1922 Rossiter edition makes this trope an "official" part of the song, ending the lyric: "I'll miss my little dad-dad-daddy." But when Vogel issued its 1937 version, in print for decades, the line was back to the simpler version: "You'll miss your little baby." In more recent times, since the song has been in public domain, the Hal Leonard company, in various editions of its fake books, first picks up and then drops again the stammering, hammering "dad-dad-daddy" line. These variations epitomize the fluid nature of the Tin Pan Alley genre. The text changes from edition to edition, so how can we identify one official version?

When Rossiter (*qua* W. R. Williams) and Klickman revised the song to publish a new edition in 1922, they kept the melody of the company's 1910 verses but changed the lyric. They drain the framing story of much of its emotional power. In particular, they make the woman who sings the song much less complex: less hurt at the start and less rebellious at the end. When the Jerry Vogel company issued their 1937 version, which stayed the same for decades, they reverted to the 1910 Rossiter verse. Tucker, in the several times she recorded the verse, stays faithful to the 1910 Rossiter edition—except for one variant line, when she stays closer to Foster's "you know I love you, honey, best of all." Could she possibly have learned the Foster verse first and somehow retained that detail? When Shelton Brooks himself is captured in concert singing the song, he does not even include the verse.

This convoluted history makes me wonder if Brooks created any of the verses we know. Perhaps the publishers wrote them. Putting all the pieces together, that seems to be the simplest solution to the puzzle.

To be accounted for are not only the changes made to the verses, but also the gender aspects: all the verses set up the song as being sung by a woman to a man who is leaving her. But the second edition of the song (the 1910 Rossiter) plus the earliest recordings all have that woman singing to her man, at the end of the refrain, "You'll miss your little daddy." Why is a woman saying to her man that *she* is the "daddy"? It would make much more sense if Brooks himself, as a man, was singing the song not as a story about a third party but as a personal statement—indeed, more as a torch song. It would make sense then for that male singer to call himself "your little daddy." Indeed, in 1940, by omitting the verse, and despite all his playfulness, Brooks delivers the lyric in an entirely personal manner—with no sense of that third-person "she moans" from "Bill Bailey."

The standard version—the 1910 Rossiter edition, which was copied by the 1937 Vogel edition—introduces a stiff, old-fashioned locution that the first Foster edition avoided—and that the vast majority of singers also avoid. The original Foster reads, conversationally, "I know it will grieve me." Rossiter, perhaps in an attempt to stick with the refrain's prevailing five-note pattern, makes the line "I know 'twill grieve me," taking us back to Shakespeare's time with the awkward "'twill." In 1911 both Tucker and the American Quartet (with soloist Billy Murray) sing "'twill," but by the 1920s this has been mostly abandoned. True, Fats Waller uses it, when he sings a fragment of the lyric on an otherwise instrumental track—but here, as was his custom, he sings in the spirit of merry parody. A few singers use it in the 1950s—Maurice Chevalier, Rosemary Clooney—in more print-influenced renditions. By and large, however, singers favor the more colloquial options: the original "it will grieve" or the even more causal substitute "it's gonna grieve."

INTERPRETING THE RECORDINGS

Sophie Tucker's 1911 recording is a remarkable audio event—one of those occasions when a great singer does a great job with a great song while it is still new. By February 1911, the entertainer had been doing the number for seven months in live performance and had time to hone her rendition. David Wondrich describes the cylinder's magical quality: "it's one of the most wrenching, emotional, and, yes, bluesy of blackface records, a low-pitched, tortured moan that gets under your skin and won't leave."[54] There are several passages in particular when Tucker creates that moaning effect, shocking the ear even after repeated hearings. Her emotional hues can be quite complex: amidst the friendly smile in her voice, Tucker often mixes a trace of tearfulness—a trait that a Jewish friend once identified to me as a part of the Hebrew heritage.[55] At the end of the verse, she slows down and mixes that sadness with a petulant quality—another vocal shading that she often uses; here, it darkens that moment of transition from verse to refrain. Even so, she is smiling—she is relishing the feel of this song under her tongue, as if she were eating a juicy steak.

In the sheet music, the start of the refrain itself has fermata marks on the pick-up notes, that little chromatic vacillation that is so compelling—and Tucker and her accompanists milk this effect beautifully. After that build-up of tension, the first downbeat, on "days," disperses into the air weakly: a moan followed by a bleating sigh. At the end of the first refrain, she elaborates on "dad-dad-daddy," improvising a rhythmic dance: "dah-ha, dah-ha, dah-ha-da-ad." Is she convulsively laughing . . . or crying?

The cylinder format allows Tucker more time than she would have had on the usual flat discs of the era, and therefore she is able to sing both verses of the song. That second verse is about the "little girlie" who decides "two can play that game." She rides away on a train: now singing with cutting irony "that loving sweet refrain" to the lover who abandoned her and who suddenly realizes, too late, that she is not going to be there to fall back on. When Tucker delivers it—and especially when she does that same semi-moaning slowdown at verse's end—she instills the saga with a triumph injected with bitter irony.

This is the New Woman in action: independent, confident, assertive, socially and geographically mobile. Tucker's persona, too, was a New Woman: aggressive, out in the world, career-oriented. She separated from her husband back in Connecticut, then cut loose from her parents, leaving her baby with her sister, to make it in show business, and struggled from the bottom to the top. An expert in comedy material, she was three-quarters tough and one-quarter vulnerable, able to make you laugh and weep. "Some of These Days" was a perfect song for her. As Robert Dawidoff poetically puts it, the song "folds the woman of passion and instinct who can take care of herself into a milk-maidenly country lass" (i.e., the heroine described in the first verse).[56] This is among the many contradictions in the song and in Tucker's persona: the serio-comic, rural-urban, vulnerable-strong woman.

Tucker's first refrain is good, but her second is sensational. Her voice emerges from that second verse confident, even indomitable. On the downbeat, "days," she leaps up a ninth and then descends through a bluesy flatted fifth—and does so open-throated, full volume. She suspends, fermata, stretching out *"far* away." She moans, "Mmm, you know, honey, I let you have your way." When she comes to the "daddy" phrase, she dances out a pattern different from her first refrain but equally fresh, leaving a syncopated gap, filled in by percussion: "your little dah" knock, knock, "ah-dah-ha-daddy." Her voice and the woodblocks are like squirrels playfully chasing each other.

In "Some of These Days," the protagonist might be a vulnerable underdog or a self-confident victor. Each singer has to create her own emotional recipe. It is laudable how well the song supplies the ingredients for a multitude of different emotional effects. This is reflected in the lyrics the stylists sing—which they change as they choose—and also is manifested through more intangible aspects of the performance: tone quality, phrasing, inflection, tempo, rhythm.

What is the protagonist's goal? The verses describe the situation clearly, but if you omit those verses—which most performers do—you are left with this question. In one scenario, the goal is to persuade the lover not to leave. In another interpretation, the relationship is over, and the only thing left to salvage is one's self-worth—"Ooo, what you're gonna be missing"—a hope that, by asserting one's value, one will actually come to believe in it. The singer is the underdog, no matter how she may protest otherwise, and we, the listeners, somehow feel her pathos and sympathize.[57]

Yet the persona of the song's protagonist is malleable, and this is reflected in how performers render the C and D sections. One-half of singers choose to retain the four switches in emotion in the second half of the chorus, dictated by the sheet music.[58] Tucker leads the way in this category, staying remarkably consistent through fifty-five years.

One-third of the singers change "I feel lonely" to "You'll feel lonely"—in which case, to follow with "You had your way" easily makes sense: it means, "You're gonna regret losing a good thing." But those singers keep the penultimate revelation—to paraphrase: "I will grieve when you go." It is inserted there almost like an unconscious slip of the tongue, because they then immediately reassert that the lover is the one who will be sorry. The song's creator, Brooks himself, makes this choice.

The remaining one-sixth eliminate all vulnerability and regret and make the song one long assertion of triumph: "You'll be sorry." Period. Full stop. Some African American icons of early jazz take this approach—Cab Calloway, Louis Armstrong, Alberta Hunter—as does early-sixties white nightclub singer Kay Stevens. Notice how the proportion closely correlates to the one-in-seven singers of "Bill Bailey" who shift the blame from Mrs. Bailey to Bill himself. The introduction of this vindictive strain is a sign, perhaps, of how society changed after 1910—or, perhaps, merely a sign of the range of human personalities: about 15 percent of singers seemingly choose to project a tough persona.

Bobby Darin typified this trend toward toughness and further popularized it. On the 1959 *That's All* album that changed his career, he swings "Some of These Days," starting off with that slightly petulant, slightly muffled tone that people take on when they are concealing the pain (or wounded vanity) that stirs within them. But soon—by the time he has gone through half of the first refrain—he has convinced himself that he is top dog, and his message is a joyful bark of triumph. For the final section of the song, he slows the tempo down (the high-kick effect for a socko finish). By this point Darin is in full swagger, confident and brash. Although he sings, "And if you leave me / You know it's gonna grieve me," through inflection he completely negates this ostensible message.

By the time Darin is captured live a few years later, at the Copacabana night-club, he relishes this moment even more, growling with gusto. While supposedly saying how sad he will be, he sounds more like he is grinding his ex-lover's face in the dust. Many singers follow Darin's lead, both in dragging the tempo for a big finish and in vindictive tone. Kevin Spacey, in playing Darin for the 2004 movie biography *Beyond the Sea*, tries and succeeds in following Darin's version step by step—understandably. But so does character actor Danny Ai-ello—with far less excuse, except that Darin's musical and dramatic conception is sensationally effective—indeed, almost addictive.

As already discussed in chapter 2, the gleeful vengefulness with which Darin, Armstrong, Calloway, Stevens, and their colleagues infused "Some of These Days" became one enduring option for the Tin Pan Alley lyric about lost ro-mance, as it evolved through the Jazz Age and later competed with rock and roll, from "After You've Gone" to "I Wanna Be Around." Will Friedwald writes of this as a major part of Frank Sinatra's mature persona: in songs like "You'll Get Yours," "he's too busy wishing the hurt on her to feel it himself."[59] As Fried-wald implies, such "swingingly cavalier kiss-off songs" became a category unto themselves; and, through the interpretations of certain singers, "Some of These Days" became the foundation for this subgenre.

Performers created other traditions around "Some of These Days." Tucker introduced to recordings the dramatic jump up to the ninth. Tucker herself used it through the 1920s, but then she probably lost those top notes: after de-cades of performing multiple live shows daily without amplification, she finds other options as she gets older. Meanwhile many other singers had adopted the device. Indeed, Brooks uses an understated version of this melodic variation in 1940 (not nearly as dramatic as Tucker's use of it)—very likely this trope originated with him. In my sample of singers, more than 40 percent use that dramatic jump, usually followed by the descent, either sliding down through an elongated "da . . . . . ays" (like Tucker) or breaking it up into short discrete utter-ances: "days, days, days" (like Brooks). It can show up anywhere in the course of the rendition, usually but not always with the title phrase. Tucker saves it for the start of the second refrain. In this tactic, she is followed by many: more than eight out of ten of those who use it. That strategy is hard to beat, because it helps the singer build toward a climax of emotion.

Performance traditions for "Some of These Days" flourished. The "dad-dad-daddy" ending persists, from the 1911 recordings of both Tucker and the American Quartet (the four singers render the phrase as a team, proving that it was a pre-planned choice), through its legitimization in the 1922 printing, and onward, at least through the mid-thirties. As soon as the repetition of the

Example 7.4. "Some of These Days," a common variant by singers of the refrain's first phrase.

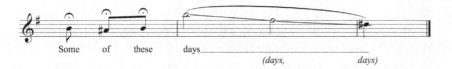

syllables of "daddy" appears, the nonsense syllables lean the phrase toward scat singing. In 1932 both the Mills Brothers and Crosby follow that implication through to its natural end. The latter transforms the conclusion into something like "You'll miss your little dah-dee-dah doo-dah-dee-doodle dwo dwee wee wee wee wee wee-ee."

With her 1926 recording, Tucker introduces her own distinctive variant for the refrain's penultimate line: "Gonna miss your big, fat mama—your mama." She would use diverse versions of that for the rest of her career. In this—a small detail but an important one because it comes at the final summation of the song—Tucker continues and even expands upon the assertiveness of the original lyric, furthered by the boldness of her self-description. From then on, one of the exciting aspects of hearing "Some of These Days" comes from eager anticipation: How are singers going to describe themselves? Female singers sometimes employ Tucker's signature phrases: "big, fat mama" and "red-hot mama." Male singers almost always use "little daddy" or variants on it. By 1940 Shelton Brooks is singing "bald-headed daddy" in the penultimate line. (He still had hair on the sides and a fringe at the front, but his top was shiny-bare (see figure 7.5). Ethel Waters (1927) and Louis Armstrong (1929) both describe themselves as "brownskin mama" or "papa," respectively. Seventy years later, Alberta Hunter elaborates that adjective into "little, long-tall, seal-skin brown-skin." Other colorful variants include Bobby Darin's "thin, little," "boney, little" and "brown-eyed" daddy; Chris Crosby's "ever-lovin', swingin', sweet daddy"; and Keely Smith's "jellybean mama." Through this device, singers custom-tailor the song to their own physiques and personas.

Brooks frequently deviates from his own printed lyric, using one of the most common methods for loosening up the phrasing of this song: using "gonna," as in "you're gonna miss me" or "it's gonna grieve me." And perhaps the introduction of that thoroughly colloquial substitute for "will" originates with Brooks. Both Brooks and Tucker alternate freely between, on the one hand, "You'll," "I'll," and "it will," and, on the other hand, "you're gonna," "I'm gonna," and "it's gonna"—and most later singers follow their lead. Indeed, both of these fountainheads for the performance tradition of "Some of These Days" are loose in their phrasing and flexible in their variations. They probably supplied the model to other singers, signaling: "Take liberties."

Brooks makes one other startling change to the lyric—although you have to listen carefully to catch it. Instead of "some of these days," he sings "some o' dese days"—i.e., he uses the title of Frank Williams's forgotten song. Once again, we are given a teasing hint—but not strong enough for conviction—that Brooks knew of the 1905 song that preceded his own.

In one more telling detail, Brooks indicates the nature of his classic when, at the end of his first refrain, he spurs on the orchestra: "Here, let's swing it!" In jazz discographies, there are numerous renditions listed of "Some of These Days."[60] One reason: the song is easy to swing. The 1922 Rossiter rearrangement implies, to any pianist who is "in the know," that the song should be swung—in an era when the feeling of swing was first being promulgated by jazz recordings—by creating dotted rhythms where formerly there were none. Muir suggests that "dotted rhythms were a convenient way of approximating swing feel in music notation" and that, starting around 1911, this convention "became increasingly prevalent in printed music."[61] Thus, Rossiter, in their 1922 edition, was simply joining the dotted-rhythm bandwagon.[62] By 1937, however, the Jerry Vogel arrangement drops the dotted notation altogether. From this I infer two things. First, they did not want to trespass on Rossiter's copyrighted 1922 special arrangement. Second, and more importantly, by 1937 the rhythmic approach of swing was so prevalent that no such signal was needed: it is assumed that an adept pianist would simply know how and when to swing, with minimal cues required from the printed score (see musical example 7.3).

What about "Some of These Days" as a torch song? Early in his career Shelton Brooks specialized in imitating Bert Williams—yet with this song, Brooks takes a leap away from the persona of that comedian. "Some o' Dese Days" by Frank Williams would fit the persona of his associate Bert Williams very well—by contrast, Brooks's song would not. In rewriting Frank Williams's motif, and in expanding the refrain, Brooks transforms its protagonist into a serious lover—a desperate person. This is not the quiet, sardonic ruefulness of Bert Williams's signature tune "Nobody." The protagonist of "Some of These Days" may still be an underdog, but he is now an underdog filled with, torn by, passions. He is now carrying a torch, and the flame burns hot.

The idea of a torch song came into the mainstream in 1927 and that of a torch singer in 1929. Therefore it is not surprising that Tucker's versions around this time are perhaps her most torchy—a bit slower and, especially in her 1929 rendition for the movie *Honky Tonk*, more plaintive from start to finish. This torchy effect is aided by omitting the verse, because the refrain of the song is very personal, while the verses are not. On her fifties album *Cabaret Days*, Tucker sings that "the verse of this song I rarely do."

Indeed, the verse is a third-person story, like that for "Bill Bailey." Yet the few performances that use the verse are among my favorites: Tucker in 1911;

Waters in 1927; Sullivan in the 1942 soundie film; and Dorothy Loudon in 1991, who takes the tempo very slow—much slower than others do—and also applies more tenderness to the ditty. Although it is in the third-person and therefore distancing the singer from the song ("She said" rather than "I said"), the verse does help the vocalist remember that this is a sincere plaint. Using the verse can place the performer more strongly in the imaginary relationship—emotionally and physically creating a different focus, and in this case a more intimate focus—than if the refrain is started off "cold."

Why was "Some of These Days" important to the development of the Golden Age ballad? Partly because the emotional meaning of "Some of These Days" is up for grabs. Almost every singer or listener will pick and choose from an assortment of wide-ranging emotions that the song potentially contains. The song might be a tough statement from a person who is actually vulnerable; or it might be a vulnerable statement from someone who is actually tough. The two original verses set it up both ways: in the first verse, the woman is pleading for him to stay; in the second verse, she is triumphantly leaving him behind. And, as we have seen, some later singers make a few simple changes and the song becomes a tough statement from somebody who is actually tough. From almost any angle, "Some of These Days" is a whirlpool of mixed-up emotions. Frantic self-boosting, pleading, grieving, bribing, threatening—it might include any or all of these.

Oddly, few singers manifest another potential I hear in the song. In this scenario, the singer is more concerned with her departing lover than herself. She truly desires his well-being. She knows she has pampered him, letting him have his way, and that he will not receive such kindly treatment from anybody else. He *will* miss her and feel lonely. She only invokes her own potential loneliness in order to convince him to stay, for his own good. When I try to see the world through the eyes of this protagonist, that is how the song comes out.

My friends and students let me collect their impressions of this song, particularly of Tucker's 1911 recording. These listeners range widely in their interpretations of the piece, while cultural critics are often more rigid. This disparity teaches writers (including myself) not to be too confident that ours is the only viewpoint. Emotional complexity is a valuable part of the legacy of "Some of These Days"—and part of the reason the song survives today.

The listeners I polled confessed to a wide range of responses. They pictured varying settings for the dramatic action: "a merry-go-round," "a saloon," "a love nest," "late at night, an empty city street." (Shades of film noir!) The song is rife with emotion: "soulful . . . heart-wrenching . . . dark," "regret, with anger and confidence." Listeners pick up on the complexity of the song's drama. "She is grieving over her loss and loneliness for her only love." "But she knows she'll recover and be okay. It's a song about a woman's confidence and high self-esteem."

The protagonist is "the dominating figure in the relationship," "manly," "the provider" (a possible explanation why, when Tucker first recorded it, she calls herself "daddy"). Along the same lines, Dawidoff declares: "Its protagonist knows her worth and makes it clear that she means to have her way, having let him have his. . . . she's not about to wait for his return."[63] June Sochen opines that this song, like others in Tucker's repertoire, "declare[s] the independence of woman over erratic lovers, difficult circumstances, and changing times."[64]

Yet some of my interviewees disagreed: "bitter . . . the protagonist is bitter," "someone who feels used. . . . heartbroken" or "taken for granted." Listeners can read into the piece a very complicated subtext: "Even when she *sounds* confident, it is only to boost her *flagging* confidence. The whole thing has a sense of comic irony." "It has a sense of humor, even though its lyrics are . . . sad. . . . complicated . . . passionate . . . competitive . . . disturbing." Some listeners register that the protagonist is transformed through the course of the song: "The dynamics have changed towards the end." And, from a woman: "That volatility is very *female*—we *are* changeable, moody, fluid, shifting."

Admittedly, the song can be extroverted, "shouting," as some listeners hear it and some singers convey it. Yet the song is also introspective: it takes us into the mind of a protagonist, a soul torn by mixed goals and confused emotions. Combine these dynamics with the conversational lyric and the swingable music, and you have, for 1910, a little miracle that presages the many miracle-songs soon to fill the Great American Songbook. An expression of internal conflicts—that is this song's legacy to the maturation, to the gradual deepening, of the Tin Pan Alley genre.

IN FILM AND LITERATURE

"Some of These Days" turns up in many movies and short films of the late 1920s, 1930s, and 1940s, usually snuck in as a sideline to the main focus of action. You can find many instances listed on the Internet Movie Database. I find it always a shock to stumble across these, such as the one (not listed on the IMDB site) in *Here Comes Cookie*, when in the grand final performance a physical comedy act does their routine to an instrumental rendition of "Some of These Days." The tune, like all of the ones in this book, became the aural wallpaper of that era.

In the 1936 movie musical *Rose-Marie*, "Some of These Days" is defined by the dialogue as an "old" song, but a "hot" one, full of "pep." The eponymous heroine, played by Jeanette MacDonald, is a temperamental opera singer. In the sophisticated urban environment where her career flourishes, she is the center of the universe, and when she sings, all listen in ecstasy. But she learns that her brother has escaped from jail and needs money, so she furtively speeds to the wilderness of Canada. Immediately, her guide steals her bags and cash. Unable to ask the police for help, she goes into a rough tavern and asks to sing for tips. Rose-Marie first tries to sing "Dinah," repeatedly falling out of tempo. (MacDonald executes a very skillful imitation of singing badly.) The crowd ignores her. She then picks up an edition of "Some of These Days"—the 1922 Rossiter arrangement with the "Radio's Big Hit" cover.[65] "Give it some pep," the pianist advises. But she cannot. Instead, the saloon's regular singer Belle butts in and takes over. (Belle is played by the great Gilda Gray, who introduced the shimmy to Broadway.) For a while Rose-Marie tries to imitate Belle's belting style and gestures and stance—but to no avail. The heroine looks at Gray askance and runs her hand up and down her own body, particularly over her breasts, seeming to think "I am not as sexy as this gal!" Gray takes over the floor, grabbing everybody's attention with her fluid, sensual movements and syncopated body isolations. Rose-Marie exits in defeat.

Within the context of this film operetta, which so celebrates classical music and its vocal style, "Some of These Days" symbolizes the vernacular culture of the rough lower classes. It serves to humble the arrogant heroine, makes her the underdog, and starts her initiation into the down-to-earth world of regular people. Rose-Marie will eventually find a doorway through which she can enter the folk culture of the American landscape, not through saloon music but rather through the panoramic beauty of the Canadian mountains and through (pseudo) Native American music, represented by "Totem Tom Tom" and "Indian Love Call." Significantly, while MacDonald sings a strictly correct rendition of the 1922 version of "Some of These Days," Gray, by contrast, freely adapts it to suit her own persona—makes it vindictive throughout ("And when I leave you / You know it's gonna grieve you") and avoids the gender entanglements of the "dad-dad-daddy" line with the simple alternative "You'll miss your little baby, baby!"

In three other Hollywood movies, the parting embedded within the scenario of "Some of These Days" takes on an even deeper meaning: the last goodbye of death. The song crops up early in *Only Angels Have Wings* (1939). Again, the context is a saloon at the edge of the wilderness—in this case, at a small airport in South America where flyers risk their lives in the foggy and stormy mountains to deliver mail and goods to isolated parts. The heroine, Bonnie (Jean Arthur), disembarks from a steamboat in the movie's first scenes and is overjoyed to encounter fellow Americans—two flyers, who compete to buy her dinner. The winner immediately dies in a plane crash, in a reckless attempt to get back to enjoy that dinner with her, and at first she is distraught, exiting in tears, appalled at the seeming callousness of the other flyers (a surface indifference that hides their great inner grief and fear). But soon she remembers the lack of sentimentality needed for a tough life, goes back in, and proves she has the same gallantry. Cary Grant is at the piano, fumbling his way into a rendition of "Some of These Days," cued by the vocal promptings of John Carroll—a macabre, perhaps unwitting, epitaph by his comrades for the young flyer who has just left this earthly sphere. Arthur takes charge, shoving Grant over on the stool, giving the band instructions, and nodding to cue when soloists should cut loose in their breaks. There is no vocal to remind us this is a song of leave-taking, but everybody knows this refrain: "And when you leave me / You know it will grieve me." Throughout the movie, issues contained within "Some of These Days" remain present: the specter of the last goodbye hangs over this little oasis of Yankee life; and whether to stay or leave becomes the central question in the life of Bonnie. (Spoiler alert: She stays.)

Jump to 1979 and *All That Jazz*: Bob Fosse's mostly autobiographical story of a work-obsessed, sex-obsessed Broadway choreographer-director who, as the story unwinds, suffers a heart attack. After his operation, the protagonist, Joe Gideon (Roy Scheider), has a dreamlike fantasy, which takes the form of a musical production number. In it, he is doubled: the sick Joe lies in his hospital bed, a passive audience; meanwhile, a healthy Joe directs a series of musical numbers. The women in his life sing goodbye in a string of torch songs, culminating in his daughter Michelle singing "Some of These Days." As throughout Joe's fantasy sequences (he has another one later), the incongruities are harsh and poignant. Twelve-year-old Michelle, cigarette holder in hand, feather boa around her neck, falters in her high heels as she slowly makes her way downstage toward her father's supine figure, singing those wisps of phrases: "Some of these days / You'll miss me, Daddy." The orchestra vamps and punctuates as if the song was from the score for *Cabaret*. In the second stanza, Joe's wife (draped over a hanging moon) and girlfriend (bounding into the air in slow motion, blowing him a kiss) contribute to the vocal for the "hugging . . . kissing" phrases. Then, for the third stanza, Michelle becomes one of the few singers who changes "I feel so lonely" to "*I'll* feel so lonely": here, the use of the future tense is both logical and heartbreaking.

In a rare instance, despite the grotesque glamour of the trappings, the song becomes something close to a genuine plea not to leave. And, for a change, the word "grieve" finds its full meaning and weight. Michelle exits, together with the two older women, disappearing into the mist riding a white limousine, with a final cry: "Daddy, don't die, please!" We cut back to Joe in the real-life hospital. He writes a question on his nurse's notepad: "Am I alive?" Yes—for the moment. "Some of These Days" has temporarily resuscitated him.

In *Beyond the Sea*, Kevin Spacey's rhapsodic spin on the life of Bobby Darin (I hardly dare call it a biopic), "Some of These Days" serves as the final capstone. In the finale, in lieu of a death scene, the duo of the adult Bobby and the child Bobby sing and dance through "As Long As I'm Singing." This is the conclusion of the formal plotline, but not the end of the movie, because then we are taken into an epilogue. Spacey-as-Darin sings "Some of These Days" in a frame-within-the-frame, as titles inform us how Darin died and what happened to the people who loved him—those characters who have inhabited the storyline—the very people who, literally, would "miss" Darin "some of these days." And when he leaves them, he grieves them. This movie was a pet project of Spacey, who co-wrote it, co-produced it, directed it, sang, danced, and acted in the role. When Spacey swings "Some of These Days" as the movie's last message, it seems like Darin is singing to the culture itself: "You're gonna miss your boney little daddy, some of these days." In 2004, in the midst of the neo-swing revival and the resurgence of lounge music, this entire movie can be seen as Spacey's and society's attempt to fill the void felt when hearing Darin: we *do* miss him. Here is "Some of These Days" as eulogy, as elegy. Singers often rattle off "Some of These Days" in a superficial manner, but these cinematic contexts remind us that the song can have deeper resonances.

Perhaps the most profound use of "Some of These Days" is in Jean-Paul Sartre's first novel, written in the mid-1930s with the working title *Melancholia* (which itself sounds as if it could be a torch song), published in 1938 as *La Nausée*, first published in English in 1949 as *The Diary of Antoine Roquentin* and later under the more accurately translated title *Nausea*. The protagonist, Roquentin, is an historian who, once upon a time, led a free-and-easy life of international travel, but now is quite solitary, hunkering down in a city in France as he finishes research on a biography. (The word "roquentin," editors tell us, means "songs composed of other songs," and with such a name Sartre's hero might well be the patron saint of Tin Pan Alley.)[66] Roquentin narrates his thoughts as he undergoes what a later generation might call a midlife crisis. His days are made painful by a self-conscious awareness of his existence, which manifests as a sweetness that makes him feel nauseated.

Frequenting the local bar, Roquentin often listens to a recording of "Some of These Days," a song that he claims he first heard the soldiers sing during World War I. His description of the record is quite specific: it is fairly old, it is on the Pathé label, it requires a sapphire needle, it starts with an instrumental segment, a saxophone comes to the fore, and then a singer—who, the narrator assumes, is "a Negress."[67] He calls the song "an old rag-time," but the rendition itself he labels "jazz."[68] Recent critics, with the lofty superiority of hindsight, assume it is "pseudo-jazz."[69] The recording is probably a fiction—a composite of various records Sartre may have heard—but most commentators assume it is by Tucker. Her best-selling 1926 rendition with Ted Lewis and His Orchestra does start with an instrumental refrain and verse before she enters for two vocal refrains, and Lewis's prominent clarinet might be mistaken for a saxophone by the less musically experienced. But the version actually released on Pathé was by the now-obscure Betty Morgan—like Tucker, a white woman who made a career (with her husband Jim) in vaudeville during the teens and twenties. I like to imagine, however, that the version Roquentin heard was that of Ethel Waters. Although Waters has no saxophone behind her (she is accompanied only by piano and violin), her husky-voiced intimacy and her second-refrain variations offer all the soulfulness and jazziness needed for "Some of These Days" to fulfill its role in Roquentin's life.

We accompany Roquentin in two listening sessions, one near the start of the novel and one at its very end. At first, the recording does nothing to relieve his existential angst—it makes him happy, but "it is a small happiness of Nausea."[70] Yet soon he perceives something else, something "outside" the music, outside the nausea of existence: a "band of steel," a "hardness" "tearing" at the dreariness of time, something outside of time: "The last chord has died away. In the brief silence which follows I feel strongly that there it is, that *something has happened*."[71] It is that "brief silence," that moment of afterglow, that would become the hallmark of the well-written, well-performed Tin Pan Alley ballad. A few years after Sartre published this novel, Oscar Hammerstein II would describe that stillness in his lyric to "All the Things You Are" (1939)—the "breathless hush of evening" that seems to hang, suspended, just beyond the song.

At the novel's end, having separated with woeful finality from the former lover who kept returning to his thoughts, about to catch a train for Paris, anticipating there a lifetime of dreary economy and loneliness, Roquentin listens once more to "Some of These Days." Sartre has his protagonist at first scoff at the idea that music can be transcendental: "To think there are idiots who get consolation from the fine arts. . . . they think that beauty is compassionate to them. Mugs."[72] Yet, here, Sartre has his protagonist soon realize that though the music is not compassionate to anybody, it can actuate our compassion for others. For, soon, Roquentin feels sympathy for the songwriter. He becomes filled with a "gentleness" for the man who sweated to create this song.[73] He envisions the composer as a fat, be-ringed Jewish man on a hot summer day in New York—and (like Hollywood) Roquentin imagines that this torch song reflects the songwriter's own romantic suffering: "there surely must have been a woman somewhere who wasn't thinking about him the way he would have liked her to."[74] When the singer's voice starts, he finds she shares in this same magic. He wishes someone, someday, could think of his life as he thinks about the singer, "as something precious and almost legendary." He is inspired with the idea of writing a book that might bring "some clarity . . . over my past" and shed a similar transforming light on his existence.[75] And so we leave Roquentin, determined—or *perhaps* determined—to travel a new path.

This resolution of Roquentin's narrative stems from an intensification of his earlier sensation that, beyond the notes of the music, the sounds that die in the

air, there is something else—the song itself, "young and firm, like a pitiful witness" of crass existence, or something even more ineffable, more intangible: "It
does not exist. . . . if I were to get up and rip this record from the table which
holds it, if I were to break it in two, I wouldn't reach *it*. It is beyond—always
beyond something, a voice, a violin note."[76] This unknown something makes
him hope, with fearful joy, "Can you justify your existence then? Just a little?"[77]
Sartre, at this very early stage in his thinking, is remarkably optimistic. He has
Roquentin discover in a simple torch song—a brief, personal, jazzy song—
"something I didn't know any more: a sort of joy," a hint that there is something
beyond existence.[78]

This concise little ditty, the changeling child of confused origin, always leaning, tempted, in the direction of the vindictive and the petty—yet never fully
yielding, somehow clinging to a redeeming core of tenderness—inspires singers,
inspires Sartre, inspires Roquentin, and inspires me. For, to me, Roquentin's
"beyond" is the sphere of the mystic philosophers. The nineteenth-century
Scottish writer William Sharp writes in his poem, "The Rose of Flame": "Oh,
fair immaculate rose of the world, rose of my dream, my Rose! / Beyond the
ultimate gates of dream I have heard thy mystical call." This is the mystical call
(the song) of the rose, of love, felt just beyond the horizon of our thoughts. John
Diamond, in his philosophical poems, imagines "the home of the Lullaby" in
terms similar to those used by Sharp and Sartre-Roquentin: "Music exists /
in another world / where Love alone / is real."[79] Another world, felt yet somehow
just beyond our imagination, lies within, yet outside, each song.

Chapter Eight

"THE SWEETHEART OF SIGMA CHI" AND THE POWER OF A SUBCULTURE

The Strange History of the American Waltz, Part Five

"The Sweetheart of Sigma Chi" was written in 1911, copyrighted in 1912, and for fifteen years slowly infiltrated society, to break out into mass popularity in 1927—at just the right moment to make a contribution to the early development of crooning and the torch song genre. Although it did not retain a connection with those modes, it has gone on to stay a standard in the repertoires of barbershop singing and Dixieland jazz. Somewhere along the way it transformed from a duple meter composition into a waltz.

In 1911 Byron D. Stokes and Frank Dudleigh Vernor (known by his middle name) were students at Albion College, Michigan, and members of the Sigma Chi fraternity. A reunion of the brotherhood loomed, and therefore that day during class Stokes wrote a lyrical tribute to the fraternity, personifying it as an ideal woman.[1] For Stokes, the thought of her—the dream of something that is "always true"—will banish sorrow during future times of trouble. Stokes put the poem on the desk of Vernor, who then spent an hour at the organ setting it to music.

In February 1912, Dudleigh's brother Richard, in Albion, copyrighted the song and published the sheet music—five hundred copies that quickly sold out. Members of the well-established and widespread Sigma Chi fraternity embraced the song. In 1916 Vernor and Stokes (now an officer of the fraternity) created a follow-up, "The Fellowship Song of Sigma Chi," which brother Richard also published to some success, but it did not spread the way "Sweetheart" did.[2] There was something particularly appealing in the earlier song's dream woman who embodied all that was comforting. Within fifteen years, Richard took "The Sweetheart of Sigma Chi" through twenty-seven editions.

There can be no precise tracing of how "Sweetheart" transitioned from collegiate culture to mass culture, but in the context of the era its rise makes sense.

As Allison McCracken has written about at some length, in the 1920s college students were "one of the most culturally influential groups."[3] Within a couple of generations, higher education enrollments had tripled, and fraternity and sorority memberships increased. Although, in the 1920s, those enrolled in college represented only 12 percent of their generation, they were a very influential elite, supporting the dance orchestra revolution of the Jazz Age.[4] They set the trends, and songs and musical comedies about them abounded. Many crooners and bandleaders had attended at least some college: for example, Rudy Vallee, attendee of the University of Maine and graduate of Yale, was closely identified with varsity life, and his band was called the Yale Collegians.

In 1922 Jan Garber led the Garber-Davis Orchestra in a recording of "Sweetheart of Sigma Chi" for the Columbia label; also, Joseph C. Smith and His Orchestra released a version on Brunswick. Starting in 1923, Victor Records issued a series of recordings of "Sweetheart." The Victor series commenced with a rendition in 1923 by Whitey Kaufman's Original Pennsylvania Serenaders, on their first record session. Marlin E. "Whitey" Kaufman started his band while a student at Lebanon Valley College, and they played many fraternity dances, so it was perhaps natural for them to include this college favorite in a medley with "Dream Girl of Pi K.A." (Pi Kappa Alpha being another fraternity).[5] In 1924 Victor sponsored another debut record, by Meyer Davis's Le Paradis Band, which also featured "Sweetheart," again in medley, this time with a university football march with a similar history, "The Washington and Lee Swing."

In June 1927, Victor elected to make a fresh rendition, to take advantage of the new electrical recording technology.[6] Fred Waring's Pennsylvanians enjoyed a major hit with it, featuring a vocal refrain by brother Tom Waring. As was the usual custom, once the dance orchestra version proved successful, the label then issued a solo vocal performance, in this case by Gene Austin, recorded in September—another huge seller.[7] (Thus, four prominent "Sigma Chi" discs were issued by the Victor label. Maybe somebody in authority at the label was a Sigma Chi brother.) Perhaps not coincidentally, both Fred Waring and Gene Austin had some college education. When Waring recorded "Sweetheart," he already had hits with "Collegiate" and "I Love the College Girls." Specializing as a cinema house live act, dressed in collegiate clothes, Waring's band was "the apotheosis of the new performance" of a varsity persona.[8] A certain mythos about college life was quickly becoming a standard pop culture trope.

In 1927, too, the Melrose Brothers publishing house in Chicago bought the rights for "Sweetheart of Sigma Chi" from Richard Vernor, tweaked the accompaniment, and issued what they proclaimed on its cover was the twenty-eighth edition. Melrose specialized in jazz-based compositions and had a strong connection with the Gennett label, who in 1927 issued a hot jazz rendition of "Sweetheart" by the Indiana-based Paul Schultz outfit. The song's vogue peaked in January 1928, with the rise of Austin's disc. Notably, its general currency as a pop hit lingered an unusually long time, with active live and radio plugs continuing until late October 1929, only fading after the stock market crashed.

Along the way, performance tradition rewrote "Sweetheart of Sigma Chi" from a composition in four-four (with a slightly odd refrain length of seventeen measures) to a tune in three-four (with a more conventional refrain length of thirty-two measures). In the 1920s, three out of four renditions alter the meter, starting in 1922 and including the most influential arrangements, by Waring and Austin. Although Richard Vernor seems to have kept publishing his brother's composition in its original duple meter, the Melrose company printed it as a waltz, presumably responding to the pressure of performance tradition. Mysteriously, at a time when waltzes were routinely starting to be adapted into fox trots, "Sweetheart" underwent the reverse transformation.[9] The sheet-music tradition permanently settled on placing "Sweetheart" in three-four time. Thus, ironically, those who chose to render it in duple meter in later decades (about two out of five) probably thought they were violating the composer's original intentions, while they were actually honoring them.

For "Sweetheart of Sigma Chi," Dudleigh Vernor composed a refrain with the standard Tin Pan Alley structure of ABAC. The very first phrase introduces sharps and flats. Indeed, Vernor avoids the tonic note for the beginning six measures. This strategy, perhaps, lends a piquancy and a touch of sophistication that is lacking in, for example, "I Wonder Who's Kissing Her Now" and "Let Me Call You Sweetheart." One can imagine the Tin Pan Alley pros being aghast.

In his poem, Stokes avoids certain specifics, thereby raising many questions. Is the protagonist reminiscing about an old acquaintance or an old fantasy? If real, why was she "the sweetheart of Sigma Chi"? Was she beloved by all the chapter members? How far did these relationships go—into sexual promiscuity? "*Each* co-ed" seems to fade at the memory of this sweetheart—does that mean she herself was *not* a co-ed? Why is her iridescence an "*after*glow"? Did she merely leave the room? Did she marry someone else? Did she die? If her figure outshines the memory of all the other co-eds, then why is the bright and beautiful image of "a rainbow trail" associated with her rivals and not with her?

As it turns out, Stokes deliberately built ambiguities into his poem. He pointed out that this sweetheart "is not a real girl; she is, in fact, just the opposite"—indeed, it "does not make sense in terms of a literal interpretation."[10] He was inspired by "the symbolic method of writing poetry," specifically by William Blake and Dante, to capture "the magic" of the fraternity initiation through a "symbol for the spiritual ingredient in brotherhood."[11] The metaphor he chose was an idealized dream girl—a generalized notion which allowed the lyric to capture the imaginations of many men for whom the Greek letter societies would remain alien.

Example 8.1. "The Sweetheart of Sigma Chi," verse and refrain, melody line.

The notion of a love relationship that takes place only (or primarily) on the level of dreams is one manifestation of the interiority slowly developing in American pop ballads. Beth Slater Whitson had already supplied the hit parade with one example in "Meet Me Tonight in Dreamland." Soon after the "Sigma Chi" vogue in 1927, Austin would have success with "The Girl of My Dreams," as would others with "Dream Kisses." Rudy Vallee, too, would achieve acclaim with another portrait of a man dreaming of women he has known or imagined, "I'm Just a Vagabond Lover." That ballad loaned its title to both his first autobiography and his movie debut, exemplifying his early persona.

The solitary figure described in "Sigma Chi," sitting with a pipe in hand, is pictured on the cover of the 1924 edition. A mirage hovers: the face of the

sweetheart in the heart of a rose. This mise-en-scène—pensive figure, seeing a dream love in the smoke—would become a common convention in Tin Pan Alley songs. Future hits such as "Smoke Dreams" (1937), "Deep in a Dream" (1938), and (a different) "Smoke Dreams" (1944) would all explore this scenario.

Austin kept "Sweetheart of Sigma Chi" firmly in his repertoire, putting his interpretation on record thrice more. With a restrained accompaniment, creative phrasing, and subtle melodic variations, he draws the listener into a convincing atmosphere of quiet contemplation. His rendering of the lonely, wistful armchair dreamer is near perfect. It is probably this scenario, so powerfully evoked by Austin, that led to "Sweetheart" attaining a place on a 1934 "list of the best torch songs."[12] For a window of time, this was a meditation not just for the varsity crowd, but for every male who lingered alone, longing for romance.

Austin's slow waltz modality, the vagueness of the situation, the "blue of her eyes and the gold of her hair" that are "the blend of the Western sky" (often

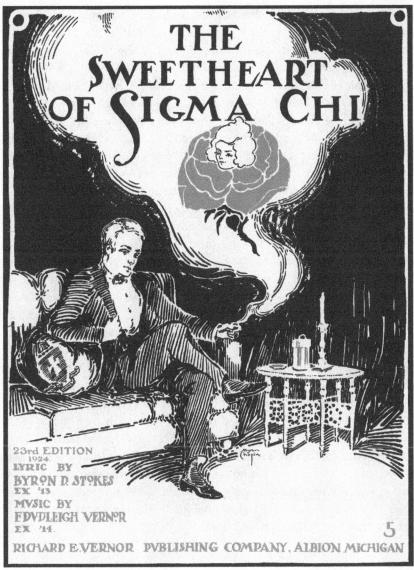

Figure 8.1. "The Sweetheart of Sigma Chi" (1911), in its twenty-third edition from small-town publisher Richard E. Vernor, the composer's brother. You did not have to be a college man—or a smoker—to relate to this wistful, semi-mystical daydream of an ideal vision of both life and womanhood. Three years after this 1924 printing, the song spread throughout American culture. Photo courtesy of the Sigma Chi Historical Initiative.

changed to "skies" by singers, to rhyme with "eyes")—all these were borrowed by "Where the Blue of the Night Meets the Gold of the Day," the 1931 song that was a hit for both Russ Columbo and, especially, Bing Crosby, who co-wrote it and for whom it became a lifelong theme song.[13] In turn, that piece seems to have inspired Frank Sinatra in his choice of theme song, "Put Your Dreams

Away"—another slow waltz about dreams with an ambiguous lyric. These resemblances are a tribute to the stamp that "Sweetheart" made on the crooner tradition. The wistful beau of "The Sweetheart of Sigma Chi," dreaming of that which "is always true," can be analyzed as yearning for the same lost or imagined port of comfort and security as the protagonists of "Kiss Me Again," "I Wonder Who's Kissing Her Now," and "Let Me Call You Sweetheart."

Although "Sigma Chi" underwent much the same trajectory in the 1930s and 1940s as did "I Wonder Who's Kissing Her Now" and "Let Me Call You Sweetheart"—a swing rendering by Tommy Dorsey, crooning versions by Bing Crosby and his rivals, appearances in movie musicals (as a title song in 1933 and 1946)—these interpretations lack luster. In the end, perhaps, the specificities in Stokes's lyric discouraged performance tradition reinvention. First, it is not adaptable to a female persona. Second, as with "Meet Me Tonight in Dreamland" and "Down by the Old Mill Stream," mentioning "the blue of her eyes" limits the general applicability of the lyric—and to this overspecificity is added the "the gold of her hair." These details strengthen the symbolism of the song for Sigma Chi members—blue and gold are the fraternity's colors—but weaken its appeal to the ragtag and bobtail. As the coup de grace, the ultimate thought, the title phrase suddenly introduces the idea of the Greek letter society, which has not before been hinted at in the lyric. Those not in that slice of culture might be excused for exclaiming, "What!?"—raising questions, just when the song should be resolving.

The cultural revolutions of the fifties and sixties altered popular images of university students, and "Sweetheart" retreated from the mainstream, to maintain a strong position within the limits of the barbershop and Dixieland repertoires and the fraternity itself. At some point, the Sigma Chi chapters began to elect an annual sweetheart who exemplifies their core values of friendship, justice, and learning (the teenage Judy Garland was one).[14] Subsequently, the order as a whole began to elect a biannual International Sweetheart—a sign of how a simple torch waltz can alter lives.

Chapter Nine

"MY MELANCHOLY BABY"

$\mathcal{T}$he longing to be comforted like a child lies at the heart of the 1911 song "My Melancholy Baby." During a chunk of American history, from the late 1920s on, to be cuddled and kissed, sympathized with and consoled in one's misery, seemed to be the wish of lovesick men. Perhaps they found catharsis through being addressed with tenderness. Take the character of Cyrus Barrett Jr., heir to a fortune, left alone by his wife, in *East Side of Heaven* (1939).

Cyrus (Robert Kent) slumps on the table, inebriated again (that's one reason his wife left him), in the diner of Ma Kelly (Jane Jones). A band of musicians encircle and droop over him, playing "My Melancholy Baby"—he has brought them along for just this purpose (see figure 9.1).

They finish, and he commands, "Play it again" (as Rick would later do for "As Time Goes By" in *Casablanca*). But those around describe the tune as "depressing," and the motherly Ma Kelly confronts him: "Haven't you had enough sad music?" The socialite strikes a match, explaining, "A torch . . . that's what I'm carrying" (see figure 9.2).

Here Hollywood presents the quintessential torch-bearing situation alongside what was then the quintessential torch song, "My Melancholy Baby." The bereft sweetheart slurring out "Play 'Melancholy Baby'" was a cliché, already crystallized by 1939, continuing through the 1950s. Yet the way "My Melancholy Baby" attained that status was anything but straightforward. What led it to be considered the first and most central torch song?[1]

Indeed, so hidden are the pathways of this song's history, it could be called "My Mysterious Baby." Several people claimed to be the writer. (Which one was it?) What was the level of its early success? (The evidence seems contradictory.) What were the steps that led it to be revived to even greater success? (There are major gaps.) To add to the muddle, the composer Ernie Burnett has a last name almost like the first publisher, Theron C. Bennett. (Therefore, I will sometimes call them "Ernie" and "Theron" to avoid confusion.) Further complicating things, Ernie originally called the song "Melancholy," but within a few years Theron retitled it "My Melancholy Baby."

Figures 9.1 and 9.2. *East Side of Heaven* (1939). Robert Kent depicts the classic torch-bearer—deserted, drunk, keeping alive love's spark (symbolized by the match he lights). In his misery he asks to be serenaded with "My Melancholy Baby."

In a fate similar to that of "The Sweetheart of Sigma Chi," also written in 1911, "My Melancholy Baby" simmered for sixteen years. Its diffusion was not even visible to some show-business insiders. It finally bubbled up into prominence in 1927, becoming a hit by late December. Between 1916 and 1927, the scanty record reveals only hints of its stirrings. Yet by 1950 it easily held its status among the top fifty most recorded songs.[2]

Different people spun different legends about the early history of "My Melancholy Baby." The cast of characters in this saga is large, and positive facts are few. There are three categories: clearly a myth; a claim that is potentially true; and sure facts. Therefore, in the discussion that follows, I will try to label when an event in this history is hearsay and when, conversely, there is documentary evidence.

MAYBELLE, BEN, AND OTHER MYSTERIES

This first section will deal with the mysteries surrounding the creation, first performances, and publication of "My Melancholy Baby."

Fact: On Halloween 1911, the Library of Congress received a copyright deposit copy from Ernest M. Burnett: an unpublished composition, "Melancholy," with music by Burnett and words by Maybelle E. Watson. Burnett's address is given as Denver, Colorado. The music manuscript has become lost (at least, the librarians could not find it in 2011), but erstwhile librarian Karen Moses found the two sheets that give the lyric.[3] Here it is. (I have added the italics, for reasons I will soon make clear.)

1.
You look so sad,
Come now be glad
Don't let little trifles ever worry you,
Something went wrong
All the day long
That is why I'm feeling oh, so awfully blue.
Tell it to me
For can't you see
Honey that I love you and I love you true,
So don't you cry
It makes me sigh
And it makes me feel so melancholy too.

Chorus: —

Oh I feel so awfully melancholy
Every time I see you sad,
Just because I think that through some folly
I have hurt your feelings made you mad.
Won't you come and tell me the real reason
What makes you so awfully blue,
Honey don't you cry
Just tell me the reason why
Or else I will feel melancholy too.

2.
I could be glad
If I just had
Someone to caress me and to love me too
All of the time
In rain or shine
Then I know that I could never feel so blue
Honey you know
I love you so
And I want to prove to you my love is strong
So let us go
Dear don't you know
Where the wedding bells will chime the whole day long.

Who was Ernie Burnett? His fellow songwriter Gene Buck described him as "a little guy, weighs about ninety pounds soaking wet."[4] His ASCAP bio says he was born in Ohio, educated in Europe, trained there for a career as a concert pianist, returned to the United States at age seventeen (1902), went into vaudeville and theatre, saw battle in World War I, worked as a bandleader, went for three years to Panama, and spent between 1921 and 1931 recovering from an illness caused by being gassed in the war.[5] Trade journals place him in a medicine show in North Dakota in 1913; writing a song in 1916 that got some plugging, "Sailing Home"; managing a tab show company in the Midwest in 1920 and 1921; working for Shapiro, Bernstein music publishers in Chicago; and being critically ill in 1924.[6] Ragtime aficionados hail him for his 1914 "Steamboat Rag."[7] In the 1910s he was a fairly prolific songwriter, and from 1933 onward he was even more prolific. Unfortunately, many of his later songs have inferior lyrics. (My comments on them get monotonous: "barely okay," "lame," "gauche," "sappy," "terrible," "trite," and "*unbelievably* trite.")[8] Today, the other Burnett tunes one is mostly likely to encounter are "Please Take a Letter, Miss Brown," which got some play in 1940, and a country-inflected comedy piece "From the Andes to the Indies in His Undies," an irresistible title that has a life of its own on YouTube.

Myth: In 1939 Ernie told the famed Hollywood gossip columnist Hedda Hopper his version of how "My Melancholy Baby" was written:[9] the day before his wedding, he waited all night at the train station in Denver for his bride-to-be, but the train never came. During his wait, he wrote "My Melancholy Baby" on the back of a railroad timetable, starting with the line "All my fears are foolish fancy, maybe." He finally fell asleep on a bench at dawn, until the newsboy woke him, shouting about the train wreck that had killed his fiancée. That is the tragic reason he never married, he told Hopper. But the line he quotes is not in the lyric he copyrighted . . . and, if his story was true, then who was Maybelle E. Watson?

Facts: Maybelle Watson, of Berkeley, California, survived the wreck of a steamship off the coast of Shelter Cove, California, in July 1907.[10] (Was this the feeble foundation for Burnett's train wreck story?) In 1910 copyright copies of three unpublished songs with lyrics by Maybelle and music by Ernie are sent by him, from San Francisco, to the Library of Congress. One year later, her name is on Ernie's copyright deposit of the unpublished "Melancholy," as lyricist. One year after that, an early printing of "Melancholy" blazons at the top of the first page: "Dedicated to Miss Maybelle Watson of Berkeley, Calif."[11] A quarter century later, from November 1938 through February 1940, Maybelle E. Watson Bergmann sued for authorship credit and royalties for "My Melancholy Baby"—and won.[12] She claimed then that she had been Ernie Burnett's wife when they wrote it together in 1911. Meanwhile, Burnett claimed "his ex-wife had nothing to do with the writing of the number. He had merely put her name on the copyright registry card and the title sheet."[13] It was while this court case was spinning through its motions that Burnett confided his heartbreaking (and self-serving) story to Hopper about why "to this day he's remained unmarried"![14]

Claims (and questions): Maybelle also at least once claimed that she had been the "stage partner" of Ernie when they wrote "Melancholy."[15] The only other clues that she was in show business are the four unpublished song lyrics. As further detailed below, the first days of "My Melancholy Baby" all trace to Denver, Colorado, but Maybelle is placed in California in 1907, 1910, and 1912. Why, one year after the period when (she claimed) she and Ernie were married and a performance team, was the sheet music dedicated to *Miss* Maybelle Watson and not to *Mrs.* Maybelle Burnett? Had they divorced within that single year?[16] Oddly, in 1939, when she finally sued, Maybelle was the wife of John Bergmann; he was a New York policeman, but meanwhile she was living in Elkhart, Indiana.[17] Could these be coincidences—or hints that Maybelle had a propensity to live far apart from her husbands?

Fact: On October 25, 1912, almost exactly one year after Burnett and Watson's copyright, the publisher Theron C. Bennett printed "Melancholy" with a melody by Ernie Burnett and lyrics by George A. Norton (see musical example 9.1).[18]

Coincidentally, within the previous thirty days, Theron had also lucked into acquiring W. C. Handy's "Memphis Blues."[19] Theron became, first, Handy's sales representative for the piece, and, then, through a bit of swift deceit, its copyright owner. As Handy's instrumental piece became well known, Theron had that same George A. Norton write a lyric for two of its melodic strains. This vocal version of "Memphis Blues" resulted in even greater popularity. Thereby, Theron and Norton together became the propagators of both the seminal torch song

Example 9.1. "My Melancholy Baby," verse and refrain, piano-vocal score.

and the seminal blues publication. This remarkable coincidence demonstrates how, at the start, the fates of the two subgenres were intertwined.

Who was George A. Norton? Born in Missouri, raised in Georgia, he became an itinerant ragtime pianist who somehow or other also developed a career as a Tin Pan Alley songwriter, particularly as a lyricist.[20] Early on he had one fair-sized hit, "Sing Me a Song of the South" (1899), and after that a prolific publication record. Through 1909 he placed the usual string of hits and misses with the established music houses—Feist, Stern, Haviland, Witmark. He temporarily disappears from the Tin Pan Alley scene, until he shows up in Denver in December 1910. He seems to be stationed there into November 1911—exactly the place and time that "My Melancholy Baby" emerges.[21] By May 1912, Norton is again being published by New York firms. His career peaked, perhaps, with the success of the vocal version of "Memphis Blues." Norton went on to make other songs in collaboration with both Ernie and Theron. He was still chugging away in Tin Pan Alley, co-founding a new company, until in 1922 he retired to Arizona for his health, where he died in 1924.[22]

Claim: The pianist Ben Light bragged that at age sixteen (which would make it 1908) he composed "My Melancholy Baby" in Denver while playing ragtime in a nightclub called Maynard's, with George Norton writing the lyric.[23]

Fact: As 1910 turned to 1911, Norton was copyrighting songs with one Jack Maynard. And on October 31, 1911, on the same day the copyright deposit of "Melancholy" arrived, so did three collaborations of Ernie Burnett and Jack

Maynard. All these Norton-Burnett-Maynard copyrights are sent from Denver. Presumption: the Maynard's nightclub of Ben Light's story was run by this same Jack Maynard. Did Light actually compose "My Melancholy Baby" at Maynard's, and Burnett falsely claim ownership?

Who was Ben Light? The pianist had a long and successful career, well documented by trade journals from 1912 through 1959, including leading vaudeville troupes, recording for Capitol Records and, at the end, easy listening albums during the golden age of lounge music. Light said he never bothered to fight for copyright on any of the songs he wrote—not even "My Melancholy Baby," because it did not become popular till many years later.[24] But, eventually, under the urging of friends, he did collect "numerous affidavits attesting to his authorship of the music."[25]

Claim: One of those affidavits was almost surely from the character actor and comedian William Frawley—the beloved "Fred" of the *I Love Lucy* show— who was perhaps the first to announce in print, in 1937, that Light was the real composer.[26] Frawley claimed he was the premiere singer of "My Melancholy Baby" in 1911 in a nightclub in Denver (perhaps the Maynard's that Light specified). Frawley was playing there with his brother Paul, and neither wanted to sing it: they thought it "a dud."[27] Bill lost and had to sing it—but it made a hit. Frawley professed to have also introduced "Carolina in the Morning" (1921), and he further staked his claim on these two standards by recording both songs for a 1958 album.[28]

Claim: On one early edition of "Melancholy" (it must be 1912 or 1913, before the title was lengthened), Theron Bennett places a blurb, stating:

> "Melancholy" the wonder song first saw the break of day in Denver's Dutch Mill, one of the show places of the West.
>
> The Dutch Mill represents a miniature town, there is a song shop, a candy shop, a curio shop, a soft drink retreat and a garden in which the "Miller" feeds over one thousand people a day.
>
> The large number of people daily attracted to The Dutch Mill were first to proclaim the merits of the wonder song "Melancholy," and from their praises spring the increasing demand from coast-to-coast until the number now stands pre-eminent in song land.

What was the Dutch Mill? On a sheet music cover in 1918, Theron gives his main address as being the Dutch Mill, Denver, Colorado.[29] In 1919 a trade journal blurb celebrates it as "Denver's famous 'dry' cabaret" (which should be taken in the context that all of Colorado went "dry"—i.e., prohibited alcohol—at the start of 1916).[30] In 1982 the Mill was looked back on as "one of the more elegant spots in the West."[31] A high-class family joint, a destination spot, almost a department store, with music performed and sold—and owned (it seems) by Theron C. Bennett.

Who was Theron C. Bennett? He was another ragtime pianist and songwriter (like Light, like Norton, like Burnett). He is credited with composing "The St. Louis Tickle" (1904), an instrumental rag which incorporates the folk tune famous in New Orleans jazz as "Buddy Bolden Blues." David A. Jasen claims that Bennett "played and sang 'Melancholy' first" (granting him priority over Frawley) "at Bennett's nightclub, the Dutch Mill, in Denver, Colorado."[32] Bennett seems to have traveled the nation almost continuously from 1905 onward, running music stores in cities across the United States. He established connections with five-and-dime music departments, working first for Chicago's Victor Kremer music publishing, in "charge of the city branches," making "extended" trips during which he "installed fifteen music departments in some of the largest retail establishments throughout the West."[33] Even during the thick of his career as a publisher, from 1910 through 1924, he lists offices in multiple cities, and the locale given priority seems to change arbitrarily on the sheet music, from cover to cover.

W. C. Handy described Bennett as having, in 1912, his own "music publishing company" (Bennett seems to have started his own publishing on a modest scale in 1908) "and also a store of his own in a Western city" (presumably the Dutch Mill). "He traveled extensively for his business, visiting retailers such as Bry's" (the Memphis department store where Handy met him) "which home he made local headquarters and spending weeks at a time with them busily demonstrating his music to their customers."[34] In the 1920s, Bennett stopped his peripatetic publishing career and settled down in California, opening another Dutch Mill in Long Beach. For the thirteen years before Bennett's death in 1937, he ran the new Mill, taught music, and became a pioneer of music broadcasting in Los Angeles with his Packard Six ensemble.[35] He had long since had to sell the copyrights for the few enduring songs he had published.

So, according to various kinds of evidence, some more trustworthy than others, in 1911 we have Maybelle Watson perhaps off in the anteroom in California, and Ernie Burnett, Ben Light, George Norton, Theron Bennett, and William Frawley all in Denver—which seems to have been a hot spot for ragtime era entertainment—the delivery room for the birth of this "Melancholy Baby." Which ones wrote the song? Which ones first performed it? There is no way to know for certain—but a guess can be made.

The relationship between Watson's lyric and Norton's lyric becomes key. Clearly the two share many elements. The overall concept is the same: the protagonist's sweetheart is acting sad, so the singer tries to find out why and urges the beloved to cheer up. Part and parcel with this is the most important resemblance: both refrains build to their concluding lines, which use almost exactly the same words.

There are many other small points of correspondence between Watson and Norton. The lyrics share the same pattern of rhymes, both in the verses and the refrain. Both embed the title word "melancholy" in the first and last refrain lines—and in other lines use "blue" as its synonym. The question of whether the singer has contributed to the sweetheart's blue mood is brought up fleetingly (Watson puts it in the refrain, Norton in the first verse). The phrase "tell me" appears (Watson puts it in the refrain, Norton in the second verse). The end of each first verse has a penultimate couplet of "sigh" and "cry." Watson's first verse addresses the beloved as "honey," Norton's as "hon." Each then returns to that endearment at the same point: the first line of the refrain's fourth stanza. Clearly one was written with knowledge of the other. There are two factors that support Watson's claim to be the first lyricist—and, by extension, Burnett's as the composer.[36]

First: the verses for Watson's lyric are clearly written to be a duet. Singer One comforts and affirms love for Singer Two (who is indicated in italics above). "Double songs" along this pattern were very popular then in performance, but not in sheet music editions (unless it was a duet from a stage musical), which were printed for home consumption with solo voice or quartet arrangements. Therefore, there must have been a particularly strong reason for this design. Watson claimed to have been working as a team with Burnett during this period. This duet version would work perfectly for such a girl-and-boy act, but it would not be welcomed by the Tin Pan Alley industry of which Norton was a veteran. While that aspect does not prove anything (after all, Watson may have been adapting Norton's lyric to her own performance needs), nevertheless it does create at least a mild presumption that Watson wrote hers first.

Second: the aforementioned dedication to "Miss Maybelle Watson" on an early edition of "Melancholy." Many scenarios are possible to explain its presence, but perhaps the strongest possibility is that it was meant as a compensatory gesture of acknowledgment from Ernie and Theron to Maybelle, a token for her being left out of the credit and royalties for the final published version. If she did write the 1911 copyrighted version of "Melancholy," then she certainly deserved both fame and money for it: the title, the overall concept and pattern, and the punchline all came from Watson. (Clearly, the courts in 1940 agreed; they awarded her credit and royalties.)

Neither circumstance is decisive, but the two together add up to a strong plausibility that Watson and Burnett were the writers.

"BABY" GAINS ITS LEGS

In 1912 Theron bought the copyright for "Melancholy" from Ernie. Probably Theron then took advantage of Norton's presence in Denver to recruit from that experienced Tin Pan Alley professional the new lyric, incorporating whatever was required from Watson's original.[37] Whether first performed at Maynard's, as Frawley remembered, or at the Dutch Mill, as Jasen states, there is a likelihood that Theron's claim was true: "Melancholy" probably became a favorite of the clientele of that bustling destination spot the Dutch Mill. Theron wrote another song with Norton at about the same time, "Ain't That Funny (That Easy, Squeezing, Teasy, Pleasing Ragtime)," and the back cover features a simple list of fourteen pop songs, three instrumentals, and six sacred pieces—his entire catalog—alongside a big ad for "The Wonder Song, 'Melancholy.'"[38]

Despite such early efforts by Bennett, he could never get "My Melancholy Baby" to break through. This is in contrast to most of the other songs focused on in this book (as well as Bennett's "Memphis Blues"), which usually spread like wildfire once they were promoted by a major firm. Instead, "My Melancholy Baby" was at first a good example of another phenomenon: many songs are neither hits nor failures, but somewhere in between. Among those, there are a few that keep on being performed for years and yet, despite that, are never very visible in the media. Such was the case with "Melancholy Baby."

What was Bennett able to achieve? He must have sold sheet music in a steady flow: in two and a half years he commissioned seven different printings, featuring at least nine vaudeville acts on the covers.[39] In the first six months alone, he gave "Melancholy" two print runs.[40] The first one, of October 1912, bears the dedication to Watson, which disappears after this. (Is that omission a sign that Ernie and Maybelle split up? Or were Ernie and Theron worried about the kind of court action that Maybelle might make—and did in fact make decades later?) In the second printing, Theron inserts the unusual blurb jointly boosting the song and the Dutch Mill. With this edition, too, he adds an additional page for a separate "chorus in march time," which is retained for years. Theron must have felt that all these print jobs were justified by sales, indicating at least a moderate popularity for the tune.

Things started to move a bit more quickly. In May 1913, a trade journal notice boasts that "Denver was no place" for Bennett "with a 'real' song hit, called 'Melancholy.' Orders were coming in so fast that he had to come to New York, and recently opened a branch in the Exchange Building."[41] Thus, it is no surprise that a fresh second edition reveals that Bennett was using a new printing firm and had moved his New York office from 36th Street to 45th Street.[42] In June, Bennett managed to get "Melancholy" reviewed by the *Player*; and in July, by *Billboard*—who recommend changing the title to "Melancholy Baby."[43]

But then, things seem to stall. From the fall of 1913, for at least half a year there are no signs of plugging "Melancholy." Perhaps Bennett got distracted by the growing success of "Memphis Blues" (which had sold fifty thousand sheets by September and had a vocal version copyrighted in November).[44]

In 1914 Bennett reissued "Melancholy" as "My Melancholy Baby," squeezing the added words into the same cover design, in a smaller font (see figure 1.1). Later, he puts out yet another edition using new plates (except for the "chorus in march time," which stays the same). In June, under the new title, Bennett convinced the Imperial studio to make a short "song portrayal in motion pictures"—and got it used in vaudeville houses.[45] This was a standard item for vaudeville and movie shows: as the vocalist sang, projected images (sometimes still, sometimes motion picture) illustrated the lyrics.[46]

In 1915, in a culmination of his efforts (or a last gasp), Bennett obtained a recording of "My Melancholy Baby" by Walter Van Brunt, for the Edison company. Whitburn charts this for one week, rating it nine (in a period when he charts ten positions). He probably only bases this, however, on the Edison announcement that heralded the record's release.

All of these events, spread over two and a half years, represent some kind of success. But it was a mild and diluted one. After that, for twelve years, "My Melancholy Baby" nearly dropped out of the media.

Nevertheless, according to a couple of autobiographies, written decades later, "My Melancholy Baby" was being performed in saloons. It was while working in Crutchfield's, a black-and-tan in Omaha, Nebraska (a city that was one of Theron Bennett's centers of operation), in 1913, that Ada "Bricktop" Smith first heard her white colleague Tommy Lyman sing.[47] Her description is vivid:

> That wistful, thin, almost shy little man had a way of singing that song ["My Melancholy Baby"] that could grab hold of you and twist your heart. Moments later he'd do another type of song and have you laughing your head off.
>
> He was working at a top cabaret in downtown Omaha. It was a Jim Crow [i.e., racially segregated] club, and I might never have gotten the chance to hear him at all if he hadn't been so generous with his talent. Every day he'd drift into Crutchfield's.
>
> I remember that the first I saw him I couldn't believe he was *the* Tommy Lyman, the saloon singer's singer, but when I saw him work in that quiet way of his I understood what it was all about. All the chatter and clinking of glasses, not to mention almost everyone's breathing, came to a standstill when Tommy sang. He'd stand at the bar, his eyes heavy-lidded, his long, tapering fingers resting on the edge, and he'd sing sooo quietly. And yet you could understand every word and exactly what each one meant.

There was no song he sang better than "Melancholy Baby," and we wouldn't let him quit until he'd done it. The way he sang it was unforgettable.[48]

Here the elements coalesce that foreshadow the later torch-song-and-crooning era: quiet singing, intent atmosphere, and heart-twisting emotions. Adding to the subtle atmosphere, perhaps, was Lyman's very high tenor range.[49] There is no other hint, however, that before 1927 Lyman actually was singing "My Melancholy Baby."[50] Bricktop might have been confusing her early memories with the many later times she heard Lyman; their paths crisscrossed for decades. As she says: "over the years I tried to see him perform as often as I could," and after 1927 "My Melancholy Baby" would become Lyman's theme song.

Yet, supporting Bricktop's memory, Lyman's repertoire was legendarily large and diverse. For example, in Paris in 1922, he won a bet with show-business crony Bill Halligan by singing any song demanded, for four hours.[51] (The stakes: the loser had to leave the city.) Halligan put Lyman to a hard test by alternately requesting forgotten old show tunes and then the latest hits fresh off the press, and he still lost. Lyman kept alive obscure songs that only became famous years after their creation (other examples: "My Blue Heaven" and "Paper Doll").[52] In that light, Lyman may well have been singing "My Melancholy Baby" in 1913—and quietly helping keep it alive for the next fourteen years.

Mezz Mezzrow also remembered "My Melancholy Baby" from his youthful days, playing in a cabaret in Burnham, Illinois.[53] Like "Kiss Me Again," it was part of a group of songs that made the prostitutes weep during their off-hours.[54] His dates are uncertain, but probably 1919 through 1921. As with Bricktop, Mezzrow's memories might be influenced by the later fame of "Melancholy Baby"—yet, really, there is nothing anachronistic about his list of "tearjerkers," and his recollections may well be accurate.[55]

Speaking of accurate (or not) recollections, now comes another . . .

Claim (the colorful raconteur-singer-historian Ian Whitcomb, passes this one on, all of which should be taken with a large pinch of salt):[56] Burnett vouched that he was felled in combat during World War I, and, in the carnage and chaos of the frontlines, his nametag got attached to a corpse. When he woke in the hospital, he had lost all means of identification—and memory. Then a performing troupe came to visit the wounded, and when the singer rendered "My Melancholy Baby," Burnett sat up and said, "That's my tune!" The entertainers argued with him, informing him that the composer of that melody had died in action. Burnett felt certain, however, and from that clue was able to reconstruct his memory and reclaim his identity.

"My Melancholy Baby" was still sufficiently well remembered for it to be mentioned in trade coverage of Burnett in 1916 and Norton in 1922.[57] In 1922, as well, the Edison company reissued the old 1915 recording by Walter Van Brunt (now going by the professional name Walter Scanlan), as the flip side of a new ballad, "The Mill by the Sea." The reviewer for *Variety* seems to have never heard of the older tune before. His verdict: "would have a chance as a popular song if properly 'plugged.'"[58] This reissue is unique in the corpus of the prolific Van Brunt/Scanlan—and perhaps in that of the Edison company as well. Maybe the slowly seeping prevalence of "Melancholy Baby" influenced the record company; or perhaps some quiet plugging *was* going on, behind the scenes.

Because, sometime or other, Bennett had sold "My Melancholy Baby" to a friendly rival, the Joe Morris firm. Bennett and Morris had offices in the same building on 45th Street, and Bennett had already handed the larger firm "The Memphis Blues."[59] George Norton had placed a lyric with Morris in mid-1913, thereby also establishing a connection with that firm. Yet the precise moment when "Melancholy Baby" was taken over by Morris remains in doubt, because varying sources indicate different dates: 1912, 1914, 1916, 1918, and 1924.[60] The year may be important, because in 1938 *Variety* claimed that "My Melancholy Baby" had a surge in sheet music sales in 1919.[61] Whether this is true, and whether Bennett or Morris was the beneficiary of this revival, is another "Melancholy" mystery.

Finally, late in 1927, "My Melancholy Baby" breaks through this veil of obscurities and becomes an undisputed, well-documented hit. The truly seismic event is when Gene Austin goes into the studio on September 14, to wax the number for the Victor label.[62] Next, Walter Winchell, in his *Vanity Fair* article on Broadway slang, defines "carrying a torch" and "torch song," and documents Lyman announcing "My famous torch song: 'Come To Me, My Melancholy Baby.'"[63] Simultaneously, Victor is pressing Austin's disc; and, on November 16, it is reviewed by *Variety*:

> Get this Gene Austin record for drunk or sober moments; . . . that ace of "torch" songs, "My Melancholy Baby," which the unique songster has revived. . . . the sobbingly sentimental "Melancholy Baby," which Tommy Lyman has been instrumental in reviving hereabouts at his Salon Royal, will make the record sell in the metropolis and nationally. When the b.f.'s are singing the blues for long-lost g.f.'s, "Melancholy Baby" is the national anthem.[64]

Clearly, the song already had a reputation as a favorite of inebriated men when separated from the women they loved. Equally clearly, "torch song" had, somehow or other, quietly become an established genre to these showbiz insiders (if not yet to the general public), with enough examples to have one stand out as exemplary: "My Melancholy Baby."

What the review does not mention is that Lyman, while appearing at the Salon Royal, was also on the radio every night.[65] In 1927 Lyman was purveying

"My Blue Heaven" over the airwaves, and he was probably doing the same with "My Melancholy Baby"—and thus spurring the popularity of these neglected gems through the paradoxical intimacy of this new electronic medium.[66] Gene Austin was surely influenced by Lyman: he insisted, against the wishes of his record label, on recording "My Blue Heaven," and thus he was probably also eager to record Lyman's other specialty, "Melancholy Baby."[67]

By New Year's Day 1928, Austin's disc of "My Melancholy Baby" was a hit, paired with an only slightly less popular flip side, "There's a Cradle in Carolina"—perhaps the "baby" and the "cradle" went together in the minds of the Victor record company executives. From here on, the pattern is a familiar one: a flood of at least eleven recordings in 1928, including two from most of the major labels; popularity spreading to England; and its establishment in the ongoing repertoire and popular consciousness.

The 1927 sheet music edition features the drawing of a doll-faced flapper (with bobbed black hair like Clara Bow) and inset photos of Austin or a host of other performers. There are new plates, but they duplicate the same old 1912 arrangement. Ukulele chords have been added, and the "chorus in march time" is gone. Most noticeably, "I am strong for you" has been changed to the less dated "I'm in love with you."[68] (Nevertheless, about half of the 1928 recordings use the original lyric line. Old sheet music editions were seemingly still in circulation.) The Joe Morris company is advertising it: "This is the Quickest Hit and Greatest Song We Have Ever Published. Sure-Fire for Everybody. An Overnight Sensation. Will Fit Any Spot. Orch. in All Keys." To label this poor, half-neglected, sixteen-year-old sleeper as "the quickest hit" and "an overnight sensation," someone at Morris must have had an ironic sense of humor.

But to say "will fit in any spot"—how true! Perhaps no other song in this book exemplifies the composition that is at once croonable love ballad, torch song, and swinging jazz piece. All the major early microphone singers of the day rendered it, either live or on radio, record, or screen—those defined as crooners or torch singers (usually as both), including: Scrappy Lambert, Seger Ellis, Austin "Skin" Young, Ruth Etting, Vaughn De Leath, Helen Morgan, Fanny Brice, Connie Boswell, Jane Froman, Cliff Edwards, Chick Bullock, Mildred Bailey, and Lee Wiley.[69] The hot players of the day gave it a thorough airing, as the Jazz Age changed to the Swing Era, including: Jelly Roll Morton, Jimmy Noone, Sidney Bechet, Paul Whiteman, Fats Waller, Red Nichols, the Dorsey brothers, Henry Busse, Jimmie Lunceford, Glenn Miller, and Benny Goodman (both quartet and orchestra outfits). Later, players of Dixieland, bop, and modern jazz embraced it. And that is just the start.

At the end of 1936, one study showed "My Melancholy Baby" was the sixth most frequently broadcast old song, with 11,375 renditions on radio that year.[70] Gazing retroactively, Whitburn guesses that three waxings of the 1930s deserve to be charted: quintessential crooners Al Bowlly (1935) and Bing Crosby (1939); and Teddy Wilson's swing outfit, featuring one of Ella Fitzgerald's earliest recorded vocals (1936). The following decade, with the rankings of *Billboard* now in place, saw Sam Donahue's big band version climb to number 5 in 1947—slow and harmonically lush. In 1959 Tommy Edwards got to number 26 with a ballad treatment tinged with rock and roll. In 1962 the Marcels made it their final charting hit, number 58, with a doo-wop treatment very much along the lines of their famous "Blue Moon" arrangement. Indeed, Whitburn credits "My Melancholy Baby" as the only song to have singles that charted in six consecutive decades.[71]

Albums got named after "My Melancholy Baby." In 1957 Matt Dennis put out *Play Melancholy Baby*, which *Billboard* judged as "a tasteful package of torch tunes, spotlighting twelve cry-in-your-martini type selections."[72] That year, too, Della Reese explored some of the same material in her debut album, *Melancholy Baby*. And 1959 saw *Georgie Auld Plays for Melancholy Babies*.

The charted LPs that include "My Melancholy Baby" are too numerous to discuss in total—there were sixteen by the end of the century—but a few deserve mention for the trends they illustrate. Crazy Otto brought the melody into the same honky-tonk piano field that had furthered the album-era fame of "Bill Bailey" (in 1955, charting for twenty weeks, peaking at number 1). Mitch Miller put his stultifying hand on it for a sing-along version (in 1961, seventy-three weeks, peaking at number 5, going gold). In 1964 Dean Martin (thirty-one weeks, peak 15) and Barbra Streisand (seventy-four weeks, peak 5) both included it on albums that went gold—representatives of the dwindling bastions of classic pop on the charts, in the new freewheelin' age of Bob Dylan and his cohort. Michael Parks recorded it in 1970, in connection with television's *Then Came Bronson*, a peripatetic, pacifistic motorcycle adventure series that spawned Parks's hit single theme song and two albums—bringing the tune into the world of late-1960s existential angst. (Parks's album with "Melancholy Baby" charted twenty-one weeks, peaking at 24.)

The preeminent place of "My Melancholy Baby" in American culture, however, was as a tune to be requested by drunks—particularly men. Perhaps this was a result of its association with Lyman, who, despite (a little bit of) vaudeville touring, (one) phono record, and (two relatively brief) stints on radio, was first, last, and finally the preeminent table-visiting nightclub singer, circling between New York and Paris and a few other favored hotspots of night life. As that 1927 *Variety* review attests, even before the song was a hit in early 1928, it had already attained its status as *the* song for men to listen to while missing their women. Secondarily, "Melancholy Baby" was also a song for men to sing together in comradely drunkenness (overlapping in this role with the previous champ, "Sweet Adeline").[73]

But primarily it became the most clichéd saloon request song. Bricktop re-counted an "old show-business joke about the entertainer who spends hundreds of dollars to buy new material and orchestrations, goes out on the floor and sings his heart out, and, when he's just about to drop from exhaustion, hears somebody call out, 'sing "Melancholy Baby."'"[74] Such was one's inevitable fate, playing at bars and in clubs.

When Dave McKenna undertook to do an album of "barroom songs," Hank O'Neal in the liner notes reports: "His idea was to play tunes he often played in some of the saloons in which he worked during his career; the kind of songs a drunk might stagger up and suggest he play, or one he might play when he was in a similar condition. Appropriately enough, he begins with 'My Melancholy Baby.'"[75] Major singing careers grew out of the public's demand for the instrumentalists to "Sing 'Melancholy Baby'!"—such was the case in the early 1930s for Tony Martin (dance band clarinetist) and in the early 1950s for Shirley Horn (classical pianist *qua* saloon ivory tickler).[76] This insistence continued even in the 1970s, when future journalist Mitch Albom played "in a dive bar where I was told by the owner that if any customers wanted to sing, I had to play along with them, no matter how wasted they were." One night, "one guy kept boozily screaming at me to play 'Melancholy Baby.' So I did." Barely able to start singing it, the drunk suddenly turned on Albom, screaming, "That's not merrrllncurly berby!" The result, Albom reports: "The owner got mad at me"—which added injury to insult.[77]

Such traumas added up. "My Melancholy Baby" is a pretty, sweet song with its own magic, but unfortunately this kind of incessant and indiscriminate demand from audiences could lead musicians to hate it. In 1936, in an English pub, George Shearing had to play it "fifteen times a night and eventually be-came sick of the song."[78] In the early 1940s, future sociologist Howard Becker, working his way through college playing in bars, made it a policy to scuttle off "the stand quickly, before anybody could ask" for it.[79] Those born around 1930 (like Clint Eastwood) and 1940 (like Dr. John) reported nightmarish visions of being reduced by fate to playing "in some little club, somebody drunkenly asking me to play 'Melancholy Baby'" or "in a cocktail lounge . . . somebody putting a dollar in the jar and me saying 'Thank you, sir. Sure, I'll play "Melan-choly Baby" one more time.'"[80]

What did audiences seem to get out of the song? For some, it was just a good song. In other instances, it was a salve for sadness—or so it seemed. Thus, the idea of singing "My Melancholy Baby" became synonymous, for a while, with consoling a person while they suffered through a bad situation.[81]

ANALYSIS

I was trying to sing the first phrases of Mendelssohn's "Spring Song," but it kept turning into "My Melancholy Baby."[82] Have a look at the schematic outline of the two melodies, with Mendelssohn transposed to the same key as "Melancholy Baby." The first four tones are the same, and eight out of the first ten notes are the same.

Example 9.2. Comparison between: the first phrase of the "My Melancholy Baby" refrain; the first phrase of Felix Mendelssohn's "Spring Song" (transposed for comparison); and the second phrase of the "My Melancholy Baby" verse. The larger sized notes are the ones that are shared.

My Melancholy Baby, start of refrain:

Mendelssohn, Spring Song, start:

My Melancholy Baby, verse, second phrase:

Thus, the main melody of "My Melancholy Baby" is pretty much a steal from the famous instrumental "Spring Song," which was the common property of all pianists at the turn of the twentieth century—and well integrated into popular culture. For instance, in 1904 James O'Dea fit "modern words" to "Spring Song" for the Remick firm, and in 1909 Irving Berlin brought it into the ragtime era as the basis of his hit song, "That Mesmerizing Mendelssohn Tune."[83] The fact that the incipit of "Melancholy Baby" has this foundation in Mendelssohn diminishes somewhat the importance of the question of originality—and puts into perspective the debate about whether Burnett or Light composed the strain.

Nevertheless, what is true of Victor Herbert's use of the motif from Albéniz's "Córdoba" in "Kiss Me Again" also applies here: from the opening kernel, Burnett unfolds a very different development from that of his classical model. Even the first phrase is transformed through an ascent to the F and the repetition of the accidental (A natural), which in this context could be interpreted as a blue fifth. This, along with other accidentals in verse and refrain, help give Burnett's melodic arches a decidedly different flavor from Mendelssohn's—an American flavor.

The structure of "My Melancholy Baby" is familiar: the refrain has an ABAC form, and its lyric has the usual limerick couplet just before the end. The chorus is sixteen measures in the main arrangement and thirty-two measures in the "chorus in march time" version. Either way the tune feels substantial, eventful, complete—unlike some earlier sixteen-measure tunes like Cannon's "Ain't Dat a Shame" or Williams's "Some o' Dese Days." As with "Kiss Me Again," the lovely arch—Mendelssohn, modified—that defines the start of the song is another harbinger, this time in duple meter, of the rise-and-fall pattern of later enduring songs such as "At Last" and "Over the Rainbow."

It is important that, for years, "My Melancholy Baby" sheet music editions featured not one but *two* arrangements under one cover. Although the note values are the same, the meters (four-four versus two-four), the piano accompaniment, and the rhythmic feeling are all highly contrasting. (There is also one difference in the lyric. "Don't be blue" is replaced by "don't feel blue"—and one out of seven singers choose that alternative.) The first arrangement indicates, at the start of the verse, "Slow with feeling." Its chorus is attired with fermata marks at crucial points (in the earliest printings, two of them for the limerick couplet; the third edition adds two more, to the initial strain).

The second rendering, however, is as a march—and not a funeral march, but a lively one. No fermata here. As with the paratextual banner on the cover of "Some of These Days," these two arrangements in the sheet music of "Melancholy Baby" are like a printed signal to performers, implying "go ahead, change it."

Example 9.3. "My Melancholy Baby," excerpt of the "march time" arrangement.

The song seems to have two tendencies inherent within it: slow, introverted, and intimate; or fast, extroverted, and trumpeted out. Indeed, in the recordings, fully two out of five change speed during the rendition. Further, among those arrangements that maintain one tempo, there are an equal number slow, medium, and fast.

Like "I Wonder Who's Kissing Her Now," Burnett and Norton's opus is multivalent, revealed by these performance traditions—and also indicated by the piece's first reviews. In 1913 *Billboard* called it "plaintive," yet in seeming contradiction also judged the lyric "highly optimistic."[84] In 1913 the *Player* deemed it "full of good cheer," while in 1927 *Variety* described it as "sobbingly sentimental."[85]

A bellwether of the particular versatility that such standards would achieve is seen in the description *Billboard* gives it: a "love ditty, set to rag ballad music."[86] As Furia and Hamm both point out, songwriters were starting to combine the stylistic modes of the ragtime song and the love ballad, and "My Melancholy Baby" is a prime example.[87] *Billboard* is struggling to find a way to describe something new, and their review is a snapshot of this change in action.

To modern ears, the melody as printed does not seem particularly like ragtime, especially because its rhythms are so predictable. The majority of measures are a rigid parade of quarter notes, and only four bars feature any shift in note values. The quarter-note drill is alleviated mostly by the pairs of lengthy notes on "baby," "maybe," and "lining." The strict, one-note-per-beat rule contrasts with the fluidity of the "Spring Song" prototype—it's more snappy than Mendelssohn, but also a bit more square than ragtime.

Therefore, of course, performers alter the rhythms. Although about one out of seven performers will at some point articulate the melody with the even-note feeling of the printed text, they seemingly do so only in order to then emphasize the exhilarating freedom of later *not* doing so. Only one recording stays in the rhythmic straightjacket: Mitch Miller's sing-along version. The others freely change note values, swinging or lingering—or both. The most common tactic, used by both vocalists and instrumentalists, is to articulate the note values to match the conversational flow of the lyrics. One odd effect of this is that the melody becomes even more like Mendelssohn's "Spring Song." The first phrase usually comes out something like this:

Example 9.4. A common performer's rhythmic rephrasing of the start of the "My Melancholy Baby" refrain.

Come_____ to me, my mel - an -chol - y ba - by

The verse is a particularly good one (despite the false rhyme of its ending couplet: "time" and "mine"). It is the most often-used verse discussed in this book: one out of three renditions include it.[88] Like the refrain, it is a sixteen-measure ABAC format. It starts off with a swinging bluesy riff, and each section ends with a little chromatic slide. Its second phrase has a certain relationship with the first phrase of the refrain—six out of its eight notes are the same—and acts as a foreshadowing of the upcoming chorus (see musical example 9.2). Similarly, the four upwardly moving chromatic notes in the last section of the verse are repeated in the penultimate phrase of the refrain. All these factors, strong and appealing in themselves, help make the song musically coherent. Surely this must be one reason why so many performers—even instrumental-ists—incorporate the verse.

Burnett's refrain melody for "My Melancholy Baby" holds special virtues. James R. Morris points out the similarities of the first three sections. He finds its "appeal is in its symmetry," with "the first phrase rising and falling" answered by the second phase "falling and rising."[89] This satisfying antecedent-consequent pattern is almost conversational, like a statement and afterthought. Morris's observation could be extended further: the B section mostly imitates the A section, but down one step—and that sequencing creates an additional, larger-scaled statement-and-afterthought pattern.

Alec Wilder lingers on the tune at greater length than Morris, but was limited in exploring its details because he was not given permission to reproduce musical passages from it. (It was not yet in public domain.) Nevertheless, Wilder gives it mild but definite praise: though it does not "rank with the great songs of later years" (fair enough, though it has held its own alongside them), "the melody is not only good" (Wilder had a keen ear for the singing line and probably admired the graceful way this one floats and flows), "containing highly unexpected phrases for that era" (I would guess he is thinking of the start of the verse, the refrain's incipit, and the first half of the C section), "but it also just might be the first torch song" (it was the first *labeled* as such, which is close to, if not quite, the same thing).[90]

Wilder, in his search for innovation, might go too far in crediting "My Melancholy Baby" with a startling uniqueness, stating "the writing is unlike that of any song of its period. . . . highly unusual for its time. . . . it's unlike any other melody."[91] Actually, it *is* like one other melody—"Spring Song."[92] Further, I don't think anybody in 1912 would have thought it much different from any number of contemporaneous "rag ballads," for instance, "I'm the Lonesomest Gal in Town."

A quick sidelight here on "I'm the Lonesomest Gal in Town" (1912), by Albert Von Tilzer and Lew Brown: it was a mild hit in 1913, again in 1940, again in 1949, and was later brushed off for a few album sets, but somehow never attained more than semi-standard status (if that). Yet it is a worthy song. Like Burnett, Von Tilzer creates an opening arch, sprinkling his tune with accidentals and short chromatic passages. Further, to his credit, Von Tilzer spells out his rhythms in a looser fashion than Burnett. Brown's lyric is also relaxed, colloquial—lamenting but humorous, a subtle combination that era was adept at. Certainly, the piece lacks the fascinating ambiguity of "My Melancholy Baby," the capacity to both romp and caress. Yet, though not a match for Bennett and Norton's number, it is also certainly in the same ballpark.

Example 9.5. "I'm the Lonesomest Gal in Town," start of the refrain, melody line.

Again, to counter Wilder's "unlike any other melody" opinion: once "My Melancholy Baby" finally became a definite hit, a couple of songs seem to imitate Burnett's original. One was a 1928 maiden effort from Kay Kyser and "Saxie" Dowell, "Tell Her (You Really Love Her)." It rises and falls in the same smooth way and settles on some of the same pitches as Burnett's tune. Another was a 1929 ditty composed by Lou Handman, "Melancholy," in which the initial strain resembles the first six notes of Burnett's tune. It is as if the beautiful arch of "Melancholy Baby" had been cut nearly in half. Even considering the narrow constraints of the Tin Pan Alley formula, these pieces can be said to display a resemblance to the Burnett composition, probably indicating the influence of its melody.

In his lyric, Norton borrowed the title, the concept, the rhyme scheme, various ideas, and a few words from Watson. Comparing the two lyrics, each has its own strengths. The following discussion will concentrate on Norton's lyric, but with occasional reference to Watson's. Norton's has a more professional feel about it—one more reason that makes it probable Watson's came first.

Norton combines two conventions that are exemplified in other well-remembered songs. From "spooning songs" such as "How'd You Like to Spoon with Me" (1905), "Put Your Arms Around Me, Honey" (1911), and most especially "Cuddle Up a Little Closer, Lovey Mine" (1908), Norton took the refrain's opening gestures, "Come to me . . . Cuddle up." Norton also draws on forebears like "Keep on the Sunny Side" (1899; a religious song somewhat secularized by the Carter family in 1928, coincidentally at the same moment "Melancholy Baby" was at the forefront) and, especially, "Wait Till the Sun Shines, Nellie" (1905; in which the title sentiment is literalized in the rainy day of the verses, but ambiguously metaphoric in the refrain). From these, Norton extracts what the *Player* called in 1913 "good philosophic advice." Within a decade, Norton's passing thought that "Ev'ry cloud must have a silver lining / Wait until the sun shines through" would dominate one of the monumental hits of the era, "Look for the Silver Lining" (1921). That, in turn, forecast decades of successful "cheer up" ballads.

By incorporating both physical intimacy and optimistic philosophy, wooing and therapy, Norton endows the situation with multiple dimensions. The two threads entwine at the end: "Smile, my honey dear, / While I kiss away each tear." This basic premise of blending courtship and comfort is an intensification of the central concept of "Wait Till the Sun Shines, Nellie." Watson's contribution lies in adding to these ingredients the further one of empathy, of reciprocal emotions, encapsulated in the refrain's final line; and Norton further intensifies these elements. The lyric is less about exploring one's own inner life and more about tuning into the inner life of someone else.

The sticking point of "My Melancholy Baby" for singers is the way the word "melancholy" lays awkwardly on its musical phrase (particularly the high note, F)—it is hard to get through that four-syllable word on those notes. About three in ten singers break there, sometimes subtly but often obviously. This tendency is satirized by Sheila K. Adams in her comic stage play, *Melancholy Baby*: eleven year-old Jane aspires to perform in nightclubs, featuring a number "about a dog like Lassie . . . (She sings) Come to me my mellon collie baby."[93] Willy-nilly, it becomes a song about a collie or a melon.[94] By contrast, Watson's first line sings more easily than Norton's. Although Watson starts weakly on "Oh," an empty word (albeit one that creates an internal rhyme with "so"), her "awf'lly" is a better fit for Burnett's two high notes.

Pitfalls of phrasing notwithstanding, Norton's first lines display his brilliance. The imperatives, "come to me" and "cuddle up," immediately thrust us into dramatic action. It commands—like "Kiss Me Again," "Cuddle Up a Little Closer," "Let Me Call You Sweetheart," and "Put Your Arms Around Me, Honey." The forcefulness of Norton's imperatives are muted by the immediate references to "melancholy" and "blue." In his study of early blues, Muir calls "My Melancholy Baby" "bluesy," partly because of the personal nature of the lyric and the slow tempo, but particularly for this atmosphere saturated with the presence of depression, of the blues.[95]

Norton's addition of "baby" is crucial. Through it, the love for a child becomes all mixed up with the love for a romantic partner: cuddling is comforting—cuddling is amorous. The refrain is sufficiently vague in this matter, allowing Gladys George convincingly to croon the song to her newborn in *A Child Is Born* (1939), and Crosby to do similarly to a six-year-old in *Birth of the Blues* (1941) (see figure 1.7).[96]

Such scenarios may seem like pure Hollywood, but they did occur in reality. In March 2018, a college student in Brooklyn interviewed a woman, born in 1922, whom we shall call Annie. The student reports: "She recalls her favorite song that her daddy would sing to her, and as she sung it to me she cried, and I cried, it was just beautiful." What was it that so affected these two women, generations apart? "The song her daddy would sing to her was, 'Mellon Collen Baby.'"[97] The power of "My Melancholy Baby" is not limited to saloons but also can be deeply moving in the nursery, in the home. Annie would have been about six years old when it became widely popular—the same age as the little girl that Crosby sings to, on screen. In that context, the altered 1927 lyric, "I'm in love with you," conveys the sort of reassurance that children often need, of being beloved.

Nevertheless, "My Melancholy Baby" is primarily a romantic love song—perhaps the earliest enduring, truly jazzy ballad about what seems to be a strong, healthy love relationship. The first verse quickly establishes the romantic modality, with the (slightly stilted) endearment "sweetheart mine." The lyric's (rather redundant) "hon," "dear," and "honey dear" reinforce the romantic point. With the title word "baby," the lyric quickly establishes itself as a quintessential example of treating the beloved as an infant. (In 1916 audiences would embrace another prime example, "Pretty Baby"—yet another wonderful and enduring song. In its playfulness, "Pretty Baby" is less conducive to hushed intimacy—though a singer like Doris Day can bring out that potential in it.)

The refrain's first lines, too, establish Norton's well-crafted internal rhymes (m*e*, melanchol*y*, bab*y*) and repetition of sounds—for instance, *c*, *m*, *b*, and *d*: "*Come* to *me*, *my m*elancholy *baby*, / *Cuddle* up and *don't be* blue." The most easily noticed alliteration is in the next section: the triple *f* in "*f*ears are *f*oolish *f*ancy." Throughout, Norton fills his lyric with subtly chiming words: *baby, wait, away; sun, honey; shines, shall;* and so forth. Indeed, in Watson's title word "melancholy" there is a built-in off-rhyme, the consonance of *el* and *ol* which Norton follows up on with *il, ile, al—silver, until, smile, while, shall—*and reverses with *lining.* The final section is an orgy of *i* and *e* sounds: sm*i*le m*y*, wh*i*le *I*; hon*ey*, d*ea*r, *ea*ch, t*ea*r, b*e*, m*e*lancholy.[98] As E. Y. "Yip" Harburg noted about the craft of Tin Pan Alley, such "tricks . . . make a song memorable."[99] They do not obtrude, but nevertheless satisfy.

"My Melancholy Baby" displays tenderness. So did "Kiss Me Again" and "Let Me Call You Sweetheart," but those were waltzes, and that distinction is important. In "Melancholy Baby," the intimate expression is poured into the mode of a jazzy one-step, two-step, fox trot–friendly duple meter. In the end, the protagonist and the beloved are physically intimate ("I kiss away each tear" is practically a stage direction, with a fermata to allow time for the kiss) and also emotionally intimate ("Or else I shall be melancholy, too").

For sixteen years the exact fame of "My Melancholy Baby" is uncertain; therefore it is hard to point at the influence of the Norton-Watson scenario on other songs. The 1915 hit "Sympathy," from the operetta *The Firefly*, is not a close parallel (a man offers a woman sympathy, but as a strategy to steal her from her fiancée). In 1925 "Brown Eyes, Why Are You Blue?" was a hit, conveying a similar tender cheering up. (Was it shaped by an insider's knowledge of "Melancholy Baby"? And did its success in 1926 pave the way for the 1927 revival of the older tune? We can only speculate.) By the mid-thirties, foreknowledge of "Melancholy Baby" can be assumed; and by then, when "Weep No More, My Baby" (1933) and "Don't Be That Way" (1935) combine romance with reassuring philosophy, they perhaps reveal the influence of Norton. In "Shoo, Shoo Baby" (1943), a World War II soldier consoles his girl as they part—again, as a mother would soothe a child.[100] Yet, all together, the mood and dramatic situation of "My Melancholy Baby" is not closely matched by prominent successors.[101] (This contrasts with long line of lyrics that can be traced forward from "Bill Bailey," "Kiss Me Again," "I Wonder Who's Kissing Her Now," and "I'm Sorry I Made You Cry.")

INTERPRETING THE RECORDINGS

I began to divide versions of "My Melancholy Baby" into three categories. Some evoke a private, even domestic setting. Some have a late-night, after-hours nightclub atmosphere. Some invite a "Whee! Let's party!" response. Such a strict classification does not quite hold water, for there are overlappings and mavericks, but to an extent it helps to make some order out of an embarrassment of riches—for "Melancholy Baby" is probably the most recorded among my focus songs. This tripartite schema also points to the tradition of the piece as a doleful inebriate's request item plus the twin modes of the early sheet music editions—"slow with feeling" versus the lively "chorus in march time" (though performers soon shifted it to "swing time").

Burnett himself, at the piano in the 1940 ASCAP concert, Carousel of Music, presents a straightforward medium-tempo reading. His solo verse is slightly florid but full of life. The orchestra joins him, as he renders the refrain with subtle hesitations and variations. His playing hints of rag, hints of swing, hints of cocktail piano. He is still creative with the tune—for him, it has not grown stale.

In many ways, the interpreters of "My Melancholy Baby" basically agree with each other. While a refrain like "Some of These Days" is open to interpretation—what is the story? what are the emotions?—it is not easy to see in "My Melancholy Baby" that kind of ambivalence or wide range of contradictory feelings and scenarios. Among the recordings, there is a general avoidance of sexiness, anger, irony, paranoia, or kinkiness.

Lacking, too, is parody as such. Even when performers place a frame around it that makes fun of its "drunken request" tradition, they still treat "My Melancholy Baby" itself with respect. This is embodied in the way the song is used in *A Star Is Born* (1954). Judy Garland plays Vicki Lester, who becomes a star by appearing in a movie showing a singer's struggle for success. In the show-in-the-flashback-in-the-film-in-the-film, Garland sings in a cheap club, then in a mid-level club. In both, drunks interrupt her, demanding "Sing 'Melancholy Baby,'" until she is able to predict just when it is coming—a comic recurrence (see figures 9.3 and 9.4). When she actually does sing "My Melancholy Baby," however, she does so in the kind of place she dreamed about, "a famous, fashionable café" (see figure 9.5). Although led up to with humor, the song rendition itself becomes a quiet, almost reverent moment of sincerity.

Two 1957 album renditions achieve the same effect. Matt Dennis, on the aforementioned *Play Melancholy Baby*, writes a special material introduction: "When the crowd thins down, and the hour gets late / And the customers are cryin' in their beer," they ask for "Body and Soul" (1929) and Dennis's own "Angel Eyes" (1944)—and "you can bet someone's gonna yell, 'Play Melancholy Baby.'" Dennis resignedly says "Sure I will." Despite his implied criticism of the request, however, Dennis then launches into a magical after-hours rendition, with rhythm section and captivating muted trumpet fills.

The Hi-Los, on their charting LP *Now Hear This*, start with crowd sounds—laughter, chit-chat, shouting—and one male voice emerges demanding "Melancholy Baby." Soloist Clark Boroughs answers (rather unctuously), "Why, thank you. We'd be glad to." Despite this jokey opening, the quartet's rendition is quiet—indeed, rather sappy (with an unnecessary chorus added to the full orchestration), albeit probably great for smooching.

The Marcels may have had the Hi-Los in mind (these male quartets tended to lend an attentive ear to each other's work) when they created their highly intertextual 1962 doo-wop single of "My Melancholy Baby." It starts with the famous vocal riff from their previous hit, "Blue Moon," before a male voice interrupts: "Nah, not that thing again. Sing 'Melancholy Baby.'" The quartet eagerly chime, "All right, then, we will!" The bass then sings irresistible vocal riffs; the other members chant "Come to me, melancholy baby" periodically; and the soloist delivers a fine vocal in the song's rock and roll tradition (more on that later). At the end of the refrain, the voice again intrudes, "Gee, that's pretty. Sing it again." The bass then takes a half-spoken solo which is clearly an allusion to the bass solos that another quartet, the Ink Spots, had featured so memorably in the forties. Then the lead soloist, in full career, unleashes "Whoa-oh, yes, smile . . ." The whole is danceable and playful. This is as close as anybody gets to making fun of the song—and, even here, the lead vocal is a straightforward (albeit 1962-styled) presentation of the piece.

This relative restraint in the performance tradition of "My Melancholy Baby" runs parallel to the simple elements of the lyric: courtship, sympathy, and philosophy as comfort-giving. There may be a hint of potentially impatient or harsh emotions: possible guilt in the first verse ("What have I done? Have I ever said an unkind word to you?"); exasperation in the command "answer me"; the admonishments "your fears are foolish fancy" or "you know"; and the near-threat "or else." Yet, these are all immediately qualified by softer phrases like "hon," "maybe," "dear," and "I shall be melancholy, too." Essentially, every interpreter agrees this is a slow, tender song or a sprightly, fun song—or both.

The first generations to record "My Melancholy Baby" convey a special kind of gentle friendliness and sweetness. Walter Van Brunt in 1915 is resonant, a bit loud for the lyrics, yet enjoyable. Although he follows the sheet music faithfully, he manages to make the composition's quarter-note parade not overly rigid. In a rare instance, he is given the chance to assay both verses. Of course, by later standards, his rhythmic feel is rather straight-laced, but even with that approach the riff-like verse manages to have some swing to it. The long fermata on the penultimate couplet is enhanced with a spell-casting shimmer of strings and harp.

Tommy Lyman never recorded "My Melancholy Baby," so Gene Austin's 1927 disc takes pride of place, defining the era's new microphone crooning, evoking an intimate personal setting for this ballad. As most of his work in these years, Austin is working high in his range; his reedy voice has just a slightly rough nap, infused here with a hint of breathiness. The simple piano and two strings accompanying him help create an intimate mood. Quietly, with clear diction and just a hint of jazziness on "li-i-ining," he creates the atmosphere of a private interlude between two lovers.

The spareness and simplicity of the accompaniment set a precedent followed many times, by Scrappy Lambert, Freddie Rose, Chick Bullock, Bing Crosby, Cliff Edwards in the 78 era; Al Bowlly and Judy Garland on film; Matt Dennis, Woody Herman, Buddy Rich (in a rare vocal from this famed drummer), and Michael Parks on LP; and in parts of the renditions of Kate Smith and Della Reese.

Many performers beautifully evoke a private setting for "My Melancholy Baby"—I will focus on three. First, Bing Crosby, in 1939, gives a very restrained, quiet, spare, beautifully modulated performance, supported at first just by solo guitar. The tempo quickens for his second refrain (almost one of out ten arrangements do this), and a discreet horn is added. The three gently swing. As always, Crosby's phrasing is superbly conversational. In the first refrain he is emotionally detached, but his second refrain is better: freer, softer, even more conversational and closely focused. On the "silver lining" lyric, he varies the melody, climbing up and dropping down to one of his relaxed basso notes. Crosby can also be heard doing "Melancholy Baby" in film and radio versions of *Birth of the Blues* (he never uses the verse), all different, yet in the same hushed, relaxed mode.

Second, Cliff Edwards recorded "My Melancholy Baby" three times for radio play: one performance is lame and two are superb (probably this pair is from 1943, for the MacGregor transcription service). They are the same arrangement, both with solo guitar (presumably played by Edwards himself); in one he sings an entire second refrain, in the other he only repeats half the refrain. He includes the verse, for which he uses some of the same inflections he later would use parodically in the verse for "I'm Sorry I Made You Cry," but, strangely, here they sound sincere. Like Crosby and others, he shifts to a faster tempo after the first refrain. Phrasing even better than Crosby, slightly husky and breathy, hushed, Edwards probably comes closest of any singer to conjuring up this intimate scenario. His voice both calms and pleads, somehow simultaneously, with an occasional slight sob in the voice, as on "don't be blue." He creates neat melodic variants on certain phrases ("all your fears," "while I kiss away"). Particularly fine is the extra breathiness behind those most personal phrases that end the verse ("something seems to grip this very heart of mine") and refrain ("or else I shall be melancholy, too")—which points to how those two concluding lines create a satisfying parallel.

Third, Frank Sinatra leaves at least three records of "My Melancholy Baby." In band vocalist mode, as part of a medley during a Tommy Dorsey broadcast, he gives a typically fine, smooth early performance. His 1945 studio recording is disappointing: he renders the whole song very, very slowly, accompanied by a sappy string-heavy arrangement (yet with a few rich, subtle harmonies from a horn). Like Crosby, he omits the verse. He gives a consistent performance, with some lovely, viola-like long notes, and lends "kiss away each tear" a touch of humorous indulgent affection. Nevertheless, he does not really capture the atmosphere of the piece. On a radio broadcast, however, the same arrangement that bored on disc now has life (even though the audio quality is muddier). Sinatra is more closely focused, evoking the story of the lyric more convincingly. The tenderness which he brings to "I'm in love with you" and the way he modulates his volume to be more quiet in the middle of a phrase, such as on "each tear," delves right to the heart of the song.

The line is thin between those intimate performances and the category I created of "late-night, after-hours"—perhaps the chief difference is more instruments, and often more jazz flavor. Indeed, some of these renditions are purely instrumental. George Rhodes's slightly pointed, jagged piano contrasts with mellow trumpet solo, to create a relaxed, medium slow, gently swinging rendering. Sam Donahue's hit 1947 arrangement is extraordinary—also medium slow, and lush, creamy, full of subtle touches. Donahue's version is restrained and harmonically rich. It seems to linger on the borders of the cool jazz style that was about to be explored.

Virtues abound in the array of other after-hours renditions—again, I will just linger on three. In 1942 Kate Smith follows the typical pattern: slow, *ad libitum* ritardando verse, into a slow, steady tempo for the first refrain (with a very spare accompaniment), then the orchestra rises forth and the tempo brightens for an additional half refrain. Her combination of velvety nap and straightforward directness, her climactic melodic variant—all makes for a fine rendition.

In 1957 Lee Wiley, her voice sounding a little tired at first, but, as usual, sexy and smiling, creates some magical moments through her shifts of tempo (with Billy Butterfield leading the accompaniment). She also does the verse slowly, *ad libitum*, with celeste alone under her, supplying delicate fill-ins. Then on "this very heart of mine," bang! The rhythm section enters in steady tempo, the speed increases. The surprise placement of this shift—not *after* but *during* the final verse phrase—seems to expand the amplitude of the music's flow. It is like a big breath in. At the track's conclusion, she slows down for the final stanza (another typical strategy), but on her last note, the band goes back into tempo to swing out a brief tag—lovely.

In 1962 Joni James and leader Jimmy Haskell create a jazz club atmosphere via a gently swinging slow groove, leaving plenty of space for the piano and clarinet to do interesting things. James displays her freedom of phrasing in the way she handles the "silver lining" line two different ways: the first, rushing through "must have" and lingering on "lining": the second, making the whole line soar, with still enough breath to add a unique "baby" on the end of the phrase. It is not convincing dramatically, yet certainly evokes a late-night atmosphere.

The jolly-party renditions commence with a large number of highly danceable jazz and swing era versions. In 1928 Red Nichols, leading essentially his Five Pennies under the moniker of the Charleston Chasers, swings hard in a fast tempo, featuring at first the counterpoint typical of early jazz, and then some solos, over a hustling rhythm section, with a competent vocal by Scrappy Lambert, and marvelous solo and duo breaks. The Benny Goodman Quartet's 1936 medium-tempo recording is a classic: finely balanced swing and, in Lionel Hampton's cascading solos, perhaps a bit more than that. Teddy Wilson's solo with Goodman is modest, but on his recording earlier in the year under his own leadership he jumps more infectiously. On Wilson's disc, Ella Fitzgerald is still a bit uninflected in her vocal, perhaps naïve (it is only her sixth recorded tune)—but already swinging like mad. Mildred Bailey, with the big band of her then-husband Red Norvo, manages to be huskily intimate in the verse and swinging in the refrains. Like Sinatra she imbues the "kiss away each tear" line with an amused tolerance. Earl Hines, Fats Waller, and the Jimmie Lunceford Orchestra all created enchanting swing era discs of "Melancholy Baby." Of two takes by Sidney Bechet, in Paris, the faster one is rollicking, danceable. A merry coordination of Bechet's saxophone with the drums in the verse, used as a middle interlude, is soon followed by an easy, rolling, swinging climactic finale.

The rock and roll era brought a wave of excellent party renditions of "My Melancholy Baby," in addition to the Marcels' semi-humorous hit. Tommy Edwards got a lush strings-and-chorus setting for his 1959 Top 40 single. Medium slow in tempo, but brought into the era with rhythmic broken phrasing ("Wait. Until the sun. Shines through.") and rock triplets—echoing Connie Francis's hit revivals of old songs—it was, without doubt, a great slow dance. Tommy Mosley's 1961 rendition is similar (lush orchestra, chorus) but was never a hit. Nevertheless, it is more creative: a tricky syncopated rhythm; holding back the rock triplets until the instrumental interlude; with conversational yet line-spanning phrasing from Mosley. Most infectiously joyful of all, however, is Damita Jo, in 1963. This single hybridizes cha-cha-cha with rock and roll. The instrumental interlude, with flute over hand clapping, is unexpectedly and delightfully spare. Damita Jo's hard-rocking vocal echoes the inflections of Dinah Washington, at times, but builds its own fervor. She starts with gripping pick-up notes "Oh, ye-es, come to me" and builds to a coda repeating the final stanza, "Yeah, yeah, yeah, smile, my honey dear, / I'm gonna kiss, kiss away each tear." You gotta smile.

Della Reese, in 1956, combines the late-night and party approaches in a manner that exemplifies the song's slow-fast, soothing-rollicking duality. No verse—she starts out with a slow, out-of-tempo refrain. Under her vocal, a celeste alternates with a lush orchestra. Her phrasing is a bit belabored, breaking up lines without creating any compelling rhythmic effect—"You know, dear. That I'm. In love. With you"—yet she does sustain the intimate mood. On her last note, the orchestra kicks in loud, and Reese starts her second refrain by shouting "Come here!" This second refrain—now in tempo, medium fast—is highly satisfying. It also brings out a rare nuance to the song—the authority of the protagonist is emphasized. Nobody would dare disobey!

Some facets of various renditions deserve mention. "My Melancholy Baby" has attracted the creative improvisations of generations of post-swing jazz players, such as Lee Konitz, Sonny Rollins, Sonny Stitt, Lenny Tristano, Thelonious Monk, and Harry Pickens—a corpus ripe for some future analyst. By contrast with their restless elaborations, Perry Como, on his 1957 album rendition, is so slow and soporific that, in a possibly inadvertent way, it works dramatically. He convincingly sounds like a guy in bed, trying to get his gal to settle down so he can sleep! In 1964, on her best-selling *Third Album*, Barbra Streisand uses (half of) the second verse, which had not been given much of an airing since 1928. (She wisely alters one line, to avoid Norton's awkward augmented rhyme of "cheer" with "tears." Dorothy Loudon, in 1991, uses both complete verses, and simply changes "tears" to "tear," which *almost* works.)[102] The Red Hot Reedwarmers, a twenty-first-century trad jazz band, does the verse in triple meter, as a waltz. It works rather well.

In 1928 Paul Whiteman got Tommy Satterfield to write a lengthy, complex orchestration of "My Melancholy Baby" that Columbia then released on a twelve-inch disc, with a vocal refrain by Austin "Skin" Young. The arrangement has some wonderful moments, including a Bix Beiderbecke trumpet solo. Nevertheless, with seven tempo changes and more textures than can be easily counted, it rather overwhelms this poor little "Baby." To modern ears, the most startling aspect is a figure in the violins during both the introduction and coda—a back-and-forth interval that Harold Arlen employed ten years later for the bridge and coda of "Over the Rainbow." Arlen, who in 1928 was deeply involved in the same world of white jazz as Whiteman, was presumably familiar with the Whiteman recording. This may well have been playing somewhere in the background of his inner ear while he was composing the classic ballad for that melancholy youngster, Dorothy, in *The Wizard of Oz.*

One prevalent performance tradition is the change of "foolish fancy" to "foolish fancies" by four out of ten singers. (This variant eventually influenced the print tradition, appearing in three editions from the mid-1980s onward.)[103] I have a sneaking suspicion that the alteration to "fancies" starts with Benny Fields, who became one of the major figures in the history of "My Melancholy Baby." He always sang "foolish fancies"—and just about the time he began to use the number in the late 1930s, others also start to sing "fancies."[104]

Who was Benny Fields? From 1917 he was the stage partner (actually, more like second fiddle) to Blossom Seeley, one of the great rhythm singers of her era. Pretty early on, the two married. Seeley always refused to work in nightclubs, favoring vaudeville (and, to an extent, Broadway, recordings, and eventually films).[105] In mid-1935, Seeley semi-retired, and Fields set out on a new path as a solo act in intimate nightclubs.[106] And here comes another . . .

Claim: In mid-1936, Fields began to brag about his early adoption of "My Melancholy Baby." He averred that Paul Whiteman revived the tune in 1926, that Fields "was one of those who helped zoom its sales" at that time, and that in the mid-thirties, "it helped Benny . . . in his recent and much discussed conquest" of nightclubs.[107] In the spring of 1937, Fields recorded the song. By 1940 "Melancholy Baby" was the biggest song in his act.[108] By 1942, it was his theme song.[109] He sang it in movies, he recorded it again in the fifties, and it was mentioned in his obituaries.[110]

Did Fields sing "My Melancholy Baby" during the crucial 1926 period? Probably not, as parts of his story seem false. If Whiteman had such an influential

Figure 9.6. *Minstrel Man* (1944). In a nightclub, Benny Fields segues straight from a traditional blues stanza into "My Melancholy Baby." The camera peeks over the shoulders of a nearby couple, to whom he intimately croons.

arrangement of "My Melancholy Baby" in his bandbooks in 1926, he would not have delayed recording it until mid-1928, when the disc market was glutted with the renditions by Gene Austin and many others. Further, no reviewers of Seeley and Fields in *Variety* or *Billboard* from 1925 through 1928 mention "My Melancholy Baby." In fact, they make it clear that either Fields did not get any solo song or, if he did, it was a comedy song. Ballads in the act were the property of Seeley. When talking pictures came, it was she, not he, who sang "Melancholy Baby" on screen, in *Blood Money* (1933).

Fields's false claim, however, does not detract from the quality of his rendering of "My Melancholy Baby." He had a plush bass-baritone and a quiet, understated vocal delivery that often went along strangely with the showbiz, hammy quality in his physical mannerisms. Bricktop praised Benny Fields (one of her youthful beaus, in a mixed-race relationship that she seems to take for granted): he "became what many people called the first crooner. . . . He had a big and lazy kind of voice that was wonderful for the blues. . . . He was big and handsome, so gentle as a lamb. . . . He was something rare then—a fellow with perfect manners, especially when it came to women."[111] The ideal singer, it would seem, for the bluesy, gentle, courtly "Melancholy Baby." His renditions of the piece reveal that he was very free in his variations on both words and music. Even when delivering the song twice in the same film, *Minstrel Man* (1944), the two performances are different and distinct. Although his claim of being one of the first to promote the tune does not hold water, from the late thirties till his death in 1959, Fields was indelibly associated with "My Melancholy Baby."[112]

"My Melancholy Baby" has two moments that hold a dramatic potential rarely taken advantage of. One is at the start of the refrain. The command to "cuddle up" could signal an audible shift to a more intimate focus. At first the beloved is at a distance, then she comes and cuddles up, and the singing should reflect that change. But nobody does that. Pity.

There are a few singers, however, who do convey the action implied with "I kiss away each tear." (Bailey and Sinatra make it a moment of amused, almost teasing, affectionate tolerance, but they do not convey that they have bestowed a kiss.) Gene Austin *almost* creates that moment. The Hi-Los sing "kiss" twice, implying that the kiss has taken place between. Finally, Michael Parks does a particularly good job: "while I kiss," pause, "away," pause, "each tear." The moment of gentle soothing becomes vividly clear.

FILMS

Ruth Etting sings "My Melancholy Baby" in a short film, *Bye-Gones* (1933), in a flashback sequence set in 1898, told to her niece and nephew as a bedtime story about her youth. In a saloon during the Alaskan gold rush, she uses it to audition for a singing job. She puts sob into her voice on "melancholy" and "smile, my honey dear." By contrast, she smiles and rolls her eyes when singing "Cuddle up, cuddle up and don't be blue"—for once coming near to making something sexy out of that moment in the lyric. For her second refrain, a bit faster and freer, she descends from the stage and walks among the saloon customers. Four tough miners wipe tears from their eyes, and the ladies of low repute are mesmerized. She gets the job. The scene draws on and reinforces the status of "Melancholy Baby" as the ultimate saloon tearjerker.

The connotations of "My Melancholy Baby" manifest subtly in many of its movie appearances. The word "baby" in the song title often connects to stories that hinge around children. *East Side of Heaven* revolves around custody of a babe-in-arms. *Bye-Gones* is a tale told to little children. Benny Fields in *Minstrel Man* at first surrenders and later is refused custody of his newborn. The separation of father and daughter is the fulcrum of the plot, which only resolves when he rejoins his now teenaged offspring on the night she revives his old show on Broadway. In *Swing It, Soldier* (1941), Frances Langford is introduced at the start of the movie rendering "My Melancholy Baby" on the radio—a foreshadowing of the fact that the character is pregnant.

As in some recordings and *A Star Is Born*, movies often frame "My Melancholy Baby" with comedy—although the renditions themselves are not comical. But a couple of these films, revealingly, follow that humor with scenes of one person sincerely comforting another. Such intimate moments occur between sisters in a low-budget Western, *The Arizona Raiders* (1936), and spouses in a gangster comedy *A Slight Case of Murder* (1938).

By contrast, in *The Roaring Twenties* (1939), "My Melancholy Baby" both plays a larger role in the film's fabric and, in two instances, is quickly followed by scenes of violence. First it is heard under the opening credits as one of several 1920s songs. Later it appears again in a scene set in 1922: the train ride home from the first date of bootlegger Jimmy Cagney (ironically, a teetotaler) and chorus girl Priscilla Lane. We get to hear her sing the final stanza a cappella—evidence of her singing talent. Cagney gets her an audition for the nightclub in which he has a concern: now we hear her sing a full refrain. Another forty-five minutes in—she has entangled herself in a love triangle, and he has entangled himself in a gang war—and she sings it at the club, with a shortened verse. While she is in the middle of her second refrain, a violent fistfight breaks out. "Melancholy Baby," a song of tender gentleness, if contrasted with brutality.

Time goes by, and at the moment Cagney learns that Lane has betrayed his affections, the bar pianist is playing "My Melancholy Baby"—and the bootlegger goes and punches his rival. After this, Cagney takes to drink; and then the stock market crash ruins him. He hits the skids and eventually goes back to his old cab driving job. When Lane comes to him, pleading with him to fend off his old gangster cronies from killing her husband, Cagney refuses. But then he hears yet another bar pianist play "Melancholy Baby." He smirks ruefully, recognizing his fate, and walks into the final bloodbath, killing the gangster who threatened Lane's happiness, and in turn getting killed. Along the way, his friends and enemies both tell him he is "still carrying a torch for that dame" and "trying to drown that torch you're carrying for her." The frequent utilization of "Melancholy Baby" in the film—rather than some other period hit—seems calculated to saturate the storyline with the important role that the failed love affair, the carrying of the torch, plays in Cagney's downfall. In this tragic melodrama, there is no humor juxtaposed against the songs, unlike many other incorporations of the tune in Hollywood screenplays.

Crosby's rendering of "My Melancholy Baby" in *Birth of the Blues* (1941) has already been touched on (see figure 1.7). It, too, is followed by a fistfight (one that ends amicably, however) and then escalating violence as the jazz-playing protagonists conflict with the strong-arm tactics of the restaurateur they have been working for in New Orleans, circa 1915. Again, this tender song—even more gentle than usual, because crooned to a young child—is followed by climactic dangers. (But, happily, the musicians escape to Chicago.)

Norton's lyric seems to pay tribute to earlier songs, perhaps particularly "Cuddle Up a Little Closer" and "Wait Till the Sun Shines, Nellie"—and all three tunes appear in *Birth of the Blues* in quick succession: "Cuddle" and "Wait" seem to combine and culminate in "My Melancholy Baby." The romance between Crosby and his co-star Mary Martin is frustrated by the fact that neither will actually say "I love you" to the other. Therefore, their love songs are directed at surrogates. She sings "Cuddle" as an audition before a group of men (not Crosby) and a couple of women; her second refrain is particularly steamy, as she focuses her gaze intently, her hand delicately touching her chin as if it were a fan used flirtatiously. She can behave this way, in performance, for others—but not in private, not in an intimate setting, not to Crosby himself.

Here comes (another) quick sidenote, this time deserved by "Cuddle Up a Little Closer, Lovey Mine." Its composer, Karl Hoschna, wrote two enduring melodies, this and "Every Little Movement"—both short songs, of unusual structure, demonstrating an idiosyncratic melodic sinuosity. Unfortunately, the talented Hoschna died young. "Cuddle" enjoyed a revival in Hollywood musicals such as *Birth of the Blues* and two Betty Grable movies, *Coney Island* (1943) and *Four Jills and a Jeep* (1945), which spurred some 1940s discs that were briefly successful and some album tracks later in the century. It is a well-remembered favorite for singers and nostalgia settings, yet never accumulated the wide-ranging performance tradition of my focus songs. Nevertheless, its sensuousness, intimate refrain lyric, plus capacity to be crooned, as Martin and Grable seductively demonstrate, combine to give it a certain historical and aesthetic importance in the history of early Golden Age ballads.[113]

Martin's audition is successful, and she gets Crosby's band hired along with her. She then sets out to learn to sing "blue music" "like the colored folk." With the help of the Black janitor and her two jazz musician friends, she succeeds in acquiring the syncopated feeling. Martin demonstrates this in a duet with Crosby on the bandstand, through a jazzed-up version of "Wait Till the Sun Shines, Nellie." At the post-debut celebration, on the rooftop of the boarding house, Crosby sees that Martin's young relative, Phoebe, is ready to sleep. He carries her to bed, in a series of tracking shots, the lights low-key, as he and the guitarist mellowly spin out "My Melancholy Baby." It is one of the most intensely domestic settings for the song. In *Birth of the Blues* as in *A Child Is Born*—both being titled after a birth—this "Baby" plays a crucial symbolic role.

As Alison McCracken writes, Crosby's love song has been displaced from Martin to, instead, a child associated with her. (Of course, Martin's love ballad also had a displaced object, from Crosby to a mostly male audience.) McCracken views this indirection as "undercutting his feminization and eroticization by making him more patriarchal and less of a sexual object."[114] Yet, from another point of view, his gentle child-caring seems very feminine. Immediately afterward, he gets into a fistfight with the fellow bandmate who is his friendly rival for Martin's attentions—as if, in compensation, he has to prove his manliness to the audience.

Figures 9.3, 9.4, and 9.5. *A Star Is Born* (1954). The new star, Vicki Lester (Judy Garland), appears in a movie in which her character strives up the showbiz ladder. In her first two nightclubs, a drunk interrupts her renditions of "Peanut Vendor" to demand, "Sing 'Melancholy Baby'!" In the third club, she actually does sing it, and, this time, everyone pays attention.

In *A Star Is Born*, the placing of "My Melancholy Baby" within an almost self-contained production number would seem to separate it from the main narrative. Nevertheless, it resonates with aspects of the storyline. The main plot starts at a benefit performance: Norman Maine (James Mason), an alcoholic movie star, interrupts the performance of Esther Blodgett (Judy Garland), but she manages to make it seem like part of the act. Later, he hears her sing a torch song, "The Man That Got Away," and realizes she is a great talent. Norman facilitates her movie contract and subsequent recording career. In her first starring film, under her new stage name Vicki Lester, she performs the "Born in a Trunk" sequence, with its penultimate section being the rendition of "My Melancholy Baby." After that, they marry—and her career rises as his falls: he cannot conquer his alcoholism and professional ennui.

In one of this tearjerker's most wrenching scenes, as Vicki says her "thank you" for receiving an Academy Award, Norman interrupts her, once again drunk. Norman's two inebriated interruptions of Vicki are echoed, comically, in the film-in-the-film scenes of the two inebriates who interrupt "The Peanut Vendor" with demands for "My Melancholy Baby." When the film-in-the-film heroine does sing that ballad, in the audience is the man who will give her a great career opportunity—just as Norman did, after he heard Esther/Vicki sing "The Man That Got Away." Again the situations echo each other. Film analyst Raymond Bellour calls this type of varied repetition *rhyme*, noting how it contributes powerfully to meaning in cinema.[115] Here it helps create parallels between song and life. In the end, Vicki becomes the "one man woman" of her first solo. Norman becomes the "melancholy baby": suckling at Dionysus's breast and needing to be taken care of like an infant. After tucking him into bed after his latest bender, Vicki determines to give up her career: "I'll be with him every moment." To prevent this, Norman commits suicide, which he successfully stages as a drowning accident. The main plotline reveals the ugly underside of the cliché about comic drunks in the "Melancholy Baby" mythos.

LITERATURE

There are so many uses of the phrase "melancholy baby" in literature—journalism, essays, novels, plays, poems, advertisements—that it is hard to realize that conjoining those two words was not common before 1927 when the song became famous. (Before that, babies might have been colicky but not melancholy.) These fall into one or several of various categories. The prevalence of texts about jazz musicians or jazz-lovers gives testament to the place of "My Melancholy Baby" in the genre's repertoire.[116] Pieces about hard luck, pity, and self-pity allude to the tradition of the song as an item requested by those who are down or as an offering to those who need solace, perhaps the most poignant being a study of how the lack of being loved in childhood can lead to depression as an adult.[117] There are powerful (or sometimes satiric) sagas about lost children, lost parents, or caring for orphans, including riveting searches for biological parents and meditations on miscarriages.[118] All these are saturated with a sense of yearning. The remarkable thing about these diverse (yet oddly interrelated) texts entitled *Melancholy Baby* is that very few of them actually mention the song. Its title phrase alone is enough to evoke an atmosphere thick with the smoke of a mystifying, ungraspable longing.

"MY MELANCHOLY BABY" AS JAZZ, AS AMERICA

Vassily Aksyonov fell in love with jazz in Russia in the 1950s, rose to fame as a poet and novelist in the 1960s, and was forced out of the Soviet Union in 1980, eventually landing in the United States. He titled his first American tome *In Search of Melancholy Baby*. In his youth, "one of the few windows to the outside world from our stinking Stalinist lair. . . . was provided by jazz," and "from the moment I heard a recording of 'Melancholy Baby' . . . I couldn't get enough of the revelation . . . that 'every cloud must have a silver lining.'"[119] At the neighborhood Fur Workers Club, he viewed *The Roaring Twenties*—a print stolen from the Germans during World War II—with the credits cut out and the movie retitled *The Fate of a Soldier in America*.[120] He remembers, "In those days jazz was America's secret weapon number one," and "Melancholy Baby" acted as a symbol of jazz, of America, of freedom.[121] Eventually, he responded to the song's invitation to "come to me."

As did all "critically thinking Soviets," Aksyonov had formed "a picture of America as an ideal society, prosperous and romantic."[122] Once in the United States, however, Aksyonov finds "neighborhoods full of crime and decay" (he thought reports of that were just Soviet propaganda), that the American smile "may hide a maniac with a knife," and that "merely by throwing in our lot with America, we play a part in her" twisted "race relations."[123] The citizens suffer from boredom (the last thing Aksyonov expected), loneliness, and provinciality.[124] And his beloved jazz is shunted to the sidelines, found in tiny, half-empty clubs.[125] With a shock, he realizes: "Jazz, which in Russia had been the epitome of America to me, has now come to epitomize my Russian youth."[126] In the Soviet Union, "come to me my melancholy baby" was redolent of "romance," it was "about fantasy, about bread, about love."[127] But now he is beset by doubt: "But *does* every cloud have a silver lining?"[128]

It is a question that remains unanswered, even as Aksyonov highlights vignettes of Americans in colorful clothes and fancy hats, with smiling, glowing faces.[129] He keenly perceives "the energy . . . the enterprise . . . the desire of the entire population to build a strong, democratic, liberal society."[130] His friend, visiting from Russia, muses, "Life is more human here"—there is "less depression, humiliation. Less wasting away."[131] One might say, life is less melancholy. Aksyonov seems to be leaving us with this thought: in the United States there are clouds—but perhaps some of those clouds do have silver linings.

A whodunit by John Daniel, *Play Melancholy Baby*, combines many of the themes of these oh-so-similarly titled works—and Daniel deftly incorporates the song itself into the fabric of the tale's unfolding revelations. The first-person narrator, Casey, is a jazz pianist-singer, wasting away his life in a small California town. He still suffers from a traumatic, fateful trip to Europe five years earlier: he fell in love, and lost her, and also fell in with a drug dealer whom he eventually helped bring to justice.

A beautiful, rich, middle-aged woman, Dixie (herself an erstwhile jazz pianist-singer, almost a star during the early 1950s), drops in to hear Casey perform. She later tries to recruit him to find her long-lost daughter. It turns out (spoiler alert) that she is his biological mother; and her daughter (his half-sister) was his lost love (an affair that was unwittingly incestuous on both their parts).

The book is enthralled with golden age American popular songs. Each chapter is titled after a jazz standard, and the dedication is to Lorenz Hart. The foreword is a brief, stammering quotation from the "Melancholy Baby" lyric: "All your fears are foolish fancy . . . maybe . . ."[132] In the course of events, Casey courageously faces his fears—and the torch he's been carrying peacefully dims, to be replaced by the illumination of truth.

When Dixie appears in Casey's audience, she requests "A Ship Without a Sail" (a less often aired Rodgers and Hart torch classic)—perhaps she thinks the title reflects Casey's aimless life. He gets her to take the vocal. When Casey hears her sing, his response is immediate and complex: competitive ("people hushed to hear her soft voice, and they stayed quiet for her as they never did for me"); enamored ("I was in danger of falling in love," despite their differences in age and wealth); and aesthetically enthralled ("I've always wanted to get to know someone who can sing like that").[133] The reappearance of the drug dealer (obviously out to wreak revenge) sends Casey up the coast with a prospective new girlfriend, Beverly. They visit Dixie and spend an evening in music-making. After playing all conceivable variations on "As Time Goes By," Casey reports that he and Dixie "looked into each other's eyes, and Dixie's were glistening, and I think mine were too. She hugged me." On the request of their obnoxious friend, Harv (also a pianist-singer, and destined to be the murder victim), "We played 'Melancholy Baby,' and I felt that perhaps all my fears were foolish fancies."[134] Despite his worries about the reappearance of his old nemesis, Casey's fears are momentarily put to rest.

When Harv gets killed, all of them are suspects. Dixie takes to drink, and in that state of inebriation, she lets the cat out of the bag: "She smiled sadly at me and sang, 'I've got the you-don't-know-the-half-of-it-dearie blues.'" After quoting that Gershwin brothers song, Dixie implicitly reveals the secret of their shared past, through a song title: "She added, 'my melancholy baby,' and I knew what she meant. . . . She shook her head, wagged it, and spoke softly, . . . 'We're a strange family, Casey.'"[135] Everything suddenly falls into place, and Casey asks himself, "How do you feel when someone has just handed you a family and said, 'Sign here'?"

Casey reunites with his half-sister, consolidates the relationships with his mother and his new girlfriend, and helps bring both the murderer and the drug dealer to justice. He ends back in the quiet backwater where he started, but now with his old torch extinguished, a new loving companion, and frequent joyful piano duets with Dixie whenever she visits. The haunting moments linger: Casey's gut response to his mother's singing—that voice he has been looking for all this life; and later, at her house, with the whole party bathing in a hot tub, under the full moon reflected in the water: "through the mist I saw the moon and Beverly's bosom and Dixie's bosom and they were the five loveliest of floating objects," and, then, "Dixie hummed a lullaby. . . . peace . . ."[136]

That promise of peace always lingers around the edges of "My Melancholy Baby."

Chapter Ten

"WHEN I LOST YOU" AND THE MUSE OF FRIENDSHIP

The Strange History of the American Waltz, Part Six

rving Berlin wrote a series of waltz ballads in the 1920s that are landmarks of American popular song. With them, he established a new standard for hushed intimacy and tenderness. His best-remembered (and there are many more) are "What'll I Do" (1924), "All Alone" (1924), "Remember" (1925), "Always" (1925), "Russian Lullaby" (1927), "The Song Is Ended" (1927), "Marie" (1928), and "Reaching for the Moon" (1930). These exemplify a distilled beauty, a seeming simplicity that hides tremendous craft.

In the history of the American waltz, Berlin's 1920s cycle represents perhaps the turning point toward a new, modern style. The famous waltzes of Richard Rodgers—a series that runs from "Lover" (1932) through "Do I Hear a Waltz" (1965)—and bop waltzes by jazz musicians, such as "Waltz for Debby" (1955) and "Bluesette" (1963), all flow forth from the spring that Berlin tapped.[1] The first generation of microphone singers embraced Berlin's waltzes and propagated them in slow tempos. It is symbolic that Russian-born Irving Berlin wrote "Russian Lullaby" as part of this cycle—a song about maternal crooning just as microphone crooning became the vogue.

Dance bands and jazz musicians seized on Berlin's waltzes, too, swinging them in lively four-four time. "What'll I Do" shared the privilege with "I'm Sorry I Made You Cry" of enjoying, right away, recordings both in triple and duple meters.[2] More than a decade later, Berlin's "Marie" was the first waltz to become the nation's top-selling record in a duple-meter arrangement. From this era on, Berlin's waltzes also existed as fox trots. These represented important steps in the Americanization of the waltz—a legacy of what jazz musicians had been doing since 1916's "I'm Sorry I Made You Cry."

This book is about ballads of the 1910s. So why am I writing about Berlin's 1920s waltzes? Because the harbinger of what Berlin accomplished in this subgenre came in 1912, with his first such hit, "When I Lost You."

Example 10.1. "When I Lost You," verse and refrain, piano-vocal score.

I lost the beau-ti-ful rain - bow, I lost the morn - ing dew; I lost the an - gel who gave me Sum - mer, the whole win - ter through, I lost the glad - ness that turned in - to sad-ness, When I lost you

THE SONG IS STARTED

Writers tend to make false claims about the uniqueness of "When I Lost You" in Berlin's early career. Laurence Bergreen posits that it was "unlike any song Berlin had previously written."[3] Philip Furia advances that, after its success, Berlin "did not try to write another ballad for several years."[4] But Charles Hamm obliterates both these claims with his discussion of at least nine Berlin songs clearly in the same mode that preceded "When I Lost You" and about a dozen more created within the fourteen months after it.[5] Indeed, since 1909, Berlin had been trying to craft ballads (many of them waltzes) that would be popular—to no avail, for his numerous early hits were rhythm songs, novelty songs, and comedy songs.

"When I Lost You" arose from Berlin's relationship to the Goetz family. Berlin and songwriter E. Ray Goetz were collaborating throughout the fall of 1911, often working at Ray's home.[6] His sister, Dorothy, came down from Buffalo for a visit. During one of the men's work sessions, Ray introduced Dorothy to Berlin.[7] Years later, Berlin told a British journalist a colorful anecdote that Dorothy and another woman had a physical fight in his office for the right to sing one of his songs.[8] Dorothy was not a performer, so the story seems implausible. Perhaps it occurred, but with somebody else. Or Dorothy might have been interested in the song for private, rather than professional, reasons—but, even if so, such an occasion was certainly not the first time Irving met Dorothy.

By November, Dorothy and Irving were engaged. Once she went back home, Berlin paid for a private telephone line to Buffalo so he could talk to Dorothy each day—demonstrating that token of modernity: intimate love speeches through electric wires, over a far distance.[9] They married in Buffalo on February 2, 1912, and went on a leisurely honeymoon cruise to Cuba.[10] The chronology of the ensuing year is one of the key elements in the mythos surrounding "When I Lost You." The delay between writing and copyrighting a song varies; therefore, the exact timing of Berlin's output must remain unknown for this early period. Nevertheless, some of the main clues about Berlin's creative flow are the copyright dates of his songs.

Somehow, in the midst of honeymooning, Berlin managed to copyright seven songs: four in February (one with Ray; and also "Spring and Fall," an arty ballad that prefigures "When I Lost You" in its story of loss told through nature imagery); one in March; and two in April (one of them, again, with Ray). In May, back home in New York City, the groom was back in high gear, registering five copyrights in one month. One of these was a pure love song, the waltz "That's How I Love You," that is easy to interpret as a reflection of the bridegroom's emotions. It is slightly arty—earnest, but a bit overemphatic—and perhaps emulates Jacob-Bond's "I Love You Truly," which was just rising again for its second round of hit status. Meanwhile, at home, Dorothy got sick, and then sicker—pneumonia—and, on July 17, 1912, passed over, probably as a result of typhoid fever caught in Cuba.

Berlin's creativity nearly dried up once he was bereaved, and Ray dragged him on a trip to Europe.[11] Berlin resumed his steady creative output in late September, with a love waltz—"When I'm Thinking of You." Despite a lovely main strain, this composition never quite jells; and there are touches that would prove to be old-fashioned—for instance, Berlin uses "thee" in the verse and more than one note per syllable in the refrain. Altogether, again, the effect is a bit pretentious. The same could be said for Berlin's next copyright, the serious ballad "Come Back to Me, My Melody," co-written with his early mentor Ted Snyder. The next month, his October copyrights include "Do It Again" and "Down in My Heart," which are sensual, playful courtship songs.

Example 10.2. "When I'm Thinking of You," start of the refrain, melody line.

Of this period Alexander Woollcott, Berlin's first biographer, writes, "the songs he brought in had no health in them."[12] Woollcott claims, "He tried to turn out jolly things about grizzly bears and bunny hugs . . . But the tunes were limp and sorry."[13] Woollcott misrepresents the situation, however. Berlin's 1912 ragtime-themed songs, supposedly "all limp and sorry"—"Ragtime Jockey Man" (a fair-sized hit) and "Ragtime Soldier Man" (which just scraped by as a mild hit)—had been copyrighted while Dorothy was still alive, albeit declining. Events flowed so swiftly, however, that these playful songs were propagated to the mass audience only after Dorothy's death.

In truth, during the months after his bereavement Berlin focused mainly on writing ballads. The songwriter's second major biographer, Michael Freedland, opines that "there was no fire in the music, no love or soul in the words" in his new creations. This opinion, however, is debatable in light of the striking main melody of "When I'm Thinking of You" (see musical example 10.2).

Finally, in November, within the space of a week, Berlin copyrights his next two monumental hits, the rhythm song "When That Midnight Choo Choo Leaves for Alabam'" (on November 2) and the waltz ballad "When I Lost You" (on November 8). All together, the editors of *The Complete Lyrics* detail nine copyrights that Berlin registered between Dorothy's death on July 17 and the registration for "When I Lost You." Therefore, it is remarkable that, in their note for "When I Lost You," the editors still acknowledge the opinion that it was "the first song that Berlin wrote after the tragic early death of his young bride, Dorothy Goetz"—despite the evidence they themselves present.[14] Legends die hard.

Figure 10.1. Madge Maitland proved her worth to songwriter Irving Berlin by singing "When I Lost You" through a megaphone. This probably earned her the status to dominate the cover of "We Have Much to Be Thankful For" (1913), Berlin's follow-up waltz ballad hit, also featuring a personal love lyric. Photo courtesy of the Lilly Library, Indiana University.

Woollcott says that "When I Lost You" gave Berlin "his first chance to voice his great unhappiness in the only language that meant anything to him" and thus "effected a kind of release" that "opened the dykes" for his renewed creative flow.[15] Freedland credits Ray, who told Berlin "not to try to forget his troubles, but to exploit them." His brother-in-law (also, of course, bereaved) encouraged Berlin: "You're a man who writes from your emotions. Let your emotions work for you."[16] This anecdote offers another fresh angle on collective innovation: friend as therapist, friend as muse.

Berlin had further success with waltzes after "When I Lost You." In 1913 he wrote another hit waltz ballad, again with a personal love lyric, "We Have Much to Be Thankful For." In late 1923, Berlin had a mild hit with his revue song "The Waltz of Long Ago." But neither of those endured as a popular standard.

The role of E. Ray Goetz in the unfolding of Berlin's talent for waltz-mongering was not yet finished. Exactly twelve years after his ill-fated first honeymoon, Berlin took another vacation trip to southern waters—Palm Beach, Florida—with Ray. There he wrote "What'll I Do"—and this did become not only a hit but a canonic standard.[17] In creating "What'll I Do," Berlin may have been encouraged by the favor won by "Waltz of Long Ago." Another spur may have been competition: in 1923 Snyder had achieved great success with a waltz ballad "Who's Sorry Now."

The new tune was, as Berlin's daughter would later describe it, "a waltz not for wheeling, . . . but for dancing close."[18] This intensified intimacy helped "What'll I Do" become a pivotal event in the history of popular ballads. Both "When I Lost You" and "What'll I Do" proclaimed ever deeper stages of emotional maturity in this celebrity songwriter. For the latter, once again, the presence of Ray—and the memory of Dorothy—may have acted as inspiration.

BRINGING "WHEN I LOST YOU" UP CLOSE AND PERSONAL

Hamm is skeptical about Berlin writing "When I Lost You" out of his bereavement, pointing out that none of its publicity material mentions Berlin's loss. It was marketed just like any other song, puffed up in ads with a photo of the songwriter pointing to the title, with the blurb "This is the best song I ever wrote."[19] In 1925, however, Berlin made no bones about it, telling an interviewer that "When I Lost You" was "the only one I ever wrote about my own personal experiences," stemming from Dorothy's death.[20] Berlin's daughter, in her book about her father, takes for granted the waltz's biographical roots.[21] Further, the link was perceived from the start by at least some of the press and the public, as the following incident illustrates.

In mid-January 1913, as "When I Lost You" was first hitting the market, Dorothy's friends in Buffalo were witnesses to an emotional landmark at Shea's, a local vaudeville theatre. As *Billboard* reported:

> Miss Madge Maitland . . . sang a song that was especially appropriate for Buffalo. It was entitled, "When I Lost You," by Irving Berlin. . . . The song feature by Miss Maitland was composed in memory of Mr. Berlin's young wife, who was Miss Goetz of this city. Many friends of the deceased woman were at the theater at each performance and the song, which was impressively sung

by Miss Maitland, made a profound impression and was loudly applauded. The singer sang through a megaphone, which helped to make the piece very effective.[22]

Perhaps, for friends grieving over Dorothy's loss, hearing "When I Lost You" sung in her hometown of Buffalo acted as a mourning ritual. They did not reject it as a commercialization of private grief; rather, they seemingly embraced the song as an authentic and sincere catharsis, not just for Berlin but for themselves as well.

Further, Maitland's performance manifested a potent combination that would become the norm in the era of crooning and the torch song: the modern personal love ballad delivered through amplification. Not until Rudy Vallee exploited the megaphone in the late 1920s would this become a widespread combination. Here it is prefigured as an important stepping stone in the popularization of "When I Lost You." Maitland was one of the first vocal soloists to regularly feature the megaphone in her act[23] (see figure 10.1). Further, she reputedly had a remarkably low-pitched range—described as "a splendid baritone voice"—as would later be the case with such microphone singers as Connie Boswell and Alice Faye.[24] In the main part of her set, Maitland wowed them with "a potpourri of . . . excellent songs on the low-comedy order" and then concluded with the contrasting "When I Lost You."[25] Her sudden shift to the megaphone probably accentuated the song's otherworldly quality. When, in February, she took her act to Manhattan's Union Square Theatre, the effect was electrifying: she had to repeat the ballad and give a speech before the audience let her off.[26]

Nose to nose with Maitland, Rene Parker was also bringing "When I Lost You" to vaudeville—and also attempting to bring a fresh intimacy to the venue.[27] Parker made her name as a table-to-table singer at the luxurious Shanley's restaurant, where she billed herself as "The Queen of the Cabarets." In mid-January 1913, she tried to transfer that success to Hammerstein's variety house in Manhattan, accompanied by solo piano, going out into the audience as she was wont to do on the cabaret floor. In seeking to reproduce that atmosphere of intimacy, she opened her set with "When I Lost You." She took her act to England in February and to the Continent in April, presumably carrying the seeds of popularity for "When I Lost You" with her.[28]

Certainly by March 1913, "When I Lost You" was an accepted item in British variety, and by the Christmas season it was "one of the big hits in the English pantomimes . . . generally being sung by the inevitable fairy queen."[29] The permissive format of panto allowed Berlin's ballad to find a place, however tenuous, in a dramatic structure. Otherwise, a hands-off policy toward this elegiac waltz seems to have been maintained by dramatists, including the Hollywood studios:

it was never featured in a movie.[30] Perhaps this boycott was imposed by the dictates of Berlin and his partners. After all, "When I Lost You" was long acknowledged to be, alongside its popular success, an expression of private grief.

ANALYSIS

In "When I Lost You," Berlin uses imagery that he had already rehearsed in unpublished lyrics that later commentators feel acted as warm-ups for his 1912 hit: "They All Come with You" and "That's Just Why I Love You."[31] Those same images also appear in the published ballads of 1912, "Spring and Fall" and "When I'm Thinking of You": sunshine, roses, the blue heaven, dew, angels, summertime, and birdsong.

In addition, Berlin follows a pattern exemplified by another 1912 hit that was finding its audience exactly when he was writing "When I Lost You": "That's How I Need You." This waltz ballad has lyrics by Joe McCarthy and Joe Goodwin and a tune by Berlin's erstwhile collaborator on waltz ballads, Al Piantadosi.[32] McCarthy and Goodwin unfurl many of the same images Berlin also explored: "Like the roses need their fragrance, / . . . Like the summer needs the sunshine, / . . . Like a broken heart needs gladness, / Like a flower needs the dew." They climax their refrain with blatant, old-fashioned sentimentality: "Like a baby needs its mother, / That's how I need you."

These are all love songs; and all the lyrics take the form of a list. Further, McCarthy and Goodwin's lyric for "That's How I Need You" and Berlin's lyrics for "That's Just Why I Love You" and "When I Lost You" all build to the final phrase, the song's title. As in "Bill Bailey," these offer examples of what Banfield terms the "melopoetic point of arrival."[33] In these 1912 examples, each line of lyric builds suspense through a repeated opening gambit: "Like a . . . needs a . . . ," "I love the . . . ," and "I lost the . . ." In his third stanza for "When I Lost You," Berlin varies this pattern once—perhaps wisely, for it helps the song avoid the over-predictability of his rivals' "That's How I Need You." Indeed, the latter, with its unexpected melismatic setting of the climactic word "mo-other," would soon sound like a joke; that is how it is treated in the 1950 movie musical *Two Weeks with Love*. People have critiqued "When I Lost You," but no one has ever treated it as a joke.[34]

"When I Lost You" has weathered the years better than "That's How I Need You"—and better than Berlin's other early ballads such as "When It Rains, Sweetheart, When It Rains," "Spring and Fall," "That's How I Love You," "When I'm Thinking of You," and "If All the Girls I Knew Were Like You." They are all appealing and the last two mentioned have melodies that could be considered superior.[35] Nevertheless, "When I Lost You" has a better lyric, which fits more naturally with the phrasing of its melody. Most of all, as Furia and Lasser state, "its simplicity is the source of its lucid emotionalism."[36] Compared to his other ballads of the period, in "When I Lost You" Berlin is disciplined to a nicety. This may be among the reasons it has endured while the others have not. The contrasts between it and Berlin's comparable ballads of that era are telling:

1) In "When I Lost You," Berlin uses vernacular diction—no "alas," no "thee," unlike "Spring and Fall" and "When I'm Thinking of You."
2) Though the syntax is expansive—it can be viewed, as Peter C. Muir points out, as "one sustained series of parallel phrases"—it is neverthe-less conversational in its word sequence.[37] This is unlike, for instance, "That's How I Love You" with its convoluted verse line, "It seemed would be my possession from one."
3) The fit between music and words is syllabic throughout—no melis-matic settings, unlike "When I'm Thinking."
4) Berlin here is not redundant, as he is in "When It Rains, Sweetheart, When It Rains" (the repetition is clear in the title), "That's How I Love You" (the refrain starts, "I love you / Darling, I love you"), or "If All the Girls I Knew Were Like You" (which ends, "If they were all like you / If they were all like you").
5) The images are coherent—Berlin makes the flow of thought compre-hensible at each step, which is not true of "When It Rains" and "If All the Girls."
7) The refrain's final statement clearly resolves the expectations that the lyric has so carefully built, unlike "When It Rains."
8) Berlin keeps a tight rein on his melodic materials. One result of that discipline: the form of the chorus is the standard ABAC, in contrast to "Spring and Fall," "That's How I Love You," and "If All the Girls," with their maverick refrain structures.[38]

"When I Lost You" just avoids being laughable. Elements skirt on the edge of being obvious, but never cross that line—for example, the flatted note that makes "heavens of blue" into a chromatic phase. The same can be said for the somewhat addictive descending figure in the accompaniment that provides the ligament to the next stanza.

In the B section, Berlin subtly plays between F natural (on "rain*bow*") and F♯ (on the next word, "I"), and between B♭ (on "*beau*tiful") and B (on the rhyming "dew"). Settling on that B natural for "dew"—the seventh degree of the scale, rather than dropping to the more obvious fifth degree or staying on the more pretentious tonic—creates a moment of tender ambiguity. If the song is ever going to convince the skeptic, this is the instant when it does.

The concluding C segment is a subtle variation on the B section. It compresses previously used melodic elements by omitting the long notes. (If you sing, from the B section, "I lost the beautiful" and then go straight into "I lost the morning"—you will get the idea.) This acceleration of the pace coordinates with the standard limerick-type couplet, to prepare for the delivering of the final punchline—the title phrase that completes the stream of thought.

Berlin seemingly imitated "That's How I Need You" in writing "When I Lost You," and he got imitated in turn. Three years later, Fred Fisher would echo Berlin's climactic phrases in "There's a Broken Heart for Every Light on Broadway," a 1915 success, occasionally aired since. In 1921 Harry Pease, Ed G. Nelson, and Gilbert Dodge wrote a waltz hit that seems to quote Berlin's 1912 elegy, albeit in a livelier context: "Peggy O'Neil" (revived in 1947).[39] Again, the relevant passage is during the penultimate limerick-like couplet. All these men pivot their final gestures around an E and (at a new measure) an F♯. They then all somehow get up to a D, with both Berlin and Fisher traveling there via the E above it. In "There's a Broken Heart," Fisher echoes Berlin most closely in the two notes before that shared pattern, while the "Peggy" trio echo him most closely in the two notes after that pattern. Despite the differences, the family resemblance is clear.

Also in 1921, lyricist Annelu Burns and composer Ernest Ball wrote the semi-standard "I'll Forget You," which follows Berlin's "When I Lost You" in the overall pattern of the refrain lyric and, in particular, the concluding couplet.[40] Burns creates her tale of lost love by mentioning that same sunshine, those same roses

Example 10.3a. Irving Berlin, "When I Lost You" (1912), penultimate couplet of the refrain. In the following two comparisons, the larger sized notes are the ones that are shared.

Example 10.3b. "There's a Broken Heart for Every Light on Broadway" (1915), music by Fred Fisher, lyrics by Howard Johnson, penultimate couplet of the refrain.

Example 10.3c. "Peggy O'Neil" (1921), music and lyrics by Harry Pease, Ed G. Nelson, and Gilbert Dodge, penultimate couplet of the refrain.

Example 10.4. "I'll Forget You" (1921), music by Ernest R. Ball, lyrics by Annelu Burns, penultimate couplet of the refrain. Burns' rhyme pair and overall effect is similar to Berlin's "When I Lost You".

When hea-ven's glad-ness_____ has turned to sad-ness_____

and heavens. Moreover, she generates similar tension with her repeated open-ing gambit, "I'll forget you when . . ." She then delivers the payoff by speaking of gladness turning to sadness in the penultimate limerick couplet. Both this and "Broken Heart" represent duple-meter transformations of Berlin's original waltz-meter ingredients. Berlin had pared down his materials, however, to an even finer simplicity than his imitators.

William G. Hyland judges "When I Lost You" "a curious composition," not-ing that its lyric identifies it "as a song of mourning," but the "melody is only slightly melancholy."[41] Berlin was striving for exactly that mixture. The song-writer proclaimed in 1913 that "no minstrel has been foolish enough to paint a song of sorrow without some redeeming point of happier sentiment that would make the spectator see the contrast," and offered specific examples: "from 'The Rosary' to my own 'When I Lost You' no ballad has met with real success that did not contain some sunshine interspersed with the account of sadness."[42] Berlin realized that "pathos devoid of contrast readily descends into the ridiculous."[43] By 1913 Berlin clearly understood that in writing "When I Lost You" and other such ballads he was treading a fine line between the sorrowful and the ludicrous. Perhaps Wilfrid Sheed is correct in arguing that "When I Lost You" is overrated, "second drawer," not a *"great* ballad."[44] Nevertheless, it is a *good* ballad, and one that proved to be the precursor to future *great* ballads, starting with 1924's "What'll I Do."

In 1947 Berlin admitted that "What'll I Do" was one of "the five most impor-tant songs I ever wrote, structurally," a "key song of forty years of songwriting," because it was one of "the basic song[s that] always suggested four or five others, each a bit different but basically the same."[45] What Berlin does not mention is that "What'll I Do" leaned on his waltz ballads of the early teens, in particular "When I Lost You" . . .

. . . and also "I Wonder Who's Kissing Her Now," because three of Berlin's twenties protagonists are obsessed with wondering about the beloved's current status. In "What'll I Do," he expects that in the future, after she leaves him, he will wonder who is kissing her. The lonely one in "All Alone" ends wondering where she is, and how she is, and if she is also all alone. Finally, the verse of "Because I Love You" features Berlin's least disguised paraphrase of the title words of "I Wonder Who's Kissing Her Now."[46] As he forged ahead with his 1920s waltz series, Berlin clearly had Hough and Adams's lyric in mind . . .

. . . and also "Kiss Me Again"—or, at least, the lyric that Henry Blossom wrote for the verse of the pop edition. In the refrain of "What'll I Do," the protagonist imagines what it will be like to be deserted, but it is not certain she has left yet—the song might be a strategy to plead with the beloved to stay. The verse, however, clearly establishes that the affair is over. Similarly, the refrain of "Kiss Me Again" is a plea for lovemaking, but the pop verse establishes that the romance is ended. Further, the second verse of "What'll I Do" echoes that of "Kiss Me Again" by mentioning the nocturnal tryst and asking whether or not the beloved has forgotten.

The verses of "All Alone" mention how the protagonist cannot get the lost beloved out of her mind, mentioning dreams—again, traits similar to the verse of "Kiss Me Again." Such faint similarities also occur in the verses to "Remember": the description of a momentary rendezvous in the past; an allusion to dreams; and a questioning of whether the lost beloved still remembers. Yet again, in the verse for "The Song Is Ended," Berlin includes the one nocturnal evening together and the description of the act of remembering.

More significant than these specific resemblances, however, is the shared atmosphere of these verses. The intro to "The Song Is Ended" is particularly evocative of that of "Kiss Me Again." Berlin uses conversational language, while Blossom's verse lyric is not colloquial, but otherwise the 1905 verse could easily lead into almost any of these Berlin waltzes of lost love.

There is one general musical trait that unites the classic Berlin waltzes: the first motif of the refrain creates an upward gesture, whether through a rising-and-falling arch or a single ascending flight. This movement starts with an upward-moving interval, stepwise or in larger jumps, sometimes in arpeggios. In "When I Lost You," it commences with a single, simple diatonic step, hurriedly rushed by. Enter the performers: the simple upward diatonic step that starts "When I Lost You" becomes more prominent because singers make the second note longer, to match the flow of the lyric. As almost always in this tradition, the performers are flexible with the note values. The main strain ends up being like this:

Example 10.5. A common performer's rhythmic rephrasing of "When I Lost You," particularly in extending the second note, on the word "lost".

I   lost   the   sun - shine_____   and   ro   -   ses_____

Many of Berlin's models also start with such an ascent: "Kiss Me Again," "I Wonder Who's Kissing Her Now," "Meet Me Tonight in Dreamland," and "Let

Me Call You Sweetheart." By contrast, however, some of Berlin's prominent earliest waltz experiments begin with a descending interval, as with "When It Rains, Sweetheart, When It Rains" (1911) and "That's How I Love You" (1912). But after Dorothy's death his more riveting examples begin with a rise, either substantial in "When I'm Thinking of You" (see musical example 10.2) or slight in "When I Lost You" (see musical example 10.1).

This holds true for all the 1920s waltzes mentioned above. One can almost hear Berlin thinking: What if I commence the refrain with a single step upward—starting on the tonic ("When I Lost You," "What'll I Do," "All Alone," "Russian Lullaby")—or how about starting on the fifth ("Always," "Remember")? Is that getting stale? Then why not begin by jumping the interval of a third ("The Song Is Ended," "Marie") or a fourth ("At Peace with the World," "Reaching for the Moon")? So it goes, for many others: "Because I Love You" (1926), "What Does It Matter" (1927), "Coquette" (1928), "To Be Forgotten" (1928), "Where Is the Song of Songs for Me?" (1928), "I Can't Remember" (1933)— even his later waltz hits "The Girl That I Marry" (1946) and "Let's Take an Old Fashioned Walk" (1949).[47] Of course, this is overly simplistic, and too much should not be made of such resemblances. Nevertheless, in light of Berlin's insistence over many decades that he based new songs on his old ones of the same type, it is not farfetched to imagine the songwriter engaging in a more subtle, complex version of such creative brainstorming. Arguably, Berlin was even more consistent in his string of waltz ballads than in his other sets of key-song-followed-by-imitations.[48]

Berlin's 1920s waltzes form a coherent group. The songwriter spoke about them together. In a 1925 interview, he discusses "When I Lost You" and then lumps together his newer hits, "What'll I Do," "All Alone," and "Remember," under the label "sob ballads."[49] In the early 1920s, the young Bing Crosby and Al Rinker focused on "fast-rhythm songs," but they "also tossed in some of Irving Berlin's waltzes into the hopper: the early ones—'When I Lost You,' 'All Alone'—things like that."[50] For Crosby these songs functioned together as a special category, with "When I Lost You" as the earliest in the set. Further, as repertoire, they seem to have helped coalesce Crosby's musical persona during his formative years.

The Berlin waltz ballads are often programmed together, with two or three being featured in one album, live performance, or broadcast. For example, in 1931 Debroy Somers's British dance band arranged eight of them in a medley, from "What'll I Do" through "The Song Is Ended." Sinatra used five Berlin waltz ballads on his eleven-track 1962 album *All Alone*. He starts with the album's title track, concludes with "The Song Is Ended," and in between moans out "What'll I Do," "Remember"—and "When I Lost You." Gordon Jenkins writes arrangements that are often symphonic in scale—lugubrious but, with Sinatra's beautifully phrased vocals, accumulating an effective atmosphere of sadness and longing. In the liner notes, Edward Jablonski places the waltzes of Irving Berlin, including "When I Lost You," unequivocally into the torch genre.

"When I Lost You" remains a standard, but it never benefited from a major revival to renewed hit status—although, after Sinatra's 1962 recording, it quickly popped up on other top-selling albums by Perry Como (1963), Jim Reeves (1964), Bobby Vinton (1964), and Wayne Newton (1968). Among my focus songs, it is perhaps the least recorded, with the lowest recognition value.[51] Aside from rephrasing the note values to match the flow of words, performers have done no indelible rewriting of the song. About one in five singers will change the lyric from "heavens" to "heaven"; that is as wild as they get.

Berlin always kept a tight control on his creations; therefore there is little variation in the print tradition of "When I Lost You"—except for one factor: an arrangement copyrighted in 1941 changes the original 1910 model only modestly, except that the piece is now in four-four meter. In the early twenty-first century, customers could still buy it both as a waltz and as a duple meter ballad. Around a third of performers transfer the tune into duple meter. Frankie Fanelli gives it the ballad-with-a-beat treatment, emulating Sinatra and his arranger Nelson Riddle at their most swinging, managing to make it quite cheerful. Jimmy Roselli manipulates it similarly, but with a Dixieland styled backing, for one of his *Saloon Songs* albums. Roselli makes it sound like the beloved is not dead, just gone away—and he knows he will win her back! Ferlin Husky also sounds like his beloved has not died but simply left him. Husky's easily loping country-western rendering creates a protagonist who could be the older cousin of Bobby Darin's woebegone drinker in "I Wonder Who's Kissing Her Now." Nevertheless, unlike the Weems-Como "I Wonder," none of these four-four renditions of "When I Lost You" established an indelible influence.

The majority of singers (seven out of ten) approach "When I Lost You" with hushed reverence. Lou Monte, in the middle of a raucous nightclub set, delivers a single simple chorus, with only trembling strummings behind. (He transitions with, "Right about here, ladies and gentlemen, I'd like to sing one of the nicest songs ever to come out of Tin Pan Alley.") Perhaps the most convincing deliveries of it are from Kate Smith, in a performance as tightly disciplined as the song itself, and Elisabeth Welch, both in the studio and live. ("It's a very touching song," Welch says, "and I love it.")

Even with full orchestra, the accompaniments for "When I Lost You" are usually very restrained, and many are admirably spare. Bing Crosby and Morton Downey, almost funereal, are accompanied just by solo organ. Tony Bennett goes to an extreme and renders the piece *a cappella*—dramatic, but austere. It is not quite clear whether all the singers are responding to the biographical context of the song—as originating in Berlin's bereavement—or to its content alone: its compositional restraint that manages to walk a tightrope, never quite falling into the outer bathos on one side and inner grief on the other.

THE BERLIN WALTZ IN HOLLYWOOD

"When I Lost You" was never exploited by Hollywood, but other Berlin waltzes were.[52] In the 1938 movie musical *Alexander's Ragtime Band*, an epic Berlin song-fest covering twenty-five years of American pop music history, a central segment is devoted to a montage of Alice Faye crooning "What'll I Do," "All Alone," and "Remember." Once again, these waltzes are treated as a set. Faye's sequences are intercut with jazzy duple meter rhythm songs rendered by Ethel Merman. The movie uses the singers and their contrasting repertoires to symbolize two halves of the 1920s zeitgeist.

This bifurcation is revealed as coming from one stem in *Christmas Holiday* (1944), through its employment of "Always." Berlin completed this love ballad in mid-1925 while he was courting his soon-to-be second wife, the socialite Ellin Mackay. When they married in 1926, amidst a blaze of unwelcome publicity and her father's disowning her, Berlin gave his bride the rights to the song as a wedding gift.[53] In 1934 it was among the first songs to be categorized by Broadway insiders as a torch song, presenting a strong argument for the most inclusive definition of that subgenre, allowing the torch canon to include pieces that induce tears through their heartwarming qualities rather than their expressions of suffering.[54] As well as being a strong standard, Ellin's wedding gift experienced a major revival to hit status in 1944 due to its inclusion in the top-grossing movie *Christmas Holiday*.

Despite its wholesome title, *Christmas Holiday* is quirky, bleak film noir in which "Always" acts as a kind of leitmotif for the doomed romance in the second half of the plot. Newly wedded, Abigail (Deanna Durbin) sings it while hubby Robert (Gene Kelly) plays the piano in their home. The domestic intimacy is intensely tender. The waltz conveys all that is gemütlich, soothing, and secure. Meanwhile, however, the shadows lurking at the edges of the frame hint at the groom's dark side. After Robert is jailed for murder, Abigail changes her name to Jackie and, filled with self-loathing at her failure as a wife, debases herself as a nightclub singer-hostess (and companion-on-demand to the club's patrons). The night of Robert's escape from jail, Jackie waits for him, now crooning to nightclub customers "Always" in duple meter as a slow fox trot. Leaning against a pillar, she is the embodiment of the torch singer. When Robert dies in her arms, shot by the police, the underscoring softly intones Berlin's waltz, then segues into Wagner's "Liebestod"—the music of their first meeting—the "love-death" aria signaling the transcendent essence of their love that will last ... always.

Figures 10.2 and 10.3. The two sides of the Tin Pan Alley waltz "Always" in *Christmas Holiday* (1944). In the domestic setting, Abigail (Deanna Durbin) embraces and croons into the ear of Robert (Gene Kelly). Later, now a nightclub chanteuse, she transforms Irving Berlin's waltz into a fox trot, with a torch-like candelabra framing her. The paean to fulfilled marital love mutates into a torch ballad of loss and separation.

THE WALTZ THAT IS AND ISN'T

Because it is both a ballad of fulfilled love and a torch number of longing, music for making in the home and music for hearing in the saloon, a waltz and a fox trot, the American waltz has taken on a freewheeling nature. By May 1922, Tin Pan Alley publishers were acknowledging this: they were all "lining up a waltz for an orchestra 'plug,'" but hedging their bets by "issuing duplex orchestra editions with fox trot and waltz arrangements to suit the musician and his demands."[55] By September even a regional publisher in Battle Creek, Michigan, Charles E. Roat, was issuing his hit "Faded Love Letters" with "the added feature of having the chorus printed as a fox-trot."[56] By February 1923, Ted Snyder was issuing his latest waltz, "Who's Sorry Now," with "jazz chorus"—i.e., in duple meter—the style that has proved dominant in later renditions of Snyder's tune.[57]

Berlin's waltzes, as much as and perhaps more than any others, became the experimental ground for this method of Americanizing the waltz. First in the Jazz Age, then to even more spectacular success in the big band era, then perhaps even more prolifically in the LP era, Berlin's waltzes were fox trotted and swung in duple meter. Within this narrative, the success of Tommy Dorsey's arrangement of Berlin's 1929 waltz "Marie" (already mentioned briefly in earlier chapters) fills a key episode.

In October 1936, Dorsey was in Philadelphia playing a gig alongside an African American band led by Doc Wheeler, the Royal Sunset Serenaders. The white musicians fell in love with their Black competitor's four-four arrangement of "Marie," with "hot vocal licks back of the vocalist" and "after a couple of days [they] all knew it by heart." The upshot: "We really stole their arrangement."[58] Dorsey exchanged eight of his orchestrations for that one from Wheeler. The Victor label chief, Eli Oberstein, at first refused to let them record it, but was finally convinced by the cheers from Dorsey's radio audiences. This reinscribing of a waltz as a fox trot was effected through a chain of catalysts: a slew of arrangers (the undocumented ones of Doc Wheeler, supplemented by Dorsey and his team, including Paul Weston, Axel Stordahl, and especially Freddie Stulce); the Dorsey band; the radio studio audiences; and Oberstein.[59]

In 1937 "Marie" clinched both Tommy Dorsey's star status and the tune's place in the standard canon—as a duple meter swinger. Irving Berlin said of swing, "I don't think it is music at all," and looked askance at his daughter's enthusiasm for Dorsey's "Marie," retaliating to her outburst of its concluding jive line with the rejoinder "Livin' in a great big way, yourself."[60] Nevertheless, he accepted the transformation of his waltz; issued a fox trot arrangement; kept his cool while Dorsey's band jumped the tune for a gala Berlin tribute on radio in 1938; and, when Dorsey did a rerecording in 1956, phoned and said "it's wonderful . . . the best version of 'Marie' ever made."[61]

It has become hard to find a waltz rendition of "Marie." The same is true of "The Song Is Ended"—and even of "Always." Ella Fitzgerald's rendition of the latter, in two halves—first as a slow waltz, then as a medium-tempo duple-meter tune—once again symbolizes the dual nature of the Berlin waltz and the American waltz in general—a triumph of the performance tradition.

While direct influence is probably impossible to trace, one can sense the sway of Berlin's waltzes in the hits of other songwriters. "What'll I Do" and "All Alone" perhaps particularly influenced two of the most enduring twenties waltzes, published by Berlin's own company, "Oh, How I Miss You Tonight" (1925) and "Are You Lonesome Tonight" (1926). "Remember" feels like a harbinger of "Together" (1927). "Always" seems continued by "You're the Only Star (In My Blue Heaven)" (1935) (called by some "the beginning of the soft-country sound"), "Eternally" (1952), and "True Love" (1956).[62] Thus, starting with "When I Lost You," Berlin's torchy waltz ballads reinvigorated the form.

Chapter Eleven

"YOU MADE ME LOVE YOU"

*J*ames V. Monaco and Joe McCarthy wrote "You Made Me Love You (I Didn't Want to Do It)" in 1913, and the song was immediately a hit. By 2000 pop music experts calculated that it was the top love song among those that arose out of the 1910s, based on its amazing performance history.[1] As a love ballad, it has done good duty in the lives of everyday people. Take the following handful of examples.

1940s: Pearl, a college student, had her frequent date, Charlie Gregory, stop the car when she heard trumpeter Harry James play "You Made Me Love You" on the radio. "You hear what they're playing? That's my song," she said. Charlie's response: "When are we gonna get married?" "I don't know, but the answer's yes," Pearl snapped back. (Soon after, they went into Manhattan to buy wedding clothes and then went to the Astor ballroom to hear James and his big band. They called the trumpeter over and told him about the proposal, and he stayed chatting at their table, for forty-five minutes.)[2]

1950s: Jerry Marshall, the New York City disc jockey, had memorized the shelf number in his radio station's library for James's single of "You Made Me Love You": 12-J-51. So he had that code engraved on all the jewelry he gave to his wife—a tiny, secret love message.

1970s: Danny Aiello, the late-blooming character actor and club singer, never crooned in public until his first time speaking at a charity benefit, in his forties. He brought his wife, Sandy, along and planned to speak impromptu—but he froze. "There were hundreds of people—all I saw was my wife! . . . I said, 'Honey, without you I'm nothing.'"[3] And he started to sing to his wife—a cappella, for there was no band on the stage—"You made me love you / I didn't wanna do it, I didn't wanna do it." (Sandy wanted to hide under the table.)

1980s: Valentine's Day: Lovers donate to the Chicago Symphony Chorus so that a vocal quartet will go to their sweethearts, at their workplaces in offices and stores in downtown Chicago, and serenade them with "You Made Me Love You." (Price: $55, or $35 for a phone call.)[4]

2000s: Susan Carpenter, a college professor, wakes up woozy from having surgery—her first time under general anesthetic. While her husband walks toward her in the post-op bay, she begins to sings to him, "You made me love you. / I wanted to do it, I wanted to do it." (I'm her husband.)

At the same time, "You Made Me Love You" displayed other facets. While it is often done slowly and sentimentally, Monaco's melody is also suitable for rhythmic treatment—it can be ragged, it can be swung. McCarthy's lyric was sometimes seen as a sad tale, oozing pathos, even tragedy. It has been, on occasion, labeled a torch song. All these aspects are shared by "Some of These Days" and "My Melancholy Baby." Unlike those two standards, however, "You Made Me Love You" has a certain exaggerated quality and a potential implied sexiness that, pretty much from the start, also made it a tool for comedy.

Two intriguing aspects emerge from the history of "You Made Me Love You." First, it became indelibly associated with three performers—Al Jolson, Judy Garland, and Harry James. But that is only the simplest part of the picture. The teenaged Garland first sang it on screen to a photograph of Clark Gable, as a tribute to his star charisma. Through this means, "You Made Me Love You" became a song about the relationship between a star and a fan, between the performer and the audience—a connotation that remains to this day. Second, it was the fate of "You Made Me Love You" to integrate early on not just into the culture of English-speaking nations, but also into French culture, perhaps functioning as an important blossom in the cross-pollination between Tin Pan Alley and the developing *chansons-realiste* tradition.

THE START

The two songwriters were both born in 1885 and represent important turn-of-the-century American ethnic minorities. James V. Monaco was brought to the United States from Italy when he was six years old. His family moved to Albany—where he taught himself to play piano and got gigs in cafes—and then to Chicago, where he became known as Ragtime Jimmy.[5] He moved to New York City, where his work at Coney Island and the Bohemian Café somehow led to a chance to get songs published. In 1912 his hits began to pour forth.

Joseph McCarthy (no relation to the notorious anti-Communist senator!) grew up in Massachusetts, where prejudice against Irish Catholics was intense. Similarly to Irving Berlin, McCarthy started in showbiz as a singing waiter. By the start of 1910, this led to him getting lyrics published, first in Boston, then Chicago, and finally New York[6] (He co-wrote the awkward, over-the-top—but successful!—lyrics for "That's How I Need You," mentioned in the previous chapter.) His early pop song successes—many of them with Monaco—advanced him to a ten-year career writing hit shows for Broadway, overlapping with nine years as president of ASCAP. His lyricist son, also named Joseph, carried the family legacy of hit-making into the 1950s (think of junior's "I'm Gonna Laugh You Right Out of My Life").

In late 1912, Monaco had a landmark hit with the enduring rhythmic comedy song, "Row, Row, Row," written with lyricist William Jerome and published by Harry Von Tilzer. Probably because of this success, when Will Von Tilzer decided to leave his brother Harry's firm and start up his own music publishing house, he recruited Monaco as his right-hand man. (Unlike with the Rossiter brothers, Will's split from Harry was amicable.)[7] Will dubbed the new business Broadway Music. (A quick sidenote on the Von Tilzer family: the brothers Harry, Albert, Jack, Julie, and Will made their fortunes in New York's Tin Pan Alley, but they grew up in Indianapolis. They were sons of Polish Jewish immigrants, a Mr. Gumbinsky, which surname got Americanized as Gumm, married to a Miss Tilzer, to whose maiden name Harry decided to add an aristocratic "Von" when he adopted it for professional purposes.)

On the other hand, McCarthy for most of his career was loyal to a long-established outfit, Feist. He must have been impressed with Monaco's talent, however, for in the spring of 1913 he strayed from Feist to team with his Italian American contemporary—and they immediately hit the bull's-eye with the successful "I Love Her, Oh! Oh! Oh!" (They also wrote the less successful "There's a Wireless Station Down in My Heart," an early song creating a parallel between romance and radio.) But even better things were still to come.

On April 25, 1913, the *Player* announced that McCarthy and Monaco had written yet another song, "You Made Me Love You." It was already being done by three acts—fast work on the part of Von Tilzer, because the song had not yet even been copyrighted.[8] One of the three was Al Jolson, who had tried out the song at the K. O. H. Ball (presumably held by the Knights of Honor, a cross between fraternal society and union).[9] Jolson was co-starring in *The Honeymoon Express*, the usual messy mélange of a musical comedy produced by the Shubert Brothers for the Winter Garden. The show was due for a revamping, because performers were being replaced: the French co-star Gaby Deslys was replaced by Grace La Rue; juvenile lead Harry Pilcer (Deslys's lover) by Charles King.[10] In what was advertised as a "Second Edition," Jolson took on a completely new set of songs for his specialty spots, and one was "You Made Me Love You."[11] Jolson kept the tune in the show through its mid-June closing—and when the musical went on tour in late August, retained it in his eleven o'clock

Figure 11.1. "You Made Me Love You" (1913). Gentle smile and gentle tears—as Irving Berlin advocated, the ideal Tin Pan Alley recipe mixes gladness with sadness. *You Made Me Love You*, Charles H. Templeton Sr., Templeton Sheet Music Collection, Manuscripts Division, Special Collections Department, Mississippi State University Libraries.

specialty spot, thereby carrying his dynamic rendition of "You Made Me Love You" around the nation.[12]

Meanwhile, between April 30 and May 6, Von Tilzer sent the Library of Congress two forms and two sets of printed copies to register what was at first called "You Made Me Love You" and, five days later, copyrighted again with its subtitle as "You Made Me Love You, I Didn't Want to Do It." There were two early covers (both heralding the song's use by Al Jolson in *The Honeymoon Express*): first a plain cover with arrows piercing or aiming at hearts; and then a soft-focus painted portrait of a woman with a small, affectionate smile and tears in her eye and running down her cheeks—an image with an ambiguity to match that of the same era's "Some of These Days" cover (see figure 7.1).

On May 12, Broadway Music got the Victor label to record the song—a jolly, raggy rendition by Will Halley (only four years before he began his career as a New Jersey judge and state assemblyman, under his real name, William J. Hanley). On May 17, Von Tilzer got the piece reviewed by *Billboard*.[13] On Sunday, June 1, Monaco himself accompanied Jolson at a benefit held by the White Rats (the predecessor of the Actor's Union). They did "You Made Me" and "I Love Her" and were one of the two biggest successes of the evening, playing before a packed audience of fellow professionals.[14] Ten days later, Jolson went into the recording studio and waxed his own disc of "You Made Me" for the Columbia label. It was the first love ballad this comedian ever recorded—and his first masterpiece. When released in September, it would become his fifth hit record, helping the composition become the number one song in the country during most of the fall.

This course of events demonstrates the tremendous clout that well-connected Tin Pan Alley firms had. Compare the speedy transition to hitdom of "You Made Me Love You" with the painfully slow plugging process that regional outsider Theron C. Bennett had to go through, trying to help "My Melancholy Baby" to success: more than nine months till he got a *Billboard* song review; more than nineteen months before he achieved a single measly recording. What a difference a powerful publisher made!

By contrast, the vogue for "You Made Me Love You" spread quickly. By July it was causing a sensation in Chicago and "rapidly heading" for the West Coast.[15] Through the summer, vaudeville acts large and small were fighting to feature it, because only one act in a bill could use a song. Whoever got there first on Monday morning laid claim to it for the week. Poor Johnny Cantwell, set to play at the Bronx Theater, waited outside from 8:30 a.m. He finally got let in at 9:00, and when the orchestra leader arrived was waiting to hand him his musical arrangement of "You Made Me Love You," only to find out the Farber Sisters had beat him to it—they had telegraphed ahead![16]

It was acknowledged from the start that "You Made Me Love You (I Didn't Want to Do It)" might be about sex. As the *Billboard* reviewer put it, although "the lyric never descends to coarseness," nevertheless "the limits of the love suggested border very closely upon the risqué."[17] Both songwriters had recent successes with suggestive songs, revealed in their final limerick couplets. McCarthy co-wrote "When I Get You Alone Tonight": "We can keep the organ playin', / So the folks will think we're prayin.'" Monaco composed "Row, Row, Row": "Then he'd drop both his oars, / Take a few more encores." They flavored "You Made Me" with some of that same lighthearted, sexy ambiguity, although it also held more serious potential.

Therefore it is not surprising that the new McCarthy-Monaco hit was quickly made a target and tool for comedy. When Fanny Brice left the cast of *Honeymoon Express* for a stint in vaudeville, she proved she could deftly "turn a rag ballad, 'You Made me Love You,' into a comic"—"You should hear her. . . . A really clever conception this," the *Variety* reviewer raved.[18] Parodies were rampant; in *Billboard* they were advertised for sale; boy singer Buttons did one in his act; the Van family (Charles, Fanny, and Fred) included theirs in eighteen minutes of "rapid-fire comedy."[19] Comedy acts favored the piece. With Johnny Cantwell and Reta Walker, "their burlesquing" of the song "was a scream."[20] Santley and Norton featured the tune and "riot was not a strong enough word" to describe the effect of these "real comedians."[21] William Bence led his troupe in a comedy dream sequence, set in a Chinese laundry, with "You Made Me" as part of the "farcical hullabaloo" that, in a working-class theatre, "before a house composed for the most part of men and boys, . . . caused a lot of laughter."[22] A gag was made famous by Dean Martin in the Swinging Sixties (one wonders if it was already being used in front of such rowdy audiences in 1913), the parodic fragment "You made me love you, / You woke me up to do it."[23] McCarthy's lyric seems to invite that kind of irreverent quip. Another prevalent trend was treating the song not as a double entendre, but rather as a "mock-sentimental product."[24] For instance, in London, Fred Kitchen "as a forlorn lover" was serenaded with "You Made Me Love You" by Ella Retford, "and much merriment was the result."[25]

"You Made Me Love You" traveled to England and, after that, to France. Its journey to England is clear-cut; the one to France is murky but important. Grace La Rue brought "You Made Me Love You" across the sea; and the London publisher Francis, Day and Hunter effectively blanketed Great Britain with it. For six weeks that spring La Rue had been listening to Jolson sing "You Made Me" every night in *The Honeymoon Express* (and, one can imagine, probably aching to get her hands on it). By mid-July she was briefly in American vaudeville, and by August 4 she made her debut in London, in variety at the Palace Theatre. "Without any preliminary booming," she "made the biggest kind of a hit," "rapidly became the big feature," even being billed co-equally with the legendary Harry Lauder.[26] La Rue was "largely responsible for the great success" of "You Made Me" in England.[27] Within three weeks of her debut, she recorded it for the His Master's Voice label, one of at least six British waxings before the year ended.

The popularity of "You Made Me Love You" was seen, then and later, as part of England's ragtime craze. This vogue resulted in a plethora of successful American popular songs (most categorized, in the loose manner of the era, as ragtime) and also revues such as *Hullo! Ragtime*.[28] Irving Berlin steamed across to visit London, riding on the wave of his mammoth hit, "Alexander's Ragtime Band"; and Nat D. Ayer came for an extended stay, helping sell his compositions "Oh, You Beautiful Doll" and "Hitchy-Koo" to the English public eager for the new dynamism of ragtime-era America. The verdict: in the summer of 1913, even after a yearlong vogue, ragtime had "not been killed off in England, by a long shot."[29]

"You Made Me Love You" was "the new London rage."[30] You could hear it across England, not just in variety, but also in multiple revues: *Hullo! Ragtime*, then on tour in the provinces; in Manchester, in *Step This Way*; and in London, in *Keep Smiling*, in *What About It?*, and in *Eightpence-a-Mile*.[31] Grande dame Lydia Yavorska (Princess Bariatinsky to you, please—she was a former colleague of Stanislavski and married to royalty) sang it in her starring drama, *I Love You*.[32] The Christmas pantomime season saw it proliferating throughout the kingdom, usually sung by the "principal boy" (i.e., a woman in the lead breeches role).[33] So completely did the English embrace "You Made Me" that I once had a hard time convincing an Englishman that it was an American song, so certain was he that it was a British music hall ditty from the turn of the century.

Harry Fragson, British singer of *chansons*, may have been the first person to sing "You Made Me Love You" in French. At least, on December 17, 1913, he was contemplating doing so, while playing at the Paris Alhambra, on the same bill as American juggler W. C. Fields (long before his movie career as a comedian).[34] Perhaps he got the idea from Fields, or perhaps from playing in London back in October, alongside an act that was parodying the McCarthy-Monaco opus.[35] Fragson may not have had time to carry out the idea. On December 30, his father, anguished over a plan for his temporary stay in a nursing home, raised his gun to commit suicide—but instead, "in a wild mad rush," killed Harry.[36]

In the end, Mistinguett popularized "You Made Me Love You" in France. She was a proponent of the *chansons-realiste* mode and already legendary as a pioneer of the French Apache dance (a choreographed physical fight by pimp and prostitute characters). She introduced "You Made Me" to Paris in *La revue légère*, at the Olympia music hall.[37] The cover of the French sheet music blazoned "Danse par Mistinguett"—"un succes sans precedent."[38] By May 1914, Elsie Janis, the new American rage in London and just back from a short trip to Paris, was performing a parody in which she portrayed Sarah Bernhardt singing "You Made Me Love You" in French.[39]

How "You Made Me Love You" got to Mistinguett was probably a tangled path that led from Jolson through La Rue. Playing alongside La Rue, for at least part of her stay at the Palace Theatre, London, were Gaby Deslys and Harry Pilcer.[40] Pilcer was a talented dancer—bisexual, oversexed, handsome, but in thrall to Deslys as they regularly hopped from his native America, to England, to her native France. In 1917 they settled in France until Deslys died in 1920, too young, as a result of the influenza epidemic.[41] The pair were part of the same crowd as Maurice Chevalier, who also played London during the 1910s; and as Mistinguett, whose greatest love was Chevalier, but who determinedly pursued Pilcer after the death of Deslys. For a while, Mistinguett and Pilcer paired both on and off stage.[42]

It was in 1920, during the Pilcer-Mistinguett affair, that one of Pilcer's rejected admirers, Jacques Charles, co-wrote the lyric for Mistinguett's most famous song, "Mon Homme," which became a touchstone of the torch genre in English as "My Man." Charles claimed that Pilcer was the *homme* who inspired him.[43] Certainly, while presenting "Mon Homme" to the world, both Charles and Mistinguett were in the midst of an obsession with Pilcer. But in fashioning the song for Mistinguett, Charles and his co-writers would also have had in mind the chanteuse's previous repertoire, which had included "You Made Me Love You."

McCarthy and Monaco had produced a very influential song, and for ten years its specific influence can be traced. Songs were "a result" of it ("Why Do I Love You," 1913); "after the fashion of" ("You Said You Couldn't Love Me, Now, Didn't You," 1914); "a second" ("Here I Am," 1914); "another" ("I'll Give Them Back to You," 1917); "in the atmosphere of" and "decidedly along the metrical order . . . having nearly the same construction" ("Somebody Stole My Heart [And You Are the One Who Did It]," 1917); and "on the same order as" ("I Hate to Lose You [I'm So Used to You Now]," 1918).[44] McCarthy and Monaco themselves found success with "What Do You Want to Make Those Eyes at Me For," a 1917 hit and standard that shares some traits with "You Made Me," though more playful. In England, during 1914, Francis, Day and Hunter sued their competitor over his imitation, "You Didn't Want to Do It, But You Did." (They lost—but, importantly, the court did affirm that copyrights registered in the United States were valid in Britain.)[45] Even as late as 1923, that publishing firm seemed to be trying to duplicate its past success by issuing "I'm Going to Make You Love Me," which ends with the line, "Just as you made me love you."[46] Perhaps its influence can even be found in "See See Rider," a blues standard first recorded in 1924, in which the protagonist states "You made me love you, / Now your gal done come."

Nevertheless, from 1919 to 1937, "You Made Me Love You" fell from public consciousness in the United States, except as an old-time ballad to be occasionally aired out, nostalgically, on the new radio music programs—or bragged about by those associated with its past success (McCarthy, Monaco, Von Tilzer, La Rue). New songs came along with the same title. To the confusion of discographers ever since, in 1926 Louis Armstrong recorded "You Made Me Love You (When I Saw You Cry)" and in 1929 Guy Lombardo put to shellac "You Made Me Love You (Why Did You)."[47] In 1927 England, too, saw a new "You Made Me Love You" in the marketplace.[48]

In *Ziegfeld Follies of 1931*, Harry Richman paid tribute to Jolson by singing "You Made Me"—as did Ruth Etting for Nora Bayes with "Shine On, Harvest

Moon."[49] The result was a major revival of "Shine On," but no action for "You Made Me." Jolson performed "You Made Me" on radio in 1932, 1933, and 1936, yet these broadcasts did not result in any renewed hit status.[50] As microphone crooning and the torch song label were being established in the 1920s and early 1930s, the public newly embraced as hits "Some of These Days," "Let Me Call You Sweetheart," "The Sweetheart of Sigma Chi," and "My Melancholy Baby"—but not "You Made Me Love You."

Enter Roger Edens. He rewrote "You Made Me Love You" for a teenaged Judy Garland, and it proved her turning point toward stardom. Edens was one of those mysterious, behind-the-scenes show-business geniuses. Hailing from Texas, by the age of twenty-five this bisexual pianist was in New York, helping Ethel Merman with her career, her accompaniments, and her special material—and he was still doing so forty years later.[51] His association with Merman brought him to Hollywood. Working for MGM from early 1935 onward, Edens composed (a few) hit songs and (more often) created magical details in classic musicals—for example, he added the "doodle-*doo*-doo" to the start of Gene Kelly's solo in *Singin' in the Rain* (1952).[52] He worked for producer Arthur Freed and himself became associate producer (that's the person who does most of the work) and then producer, on favorites from *Meet Me in St. Louis* (1944) to *Hello, Dolly!* (1969). Along the way, Edens shaped material for Judy Garland until she died in 1969. One year later, he too passed over.

Edens was among the excited parties who were in the room when thirteen-year-old Garland auditioned for MGM in the fall of 1935. Immediately hired, she nevertheless stagnated—only being given radio work (which she had been doing before MGM anyway), one loan-out, and one short. One of the problems was in establishing a salable teenage persona for her: she already had a prematurely full-bodied, mature voice and, moreover, was accustomed to singing torchy adult songs like "Bill."[53]

In an unpublished Garland biography, John Graham gives the most plausible version of what happened next.[54] Early in 1937, Edens created a special sung introduction and a spoken monologue, as a fan letter expressing a teenage crush, to go along with "You Made Me Love You." At first, Garland was going to sing about comedian-bandleader Ben Bernie (she was set to appear on his radio program)—a joke, for Bernie was far from being a romantic idol. But then Edens and his fellow Garland-champions (producer Arthur Freed, executive secretary Ida Koverman, fellow contractee Mickey Rooney) realized that Clark Gable was about to have an on-set birthday party, on February 1, attended by all the studio bigwigs, and this was the chance for Garland to show off her talent. Edens changed the special intro from "Dear Mr. Bernie" to "Dear Mr. Gable." Performed at the festivities, it charmed Gable and wowed studio head Louis B. Mayer, who ordered that the number be inserted into the movie Garland was

Figure 11.2. *Broadway Melody of 1938.* Fans, too, can carry a torch: the audience (Judy Garland) centers its gaze on the performer (Clark Gable, in the scrapbook) and sings "You Made Me Love You."

already set for, the loosely structured *Broadway Melody of 1938.* (This, of course, was the same movie in which Sophie Tucker rendered "Some of These Days"; see figures 7.2, 7.3, and 7.4.)

Edens was probably inspired by Carmel Myers, the beautiful vamp of 1920s Hollywood, now raising a family. Myers spent from winter 1936 through spring 1937 guesting on many radio shows, doing her own "song dramatizations."[55] One of these was a dream date with Clark Gable, incorporating the 1934 hit "Let's Fall in Love." Edens arranged the music for Myers's soliloquy. Then, later, he adapted Myers's notion of a song-monologue tribute to Gable, fitted it to a teenager's persona, and mated the idea with "You Made Me Love You."[56]

McCarthy and Monaco later told the tale that MGM offered them $250 each to use "You Made Me Love You" in the new movie.[57] Both men were in career slumps. After their 1913 success together, the two men had quarreled, but patched it up by the end of 1914 to create still more hits as a team for a few more years.[58] McCarthy had gone on to a series of Broadway shows with composer Harry Tierney, including the blockbusters *Irene* (1919) and *Rio Rita* (1927). Thus, McCarthy was on the top tier of the popular music hierarchy for about ten years. Meanwhile, Monaco's hit tunes had dwindled to about one every two or three years. The songwriters reunited for one more success, "Through," in 1929, and soon after that it seemed their major careers were . . . through. Their attempts in the Hollywood industry fizzled out as the early movie musicals lost popularity. By 1937 McCarthy had not had a hit since 1930 and Monaco since 1933. So they accepted the low payment from MGM "on the theory that it was a plug and might spark a revival."[59]

It did and it didn't. Garland, Chick Bullock, and Ben Pollack all recorded it for Decca, but none of these releases were top-of-the-chart events. Nevertheless, Garland created a sensation in *Broadway Melody of 1938*. Headlines blazoned "Singing Torch Song of Yesteryear, Judy Garland Scores Mightily."[60] Reviewers always praised and sometimes raved: "In itself worth the ticket fee"; "thrilled this writer"; "sensational work"; "her torch singing being unquestionably first-rate"; and "probably the greatest tour de force in recent screen history."[61] Ever after, Garland was associated with "You Made Me Love You," and her movie performance of it set the pattern for her to revive onscreen other old ballads, such as "I'm Nobody's Baby" (1921) and "I Cried for You" (1923), with Edens again creating a soliloquy to accompany the latter.

Further, Garland's rendition of "You Made Me Love You" resulted in Monaco having a spectacular comeback. MGM previewed *Broadway Melody* in mid-August—and on September 1, Monaco was flying out to Hollywood, holding a new contract with Paramount to compose a score for Bing Crosby.[62] This was followed by six more Crosby movies over the course of three years, with a total of sixteen hit songs. None of them, oddly, endured as strong standards, although "I've Got a Pocketful of Dreams" might qualify (just). Nevertheless, Monaco had more successes in just those three years than he had in the previous two decades.[63]

Jack Kapp of Decca Records flew to California to view the preview of *Broadway Melody* and went right back to his hotel and drew up a record contract for Garland.[64] The first single: "Dear Mr. Gable—You Made Me Love You." Throughout 1937, Garland performed the song on radio, at industry events, and in movie theatres. Though she soon set it aside (for a while), the few radio disc jockeys of that era kept spinning her Decca single on the air.[65] Although Garland's rendition of "You Made Me Love You" did not boost the number into the Hit Parade, it did strengthen the tune's status as standard repertoire.

Slowly, over the next few years, performers in nightclubs, on radio, and record increasingly used it. In the fall of 1940, Jolson returned to Broadway after a long absence, starring in *Hold onto Your Hats* and revisiting "You Made Me Love You" in his eleven o'clock specialty spot. The same season, Decca issued a fast-tempo rendition by Bing Crosby and the Merry Macs, which perhaps corresponds to a new sheet music edition about this time featuring the indications "bounce tempo" (at the start of the verse) and "slow rhythmic swing" (for the refrain). The disk only made a slight splash, but it boosted the profile of the song. "You Made Me" was proving well adapted to the Swing Era.

One of the performers who began to tour with the McCarthy-Monaco standard in their repertoire was Sue Raney, "singing comedienne."[66] One of her best bits was "her 1913 version of 'You Made Me Love You,' followed by a swing rendition as of 1941."[67] On January 3, 1941, she was in Providence, Rhode Island, playing on the same bill as Harry James and His Music Makers—a swing band that had been struggling ever since its start in 1939 and seemed about to fold. But James—one of the jazz trumpet idols of the thirties—had a plan: add three violins and a cello, hire a second singer, and start playing some sweet music along with the hot jazz.

Perhaps appearing in the theatre with Raney gave James an idea, along with hearing Garland and Crosby's discs on radio, because the bandleader soon had his arranger, Gray Raines, create a slow-tempo, string-heavy setting of "You Made Me Love You" to set off his sentimental solo trumpet work.[68] The Columbia label recorded the instrumental by mid-July and released it near the end of August.[69] In *Billboard*, M. H. Orodenker presciently gushed: "typically terrific . . . bringing new life to an always appealing number. . . . It's practically a new number as given here, and Harry's horn lifts it way out of the world. It's the sort of draw that should build steadily."[70] And it did.

Sales of the disc grew for nine weeks, and then by mid-December it began to get a lot of play on the jukeboxes, too. Belatedly, the music industry realized it had a major hit revival on its hands, and finally people began to broadcast it, other acts rushed to get it into their books, and labels scrambled to release rival waxings—ten in all, according to one report, including Ina Ray Hutton for the small Elite label.[71] Decca, amazingly, not only kept the Garland and Crosby discs in circulation, but also released new renditions by Guy Lombardo, Jimmy Dorsey, Hildegarde, and Carmen Cavallaro! (Perhaps Kapp was fond of the tune, which may offer an additional explanation of his prompt signing of Garland after witnessing her version.)

The song became, willy-nilly, a trumpet soloist's staple. Will Osborne had his usually "torrid" Black horn player "Red" Mack mute down for a sweet solo on it.[72] Out in Des Moines, novice bandleader-trumpeter Charlie Fisk performed "a thrilling duplication of the James record."[73] These were only the start of decades of trumpet tributes to James using "You Made Me."

"You Made Me Love You" was widely acknowledged as having *made* Harry James.[74] In two years the disc sold over a million copies, and it remained a jukebox staple through the fifties.[75] James performed "You Made Me" on screen twice in 1942 for the Universal studio: as part of a short, *Trumpet Serenade*; and to kick off the movie musical *Private Buckaroo*, where band canary Helen Forrest's vocal got nestled in amidst James's trumpet flourishes. ("You Made Me" brought James to Hollywood, where he was cast in *Springtime in the Rockies* alongside box-office star Betty Grable. Within seven months they were married;

twenty-two years and two children later, they divorced.) The trumpeter rere-
corded "You Made Me" in hi-fi in 1955 and for the rest of his life could not fill
a gig without playing it.

The converse was also true: James *made* "You Made Me Love You."[76] *Variety*
(a trifle exaggeratedly) claimed that the "tune [was] completely overlooked
when it was revived by Judy Garland," but it became a hot item after the extended success of James's version.[77] From then on it was, essentially, a timeless
standard first and a nostalgic, old-time song second, if at all.

The ditty's new status also seems to have given Monaco's career yet another
boost. Despite his successful run of hits with Crosby, Paramount had let him
go in 1940, and he did not produce another film tune for over three years. But
after the revival of "You Made Me Love You," he went on to compose five top
movie ballads over the course of two years—several of them for Betty Grable
movies. He died in the fall of 1945, with one of his biggest successes just about
to chart: "I Can't Begin to Tell You." Fittingly, one of the top discs was by Harry
James, with a vocal by wife Betty Grable.[78] (McCarthy also lived to see "You
Made Me Love You" reborn, before passing over in December 1943.)

Even as "You Made Me Love You" surged in renewed popularity, the United
States was mobilizing to join the military conflicts of World War II. *Variety*
pointed out that "because the younger men are being drafted," therefore "much
of the danceries" were left "to the older, more conservative clientele."[79] In Al-
lentown, Pennsylvania, Andy Perry, proprietor of the Empire Ballroom, asserted
"there has been a noticeable increase in the attendance of older persons at dates
played by name bands," and "those outfits that have helped build their reputa-
tions on click recordings of old-time standards have particular attraction for
the older people in his territory."[80] His example: Harry James and "You Made
Me Love You."

But the song's attraction to older audiences must have been only half the
story, for college students and their peers in the army were also enthusing about
the tune. Male students at Syracuse University vouched that "James's version"
of "You Made Me Love You" "has had widespread campus appeal."[81] The annual
survey by *Billboard* of 158 campuses documented "Harry James's phenomenal
rise from nowhere to third" place in their poll; and this "sensational quick
rise to fame on the country's campuses" corresponded to "those round, black
platters [that] had everything to do with the ork's popularity among the col-
leges"—foremost among them, of course, "You Made Me Love You."[82]

Representative of the draftees was Pvt. Jesse W. Hoagland, from Bridgeport,
Oregon, who was "a Harry James booster, and especially his record of 'You
Made Me Love You.'"[83] A typical scene: at the USO canteen in Wrightstown,
New Jersey, William Achtel "was swinging out on the piano a tricky arrange-
ment" of Monaco's tune, while around him fellow soldiers chatted, slept, and

wrote letters home.[84] Two generations embraced anew "You Made Me Love You," contributing to its revival.

Alongside the James connection, the association of Jolson and Garland to the song was not forgotten. Jolson was among the first to tour the nation (and, eventually, the world) performing for soldiers, usually including "You Made Me Love You" in his sets. At his first such junket, at Jacksonville, Florida, "the ovation was thunderous and overwhelmed the comedian, who repeatedly wanted to know 'Do you mean it?'"[85] Garland had her first solo concert, outdoors at Fairmount Park in Philadelphia in 1943, for 15,000 customers (at least as many were turned away). She had the "crowd in her mitts almost immediately," right through her "Garland medley" of "faves from her pix" that, of course, included "You Made Me."[86] She followed this with army camp and bond rally tours, likely featuring her first trademark number; she certainly sang the "Dear Mr. Gable" version on *Mail Call*, the military transcription radio show.[87]

Each unfolding added to the web of associations that the tune carried. The Garland revival of 1937 had perhaps encouraged Jolson to return "You Made Me Love You" to his radio, recording, and stage repertoires; and the James hit of 1941, likewise, probably even further encouraged both Jolson and Garland to propagate the number. Jolson kept singing it, including for the soundtrack of the movie based on his life, *The Jolson Story* (1946), and its sequel, *Jolson Sings Again* (1949). Garland regaled audiences with it on radio, television, LP, and especially in the live performances that became her major forum after her long-term contract at MGM ended in 1950. Nevertheless, it was the impact of the James disc that led to the song becoming foundational for bands and singers through the ensuing decades, paving the way for uncounted nightclub performances, as well as the 1959 charting single by Nat King Cole (simple, sweet, smoochy) and 1965 Easy Listening hit by Aretha Franklin (slowly climaxing), plus other notable singles by the Eddie Heywood band, Patsy Cline, and Dean Martin, and inclusion in over a dozen best-selling albums.

"You Made Me Love You" also had a mysterious 1954 surge of popularity. It began in late January; suddenly "You Made Me" was getting the same kind of radio play as the newest hit songs.[88] This vogue may have started merely as a lead-up to Valentine's Day; the intense play the song was getting spread to television, too, during that romantic holiday week. But then it kept appearing on the lists of pop tunes with the biggest audience share for either television or radio, right through to the third week of March. It is enigmatic. This revival to hit status was brief, just for two months, and was not associated with any particular recording or artist.[89] Instead, everybody was performing it.

ANALYSIS

McCarthy and Monaco organize "You Made Me Love You" in the typical manner: sixteen-measure verse, followed by a thirty-two measure refrain with an ABAC structure.

The lyric features a penultimate couplet that corresponds roughly to the usual "limerick" device, but because the phrases are not as symmetrical as usual (eight notes, then thirteen notes) the effect is somewhat different. The hallmark of the song lies in its repetitions, both obvious and subtle. (Perhaps there is too much repetition: one in five singers omits at least one line at some point in their arrangement.)

Commentators have admired and analyzed McCarthy's lyric for almost a century. Picking up the thread that unspools from "Some of These Days," McCarthy further limns the lyric about internal conflict. He paints a portrait of the protagonist's inner life. Both songs are remarkable because they manifest ambivalence, expressing not one simple emotion but a mix of emotions.

By contrast, critics have ignored Monaco's music, except to notice that it fits the words. His refrain starts with another of those arching phrases, like the ones that start "Kiss Me Again," "My Melancholy Baby," and "I'm the Lonesomest Gal in Town." Commencing his own little arch, Monaco jumps up a fifth. In the middle of the phrase he places a whole-step descent on "me love," which is echoed later in the song with "me want," "me sigh," and finally "some love." As the lyric mentions, it is like a sigh. The phase then subsides down to a tone just one-half step above the initial note, reinforcing a mood of irresolution. Thus, he settles his two-measure arch on a note not in the key—a sharp that could be interpreted as a blue note, a flatted fifth. This is the kind of gesture that would later become standard in songs like "Little White Lies" (1930).[90]

Overall, Monaco uses eighteen accidentals in the refrain, a higher incidence than any of the other tunes focused on in this book. (Perhaps this is why Alan Lewens labels it a "bluesy melody.")[91] Monaco's rhythms are very supple (particularly in contrast with the rigidly written note values of "My Melancholy Baby"). Through the main strain's leap up to a long note on the second beat of the measure, the rests at the start of five bars, and dotted rhythms in ten of the phrases, the composer creates a lively sense of syncopation throughout the refrain.

The wistful little opening arch is followed by a raggy repeated phrase. This kind of insistent, swinging repetition is a ragtime riff, a jazz riff. It conveys that Yankee quality that George Gershwin would later emulate: "jazzing up" a phase, "by repeating the words . . . in a stammering rhythm," in order "to Americanize it."[92]

Example 11.1. "You Made Me Love You," verse and refrain, piano-vocal score.

speak this   way,___   Why, oh! why   should   I   feel   blue,___
thought of   you,___   Now my   dream   of   love is   o'er___

Once I   used___ to   laugh at   you,___ But now I'm   cry - ing,_____ No use de -
I want   you___ and   noth-ing   more,   Come on, en - fold   me,_____   Come on and

ny - ing_____   There's no one   else   but you will   do,___
hold me,_____   Just like you   ne - ver   did be -   fore,___

Refrain

You   made   me   love   you,   I   did - n't want to do it   I

p - f

This kind of repetition of both words and notes was exploited in hit songs that closely preceded "You Made Me Love You." In "Alexander's Ragtime Band" (1911) Berlin repeats "come on and hear, come on and hear"; and in "Everybody's Doing It Now" (1912) he reiterates "doing it, doing it." In "Waiting for the Robert E. Lee" (1912), Maurice Abrahams repeats "come down to the levee, I said to the levee"; and his "Hitchy-Koo" (1913) repeats the title phrase three times. All of those repeated musical phrases are in ragtime-themed songs, attached to reflexive lyrics that are about the music itself. In contrast, McCarthy and Monaco yoke that sort of pattern to an emotion-tossed personal love lyric, creating a fascinating dynamic. Even more than "My Melancholy Baby," it seems to deserve the new appellation that *Variety* soon applied to it: "rag ballad"—a combination of rhythm song and love ballad.[93]

The "didn't want to" lines are infectious repeated figures. People often join in singing along with them, embracing them with a kind of joyous recognition.[94] In fact, from one perspective, Monaco's music and McCarthy's words go together to make the song a jolly ride throughout.

In the second pair of riff-like phrases, the "you knew it" lines, Monaco introduces the sharpened fifth, making these phrases quite jazzy—again, almost bluesy. Yet all these repetitions also hold a danger of retarding the momentum, particularly when taken at a slow tempo. The tune drags yet propels, pulsates yet soars. These repeated patterns and near variants may help it be more American, but also make it full of redundancies. There are two pairs of "I didn't want to"; two "knew" plus at the end "know"; a sextet of "want," used with two different meanings; the echoing of "times" with "sometimes" (and the verse's "there were times"); the trio of "I do"; the seven uses of "made." These repetitions reinforce what David A. Horowitz describes as the piece's "obsessive qualities," which are "literally climaxed with the love addict's naked plea of dependence": "Give me, give me."

The B section starts with another "made me" lyric, but varies it by adding "sometimes." With the melody trailing downward, the word sort of hangs there, a parenthetical appendix. The strain stays in its lower range for "You made me glad," another redundant statement—the phrase feels, again, like a parenthesis, creating a lull in the proceedings. The three-note chromatic descent on "made me glad" seems very barbershop-quartet-like (and is similar to moments in the verse of "My Melancholy Baby"). The next phrase starts with a dramatic ascent, up through a sharpened third, to the octave, "but there were times"; verbally and musically, it is a gesture of contrast with what preceded. The end word, "dear," seems like a filler, an empty word, except that the endearment softens, in retrospect, the coming negative statement: "feel so bad," set to another three-note chromatic descent.

"Bad" is ambiguous: unworthy? unhappy? depressed? naughty? sinful? McCarthy's lyric here encapsulates the ambivalence of the protagonist: love makes her feel "happy" and "glad," but also "bad." This is the emotional confusion that would become a frequent element of classic pop from the mid-1920s to the mid-1950s, whether "It Had to Be You" (1924), "Between the Devil and the Deep Blue Sea" (1932), "Ol' Devil Moon" (1947), or "Mixed Emotions" (1951). In "You Made Me," this characteristic ambivalence is encountered in its early stage of development.

The frisson comes from the way McCarthy and Monaco subtly shift and vary their repetitions. The A section is in two halves, and the second half does not exactly repeat what came before. Instead, the opening arch is altered to a ski slope by omitting the first jump: it starts up on two repeated notes. Then Monaco changes the riff phrase to introduce the sharp G, a chromaticism that intensifies the riff gesture. When he comes back to that point in the second A section, he creates a new pattern, repeated not twice but three times and varied the third time to include an extra note—while McCarthy, of course, introduces an additional syllable ("Yes, I do / 'Deed I do / You know I do"). Just before that, where in the first A section Monaco had a rest, instead the flatted note on "true" falls strongly on the first beat, which also helps build tension.

The penultimate line has attracted praise from the beginning. *Billboard* pointed out that "the climax lyric line of the chorus is accompanied by a climax melody line that should do much to popularize the song."[95] While the riff phrases used one pair of a dotted eighth then a sixteenth, building up to the conclusion Monaco links up *four* of those pairs. This is another satisfying variation, an amplification of what came before. Meanwhile, the composer takes the melody line up, and up, to finally rest on the highest note of the song, "I'd"—soon matched by a repetition of that note on "You." At the climax of the song, "I" and "you" are united in a peak experience.

If I make all this sound sexual, I am not alone. Not only did *Billboard* remark about the risqué nature of the overall lyric in 1913; in 1946 the editor of *Musical Express* wrote specifically about the ending of the song: "What do you 'sigh for' at the climax of this 'lovesick' theme? To me it has only one significance." At first he gets the lyric slightly wrong, but the correct words, "give me what I *cry* for," only make that sexual significance even clearer—as he soon elaborates: "to 'die for' a kiss is surely carrying the ecstasy to the heights of eroticism."[96] The unexpected fall onto the flatted "true," the snowball effect of the three "I do" phrases, the hammering demand "give me," capped by the ascending final phrases—all these elements contribute to the creation of a metaphorical orgasm. One out of three performers intensify this further by repeating the final lines or creating some other tag, milking it for all its worth.

This effect was prefigured in "Kiss Me Again"—but, in that work, the waltz time and large vocal range of operetta makes it feel different. In a raggier style, this sort of climax can also be found "Oh, You Beautiful Doll," with its final "Oh! Oh! Oh! Oh! Oh, you beautiful doll." The orgasmic effect created in "Kiss Me Again," "Oh, You Beautiful Doll," and "You Made Me Love You" is echoed in many later standards. For example, Cole Porter creates such a climax in "I've Got You Under My Skin" (1936), as do Rube Bloom and Johnny Mercer with "Day In, Day Out" (1939). The way McCarthy and Monaco build the intensity in their "rag ballad" is compelling and masterful—and particularly remarkable for coming in 1913, demonstrating what "You Made Me" helped crystallize for the canonic style of the ensuing golden age.

Among the weaknesses of the song is its tendency to bleat, to blare. The opening notes, jumping up and lingering on "made," itself is a rather blatant, shrill call. The insistent repetitions, the chromatic slides, the hyperbolic "kisses that I'd die for," all contribute to a kind of crudity in the piece. The final climax is tremendously satisfying—however, it is also a trap. So many singers exploit the mounting intensity of "You Made Me Love You," shouting out the final section, that this approach becomes routine. It is a temptation to ride this wave to the top in order just to show off, to milk from the audience a knee-jerk ovation. Singers forget to delve into the more complex and tender aspects of the piece.

The lyric is complex. The basic message is: I can't resist you—I'm yours—even though you are far from perfect, and I feel far from idyllic in my love for you. There's a kind of reality to this portrait. Philip Furia has (twice, the second time with Michael Lasser) analyzed some of its subtleties. Furia calls the exclamation "you made me," a "street taunt," but it is more an accusation; Furia labels "I didn't want to" as a "vernacular, but limp, apology," but it is more an excuse.[97] Yet, Furia and Lasser are correct in identifying the allusion to a "childishly helpless point of view."[98] The lyric is full of phrases a kid in trouble would use when trying to blame her mischief on somebody else. Equally valid is Furia's noting of McCarthy's deft "slang collage" and the oscillations in emotion, the "juxtaposition of images that portrays the singer as at once helpless and aggressive," the "erotic anger," the "paradox of passionate impotence with comically angry accusations."[99] Passion, powerlessness, eroticism, comedy, and anger—to which can be added greed—are all lurking within the song.

Each singer and listener decides the level or kind of making (charming, persuading, forcing), loving, wanting, sighing, crying, and kissing that the piece refers to. At its most extreme, the lyric carries an aura of sexual coercion—that the lover seduced her, made her have sex, perhaps even raped her. Yet, another scenario is hinted at near the end: under the pretext of saying the love object has got his way, the singer is actually demanding *her* own way—and blaming it on him. Perhaps this lyric is a strategy for seduction, rather than the fallout from it.

At the other extreme, it can mean the sweetheart is just so loveable, so full of love, that the protagonist's pride, stubbornness, and fears have been dissolved. There is a long line of lyrics that follow "You Made Me Love You" in this: for example, the coy 1934 "Don't Blame Me" (instead, blame my desire for you on your charms, your arms, your kiss); and the negative 1947 "I Wish I Didn't Love You So" (because I should have moved on after we broke up, but I'm still attached to you). In the end, however, the underlying message of such lyrics is always: I love you. That is the bottom line. And so it is in "You Made Me Love You"; the seeming contradictions resolve. In the end, the singer asks for love, for kisses, now. This is the tender thing about the song: there is happy eagerness, not regret.

McCarthy uses the startling phrase "brand of kisses," language out of the field of commerce, of advertising—very modern, very consumerist. Horowitz creates a lengthy discussion about such "commodity fetishism" in Tin Pan Alley songs. He says that the lyrics present the desire for the sweetheart as being like the desire of the consumer for industrial products. (Obviously, one could easily argue the opposite.) The only song, however, that he cites using the language of merchandising is here, with the use of "brand of kisses" in "You Made Me Love You." One in six singers, however, get rid of "brand," usually changing it to the less mercantile "kind."

Nevertheless, popular songs were a commodity, in part—art and artifact, products of both Muse and Mammon. Horowitz's ultimate point is valid: "Popular culture succeeded in commodifying romance as an essential experience for the young"—it was in the commercial interests of the pop song industry that the customer view romance as important.[100] In such a culture, "lovers and potential mates" became "the object of deeply embedded fixations and fetishes."[101] Ironically, by so describing them, "the creators of popular songs were" being realistic, "unconsciously commenting on the very commodification of romance their work helped to create."[102] The song makes us love it—however much we didn't want to do it.

I have so far ignored the verses of "You Made Me Love You," partly because most performers do. The early artists to record the tune included the verse (in fact, Halley and La Rue include both sets of verse lyrics). But, after that, it has been largely neglected—no surprise, for so have the verses to all the songs in this book (except "My Melancholy Baby") and, in fact, most classic pop ballads. Yet, out of respect for the writers and those few performers who have used the verse, some observations are in order. It is a personal "I and you" statement throughout (no "she did this, he did that"), and both sets of verse lyrics are worthy of being performed, perhaps with a little tweaking to a few lines here and there.

There are musical effects in the sixteen-measure verse that are echoed in the refrain, creating some coherence and unity in the song as a whole (as is also the case with "My Melancholy Baby"). Like the refrain, the verse is structured ABAC and uses wonderfully insistent repeated melodic units—except here it is only bits of tune that repeat, not words. In the verse B section, we hear a three-note chromatic descent similar to the one in the refrain B section (and similar to those in the verse of "My Melancholy Baby").[103] The transition from the verse's second A section to its C segment is rushed—no long note, no rest, no pause. This is like the hypermetric shift in the verse of "Bill Bailey, Won't You Please Come Home?" and other blues ballad structures. As with such proto-blues, the rushing ahead adds a very American sense of propulsion. What is rushed into is another repeated musical figure, but this time repeated three times rather than merely twice. (This will be later paralleled in the chorus, when what had previously been pairs of riff phrases are replaced by the triple "I do" phrases as the refrain transitions to its final stanza.)

The lyric paints a jumble of emotions. The most unusual touch is the revelation "Once I used to laugh at you." There is something very realistic in this scenario: you didn't used to take someone seriously, but now you desire them. The second set of lyrics for the verse continues the synopsis of two people who have known each other a long time, and only gradually has the singer fallen in love. (This second verse was omitted from one of the major sheet music editions, issued when the Harry James disc became a hit.) The protagonist used to dream of an ideal lover—handsome and true. The singer never considered the laughable acquaintance a possible candidate for romance. Here, McCarthy offers a prefiguring of P. G. Wodehouse's early torch lyric, "Bill" (1918; revised by Oscar Hammerstein II in 1927), wherein the verses describe the protagonists' youthful ideal fantasy lover and the prosaic everyman she ended up falling for. The word "handsome" implies the love object is male (though of course women are sometimes called handsome too). Presumably by "true" she means sexually and romantically faithful. Yet there is also a kind of play of ideas there: her *untrue* fantasy is about someone *true*.

The point is that she has erased her fantasies to come down to reality, which includes accepting, indeed *desiring* a man who is not handsome—and, sadly, perhaps not true either. Reality is a mixture of good and bad and, unlike fantasy, is out of one's control. The final section of the second verse—begging to be held, enfolded—echoes the pleading demands for physical intimacy at the end of the refrain. "Just like you never did before" is ambiguous, but may imply the pair have not yet had sex. Perhaps this is why *Billboard* particularly praised this section: "McCarthy shows himself to be a master of the art of writing a real second verse in this number, for the chorus sentiment is considerably strengthened by its clean-cut explanation."[104]

Early discussions of "You Made Me Love You" reveal further aspects of the refrain. *Billboard* pointed out to its professional audience that "the peculiar semi-patter chorus effect makes the song one which can be acted throughout by a performer in such a way that individual lines receive individual interpretation."[105] The shifts and vacillations allow for a wide range of emotional expression within one short refrain. In addition, even the repetitions allow for each riff phrase to be given a shifting intonation and emotion; for example: "And all the time you knew it" (resentment), / "I guess you always knew it" (affectionate resignation).

Perhaps most remarkable in the early literature is a 1917 piece written by theatre critic Percy Hammond—in his early Chicago years but already featuring his characteristic erudite, lightly ironic style—in interaction with Al Jolson, in the Windy City on tour with yet another Schubert hodgepodge musical comedy, *Robinson Crusoe, Jr.* The star defends American popular songs and their songwriters from Hammond's highbrow disdain. The example Jolson chooses is "You Made Me Love You," which he interprets in the most serious possible light:

> A human investigation of its content, says he, will disclose that it is not less than the hurt outcry of a simple soul, suffering, not ignobly, the anguish customary to a wrecked amour. He believes it to be the understandable epitome of a myriad of minor amatory crises, voicing the desperate lamentation of all the little people who love and lose. It is, he thinks, the threnody of many dead kisses from lips that lie to lips that trust. . . . "Can't you see," he queries, "the thin, white arms reaching up out of the darkness? It is the dirge of seduction, and it has kept more innocent lady barbers out of the primrose path than all the Brahms concertos ever played by a symphony orchestra. . . . when I tell them about sex in words and music that they understand they realize a propinquity of life and the theater that they get in a cheap song."[106]

Most singers render "You Made Me" as a story about a "minor amatory crisis," with a potentially happy outcome. In his 1940s renditions, Jolson conveys just such a positive scenario with playful excitement. Throughout most of this 1917 passage, however, he predominantly lingers on the tragic undertones of the ditty. This protagonist is "desperate," in "anguish," lamenting and singing a "dirge"—a fallen woman, seduced, betrayed, and abandoned. The description of "thin, white arms reaching up out of the darkness" foreshadows the later image of the profoundly suffering female torch singer.[107]

Indeed, from the start, alongside the comic extrapolations on "You Made Me Love You" were the serious ones. *Billboard* praised both the Jewish American vaudeville headliner Belle Baker and the team of George Whiting and Sadie Burt for singing it "seriously."[108] The *Player* called Baker's rendition "a revelation."[109] Whiting and Burt, singing it in duet, make it "more effective," indeed, "make a new song of it," by rendering it as a dialogue and putting "feeling and heart into their interpretation."[110]

Similarly in England, in 1913 the *Manchester Guardian* journalist known as W. H. M. wrote, "the song expresses something which someone has rather strongly felt—it has in it an authentic, credible quality."[111] Yet, he "heard it a week or two ago sung with much archness by the 'Sisters Someone' as the irrelevant prelude to a step dance."[112] The true potential of the song, however, was brought out in the Hippodrome revue *Step This Way*, by a "young lady in the red frock . . . a broken and, for all her finery, forlorn presence among us."[113] She rendered the song as a "tragedy expressing itself by the means readiest and nearest to hand, these means happening to be the contemporary slang of the streets. She was a forlorn and broken presence among us. And she was among us, for she sang not from the stage but from a bridge" that spanned the space between the audience and the stage.[114] As with the table-visiting of Tommy Lyman and his peers, or the megaphone into which Madge Maitland crooned "When I Lost You," the staging of "You Made Me" in *Step This Way* sought to create greater intimacy between the performer and the audience, using the vehicle of the new American rag ballad.

These contemporaneous descriptions are a reminder that these songwriters, in crafting material such as "You Made Me Love You," were pioneers in doing something radical: making statements about love that carried emotional heft, yet that unspool in the vernaculars of a boisterous, modern, urban world.

RECORDINGS AND THE PERFORMANCE TRADITION

If you want to hear what "You Made Me Love You" sounded like as a product of the ragtime era, listen to William J. Halley's medium-fast rendition in 1913—he has time to do both verses. Or Tommy Handley's 1927 British comedy sketch "The Dis-Orderly Room"—skim through to the climactic trial scene, when the accused sings a parody, emphasizing he "didn't want to do it." These lively figurings of the song contain a revelation to those who are bored with the many slow and spineless renditions of later decades.

But it is the transformation of the song by Al Jolson that grips—still raggy, but with complex emotions. His later recordings of it pale by comparison (good as they are). In 1913 he approaches it with rhapsodic freedom. He changes the lyrics to half the lines. In the most mysterious alteration, he makes "I want some love" into the elliptical "Some love from you." Rather than creating confusion, the lack of grammar is convincing as a depiction of emotional turmoil—rather like the odd juxtapositions in "Some of These Days." He slides downward on "ma-ade (me) lo-ove (you)" and upward on "(made me) wa-ant (you)." He moans, almost apologetically: in the verse, on "Your love makes me this way—aw," thus eliminating the awkward "speak"; and in his second refrain, with "O-aw, I felt so bad."

He is singing full out on "You made me glad"—which he takes up an octave, making that rather limp line into something dramatic. Yet in general, he sounds intimately focused, his tone soft like raw dough. On top of changing the lines themselves, his phrasing throughout is beautifully pliable, mercurial. He creates an emotional ambience that is mostly anguished, but occasionally playful, as on "I didn't think you'd do it" (which is his alteration of "I didn't want to do it"). This hint of kittenishness culminates in his altering the insistent but potentially plodding "Give me, give me" to a triple "Give me. Give me. Give me"; and, after the second refrain, a sevenfold "Give me, gimme gimme gimme, gimme gimme gimme." (That is more "gimmes" than any other singer would ever use again.) He is eager but suffering, his very neediness creating his suffering. He is a ma-cho guy, yet vulnerable and distressed by his own, unexpected vulnerability. Yet underneath still lies the cock-o'-the-walk confidence: "gimme gimme gimme" is a pathetic plea, but he still feels entitled to receive it.

Grace La Rue's rendering is, by modern standards, a bit screechy and rhyth-mically sometimes stodgy—though at other times flexible—but compelling nevertheless, and certainly effective for an acoustic era theatre. She follows Jolson in going up an octave on "You made me glad" (which sounds even more dramatic in a soprano range). She also expands the "Give me" line, to "Give me, gimme gimme gimme." There is an implied double-time tempo in this choice.

Both the colloquial "gimme" and the double-time feeling would prove im-portant in the history of the song. After the initial sheet music editions of "You Made Me Love You," Broadway Music capitulated to what Jolson had been do-ing from the start—and, once again, the performance tradition transformed the printed tradition: every later printing alters "I didn't want to" to "I didn't wanna"; and "Give me, give me" becomes "Gimme, gimme." (Oddly, the front covers and inner title pages continue to display the subtitle as "I Didn't Want to Do It," even while the lyric reads "I didn't wanna do it.") Singers make their own choice: two out of ten vocalists change "want to" to the slangier "wanna." One out of ten uses only "gimme"; three out of ten intermix "gimme" and "give me"; and six out of ten singers just stay with the original "give me."

Singers insert additional instances of "give me" or "gimme," which allows them to play with the rhythms of that line. About one in six will use differ-ent numbers of them at different points in a rendition, like Jolson in his 1913 recording. About half of singers stay with the original pair of them. The other half, or just slightly more, multiply them to three, (even more often) four, or (not as often) five or six.

The tune seems to invite the use of double time using "Gimme, gimme, gimme, gimme."[115] (Perhaps this is caused by anticipation of the next phrase, which does use shorter, quicker notes.) Even so, no print edition changes that vocal line. One edition, however (the "bounce tempo" one), does go into double time in the *piano accompaniment* at those measures. While the upper stave continues in four even quarter notes, "gimme, gimme," the piano is ragging away in dotted-eighth and sixteenth notes, as if chanting "gimme, gimme, gimme, gimme," seeming to encourage the vocalist to stray from the vocal line.

Garland's renditions have influenced many other singers—thereby making Edens, too, one of the major shapers of the "You Made Me Love You" performance tradition. Unlike most special material items, "Dear Mr. Gable" was copyrighted as a song in its own right. In Garland-related printed editions, the two are often joined, as verse and chorus, even though the refrains never include Edens's alterations of it. Garland's movie vocal is a shade more delicate than her waxing of it for disc, but otherwise they feature only the minutest differences in text and delivery. And what a text and what a delivery!

Garland (and Edens) deserve all the accolades given at the time and over the decades for this masterful sequence. The "Dear Mr. Gable" verse is catchy and well shaped. (Use of it in later decades is often mentioned in reviews of club acts; and Steve Lawrence and Connie Francis are caught on disc delivering adaptations of it.) With the refrain, Edens appropriately desexualizes the lyric, adapting it to an adolescent persona. In the first A section, Edens alters "want" to "love" (one out of four later singers follow his lead). "Bad" becomes "sad" (a variation La Rue had already used, but the one out of four singers who later make that change are probably more influenced by Garland and Edens). "I need some love" is replaced by "I think you're grand" (a change that Garland and her daughters Liza Minnelli and Lorna Luft retain—and Barry Manilow, whose rendition is very Garland-influenced). The "gimme, gimme . . . brand of kisses" stanza is supplied with two sanitizations: the first about the youngster's "heart reeling" (utilized by Francis and Manilow, as well as Garland and her daughters); the second declaring "let the whole world stop . . . you'll always be the top" (a variation of this is always used by Dean Martin). All together, touches of Edens's refashioning of "You Made Me Love You" are manifested in more than three out of ten performances.

I first encountered "You Made Me Love You" in Garland's 1937 renditions—originally in a shortened version (minus one stanza and the spoken interlude) in *That's Entertainment!* (1974). For this movie tribute to MGM, Garland's voice underscores a montage of clips of Clark Gable, scowling, grinning, winking, and kissing. The excerpt helped to create a mythic aura around both stars.

I felt shocked—and vaguely disturbed—by Garland's combination of innocence and passion. Her intensity seemed alien amidst the seventies' cool, damp, gray, post-Watergate atmosphere. But the scene was also unforgettable, doing its part to make the film a pivotal experience in my life. (Soon after, among the first albums I bought was *The Best of Judy Garland*, with her Decca version.) The movie scene had already been extracted in the 1950s for the *MGM Parade* television anthology series, and Decca had been reissuing the single on albums since Garland's resurgence in the early fifties. The success of *That's Entertainment!* led to further uncounted "Dear Mr. Gable" repackagings in song folios and on LP, CD, VHS, Laser Disc, DVD, downloads, and streaming. All these helped make Garland's version the one people most remember at the start of the twenty-first century.[116]

At age fourteen-going-on-fifteen, Garland already displays hallmarks of her mature style: the swift, subtle modulations in volume and intensity; the alternation between flowing ease and quivering nervous energy.[117] Riveting. Admittedly, in *Broadway Melody*, the way she wrinkles her nose, and some of the soft-spoken, naïve passages are almost *too* cute; and yet, they still seem fresh, and she soon grew out of those affectations.

In later years, Garland would render only a single chorus of "You Made Me Love You" as part of a medley. Only on a 1951 radio transcription does she display what she can do with it full-length, using her adult persona. She starts by crooning and continues the first refrain using most of the Edens's details. Very good.

But then! Her second half-refrain starts with a long "Oh!" that signals the huge climax to which she is going to build, discarding the jejune Edens variants. This may be the only time Garland begged "give me, give me, give me, give me" for his "brand of kisses." When she gets to "that I'd *die* for" (in a fine and perhaps unique melodic variation from the original), she mixes heartache and excited eagerness, all rolled together in one, in a complete fulfillment of the song's (and the genre's) potential.

This may be the earliest recording in which the second half-refrain so completely comes to a climax—a tendency that would become one of the most often-found traits in renditions of "You Made Me Love You." During the album era, most recordings (when they are not bland and sappy) went for this applause-milking climax: Dion, Della Reese, Aretha Franklin, Anthony Newley, Joan Shaw, and Eve Graham.[118] The tendency is even more blatant in live performances captured of Tony Martin, Vic Damone, and Ray Charles (many times—2002 being one instance). The song's potential in this direction has, unfortunately, become a kind of trap, a knee-jerk artistic choice that prevents fresh approaches. Perhaps the best of the strutters caught live are Eddie Fisher, in 1962 at the Winter Garden (where Jolson originally purveyed the tune), and Debbie Reynolds, on a 1985 PBS live television special.[119] Fisher, in good voice, floats, struts, builds, understates, then climaxes in an economical refrain and a quarter, plus a brief tag. Reynolds is remarkable for stringing it out—two and a half refrains and a very lengthy tag—and making it work!

Reynolds had reintroduced "You Made Me Love You" on the Broadway stage in a 1973 "revisical" of McCarthy's 1919 hit musical *Irene*. It served as the second act expression of romantic reunion of the eponymous heroine and her beau. Seemingly it is included because of its familiarity: almost any other ballad could have filled the spot just as well. Patsy Kelly, playing Irene's mother, also reunites with a past lover, and "You Made Me" is the song marking this consummation, as well. On the cast album, a delightful spoken dialogue version of the lyric ends with Kelly belting out a hilarious climactic C segment, which satirizes the strident aspect of the song's performance tradition.

From 1973 on, Reynolds kept the song in her act. She croons half of it to her daughter, Carrie Fisher, on the *Oprah Winfrey Show* in 2011: "I didn't wanna do it" (and then, spoken, "I did"); followed by "You made me happy sometimes" (and, spoken, "always"). After the poignant deaths of daughter and mother within a day of each other at the end of 2016, the Golden Globes awards show paid tribute to both actresses. Portions of the Oprah video were used to bookend a montage of cinematic moments of the two, underscored by part of Reynolds's *Irene* recording. It is an imitation of the Gable montage in *That's Entertainment!*—testifying to how strongly the song has become associated with the mythologizing of star performers.

In jazz history, "You Made Me Love You" has played a different role. Warren Vachè relates a revealing anecdote concerning "You Made Me" after Harry James came out with his 1941 disc:

> I have an amusing recollection of an incident that took place around this time at Nick's, the jazz club in Greenwich Village. Somebody in the audience requested the band to play the song—disregarding the fact that it was not in the usual repertory—and they complied. Wild Bill Davison was the trumpet player, and he gave it his customary steamy rendition. Then as the band was about to leave the stand for the intermission, I overheard him remark to one of the other musicians, "Hey, that tune ain't half bad when it's played like that. But have you heard that thing by Harry James?"[120]

In 1941 the struggle between supporters of "sweet" music and "hot" music was intense. Fans had treasured James as a hot trumpeter and a bandleader of swing, swing, swing. They were shocked by him taking on a string section—and alarmed when his sweet rendition of "You Made Me Love You" swept the country and became an identifying number for James. The outrage was both immediate and long lasting—as Dan Morgenstern reports, "jazz critics never forgave Harry."[121] The offense was all the worse because of its ripple effect.

The sensuous feel of the arrangement attracted singer Helen Forrest, who took a drastic pay cut to mate her sound with those textures (and, also, to both start and end the arrangements that featured her vocals). Together, the trumpeter and singer fused—soon, in bed as well as on the stand. Forrest pointed to "a cry in our music," "like a couple of rabbis chanting together," and a "warmth" that she brought out in James.[122] The ambience could have been fulsome, but instead was luxuriously full-bodied. The hits (many of them ballads) poured forth. As Gunther Schuller opines, they "affect[ed] the future course of jazz. . . . other bands . . . copied the formula, singers took over . . . , [and] jazz as swing was more or less driven out—certainly as a *leading* force."[123] Ironically, James's instrumental of "You Made Me Love You" indirectly ended an era of instrumentals.

James opens with seven pick-up notes that provide an irresistible launching pad for the first phrase, where his brassy trumpet is joined by the sighing strings. James slides and slurs ("I di-idn't wa-anna do-o it") and, on the long notes, opens up his vibrato like a French kiss. Raines's arrangement arches its back like a kitten, sprightly skips, ambles, builds, shimmers to support a moment of cantorial trumpeting, and fades for a quiet finish.

In the spring of 1941, James's mother suddenly died, age forty-nine, just after visiting James's newborn son. Within months, James was in the studio, poised to put Raines's arrangement of "You Made Me Love You" onto wax. James "suddenly remembered" his mother's advice: "he should play the way she sang."[124] Focusing on the memory of his mother's singing, he recorded the track that saved his band and set the pattern for his ballad playing for the rest of his life.

Forrest got her chance to join James on "You Made Me Love You" in the opening sequence of *Private Buckaroo* (1941). His solos prove that he did not grow stale—his phrasing here varies in a creative manner from his studio recording (as is also the case with his 1950s hi-fi recording). Forrest enters to take her own refrain. Smiling, sensuous, restrained, her voice like plush, she comes as close as anyone to making the storm-tossed lyric into a simple, fond, affectionately amused "I love you." (Forrest kept the song in her repertoire to the end of her lengthy career. Away from the restraints of the band setting, her renditions tend to become overblown, with her wide open vibrato and emotionalism taking over.)

The song thrived in many contexts. The uptempo, jolly, rollicking renditions are some of the best: Miff Mole and his Little Molers giving it that 1920s jazz kick (especially the drums at the end of the B sections).[125] Bing Crosby and the jivey Merry Macs use the uncomfortably fast tempo to play around the beat like chipmunks. The twenty-first-century Israeli gypsy-swing group Swing de Gitanes race through it, like a comic chase scene.

In contrast to "Let Me Call You Sweetheart," "I Wonder Who's Kissing Her Now," and "My Melancholy Baby," few rock and roll era stylists were attracted to "You Made Me Love You."[126] Yvonne Mills and the Sensations give it a fine, *echt* high-school-gym ballad treatment. Screamin' Jay Hawkins spouted it, chortling, rasping, spewing nonsense syllables, in a unique and wild rendition, climaxing with call-and-response ejaculations. The song fits nicely over the usual rock triplets, yet hardly anyone felt impelled to tackle it in this vein.

Though later jazz generations ignore the tune (probably put off by the James aura), some swing-era greats created intelligent articulations.[127] Earl "Fatha" Hines's piano solo is full of gorgeous harmonies and hesitations. A prominent version by the Eddie Heywood band, in a leisurely medium-slow tempo, has the band-chorus playfully call and respond to the "talking" trombone soloist. Maxine Sullivan, in her 1981 rendition with a Swedish small jazz group, opts for playful swing—jolly and sweet—understating the drama.

The classic three—Jolson, Garland, James—were all highly emotional performers with big, even vibratos. Among others, however, those who understate the song are most riveting. Una Mae Carlisle (on piano and vocal) starts with half the verse—a nice touch also used by Ina Ray Hutton. Carlisle then delivers a gently rolling, sexy, smoky-voiced, after-hours, small-group jazz version. Hildegarde, that sophisticated chanteuse, gave it her elegantly gloved touch, led into with a wistful vamping figure.[128] Intimate, restrained, filled with quiet yearning, quiet beseeching, she sings it with intelligence. (Her sophisticated approach makes it sound as if it were by Cole Porter, pointing to how much he may have been influenced by "You Made Me" in his portraits of ambivalence, such as "I Hate You, Darling.") Carlisle and Hildegarde are united in creating a close focus: the beloved seems to be right there on the couch.

FILM AND LITERATURE

Jolson was never filmed singing "You Made Me Love You." Instead, we can only imagine him in 1913, rendering it in *Honeymoon Express*, helping the heroine prevent her divorce, as Gus, the crafty, comic servant, in blackface.[129] To those like myself, raised during or since the civil rights era, the idea is repellant: blackface makeup and conventions nauseate. We have to work hard to see the artistic genius behind the many (white and Black) who appear in drawings, photos, and films in that guise. Except for Jolson's use of it in *Honeymoon Express*, "You Made Me" never became connected with blackface conventions. Other stars associated with the ditty in the 1910s—Belle Baker, George Whiting, Fanny Brice, Grace La Rue, Mistinguett—were not blackface performers. Their adoption of this rag ballad once again represents the gradual interweaving of slangy, raggy songs into the white mainstream.

In all his Winter Garden shows, Jolson was given the privileged eleven o'clock spot for his set of solo songs. During this, he would break character. Thus his

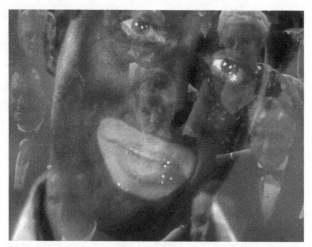

Figure 11.3. *The Jolson Story* (1946). The performer centers his gaze on the audience and sings "You Made Me Love You." "Al Jolson" (played by Larry Parks, in blackface, on the visual track and sung by Al Jolson on the soundtrack) makes love to the theatre crowd—with an assist from the optical effects technicians—sealing the compact between audience and star.

shifting repertoire would have only accidental relevance to the surrounding plot—and instead was an expression of his own persona, each number adding to his star mythos. This must have held true for "You Made Me Love You."

Posterity cannot see Jolson, in all his dynamic physicality, deliver "You Made Me Love You"—instead we have Larry Parks embodying a fictionalized Jolson in *The Jolson Story* and *Jolson Sings Again*. Parks is compelling in his own way, but there is no substitute for the way the music flowed through Jolson's body, as seen in his earliest movie vehicles. In the first biopic, Parks appears in blackface for this number. In the sequel, he appears both in and not in blackface. This becomes another symbol of the peeling away of the blackface tradition from the classic pop gestalt: in 1949 blackface is framed as history.

Many renditions of "You Made Me Love You" are in tribute to Al Jolson (in the many club acts and biographical plays), Judy Garland (even Frank Sinatra performed it in a nightclub with a "Dear Judy Garland" intro), or Harry James (the number of trumpet versions! Oy!).[130] Performers who exploited the song as long as (indeed, sometimes longer than) those three, nevertheless, never became associated with the tune—not Dinah Shore, for instance, or even Ray Charles. (Many imitate Charles's "I Wonder Who's Kissing Her Now," but none do his "You Made Me.")

Because of "Dear Mr. Gable," the connotations surrounding "You Made Me Love You" came to include the relationship between the audience and the performer, with a self-consciousness about the mythos of a star persona. There are some discrepancies between the lyric and the situation of Garland singing

Figures 11.4 and 11.5. *Jolson Sings Again* (1950). The performer centers his gaze on himself. On the right, "Al Jolson" (played by Larry Parks on the visual track) is intently involved as "Larry Parks" (on the left, also played by Larry Parks on the visual track) lip-synchs to a recording by "Al Jolson" (sung by the real Jolson on the soundtrack). The sequence that "Larry" is supposedly filming is the one in Figure 11.3, singing "You Made Me Love You." The two figures mirror each other's fervent facial expression and shoulder twist. The performer becomes, narcissistically, his own fan, his own object of adoration, in a moment that mythologizes mythologizing.

to Gable. Some lines make little sense when addressed to someone you have never met: "and all the time you knew it" (how? mental telepathy?) and "I didn't want to tell you . . . I think you're grand" (the point of writing a fan letter is to tell the person they are grand). Nevertheless, Horowitz points out that the song's "obsessive qualities" of "emotional dependence and romantic fixation," depicted in "ambivalent and psychologically complex terms," equally fit both Jolson's "love addict" and Garland's media addict[131] (see figure 11.2).

In *The Jolson Story*, the idea of a love song from audience to star is reversed. The fictionalized Jolson is played by Parks, who lip synchs to the singing voice of the real Jolson. In the plot, Jolson finally gets a chance on Broadway. He seizes the opportunity to implement his long-held dream: raise the house lights up, so that he can see into the eyes of the audience. Through this increased intimacy, the love affair of star and crowd is made complete.

In the sequel *Jolson Sings Again* (1949), the mythologizing of the star is intensified. Parks plays both the middle-aged Jolson and also himself, Parks. He can then play a scene in which the middle-aged Jolson watches Parks play the youthful Jolson. The song: "You Made Me Love You." The narcissistic leanings of the song and its mystique are brought to the forefront.

Figures 11.6 and 11.7. *Love Me or Leave Me* (1955). While Moe Snyder (James Cagney) cannily registers the magnetism that she holds not only for him but the audience too, Ruth Etting (Doris Day) sings "You Made Me Love You," clearly relishing her newly proven power over her listeners.

"You Made Me Love You" also functions as a fulcrum in *Love Me or Leave Me* (1955), a biopic in which Doris Day plays Ruth Etting. The singer finally gets a chance to prove her worth as a soloist in front of a nightclub audience and her mentor (and would-be boyfriend), Moe Snyder (James Cagney). The bond immediately created between Etting and her audience is almost palpable. As they applaud, smug triumph fleetingly flickers across her face. So effective was the mythologizing accomplished by this movie that Etting's obituaries (and books that rely on them) proclaimed that she purveyed the song in her heyday.[132] I have found no evidence that Etting ever sang "You Made Me Love You."

Xanadu (1980) is another musical intent on mythologizing. Gene Kelly stars as Danny McGuire, the same name as his role in *Cover Girl* (1944), in which he starred with Rita Hayworth. The unacknowledged bases for the script of *Xanadu* are *Cover Girl* and another Hayworth musical, *Down to Earth* (1947), in which she costarred with Larry Parks (he who mimed "You Made Me Love You" for Jolson in the examples above). *Down to Earth* and *Xanadu* both concern literal mythologizing, with a Muse coming down to earth and falling in love with a mortal. In the 1980 version, Terpsichore (Olivia Newton-John)

Figures 11.8 and 11.9. *Xanadu* (1980). Danny McGuire (Gene Kelly) dreams of his past, when the muse of his youth (Olivia Newton-John, ghostly in the background) sang "You Made Me Love You." Under the spell of her song, he gazes like Narcissus in the mirror—and can't keep a straight face. He mocks his own self-involvement and torch-bearing regrets.

inspires first Danny, in the 1940s, to open a jazz club, and then, in 1980, Danny and Sonny (Michael Beck), together, to open a roller disco. Sonny falls in love with his muse; Danny had done the same in his youth, when he was a swing clarinetist-bandleader.

Now, Danny listens to a 1940s record of his muse singing "You Made Me Love You." (Newton-John includes the verse, but unfortunately the track is barely audible until the refrain is halfway through.) Kelly-as-Danny gazes in the mirror, contemplating himself just as Parks-as-Jolson had done in *Jolson Sings Again*. His self-mythologizing is undercut by self-deflation: he makes faces at himself. Then, however, Kelly launches into a duet with Newton-John, using many of the dance moves he used in the 1940s, reaffirming his grace and powerfully reinscribing his star mythos.[133]

Even the use of "You Made Me Love You" by the highly political, androgynous British performance artist David Hoyle links to the traditions of the song. Interviewer Dominic Johnson names his chapter on Hoyle after the ballad, calling it "Judy Garland's traditionally plaintive" piece.[134] Thereby, Johnson furthers the Garland mythos, even as Hoyle self-reflexively admits that this interview itself has become part of Hoyle's own "self-mythologizing."[135] (Johnson witnessed Hoyle live, singing the McCarthy-Monaco standard "in his barbaric warble," "to the accompaniment of a MRI scanner alarm.")[136] Hoyle carefully admits, "I say I only know two songs all the way through"—the implication of "I say" is that this claim, too, is a colorful bit of self-mythologizing.[137] In reality, his oft-used repertoire includes "You Made Me Love You," "Maybe This Time," and "Where Have All the Flowers Gone." All three he categorizes as "camp, of course," but adds, significantly, "camp is a very effective tool."[138] There is a notion contained in the progression from Garland, to Parks-as-Jolson, to Day-as-Etting, to Kelly-as-Danny, that is brought forth by Hoyle's practice and his discussion of it: "You Made Me Love You" is a *performance* of love—or, as Hoyle puts it, of "what it is to yearn, and to want." Seen in this light, "Some of These Days" and "You Made Me Love You" can be interpreted as *flaunting* ambivalence—inner turmoil becomes exteriorized, becomes crafted, becomes performance.

A final sign of how "You Made Me Love You" became associated with the relationship of performer and audience is the tradition of singing it to an audience member. It starts in World War II, with female vocalists getting a soldier volunteer up on stage (result: hilarity all around).[139] Then a handful of club singers adopt the routine during the late 1950s to mid-1960s, sometimes going around the ringside, table-to-table.[140] In the 1980s, Suzanne Somers resurrected this saucily flirtatious practice.[141] The recurring themes of sex, humor, and audience-performer relationship here become intermingled.

Most of the novels entitled *You Made Me Love You* are romances that never mention the song.[142] By contrast, Joanna Goodman's 2006 saga of three Jewish Canadian sisters and their parents weaves the song, the title phrase, and the ideas associated with them throughout the story. In an interview, Goodman reports how she "loved the malleability of that song title," relishing its ambiguities.[143] She identifies two "main sentiment[s]" behind the song and its title. First, "how people can almost inadvertently come to love other people, as opposed to that romantic concept of love at first sight. . . . love is something that can develop slowly over time, or creep up on us when we least expect it." This is the realistic idea contained in McCarthy's too often neglected verses: "once I used to laugh at you," because "I had pictured in my mind . . . someone handsome, but . . . now . . . I want you and nothing more." Love takes us by surprise.

The second meaning, says Goodman, is that "love is something that can be manipulated." Indeed, most of the characters can be interpreted as manipulating their love partners—and, in turn, being manipulated—each with their eyes partly open and partly shut. When the youngest sister, Erika, vacillates about leaving her not-really-committed live-in boyfriend, Paul, her other beau, Mitch, makes the theme explicit: "You made me love you. So either it was part of some perverse game, or else you have feelings for me too."[144] The truth about love tends to ooze out, wittingly or not.

The song has most direct meaning for the parents, Lilly and Milton. He was a famous Canadian crooner, paired on television and later as a restaurateur (and in a longstanding extramarital affair) with Gladys. Lilly was his first television partner, till he wooed her into marriage and domestic life. Now retired, he sits at home, mourning Gladys as she dies of cancer, watching a broadcast of his life story as it "take[s] on a grander, fictional quality."[145] The mise-en-scène from *Jolson Sings Again* and *Xanadu* is replicated: the middle-aged star contemplates his own image.

His wife, meanwhile, remembers: "Once upon a time, Milton had been crazy about Lilly. Always singing to her . . . that famous Judy Garland song—she can't remember it now. God, she loved it. It was always her favorite. What *was* it?"[146] The song symbolizes the loving connection between wife and husband, now half-forgotten. After Gladys dies, Milton slowly realizes that Lilly, the leader of this clan of women, has a strength: "an all-encompassing love that tends to bleed into controlling, but it comes from a place of purity and good intention."[147] After Lilly survives a stroke, her prognosis is good but her spirit is broken: she can no longer be a leader.

Milton searches in vain for a way to reawaken Lilly, to reconnect. One day, in anticipation of singing at their daughter's wedding: "He clears his throat and starts singing to her, a song he used to sing back in the days when he was courting her. It was always her favorite, an old Judy Garland tune, 'You Made Me Love You.' She looks up at him. Her face is suddenly full of recognition." He dances across the room, takes her hand, pulls her up, "sweeps her across the floor."[148] The moment is exhilarating. Lilly grins, laughs: "Is this all he ever had to do? Could it always have been this easy? . . . Even if it couldn't have been this easy with her in the past, perhaps it can be now. Perhaps this is enough for both of them."[149] So the novel leaves them, sparkling with delight, as they twirl around the living room, crooning "You Made Me Love You."

Milton and Lilly's quiet reconciliation echoes the love stories told at the start of this chapter—and so does the place of "You Made Me Love You" in the autobiography of Shirley Cunningham.[150] Hers is a spiritual odyssey: she left behind her first path as a nun, and eventually traveled a road of increasing

New Age ecumenism and feminism. After a divorce from her first husband, she enters into a protracted on-and-off relationship with a new love, Jerry, and eventually marries him. At the reception, she unexpectedly delays the first dance, taking the microphone:

> "I guess every last one of you wondered if I'd ever marry Jerry. I'd broken up with him so many times." . . . "Well, this song is my explanation." Blushing, I cued the piano player, and opening my arms wide, belted out the old familiar hit from the forties: "You made me love you. I didn't want to do it . . ."
>
> Jerry's eyes were soft. I hugged my new husband as laughter and applause drowned out my last notes. The song said it all! After so many fits and starts, I was still dazzled by the miracle of this wedding.[151]

Although this is only a passing incident in Cunningham's bildungsroman, it can be interpreted as having a larger significance in her narrative. Throughout, she makes it clear she sees herself as guided—despite her inner resistance—by God, by the "feminine divine," "the Great Mother," through the means of forces that are mystic and psychic, to her fate: as a counselor, as an artist, as a writer, and as a love-partner.[152] That higher power helps her shed her narrow-mindedness, judgmentalism, resentments, griefs, and fears. In this marriage, as in all these aspects of her life, God "made her love." Cunningham's story yet again reveals how these ballads weave into the lives of individuals, and the life of society, imbuing and receiving significance during moments of tenderness and revelation.

Chapter Twelve

CONCLUSION

Authors and Torch Songs

*U*nder the hammers of thousands of known and unknown crafters, a mature ballad style came to be forged. The impression that it was an innovation led by a handful of famous geniuses is disproved by the saga unfolded in the previous chapters. Innovation was caused by a mass of people, moving together. Who are those "great innovators" that Alec Wilder and his editor James Maher glorified? The famous Frank Williams? The celebrated Beth Slater Whitson? The charismatic Maybelle A. Watson? They are forgotten, along with most of the performers who shaped the songs through the formative years. Nevertheless, by their efforts a genre both jazzy and intimate was born.

These innovators were operating across the nation. This book's focus songs sprang from all over, Louisiana to Michigan, California to New York. Among these seminal songs are examples that draw from classical music (as with the incipit melodies of "Kiss Me Again" and "My Melancholy Baby") and the blues (as with the verse of "Bill Bailey, Won't You Please Come Home?"). The repertoire fused divergent influences, as American print and oral traditions intermingled.

The trickle of enduring personal ballads continued throughout the 1910s. I have already been forced to jump ahead to 1916 to discuss "I'm Sorry I Made You Cry," and before the 1910s ended other such examples emerged. These are songs that maintained their place among the throng of later classic pop ballads. Each of them has origins as complex as the ones covered in this book. Some have motifs shared with earlier tunes ("The St. Louis Blues" [1914], "After You've Gone" [1918]), including theft from classical music ("I'm Always Chasing Rainbows" [1918]). Others have disputed and confused authorship, as with "I Ain't Got Nobody" (1914). Some underwent major alterations over time ("If You Were the Only Girl in the World" [1916], "Bill" [1918], "Baby, Won't You Please Come Home" [1919]). Others experienced quirky delays in popularity ("They Didn't Believe Me" [1914], "Paper Doll" [1915], "Somebody Stole My Gal" [1918]). Meters shifted, new lyrics sprang up from unknown sources, traditions accumulated, influence blossomed. And, bang! A classic style and a valued corpus were fashioned.

The electronic microphone starts its reign in the mid-twenties. The flourishing of radio and talking pictures follows soon upon its heels. The earlier songs were revived through these media. Between 1926 and 1931, "Let Me Call You Sweetheart," "My Melancholy Baby," "Some of These Days," "I Ain't Got Nobody," "St. Louis Blues," "If You Were the Only Girl in the World," "After You've Gone," "Bill," and "Somebody Stole My Gal," were resurrected; and meanwhile, "Kiss Me Again" and "I Wonder Who's Kissing Her Now" were being featured in early film musicals. Thereby, these songs became permanently yoked to the microphone—to the extent that they seem to have predicted its advent.

Sometimes these vogues appear to occur in patterns. For instance, as the 1950s gave way to the 1960s, "Bill Bailey," "Some of These Days," "My Melancholy Baby," "You Made Me Love You," and "I'm Sorry I Made You Cry" all hit the charts once more. In 1962 *Variety* surveyed the "most 'active' pop standards," the "Golden 100," and, alongside the most mature products of the era, these progenitors fit right in: "After You've Gone," "I Wonder Who's Kissing Her Now," "Kiss Me Again," "Let Me Call You Sweetheart," "My Melancholy Baby," "Some of These Days," "St. Louis Blues," and "You Made Me Love You."[1]

Elements of the crooning that developed then still continue today—it is hard to imagine that such microphone techniques shall ever cease. McCracken emphasizes how patriarchal critics exhibit "effemiphobia and casual sexism" as they put down male crooners who sing softly and emotionally in a high voice.[2] The result: "crooning's queer sounds were culturally marginalized in the decades following the 1930s," right through the turn of the twenty-first century[3] Just as striking, however, is how successful these latter-day male crooners have been, whether stolid Frank Fontaine in the early 1960s or flamboyant Prince at the turn of the twenty-first century. McCracken elides over a larger point: as recently as the mid-1920s no one could have conceived of anybody, whether male or female, making a living and earning international fame by singing *quietly*—sometimes as quietly as a parent lulling a baby to sleep.

In contrast to the endurance of the pop category of *crooning*, the term *torch song* may fade from use. Harvey Fierstein's three-act play *Torch Song Trilogy* can act as a symbol of this process. The protagonist, drag queen Arnold, wrestles with sexual-romantic-domestic longing, ambivalence, fulfillment, rupture, and bereavement—the stuff of torch songs. When it originally debuted in 1983, a character outside the action, named Lady Blues, sang at regular intervals. Fierstein did not specify which songs, except that each should be "a 1920s or 1930s torch song in the manner of Helen Morgan or Ruth Etting."[4] He dictated that her repertoire should vary from production to production. (Thus, as with the torch songs we have traced, the play's performance text was fluid and the product of multiple authors.) Lady Blues's songs "should not comment on the action as much as conjure it."[5] (Atmosphere is all.)

For the 2018 revival, the trilogy was shortened to two acts, so the title is now truncated to *Torch Song*. Yet, in this iteration, Lady Blues and her torch songs have also been ejected from the proceedings. All that remains is a hollow name, reverberating faint echoes of a phrase that once had meaning. (So, in those parts of Arnold's life we witness, his love relationships with Ed and Alan exist more as echoes of the past than fulfillments of the present.)

Amidst his discussions about the thrill of buying Morgan albums and the poignancy of remembering romantic call-in show requests for "My Funny Valentine," Arnold defines "torch ditties" as "music to be miserable by."[6] Earlier in the century, the definition would more likely have been "music to touch the heartstrings of the miserable." This fits the context in which the phrase was first used: Tommy Lyman's intimate club performances, going table to table, crooning "to the hand-holding set."[7] In a 1946 profile of Lyman, Herb Graffis offers a definition of the torch genre that emphasizes response:

> He's the premier troubadour of the torch song, that sentimental sort of a lay
> that made the old-time girls in the back room dribble tears into their drinks,
> causes the sophisticated deb[utante] to blink and lose her dull, hard look,
> and which softens the heart of the predatory male and makes him want to
> hold hands and be a pushover for a penthouse.[8]

A list of "the best torch songs," created and debated by showbiz insiders in 1934, reveals thirty-two lyrics seemingly designed to do just what Graffis says, soften the heart. The privileged selection includes the expected depictions of unhappiness, such as "My Man" and "Body and Soul," but also, surprisingly, paeans of happy romance, such as "Always" and "Love in Bloom"—*and* "My Melancholy Baby" and "Sweetheart of Sigma Chi."[9] This is a repertoire to be performed *for* someone who is full of longing, rather than *by* someone who is full of longing. I suggest that it is this viewpoint that explains why "My Melancholy Baby" was for thirty years described as the "ace of 'torch' songs," "the greatest torch song ever written," "the torchiest of all torch songs," "the greatest torcher of them all," "an old torch ballad," and "the champ torch song."[10] In 1972 Alec Wilder credited it as "an example of the emergence of . . . the torch song," and in 1993 Loonis McGlohon opined it "may well have been the first torch song."[11] Not until after the early 1960s did the definitions offered for "torch song" became strongly dominated by the notion of unrequited love.

Added to that recent trend has come a focus on abusive relationships, through an emphasis on "My Man," with its line in the verse "he beats me." In their discussions of torch singers, John Moore and Stacy Holman Jones use this French-into-English *chanson-realiste* as a starting point and springboard.[12] Moore asserted that "My Man" "provided the formula for the torch song," and Holman Jones followed him and went further, claiming that it "supplied *the* musical formula for the Tin Pan Alley ballad," presumably of all types.[13] The history supplied in the previous chapter demonstrates the contrary: Tin Pan Alley may have supplied the formula for "My Man," at least in part.

My study has sought to shift the focus from the torch singer to the torch song. Instead of "My Man," I use "My Melancholy Baby" as the starting point and springboard, with the rationale that it was actually the first song to be labeled as "torch" and was accepted as the quintessential example for over half a century. Through doing so, I end up with this definition: a torch song is a love ballad that makes the listener acutely aware of the flame of love within their heart. This response depends not just on the song but also on many other factors, including the listener, the performers, and the context, all of which may vary.

Rick Altman has written extensively about the many ways to define a genre (such as "torch song") and decide what texts fit into it (such as "My Melancholy Baby" and "My Man"). "Producers, exhibitors, viewers and critics"—all seem to disagree.[14] Therefore, "we need to recognize their differing purposes and the resultant differences in generic categories, labels and uses."[15] As critics, Moore and Jones aim to explore how the female torch singer functions "as naysayer, as critic, as the voice of resistive and radical possibilities" and her performance becomes "a militant affirmation of her integrity . . . an assertion" that "creates an ethical victory."[16] Many of the female singers whose renderings are described in this book can easily be viewed as triumphing with exactly this agenda, from Nancy Wilson shifting blame from herself to Bill Bailey, to a teenage Judy Garland infusing the helplessness of "You Made Me Love You" with an intensity that sweeps away all passivity.

As a critic, I aim to explore how both men and women have used torch songs to achieve three things. First, freedom—the freedom exemplified by jazz. Second, tenderness—the tenderness exemplified by the lullaby. Since at least the first nation-states, with their hierarchies and military specializations, freedom and tenderness have been among the most radical of modalities. Third, introspection—the soul-searching of the existential wanderer. In this last mentioned, I commune (in spirit) with psychologist Gregory F. Pickering, who finds in "each torch song . . . a dream—a comment on the individual's inner condition."[17] I seek the roots of this interiority in the saga of the ballads of the early twentieth century. As a result (and as Altman would predict), I emphasize "generic categories, labels, and uses"—and a corpus and an origin story—that differ from those of Moore and Jones.[18]

Altman applies his theories to movies—and emphasizes that they need to be "feature length" movies.[19] For example, any depiction of the Southwest, horses, and gunslingers will conjure up the western (these are the *semantic* units of the genre). But these also have to be used in a particular plot pattern, to symbolize the taming of the American wilderness (this is the *syntax* that makes sense and meaning out of the ingredients). To give full significance to short works, like torch songs, "narrative situation and development" need to be supplied.[20]

As has been recounted again and again throughout my study, these narrative situations are supplied through plays, movies, and books, through our own life stories, and through scholarly criticism. Moore positions the torch song in a tableau of women who performed urbanity and exoticism at the pivot between the Jazz Age and the Great Depression. For Jones, torch songs are a thread in the life chronicles of herself and other women as feminists, lovers, cabaret audiences and performers, daughters, and mothers: one of her most vivid episodes tells of hearing her mother sing in a nightclub. For me, torch songs also stem from my mother, but are rooted in the domestic sphere. They appear in my life's saga as bedtime lullabies and recordings to enliven cooking while the chef dances around the kitchen. Therefore, I see in the microphone the intimacy of the nursery and, in the torch song, the dance through life.

Because torch songs are from my mother, for me they are ancestral. That is why I have attempted to trace their lineage. As an historian, I gaze at the past. But now, too, I look to the future, to others who will create new narrative situations and developments—for the torch song.

APPENDIX

A Summary of the Development of the Personal, Intimate, and Internal

This is a summary of how each of my focus songs contributed to the development of the personal, intimate, or internal qualities (and jazziness) found in many classic pop ballads.

"Bill Bailey, Won't You Please Come Home?" (1902)
The earliest of the enduring jazz standards about the loss of love. An impersonal, comic, ragtime-style song that influenced later ballads and was itself eventually performed as a personal ballad.

"I'm Sorry I Made You Cry" (1916)
Discussed ahead of chronology, because it is perhaps the earliest personal waltz ballad to be performed and printed in duple meter in jazz style. This performance tradition set the pattern for the waltzes below (and many others).

"Kiss Me Again" (1905)
The earliest of the enduing ballads about nocturnal lovemaking. An operetta waltz that was eventually occasionally crooned or jazzed up. With the verse written for the pop version, it became a personal song throughout and the earliest enduring ballad about the loss of love among my focus songs.

"I Wonder Who's Kissing Her Now" (1909)
The refrain is ruminative, taking place in the imagination and memory of the protagonist. (The verse is more impersonal.) A waltz ballad that was eventually often done in duple meter.

"Let Me Call You Sweetheart" (1910)
A ballad with a personal lyric throughout verse and refrain. The verse dwells on the imagination and dream life of the protagonist. The refrain is a direct,

personal statement of love and plea for reciprocation. A waltz that was eventually sometimes done in duple meter.

"Some of These Days" (1910)

A song in which the protagonist anticipates the impending loss of love and expresses inner ambivalence through several shifts of emotion and tense. Meanwhile, the bluesy, jazzy music also shifts restlessly.

"The Sweetheart of Sigma Chi" (1911)

The protagonist lingers, in ambiguous language, on dreams about women, particularly the sweetheart of the title, foreshadowing many such later songs. A duple meter ballad that was later printed and most often performed as a waltz.

"My Melancholy Baby" (1911)

The protagonist pleads for his sweetheart to cuddle and cheer up, exhibiting empathy for the inner emotions of another person. A personal lyric throughout, supported by a riff-like verse melody and a sinuous refrain melodic arch, published in both slow ballad and fast march versions.

"When I Lost You" (1912)

A ballad with a personal lyric throughout, widely accepted as an autobiographical statement by the songwriter, Irving Berlin, of loss and grief over the death of his wife. A waltz that was sometimes later done in duple meter. It foreshadowed Berlin's many famous personal, intimate waltzes of the 1920s, many of which are also regularly transformed into duple meter.

"You Made Me Love You" (1913)

A personal lyric throughout. The protagonist expresses and pleads for love, but also articulates the ambivalence of a complicated inner life, set to music with bluesy notes and riff-like repeated phrases.

NOTES

PREFACE

1. Gregory F. Pickering, "The Torch Singer: A Depth Psychology Study" (PhD diss., Pacifica Graduate Institute, 1999), 6.

2. Philip Furia and Michael Lasser, *America's Songs: The Stories Behind the Songs of Broadway, Hollywood, and Tin Pan Alley* (New York: Routledge, 2006).

3. I consider these the Tin Pan Alley generations: first, those born from 1865 to 1885; the second, born 1885 to 1905; the third, from 1905 to 1920; the fourth from 1920 to 1940. Among histories of Tin Pan Alley, there are many fine tomes. Two of the most thorough are Russell Sanjek, *American Popular Music and Its Business* (New York: Oxford University Press, 1988); David A. Jasen, *Tin Pan Alley* (New York: Primus, Donald I. Fine, 1988). Many fine popular summaries are found, such as Ian Whitcomb, *After the Ball* (New York: Limelight Edition, [1972] 1986); Jody Rosen, *White Christmas* (New York: Scribner, 2002).

4. For example, in a different category from the popular style are pieces such as the score from the 1911 Broadway hit *Everywoman (Her Pilgrimage in Quest of Love)*, by Walter Browne and George Whitfield Chadwick; and songs by Erich Wolfgang Korngold for the swashbuckler *The Sea Hawk* (1940), despite the classical composer's teaming with Tin Pan Alley lyricist Jack Scholl for two of them.

5. Ted Gioia, *The Jazz Standards* (Oxford: Oxford University Press, 2012). See also Richard Crawford and Jeffrey Magee, *Jazz Standards on Record, 1900–1942* (Chicago: Center for Black Music Research, Columbia College Chicago, 1992).

6. Gioia, *Jazz*, discusses the differing jazz repertoires in passing, in many places starting 29–30.

7. Relevant genre terms can be seen in book titles: David Ewen, *The Life and Death of Tin Pan Alley: The Golden Age of American Popular Music* (New York: Funk and Wagnalls, 1964); Allen Forte, *The American Popular Ballad of the Golden Era, 1924–1950* (Princeton, NJ: Princeton University Press, 1995); Allen Forte, *Listening to Classic American Popular Songs* (New Haven, CT: Yale University Press, 2001); Max Morath, *The NPR Curious Listener's Guide to Popular Standards* (New York: Penguin Putnam, 2002); David Jenness and Don Velsey, *Classic American Popular Song: The Second Half-Century, 1950–2000* (New York: Routledge, 2006), who also refer to the terms "classic pop" (xii) and "Great American Songbook" (2). The current denotation of the latter term perhaps stems from the 1972 Carmen McRae album, *The Great American Songbook*, and, judging by a search of Ebsco databases, consolidates in 1987. I use "American" to designate "of the United States of America"; this is deplorable in its ethnocentrism, but convenient and used throughout past literature on this topic. As of this writing, alternatives like "Usanian," "Usonian," and "United Statesian" would confuse many readers.

8. Traditionally, *ballad* means usually a folk song, usually strophic, usually narrative, usually in the third person. This older meaning of *ballad* continues to coexist alongside the later pop meaning of the term.

9. *Love song* equals *ballad*, in Forte, *American Popular Ballad*, 3; Morath, *NPR*, 208. This conflation leads Forte to classify as ballads such sprightly airs as "Thou Swell" and "Isn't It a Lovely Day," pieces that Lehman Engel would probably categorize as *charm songs*, "songs with . . . optimistic lyrics . . . [and] a steadier sense of movement" than a ballad; Lehman Engel, *The Making of a Musical* (New York: Macmillan, 1977), 13.

10. "Unrequited" is used by Forte, *American Popular Ballad*, 238; Isaac Goldberg, *Tin Pan Alley* (New York: Frederick Ungar, [1930] 1961), 215; Stacy Holman Jones, "Torch," *Qualitative Inquiry* 5, no. 2 (June 1999): 280; John Moore, "'The Hieroglyphics of Love': The Torch Singers and Interpretation," *Popular Music* 8, no. 1 (January 1989): 32; James R. Morris, "The Selections" *American Popular Song*, booklet for phonorecord anthology (New York: CBS Records, and Washington, DC: Smithsonian Collection of Recordings, 1984), 31; Sheldon Patinkin, *"No Legs, No Jokes, No Chance"* (Evanston, IL: Northwestern University Press, 2008), 123; Mel Tormé, *My Singing Teachers* (New York: Oxford University Press, 1994), 23.

11. Respectively: David Horn, "Torch Singer," *Continuum Encyclopedia of Popular Music of the World, Vol. II* (London: Continuum, 2003), 115; Robert Parker, CD liner notes, *Torch Songs* (New Orleans: Louisiana Red Hot Records, 1997), 2; Loonis McGlohon, "Torch Song," *Facts Behind the Songs*, edited by Marvin E. Paymer (New York: Garland, 1993), 296–97. Historically, songs that are especially known as torch songs have included lyrics about unhappiness in one's love life, such as "My Man," "The Man I Love," "Moanin' Low," "Body and Soul," "Stormy Weather," and "One for My Baby," but also some about ongoing, seemingly healthy and happy love relationships, such as "Bill," "Come Rain or Come Shine," and, as will be discussed, "My Melancholy Baby."

12. Bradford Gardner, "Why You Sing the Songs You Do," *Los Angeles Times*, March 12, 1933, F3, 20.

13. Songs might or might not be done as a torch song: Muriel Babcock, "'Torch Song' Defined," *Los Angeles Times*, February 8, 1931, B11, quoting actress Mayo Methol; Bert Leston Taylor, "A Line o' Type or Two: After Life's Fitful Fever," *Chicago Daily Tribune*, October 14, 1941, 12. See also Tormé, *My Singing*, 23–24.

14. Alec Wilder, *American Popular Song: The Great Innovators, 1900–1950* (London: Oxford University Press, 1972).

15. Rennold Wolf, "The Boy Who Revived Rag-time," *Green Book Magazine* 10, no. 3 (August 1913): 201–9. Library of Congress Irving Berlin Collection Scrapbooks, microfilm 92/20013, reel one.

16. I hope in the future to present a survey that examines a larger, more representative body of these songs and looks at the output of Tin Pan Alley more in terms of its own time. This project started out to be that, with a charting of information about 2,400 songs, but I got mesmerized by the histories of these enduring early ballads. Nevertheless, I retain ambitions for a study of broader scope.

17. As this book comes to completion, copyrights of additional years are falling into public domain—1923 works in 2019, 1924 songs in 2020, etc., as of each January 1.

18. Wilder, *American*; Philip Furia, *The Poets of Tin Pan Alley* (New York: Oxford University Press, 1990); Morath, *NPR*; James R. Morris, "Introductory Essay," in *Six Decades of Songwriters and Singers*, record booklet, 3–27 (Washington, DC: Smithsonian Institution Press, 1984); the selections for this album were made by Morris and Dwight Blocker Bowers.

19. I have been the beneficiary of varying institutional resources, covering at different times Ebsco's *Entertainment Industry Magazine Archive* and *Historical Newspapers* for the *New York Times, Chicago Tribune, Los Angeles Times, Washington Post, Christian Science Monitor, The Stage, Variety, Billboard*, and other periodicals.

20. Musicology: Wilder, *American*; Furia, *Poets*; Nicholas Tawa, *The Way to Tin Pan Alley* (New York: Schirmer Books, 1990); Charles Hamm, *Irving Berlin* (New York: Oxford University Press, 1997); Peter C. Muir, *Long Lost Blues* (Urbana: University of Illinois Press, 2009); Forte, *American*; Forte, *Listening*. Various works by Stephen Banfield, including "Popular Song and Popular Music

on Stage and Film," in *The Cambridge History of American Music*, edited by David Nicholls (Cambridge: Cambridge University Press, 1998), 309–44; "Sondheim and the Art that Has No Name," in *Approaches to the American Musical*, edited by Robert Lawson-Peebles (Exeter, UK: University of Exeter Press, 1996), 137–60; and *Jerome Kern* (New Haven, CT: Yale University Press, 2006).

21. Literary analysis: Furia, *Poets*; Lehman Engel, *Their Words Are Music* (New York: Crown, 1975); Timothy E. Scheurer, "'Thou Witty': The Evolution and Triumph of Style in Lyric Writing, 1890–1950," in *American Popular Music: Readings from the Popular Press, Vol. I*, edited by Timothy E. Scheurer (Bowling Green, OH: Bowling Green State University Popular Press, 1989), 104–19.

22. Melopoetics: Banfield, "Sondheim"; Stephen Citron, particularly in *Noel and Cole: The Sophisticates* (New York: Oxford University Press, 1993); Furia, *Poets*; Jenness and Velsey, *Classic*.

23. Roger D. Kinkle, *The Complete Encyclopedia of Popular Music and Jazz, 1900–1950*, 4 vols. (New Rochelle, NY: Arlington House, 1974); Brian Rust, *Jazz Records, 1897–1942*, 4th rev. and enlarged ed. (New Rochelle, NY: Arlington House, 1978); Brian Rust with Allen G. Debus, *The Complete Entertainment Discography: From the Mid-1890s to 1942* (New Rochelle, NY: Arlington House, 1973); Tom Lord, *The Jazz Discography* (West Vancouver, CA: Lord Music Reference, 1992); Robert M. W. Dixon, John Godrich, and Howard Rye, *Blues and Gospel Records, 1890–1943*, 4th ed. (Oxford: Clarendon Press, 1997); Ross Laird, *Moanin' Low: A Discography of Female Popular Vocal Recordings, 1920–1933* (Westport, CT: Greenwood Press, 1996); Tony Russell, *Country Music Records: A Discography, 1921–1942* (Oxford: Oxford University Press, [2004] 2008). Online: *Discography of American Historical Recordings*; *Red Hot Jazz Archive*; and, in a slightly different category, *Second Hand Songs*.

24. Edward Foote Gardner, *Popular Songs of the Twentieth Century, Vol. I* (St. Paul, MN: Paragon House, 2000); Joel Whitburn, *Pop Memories, 1890–1954* (Menomonee Falls, WI: Record Research, 1986). Tim Brooks points out problems with Whitburn's methodology, sources, and the precision of his chart positions before the 1940s; "*Pop Memories*," book review, *ARSC Journal* 21, no. 1 (spring 1990): 134–41. Yet Brooks does not express doubt (and indeed no one does) that the recordings Whitburn charts were prominent at least to some extent.

25. Sean Wilentz and Greil Marcus, eds., *The Rose and the Briar* (New York: W. W. Norton, 2005).

26. Many of Diamond's foundational thoughts can be found in *Life Energy* (New York: Paragon House, 1985), and, concerning music, *The Life Energy in Music, Vols. 1–3* (Valley Cottage, NY: Archaeus Press, 1981–86). The book you are reading is in many ways simply one academe's exploration of the critical issues raised by Diamond in many unpublished recorded lectures, including "Ballad Is Best," August 27, 1992; "Composing: We Gotta Write Love Songs," 1998; and "Songs and Intimacy," February 12, 2004. Another general influence from Diamond is an etymological love of tracing word roots and meanings.

27. Wilder, *American*, 21.

28. For the etymology of "repertoire," I draw from the American Heritage Dictionary, 4th ed.

CHAPTER ONE: THE WORLD OF THE GREAT AMERICAN SONGBOOK

1. The occasion was a book-signing in a Borders bookstore. The chain, at that time, did not pay ASCAP or BMI for the playing of copyrighted musical materials in their branches.

2. "The Man I Love" was written in 1924 but not popularized until 1928; this famous story is told many places, including by Ira Gershwin, *Lyrics on Several Occasions* (1959; reprint, New York: Limelight Editions, 1997), 3–7; and Wilder, *American*, 129–31. In a less famous instance of delay, "My Blue Heaven" was not published until 1927, but David Ewen reports it was written in 1924; *All the Years of American Popular Music* (Englewood Cliffs, NJ: Prentice-Hall, 1977), 226. In addition, enduring standards emerged in 1924 that do not fit as easily into my discussion: rhythm songs ("Fascinating Rhythm," "Copenhagen," "Doodle Doo Doo"); operetta classics that did not become standard jazz repertoire items ("Rose-Marie," "Deep in My Heart, Dear," and "Serenade");

and others ("Hard-Hearted Hannah," "California, Here I Come," "Spain," "Charley, My Boy," "Last Night on the Back Porch").

3. Ironically, in 2020, while final work was being done on this book, the pivotal songs of 1924 fell into public domain.

4. "Bill Bailey" is called a ballad: Corb, "House Review: Keith's, Indpls," *Variety*, August 11, 1943, 23; "Marilyn Chandler of Monroeville Recreates the Past and Writes About," *Pittsburgh Post-Gazette*, August 1, 1996, VN-4.

5. Furia, *Poets*, 44.

6. Perhaps this neglect is due to the fact that high-profile stars often choose repertoire based on that of an idolized star of the past; thereby, dominant repertoire becomes self-perpetuating. Among my focus songs, "You Made Me Love You" is the most recorded by later high-profile stars (Anne Murray, Neil Diamond, Crystal Gayle, and Gloria Estefan); and presumably this is because of the connection to Judy Garland, whose cultural cache stays strong and, indeed, has perhaps grown, partly through the continued popularity of *The Wizard of Oz*.

7. Along with those already mentioned, histories of Tin Pan Alley include Goldberg, *Tin Pan Alley*; Edward B. Marks, *They All Sang* (New York: Viking Press, 1934); Charles Hamm, *Yesterdays* (New York: W. W. Norton, 1979).

8. For a discussion of sheet music inside-cover advertising, see Daniel Goldmark, "Creating Desire on Tin Pan Alley," *Musical Quarterly* 90 (2008): 197–229.

9. Sanjek, *American*, 42–43.

10. Wilder, *American*, chapters 2 through 7.

11. James Maher, "Introduction," in Wilder, *American*, xxix.

12. Maher, "Introduction."

13. Forte, *American*. Forte devotes one chapter to each of the "Big Six" composers (representing 55 percent of the book), and in addition also extensively utilizes their songs as examples in his introductory opening chapters.

14. Furia, *Poets*.

15. Probably the most widely known study of the social processes of innovation is Malcolm Gladwell, *Outliers: The Story of Success* (New York: Little, Brown, 2008). See also James Surowiecki, *The Wisdom of Crowds* (New York: Doubleday, 2004); Nicholas A Christakis and James H. Fowler, *Connected* (New York: Little, Brown, 2009); Steven Pinker, *The Better Angels of Our Nature* (New York: Penguin, Viking, 2011), especially 478, 522, 650.

16. The collective innovation phenomenon is explicitly argued in Randall Collins, *The Sociology of Philosophies: A Global Theory of Intellectual Change* (Cambridge, MA: Belknap Press of Harvard University Press, 1998). In addition, it is implicitly sketched in books on a wide range of topics, such as Peter Biskind, *Easy Riders, Raging Bulls: How the Sex-Drugs-and-Rock-'n'-Roll Generation Saved Hollywood* (New York: Simon and Schuster, 1998); Jennifer S. Uglow, *The Lunar Men: Five Friends Whose Curiosity Changed the World* (New York: Farrar, Straus and Giroux, 2002); Tom Shales and James A Miller, *Live from New York: An Uncensored History of Saturday Night Live* (Boston: Little, Brown, 2002); Patrick Burke, *Come In and Hear the Truth: Jazz and Race on 52nd Street* (Chicago: University of Chicago Press, 2008). Gladwell's essay review sketches a parallel between the principles Collins outlines and the phenomena documented by Shales and Miller; "Group Think: What Does 'Saturday Night Live' Have in Common with German Philosophy?," Malcolm Gladwell, *New Yorker*, December 2, 2002, 102ff.

17. Anne Dhu McLucas, *The Musical Ear: Oral Tradition in the USA* (Farnham, UK: Ashgate, 2010), 2.

18. McLucas, *Musical*.

19. McLucas, *Musical*.

20. McLucas, *Musical*, 3.

21. Morath, *NPR*, 4.

22. Banfield, "Sondheim," 146. The first version of "Bill" was written in 1918; see Miles Kreuger, *Show Boat* (New York: Oxford University Press, 1977), 57–63. Banfield analyzes its 1927 revision.

23. Will Friedwald, *Stardust Memories* (New York: Pantheon Books, 2002), xiii–xiv.

24. McLucas, *Musical*, 1.

25. When I discuss the "American melody," I draw on John Diamond, unpublished lectures and conversations with the author, 1991 on; and Henry Pleasants and his discussions and definitions of "American music" in *The Agony of Modern Music* (New York: Simon and Schuster, 1955); *Death of a Music?* (London: Victor Gollancz, 1961); and *Serious Music—And All That Jazz!* (New York: Simon and Schuster, 1969). On the development of the conversational lyric: Engel, *Their Words*; Furia, *Poets*; Scheurer, "'Thou Witty.'"

26. I draw on Diamond, *Life Energy in Music, Vol. 3*, 88–90; Diamond, "Songs"; and Diamond, unpublished lectures and conversations with the author, 1991 on.

27. The Fields interview probably dates from the early 1930s; quoted by Deborah Grace Winer, *On the Sunny Side of the Street* (New York: Schirmer Books, 1997), 48. Similar statements are found from various sources, including historian Isaac Goldberg, *Tin Pan Alley*, 212; and singer Sylvia Syms, in an interview for *Down Beat* magazine, quoted by James Gavin, *Intimate Nights* (New York: Grove Weidenfeld, 1991), 11.

28. Vallee's fans are quoted in Alison McCracken, "'God's Gift to Us Girls,'" *American Music* 17, no. 1 (1999): 378.

29. Ada "Bricktop" Smith and James Haskins, *Bricktop* (New York: Atheneum, 1983), 51.

30. Smith and Haskins, *Bricktop*.

31. Smith and Haskins, *Bricktop*, 51–52.

32. Walter Winchell, "A Primer of Broadway Slang," *Vanity Fair*, November 1927, 132.

33. Winchell, "Primer."

34. Arlen's interview, probably from 1961 or 1964, is excerpted in the documentary *Somewhere Over the Rainbow*, DVD, directed by Don McGlynn (New York: Wellspring, 1999).

35. Tormé, *My Singing*, 23.

36. We do not know when Lyman dubbed the "torch song," for Walter Winchell is unspecific: "he announced one night." But I am presuming that it was more or less within the three years preceding Winchell's November 1927 article; Winchell, "Primer," 132.

37. As a temporary measure, I here refer to a male protagonist of "My Melancholy Baby" in tribute to the influential renditions by Lyman and Gene Austin—and the rhetoric of Winchell.

38. "Always" as a torch song: "Night Clubs: Torch Songs," *Variety*, September 25, 1934, 48. "Violets for Your Furs" as a "lush torch ballad": M. H. Orodenker, "Music Reviews: On the Records," *Billboard*, November 29, 1941, 10.

39. I surveyed 105 torch-labeled songs, particularly focusing on the seminal years from 1927 through 1934. I paralleled it with an online string by Frank Sinatra fans of 74 torch performances; "The Torch Song Sinatra," *Sinatra Family Forum*, 2004, http://sinatrafamily.com/forum/showthread.php/25356-The-Torch-Song-Sinatra (accessed July 8, 2015). The two lists yielded very similar results, and I have combined results from the two corpuses for the percentages given here.

40. Starting with Alec Wilder in 1972, the torch song has been credited by a string of commentators for its "personal point of view"; *American*, 21. Others following in this trail include: Diamond, *Life Energy in Music, Vol. 3*, 88–90; John Potter, "The Singer, Not the Song," *Popular Music* 13, no. 2 (May 1994): 193–94, writing about k.d. lang; Pickering, "Torch Singer," 110; Larry David Smith, *Elvis Costello, Joni Mitchell, and the Torch Song Tradition* (Westport, CT: Praeger, 2004), 260.

41. The Historical Newspapers database supplies eighteen examples of "love ballad" through 1907, when the early torch songs were about to be written, and many after that date as well. The earliest is "Music," *Chicago Daily Tribune*, December 22, 1872, 7, which contrasts composer Dudley Buck's "religious sentimentalism" with the "would-be passionate sentimentalism of the modern love-ballad." Skipping ahead past many examples to the eve of the pioneer torch song years, in

1907 we find Clare Kummer's "Egypt" described as "different from the conventional love ballad"; "Women Song Writers," *Chicago Daily Tribune*, November 17, 1907, G8.

42. "Rag ballad" was used for some years to mean the type of narrative (often satirical) song exemplified by "The Bully Song" (several versions of which were popular from 1895 onward; see Muir, *Long Lost*, 210–11). As a later chapter will demonstrate, around 1913 it starts to be used to describe "My Melancholy Baby" and similar songs.

43. "Syncopated ballad" is found in "Irving Berlin and Modern Ragtime," unidentified and undated clipping, in the Irving Berlin Collection of scrapbooks at the Library of Congress, reel one. The article says it is an exclusive for "the *Mirror*" (perhaps the *Daily Mirror* or the *Dramatic Mirror*), and the song about to come out when the article was printed was "Daddy Come Home," which Berlin copyrighted on December 16, 1913. The term "syncopated ballad" is also utilized in 1924 for lyricist L. Wolfe Gilbert's "Why Live a Lie," with which he wooed back his ex-wife less than a year after their divorce—a quintessential torch song anecdote; "Song Heals Marital Rift," *Los Angeles Times*, June 27, 1924, A19. Charles Hamm also discusses the article "Irving Berlin and Modern Ragtime" and uses the term "rhythmic ballad," implying that this is the modern-day equivalent of Berlin's "syncopated ballad"; *Irving Berlin*, 169.

44. On January 26, 1928, a British advertisement, for Campbell, Connelly Publishers, plugs the American song "Just Another Day Wasted Away" as "that wonderful sob rhythm ballad"; *Stage*, 7. This is, of course, just as the term "torch song" is starting in the USA, and "sob rhythm ballad" seems to be striving to describe a similar phenomenon. Later that year, in the American showbiz trade journal *Variety*, an advertisement, for DeSylva, Brown and Henderson Publishers, also brags of "a rhythm ballad that is a 'stand-out'"; *Variety*, November 21, 1928, 33. The stream of usages is only a trickle through the 1930s. Although by 1941 the phrase is in the popular press ("New Girl Trio to Make Debut on Steelmakers," *Chicago Daily Tribune*, May 25, 1941, NW4), it is rare, even in trade journals—for instance, only two instances in 1944. Then, in 1945 there are suddenly twenty uses of the phrase in *Billboard* and *Variety*. Writing in 1972, Wilder uses the term "rhythm ballad" to describe many songs, starting with "Some of These Days"; Wilder, *American*, 14.

45. "Irving Berlin and Modern Ragtime."

46. Milton "Mezz" Mezzrow and Bernard Wolfe, *Really the Blues* (New York: Random House, 1964), 60. Pinky Tomlin, eight years younger than Mezzrow, describes "Ace in the Hole" using the same "tearjerker" genre label, *The Object of My Affection* (Norman: University of Oklahoma Press, 1981), 64. This "Ace in the Hole" is not the Cole Porter song of 1941with the same title, but rather a 1909 song by G. Mitchell and J. Dempsey that had become a semi-standard by the late forties.

47. "Berlin-Mackay Engagement Denied," *New York Times*, June 11, 1925, 14.

48. Admittedly, the story context of *Gold Diggers of 1933* somewhat belies Dick Powell's sentiment "I've Got to Sing a Torch Song," for his character is shown happily engaged in a playful courtship at the time. Nevertheless, as we eventually discover, he actually is unhappy, for his wealthy family want to stop his career in popular music and prevent him from marrying his working-class beloved. Therefore, his sweetheart matches the description of the lyric—she is "someone far apart."

49. *Rose of Washington Square* is a disguised biography of Brice, not an explicit one. Other examples of disguised biography of a famous torch singer are three movies loosely based on Libby Holman's tragic first marriage, which also sketch the life-art parallel: *Sing, Sinner, Sing* (1933); *A Brief Moment* (1933); and *Reckless* (1935).

50. Although McCracken details many of the changing connotations of "croon" and "crooner," even she has not pinpointed exactly when "crooning" became applied to microphone-friendly popular singing styles. As early as 1924–25, Andy Razaf (already a budding lyricist) was being billed on radio and on the Harmony Records label as "Crooning" Andy and His Ukulele; Barry Singer, *Black and Blue* (New York: Schirmer, 1992), 134, 152–53. An early newspaper instance of "crooner" being applied to the new singers is found in an anonymous blurb about singer-songwriter Gene Austin; "Writing of Songs Declared Great Fun by Crooner," *Los Angeles Times*, December 4, 1927,

C32. (Since the first journalistic appearance of "torch song" in print is from November 1927, the close timing of the rise of these two terms is almost uncanny.) The "quiet delivery" of Ruth Etting is described by Sime Silverman in 1927: "She more croons than throws her songs over"; *Variety*, June 15, 1927, 26 (see also Silverman's similar description of Etting in the same issue, 28); also quoted in Anthony Slide, *The Encyclopedia of Vaudeville* (Westport, CT: Greenwood Press, 1994), 165. By 1931 Etting is included in a list of crooners by Richard B. O'Brien, "Crooners in the Spotlight as Year Nears an End," *New York Times*, December 6, 1931, XX29. In a December 1928 review of *Whoopee*, Walter Bolton praised Etting as "the first of torch singers"; quoted in Kenneth Irwin and Charles O. Lloyd, *Ruth Etting: America's Forgotten Sweetheart* (Lanham, MD: Scarecrow Press, 2010), 83. Helen Morgan is dubbed "the little crooning torch singer" in "Color Camera Takes a Place Beside Talkies," *Chicago Daily Tribune*, September 15, 1929, G1, in subsection "Helen Morgan's Film Ready." For Crosby as a torch singer: Ruth Morris, "Uncommon Chatter," *Variety*, November 10, 1931, 48; Bud Budwin, "Times Square: Chatter—Spokane," *Variety*, April 12, 1932, 44.

51. Bing Crosby and Pete Martin, *Call Me Lucky* (New York: Simon and Schuster, 1953), 148. The phrase "soft-songsters" is from the subheader of O'Brien, "Crooners." Rudy Vallee explains his use of the megaphone in *Vagabond Dreams Come True* (New York: Grosset and Dunlap, 1930), 67–69. For De Leath as "the original radio girl," there are numerous newspaper entries, including "Today's Radio Programs," *Washington Post* August 8, 1923, 11, through to "Telecasts This Week," *New York Times* December 31, 1939, 94.

52. Sophie Tucker is characterized as a "torch mamma" by Larry Wolters, "Eighty Voice Choir to Sing 'St. Louis Blues,'" *Chicago Daily Tribune*, July 17, 1932, F4. Much later, conversely, John Moore drew a sharp distinction between the "red hot mama" and the "torch singer" personas: "'Hieroglyphics,'" 46. Peter Stanfield does similarly in *Body and Soul* (Urbana: University of Illinois Press, 2005), 114. But Wolters's contemporaneous labeling of Tucker breezily conflates the two types, proving that, at the time, these categories were fluid.

53. In film and commercial recordings of the 1930s, we hear Ethel Merman sing in a slightly more subdued and lyrical manner than in the post-1945 era; but, in a probable explanation, she comments in her first autobiography that filmmakers and recording engineers demanded she modify the style that she was accustomed to using in live performance; Ethel Merman as told to Pete Martin, *Who Could Ask for Anything More?* (Garden City, NY: Doubleday, 1955), 124, 238. Even at the very start, she is a "comely ballad singer" who is having her "torch singing premiere" on New York's Palace vaudeville stage; "Ted Healy Returns with His 'Racketeers,'" *New York Times*, September 15, 1930, 33. This label lasts at least through "'Here Comes the Bride'—Torch Singer Marries," *Washington Post*, November 16, 1940, 3. Merman was cast as the epitome of the torch singer in her early one-reel musical shorts, such as *Her Future* (1930). For over a decade a Merman Broadway appearance hardly seemed complete without her torch ballad solo, including "I Get a Kick Out of You" (1934), "Down in the Depths" (1935), "I'll Pay the Check" (1939), "Make It Another Old Fashioned" (1941), "He's a Right Guy" (1943), and "I Got Lost in His Arms" (1946). She herself noted the "torchiness" that was important in correctly rendering "Down in the Depths" (Merman, *Who Could Ask*, 136).

54. Ethel Waters, *His Eye Is on the Sparrow* (New York: Jove/HBJ, [1950] 1978), 75.

55. On early American cabaret, see Lewis A. Erenberg, *Steppin' Out* (Westport, CT: Greenwood Press, 1981), 75–76, 114–15; Hamm, *Irving Berlin*, 120–22.

56. Smith, *Bricktop*, 49. Cliff "Ukulele Ike" Edwards told of going "from table to table . . . and be given anything from a quarter to a dollar bill by the diners and drinkers" in Chicago in the years 1917 and 1918; Larry F. Kiner, *The Cliff Edwards Discography* (New York: Greenwood Press, 1987), x. Kiner is probably drawing from a 1932 interview (that he mentions just after) of Edwards with Alissa Keir of the *New York Daily News*. Ruth Etting describes a similar table-hopping norm for the early 1920s nightclub singing: Carroll Nye, "Ruth Etting Scorns 'Dance Band Cuties,'" *Los Angeles Times*, September 22, 1935, A6; and in Irwin and Lloyd, *Ruth*, 41. Other biographies that

describe this set-up in the 1920s include Mezzrow and Wolfe, *Really*, 60; and Marks, *They All Sang*, 212, describing Tommy Lyman.

57. Victor Ganzl discusses the international trend toward intimate musicals in the teens; Victor Ganzl, *The Musical* (Boston: Northeastern University Press, 1997), 161–62, 167.

58. Ganzl, *The Musical*, 173–76. For the audience capacity of the Princess and Vanderbilt theatres and their history of productions, see those theatres' entries in the Internet Broadway Database, as well as entries for the shows under discussion in Richard C. Norton, *A Chronology of American Musical Theater*, 3 vols. (Oxford: Oxford University Press, 2002).

59. Please note that Von Tilzer's "All Alone" is a very different song from Irving Berlin's better-remembered "All Alone," of 1924, discussed later and in chapter 10.

60. The staging of Berlin's "All Alone" is described by John Murray Anderson, *Out Without My Rubbers* (New York: Library Publishers, 1954), 86. As Jeffery Magee points out, Gerald Bordman describes the scene differently, saying they are sitting and dressed in white; Jeffrey Magee, *Irving Berlin's American Musical Theater* (Oxford: Oxford University Press, 2012), 128, and 323n73, citing Gerald Bordman, *American Musical Revue* (New York: Oxford University Press, 1985), 83. Robert Baral agrees with Anderson in *Revue* (New York: Fleet Publishing, 1962), 157. Whatever the details, the staging clearly combined the telephone with an intimate love song.

61. R. Murray Schafer, *The Tuning of the World* (New York: Alfred A. Knopf, 1977), 89.

62. Schafer, *Tuning*, 88.

63. For the telephone's dual effects, see Ithiel de Sola Pool, *The Social Impact of the Telephone* (Cambridge, MA: MIT Press, 1977), 4. Although the telephone became a thriving commercial technology by 1880, by the turn of the century it was still predominantly used for business; see Pool, 26–28. Therefore, its potential use as a mode of personal intimacy did not have much effect until the decades when the torch song was developing.

64. Nellie Revell, "Remarks at Random," *Variety*, April 25, 1928, 49; for this, plus an early use of "torch singer," see Myra Nye, "Society of Cinemaland," *Los Angeles Times*, January 27, 1929, C27, under the subheading "Cupid's News."

65. McCormack "added one song as an encore . . . 'All Alone', not on the program, which was announced as a song he had just recorded," as reported in "Famous Stars Sing First Time by Radio to 6,000,000 People," *New York Times*, January 2, 1925, 1.

66. Lawrence Bergreen, *As Thousands Cheer* (New York: Penguin Books, 1990), 201; and entries for "All Alone" in Whitburn, *Pop*.

67. Regarding the low pitch in crooning: Ruth Etting "found a lower register when she entered radio"; Carroll Nye, "Ruth Etting Scorns." The *New York Times* reported that De Leath pioneered "the 'crooning style,' a delivery made necessary by the imperfect microphones of the period, when a high note was likely to shatter a transmitter tube"; "Vaughn De Leath, Radio 'First Lady,'" *New York Times*, May 29, 1943, 13. Ian Whitcomb points out that "around 1932, condenser microphones and loudspeakers with a warmer bass response were introduced," favoring these lower ranges; Ian Whitcomb, introduction to *The Rise of the Crooners*, by Michael Pitts and Frank Hoffman (Lanham, MD: Scarecrow Press, 2002), 49n38. This technological advance encouraged performers to sing in the same pitch range as their speaking voice, thereby even more strongly matching the conversational qualities of the era's songwriting.

68. This is my own interpretation of the information on proto-blues and early blues given by Muir, *Long Lost*, 38–48, 181–216. My brief summary should not be taken to imply that, after the "blues proper" became popular, the older form of "blues ballad" did not continue in American music; it did.

69. Muir, *Long Lost*, 11–15.

70. Wayne D. Shirley, "The Coming of 'Deep River,'" *American Music* 15, no. 4 (winter 1997): 515, see also 512–13.

71. Shirley, "Coming," 515.

72. "Science Discovers Reality of Dreams," *New York Times*, May 8, 1910, SM14. The important term "unconscious" is soon introduced into public discussion; it is used in "Mothers of Married Sons," *New York Times*, August 14, 1911, 6.

73. "Science Discovers"; "Every Dream Has Its Meaning," *New York Times*, May 12, 1912, MS3; "Is an Only Son a Menace to Society? This Doctor Says He Is," *New York Times*, September 8, 1912, SM12; "Soul Analysis and Nerves," *Washington Post*, July 18, 1911, 6.

74. Jerome Kern, "Letter from Jerome Kern to Alexander Woollcott from *The Story of Irving Berlin*," in *The Irving Berlin Reader*, edited by Benjamin Sears (Oxford: Oxford University Press, 2012), 81. The Kern letter probably was written in late 1923 or early 1924. This was just before Irving Berlin began writing his series of waltzes suffused with hushed intimacy, discussed below, starting with "What'll I Do" (copyrighted March 10, 1924).

75. Muir presents copyright and publication evidence for the blues developing in the American South; Muir, *Long Lost*, 141–42.

76. Muir, *Long Lost*, 81–83.

77. "Science Discovers."

78. "Influence of Mind on Body," *Washington Post*, March 5, 1911, MS3.

79. Harburg may be heard using this phrase on disc four of *The Songwriters Collection*, DVD, (New York: Wellspring Media, Lance Entertainment, 2004).

80. In tracing the lineage of *croon*, as elsewhere, I depend on the Oxford English Dictionary, accessed online.

81. "Man Is Divine, Says Rector in Sermon," quoting H. L. Durant, *Washington Post*, August 14, 1922, 5; Helen Frances Scott, in a poem titled "Berceuse," *Los Angeles Times*, May 21, 1924, A4.

82. "Lyon and Healy Draw Your Attention to These Victor Records," advertisement, *Chicago Tribune*, January 6, 1919, 8. I presume "Lullaby" is a piece by British composer Adela Verne. Grace Kingsley, "Personal Grief and Dramatic Talent Blend in Portrayal of Actress in 'Copperhead,'" *Los Angeles Times*, March 21, 1926, 23.

83. Maude Nooks Howard, "Black Mammy's Apotheosis," *New York Times*, January 28, 1923, XX6. This is a critique of white Southern hypocrisy toward Blacks, with a sharp satire of the "mammy" stereotype. "Coming Radio Events Cast Their Shadows," *New York Times*, October 11, 1925, XX18. There are also numerous songs that include "mammy" figures "crooning." Of thirty-eight early twentieth-century songs indexed at online sites with the word "croon," forty percent were Southern-themed, and more than half of those specifically mention "mammy" crooning (i.e., slightly more than one in five of the total). Allison McCracken discusses this phenomenon, *Real Men Don't Sing* (Durham, NC: Duke University Press, 2015), 41–65.

84. "Alabam's Sing-Copated Star," advertisement, *New York Times*, March 9, 1926, 20.

85. National Child Welfare Association, *Music and Childhood* (New York: National Child Welfare Association, 1919), 26. This slender booklet was the basis for a news feature by Lucy Calhoun, "Musical, Instead of Noise-Making, Toys Urged for Children," *Chicago Tribune*, September 4, 1919, 19.

86. National Child Welfare, *Music*, 26.

87. National Child Welfare, *Music*, 6.

88. Irving Berlin, "Song and Sorrow Are Playmates," from an unidentified journal of 1913; in Sears, *Irving*, 169.

89. McCracken, "'God's Gift,'" 392n31; 368.

90. McCracken, "'God's Gift,'" 390n5.

91. Ralph M. Pabst, *Gene Austin's Ol' Buddy* (Phoenix, AZ: Augury, 1984), 68.

92. McCracken, "'God's Gift,'" 377.

93. British crooner Al Bowlly had a book credited to him that attempts to discuss the new crooning. The text derisively bristles at any possible comparison of disciplined "quiet singing

into a microphone, in the modern dance-band style" to infant-directed song; it states that the label "crooning" is "a horrible expression. . . . Different dictionaries give varying definitions . . . between 'a low moaning sound, as of animals in pain' to 'the soft singing of a mother to her child.' Neither of those is very complimentary, but at least the former supplied a new joke for hard-up humorists!" *Modern Style Singing ("Crooning")* (London: Henri Selmber, 1934), 10. In flagrantly denying this parallel, perhaps the writer felt its underlying validity potentially threatening; and this may be the reason for his defensive rhetoric.

94. The transitions in the connotations of "crooner" are traced by McCracken in some detail; *Real*, 37–64, 74–83, 208–37, *et passant*.

95. In *Pennies from Heaven*, Crosby sings the title song to his young ward at bedtime at a slow, lullaby-like tempo. In *East Side of Heaven*, he sings to a babe-in-arms "That Sly Old Gentleman (From Featherbed Lane)." In *Blue Skies*, he plays and sings to his young daughter, as a pre-bedtime treat, "Running Around in Circles." In *Here Comes the Groom*, he lullabies two juvenile émigrés from France with "Bon Nuit." In *High Society*, Crosby's character mollifies his young erstwhile sister-in-law by extemporizing a new song just for her: "Little One."

96. In *Going My Way*, Crosby's character attempts to sing to sleep his fellow priest with "Too-Ra Loo-Ra Loo-Ral," thus reviving a 1914 Tin Pan Alley hit that henceforth became indelibly associated with Crosby—and that has been assumed by many I have encountered to be a folk song. In *White Christmas*, Crosby offers advice to Rosemary Clooney on how to fall asleep when troubled, with "Count Your Blessings (Instead of Sheep)."

97. John Diamond, *Life-Energy Analysis* (Valley Cottage, NY: Archaeus Press, 1988), 58; John Diamond, *Music and Song, Mother and Love* (Bloomingdale, IL: Enhancement Books, 2001), 3.

98. Diamond, *Music and Song*, 14.

99. Eric Lott, "'Love and Theft' (2001)," in *The Cambridge Companion to Bob Dylan*, ed. Kevin J. H. Dettmar (Cambridge, UK: Cambridge University Press, 2009), 172.

100. Diamond, *Music and Song*, 21.

101. About the time Buddy Clark was being conceived, "I Wonder Who's Kissing Her Now" was dubbed "the most popular selection among ivory ticklers for 'for variations'" in vaudeville; Sime Silverman, "Fairman and Manion," *Variety*, November 25, 1911, 18. This train of thought derives from John Diamond, conversations with the author, July 1999.

102. Whitcomb, *After*, 43. Edward Marks made a similar declaration about one late nineteenth-century forum for getting songs known to the public: "Minstrel songs fell into three categories: ballads, bass songs, and end songs. The ballads sold best"; Marks, *They All Sang*, 63–64.

103. *Frank Sinatra Concert Collection*, DVD (Los Angeles: Shout! Factory, 2010); the quote is from the November 24, 1965, special on disc one.

104. Liner notes and track selections for Frank Sinatra, *Everything Happens to Me*, CD, (Burbank, CA: Reprise Records, 1996).

105. Even their early proponents point this out. The pioneer Alley publisher-songwriter Edward Marks wrote that, in contrast to Broadway songs, "Tin Pan Alley specialized in the meretricious type of thing that reflected the demand for potted palms. Full of quavers, fake notes, and fake sentiment"; Marks, *They All Sang*, 144. Sigmund Spaeth said in 1934, "in every . . . branch of popular song-writing, a great many artificial insincerities are balanced by a small number of really honest expressions"; Sigmund Spaeth, *The Facts of Life in Popular Song* (New York: Whittlesey House, McGraw-Hill, 1934), 70.

106. For my insights into courtly love, I draw on conversations with John Diamond as well as his "Courtly Love, Wonderland and Marriage," *The Diamond Report* 112 (June 1986); supported by the discussions of Rick Altman, *The American Film Musical* (Bloomington: Indiana University Press, 1987), 212, 262–63; and Barbara W. Tuchman, *A Distant Mirror: The Calamitous Fourteenth Century* (New York: Ballantine, 1978), 66–67, 215.

107. S. I. Hayakawa, "Popular Songs vs. the Facts of Life," in *Mass Culture: The Popular Arts in America*, edited by Bernard Rosenberg and David Manning White (Glencoe, IL: Free Press, Falcon's Wing Press, 1957), 394–96. Hayakawa originally published this in *Etc.* 12 (1955): 83–95.

108. Hayakawa, "Popular," 398–99.

109. Hayakawa discusses the pop song "Tired" as if it were a blues. He also presents some songs that are admittedly bluesy but not really blues; for instance, "A Good Man Is Hard to Find" (1918) and "St. James Infirmary" (a blues ballad derived from folk sources). Among other contradictions are Hayakawa's presentation of sophisticated Tin Pan Alley blues by W. C. Handy and Spencer Williams as outside of popular song, and a footnote that acknowledges virtues in the lyrics of the 1953 pop hit "Little Things That Mean So Much." In addition, he derides the music of popular song and praises jazz music, yet does not address the seeming contradiction that jazz musicians embrace (and create) popular songs. For further debates with Hayakawa's argument, see David A. Horowitz, "The Perils of Commodity Fetishism: Tin Pan Alley's Portrait of the Romantic Marketplace, 1920–1942," *Popular Music and Society* 17, no. 1 (1985): 37–53; and Rose Rosengard Subotnik, "Shoddy Equipment for Living? Reconstructing the Tin Pan Alley Song," in *Musicological Identities: Essays in Honor of Susan McClary*, edited by Steven Baur, Raymond Knapp, and Jacqueline Warwick (Aldershot, UK: Ashgate, 2008), 205–18.

110. Gerald Mast, *Can't Help Singin'* (Woodstock, NY: Overlook Press, 1987), 27.

111. Whitcomb, *After*, 56.

112. LaRosa is quoted by Gene Lees, *Singers and the Song* (New York: Oxford University Press, 1987), 104.

113. When a melodic section is repeated but not quite exactly—for instance, the B section of "Fly Me to the Moon"—then it is called, in that instance, "B prime," and indicated with an accent mark like this: B'.

114. Peter van der Merwe, *Origins of the Popular Style* (Oxford: Clarendon Press, 1992), 270. Van der Merwe points out that this penultimate limerick-like rhythm is common in the Anglo-American folk song tradition going back to the sixteenth century, with "Go from My Window, Go," and in Tin Pan Alley songs through the 1920s, with examples such as "Sweet Georgia Brown" (1925).

115. Van der Merwe, *Origins*.

116. The importance of verses before 1900 is often noted: Goldberg, *Tin*, 94, 228; Hamm, *Yesterdays*, 254–55, 291–93; Nicholas Tawa, *Way*, 96–97; van der Merwe, *Origins*, 269.

117. Several writers note the variety in verse length and form. Tawa gives data on verse and refrain structures for the period from 1890 through 1910; Tawa, *Way*, 170, 179, 190, 196. Engel discusses how "there is no *single* recommended form or length for this verse section"; Engel, *Making*, 4. Wilder comments on the "rhapsodic, free potential" of verses, which he finds manifested in the verses of Richard Rodgers; Wilder, *American*, 170.

118. Wolf, "Boy."

119. Charles Hamm briefly tells the tale of the vanishing verses; Hamm, *Yesterdays*, 359. As of this writing, there is still no methodical survey of this trend. One piece of the story may be found in the report of radio policy of Lucky Strike, with their dance music broadcast, starting in 1928, which banned verses and only played choruses, as reported by Sanjek; Sanjek, *American*, 166. Another bit of evidence is supplied by the much-imitated Rudy Vallee, who wrote in 1930 about his rule to "to play only choruses"; Vallee, *Vagabond*, 93.

120. Raymond Knapp, *The American Musical and the Formation of National Identity* (Princeton, NJ: Princeton University Press, 2005), 78.

121. Knapp, *American Musical*.

122. Banfield, "Sondheim," 155. In this article, Banfield recruits the term "melopoetics" for, in a song, "the interplay between verbal and musical factors giving rise to a unitary perception dependent upon them both," 138; I have borrowed the term from his usage.

123. Johnny Mercer, *The Complete Lyrics of Johnny Mercer*, ed. Robert Kimball, Barry Day, Miles Kreuger, and Eric Davis (New York: Alfred A. Knopf, 2009), 275; Sammy Cahn, *I Should Care: The Sammy Cahn Story* (New York: Arbor House, 1974), 75.

124. Titles inspired some famous melodies. Richard Rodgers made a note when Lorenz Hart identified the phrase "My Heart Stood Still" as a good title and later wrote a melody inspired by that hint; Richard Rodgers, *Musical Stages: An Autobiography* (New York: Random House, 1975), 101–3. Sammy Cahn gave Jule Styne the title and first stanza of "It's Been a Long, Long Time"; Cahn, *I Should*, 97. E. Y. Harburg gave Harold Arlen the title "I Want to Go Beyond the Rainbow" (which became "Over the Rainbow") and Burton Lane the phrase "There's a Glen in Glocca Mora" (which became "How Are Things in Glocca Morra"); Harold Meyerson and Ernie Harburg, *Who Put the Rainbow in the Wizard of Oz? Yip Harburg, Lyricist* (Ann Arbor: University of Michigan Press, 1995), 132, 232.

125. Berlin is quoted by Isaac Goldberg, in an excerpt of "Words and Music from Irving Berlin," from an unidentified journal, circa 1933 or 1934, in Sears, *Irving*, 182. Even after 1924, when true rhyme became the rule for lyrics of serious sentiment, an odd convention of the time allowed wordsmiths to rhyme "again" at times with "then" and at other times with "rain."

126. Admittedly, Tin Pan Alley songwriters often skirt around the edges of correct emphasis with words ending in "y"—for instance, making "*eternally*" into "eternal-*lee*."

127. Will D. Cobb, "The Business of Song Writing," *Variety*, December 16, 1905, 4.

128. Cobb, "Business."

129. Irving Berlin and Justus Dickinson, "Love Interest as a Commodity," *Green Book Magazine* April 1916, 695; quoted in Goldberg, *Tin*, 220.

130. Berlin, "Song," in Sears, *Irving*, 169.

131. Undated quote in Sears, *Irving*, 8.

132. Bert Williams is quoted in Jasen, *Tin*, 21.

133. Paul Whiteman and Mary Margaret McBride, *Jazz* (New York: J. H. Sears, 1926), 180–81. The bandleader's claim is that "at least nine-tenths of" these melodies derive from "classical music" by "the masters"—an exaggeration, but a subject that I will return to in later chapters.

134. Marks, *They All Sang*, 172.

135. Marks, *They All Sang*.

136. As with all such instances in this book, unless otherwise noted, the hit statuses in the United States of "Ma Blushin' Rosie" (a.k.a. "My Blushin' Rosie," introduced on Broadway in *Fiddle Dee Dee*) and "Ida" are charted by Gardner, *Popular*; and Whitburn, *Pop*.

137. Given its priority in print, "Rosie" would seem to be the model for "Ida." Nevertheless, Eddie Leonard stated later, in an advertisement seeking to guard his style and songwriting credits from the theft of others, "'Ida' was written by Eddie Leonard and Eddie Munson in 1895"; *Variety*, March 19, 1910, 40. Contradicting that claim, David Ewen reports: "As a member of the Primrose and West Minstrels in 1903, Eddie Leonard wrote the words and music of 'Ida, Sweet as Apple Cider.' At that time, Leonard was about to lose his job. But when the premiere of this song inspired an ovation, the manager of the minstrel company kept Leonard on"; Ewen, *All the Years*, 48. It is not hard, admittedly, to reconcile the two accounts: Leonard may have written "Ida" in 1895 and kept it in reserve until his 1903 job crisis. Nevertheless, both accounts seem partial: Leonard does not explain why he held back the song for eight years; and Ewen depicts Leonard as the sole creator. Further, Ewen's version seems almost too colorful to be true. Neither story accounts for the strong resemblance of "Ida" to "Rosie."

138. Richard Peters, Ed O'Brien, and Scott P. Sayers, *The Frank Sinatra Scrapbook* (New York: St. Martin's Press, 1982), 74. Although undated, internal evidence suggests this quote is from a newspaper interview of the mid- to late forties.

139. Scott Yanow, *Jazz on Record* (San Francisco: Backbeat, 2003), 775.

CHAPTER TWO: "BILL BAILEY, WON'T YOU PLEASE COME HOME?"

1. For the importance of "The Bully Song" for this genre, see Douglas Gilbert, *Lost Chords* (Garden City, NY: Doubleday, Doran, 1942), 244. Gilbert quotes the *New York Herald*, "In an unsigned article dated Sunday, June 20, 1897," probably by the songwriter-journalist Monroe Rosenfeld. For analysis of the six published adaptations of "The Bully Song," see Peter Muir, "Before 'Crazy Blues': Commercial Blues in America, 1850–1920" (PhD diss., City University of New York, 2004), 254–70.

2. Jasen, *Tin*, 5.

3. Haviland's career is discussed in Jasen, *Tin*, especially at 4–5, 14–15; on his Quaker religion, see "F. B. Haviland Dies; Music Publisher," *New York Times*, March 31, 1932, 21. Dresser's character is outlined in Marks, *They All Sang*, especially at 122–26; for both Dresser and Howley see Goldberg, *Tin*, 112, 118.

4. Muir, "Before," 234–36; Muir, *Long Lost*, 189–93.

5. Muir, "Before," 243.

6. Muir, "Before," 244.

7. I patch together Cannon's life story from various sources, including Muir, "Before," 222–30; Frank Leighton and Bert Leighton, "Origin of 'Blues' (or Jazz)," in *Jazz in Print (1856–1929)*, edited by Karl Koenig (Hillsdale, NY: Pendragon Press), 164–66; originally in *Variety*, January 6, 1922, 27.

8. Richard Robbins, "'Bill Bailey, Won't You Please' . . . Composer's Star Twinkled a Century Ago," *Tribune-Review*, May 13, 2001, Focus section 2–3, 10.

9. Leighton, "Origins," 165.

10. I base this statement on Muir, "Before," 591–94, Appendix 4, which lists thirty-five songs that can be called true prefigurings of the blues. ("The Bully Song," which was published in six versions, I count as one song. There are also a handful of other songs that are only marginally related to later blues structures, plus ten instrumental pieces.) Of those thirty-five, the "pioneer" group mentioned by the Leightons (i.e., the Cannon circle plus Ben Harney) have their names on sixteen, or 46 percent.

11. Leighton, "Origins," 165, 164.

12. Muir, "Before," 244.

13. Muir, "Before," 245.

14. See: Tom Fletcher, *One Hundred Years of the Negro in Show Business* (New York: Da Capo Press, 1984), 147. See also: Richard D. Barnet, Bruce Nemerov, and Mayo R. Taylor, *The Story Behind the Song* (Westport, CT: Greenwood Press, 2004), 10. Sigmund Spaeth also mentions "Creole Belles" (1900) as a "higher type of 'coon song'"—perhaps a sign of the same trend; Sigmund Spaeth, *A History of Popular Music in America* (New York: Random House, [1948] 1958), 313.

15. Daniel I. McNamara, ed., *The ASCAP Biographical Dictionary of Composers, Authors, and Publishers* (New York: Thomas Y. Crowell, 1952), 300. As "Bill Bailey, Ain't Dat a Shame," the brothers claim joint authorship in their 1922 article; Leighton, "Origins," 165. Muir reports the copyright card credits Queen and Bert Leighton; Muir, "Before," 275.

16. Muir, "Before," 301–2.

17. There is a slight question whether or not Bill Bailey and the lady are actually married. "Ain't Dat a Shame" calls her his "lady friend" and Cannon's big hit at first dubs her his "lady love." Such ambiguous terms might indicate they are living together out of wedlock. But Cannon's lyric goes on to say that she "married a B. and O. brakeman," meaning Bill—so we can assume they are married. In this era, however, common-law marriages were common among the lower working classes, including among many African Americans. Nevertheless, in another song the Baileys are considered by their friends to be married: Bill's pal, Eli Crosby, refers to her as "Mrs. Bailey" in the song "Won't You Kindly Hum Old 'Home Sweet Home' to Me."

18. I examined the lyric of Cannon's "Won't You Kindly Hum Old 'Home Sweet Home' to Me" at the Library of Congress. Muir assured its verse music and harmonies relate to the blues ballad intros of the rest of the "Bill Bailey" cycle; email correspondence, January 23, 2019.

19. "Sporting Sidelights," *Washington Post*, March 26, 1908, 9; Ewen, *All*, 169.

20. Joe Laurie Jr., *Vaudeville* (New York: Henry Holt, 1953), 64; Robert Trumbull, "Bill Bailey Isn't Budging," *New York Times*, September 1, 1962, 5; John Gregory, "How It Was During the Bill Bailey Era," *Los Angeles Times*, July 22, 1973, I1.

21. The Bill Bailey of Singapore said, when asked why he stayed abroad, "Hell, I like it here!" Trumbull, "Bill"; Gregory, "How."

22. James J. Geller, *Famous Songs and Their Stories* (New York: Macaulay, 1931), 205.

23. That Bill has the upper hand in "Bill Bailey" may be one reason that (a) it survived more strongly than "Ain't Dat a Shame" (in which Mrs. Bailey has the upper hand); and (b) it turned up so often, usually parodied, in the twentieth century's male-dominated preserves of sports, politics, and business.

24. Jennings Parrott, "Apron Strings Entangled in Red Tape," *Los Angeles Times*, April 12, 1976, B2.

25. Parrott, "Apron."

26. Muir, *Long Lost*, 196; see also Dorothy Scarborough, *On the Trail of Negro Folk-Songs* (Cambridge, MA: Harvard University Press, [1925] 1963), 89–90.

27. John M. Willig, "'Follies' a Homecoming for Ethel Shutta," *New York Times*, November 14, 1971, D32.

28. "Juvenile Operetta at Gonzaga Hall," *Washington Post*, November 26, 1902, 10.

29. "Beer Shower for a Singer," *Chicago Daily Tribune*, December 19, 1902, 2.

30. "To Diplomatic Corps: First State Reception of the Season at the White House," *Washington Post*, January 9, 1903, 3.

31. "Why One Man Likes Housecleaning," *Chicago Tribune*, September 13, 1903, 42.

32. "Battle of the Hand Organs," *New York Times*, March 27, 1904, SM2.

33. Ewen, *All*, 308.

34. George Bernard Shaw, *Passion, Poison, and Petrification, or, The Fatal Gazogene*, in *Translations and Tomfooleries* (New York: Brentano's, 1926), 237.

35. Edith Nesbit, *The Railway Children* (Harmondsworth, UK: Puffin, Penguin, [1906] 1974), 137.

36. Shaw, *Passion*, 220.

37. Nelson Bell, "The New Week's Bills," *Washington Post*, April 29, 1929, 14.

38. Russell lists six country "Bill Bailey" discs between 1927 and 1930 and one in 1937; *Country Music*, 1022.

39. An advertisement includes Durante's disc; "MGM List of Hits," *Billboard*, September 23, 1950, 22.

40. "Night Club Reviews: Olympic Hotel, Seattle (Georgian Room)," *Variety*, April 25, 1951, 54; with both *Billboard* and *Variety* thereafter reporting Kay's use of the song at various dates, through to "Night Club Reviews: Fire Station House, Garden Grove, Cal.," *Variety*, August 23, 1967, 81.

41. "Night Club Reviews: New Frontier, Las Vegas," *Variety*, June 29, 1955, 53; also "Night Club Reviews: 500 Club, Atlantic City," *Variety*, August 31, 1955, 53.

42. "Night Club Reviews: New Frontier, Las Vegas," *Variety*, August 29, 1956, 53.

43. Gilbert Milstein, "Jazz Temple on Times Square," *New York Times*, 29 November 1953, SM25.

44. Will Leonard, "On the Town: Improved Haymes-Jeffries Act," *Chicago Daily Tribune*, December 3, 1961, D14.

45. Bill Henry, "A Window on Washington," *Los Angeles Times*, January 31, 1961, B1.

46. Mary V. R. Thayer, "Sen. Kennedy Gets Two More Supporters—by Mistake," *Washington Post*, July 11, 1960, B3.

47. Jim Murray, "A Place to Ponder," *Los Angeles Times*, July 12, 1962, B1.

48. Ironically, "Bill Bailey" beckons the listener back home, while the melodically similar "Cabaret" urges them to leave home. Jerry Herman simultaneously points out and dismisses such resemblances as that between "Bill Bailey" and "Cabaret": "No one sits down to try to sound like 'Bill Bailey' . . . Not deliberately"; Joyce Haber, "Eight Notes to Immortality," *Los Angeles Times*, August 18, 1974, O21.

49. Early on, "Bill Bailey" is linked to the honky-tonk piano style, in "Record Reviews," *Billboard*, January 7, 1950, 80, in a pair of singles on "slightly gimmicked piano" and "in fine pianola style" by pianist Freddie Mendelssohn and rhythm section.

50. Perhaps the first sing-along LP, the 1956 Mercury album *Everybody Sing*, with Guy Cherney, claims in its liner notes, that it is "a new departure in record albums, for . . . it marks the first time that the entire music repertoire consists of songs that invite you to sing along." Indeed, the reviewer in *Billboard*, nonplussed, writes of it with the skepticism that often greets a novelty; "Reviews and Ratings of New Albums," *Billboard*, April 7, 1956, 24.

51. Before the success of *The Five Pennies* soundtrack and Darin's "Bill Bailey," the jazz trumpeter Jonah Jones had featured a breakneck "Bill Bailey" on his best-selling album that charted in September 1958, *Jumpin' with Jonah*, featuring a restrained piano solo by his combo member George Rhodes that took the song out of the realm of the usual Dixieland style. Brenda Lee, Darin's peer on the pop charts, subsequently had her rockabilly-styled single of "Bill Bailey" released in December 1958; however, it did not chart.

52. Jeff Bleiel, *That's All* (Ann Arbor, MI: Popular Culture Ink, 1993), 49.

53. Singles by both Reese and Darin (in US pressings) use the de facto alternative titles "Won't You Come Home, Bill Bailey" and "Won'cha Come Home, Bill Bailey," respectively. In fact, the title appears in many forms throughout the years, including the brief forms "Bill Bailey" and "Come Home"—perhaps one more sign of the song's quickly developed folk-song status.

54. Paul Hume, "New York Report: From Pengo to Ella to 'Ariadne,' Too," *Washington Post, Times Herald* February 10, 1963, G1.

55. Leo E. Litwak, "A Fantasy That Paid Off," *New York Times*, June 27, 1965, SM22.

56. Leonard Feather, "Month at Flamingo: B. B. King Opens in Vegas," *Los Angeles Times*, December 13, 1971, G23.

57. Dan Sullivan, "*Tintypes*: Nostalgia Songbook," *Los Angeles Times*, March 20, 1981, H1; Frank Rich, "Revue: *Tintypes* Scrapbook of Nostalgia," *New York Times*, October 24, 1980, C3.

58. In using the term "hypermetric shift," I am drawing from its use by Muir, who explains it more fully in "Before," 239, 264.

59. Van der Merwe, *Origins*, 194, 280.

60. Van der Merwe, *Origins*, 269.

61. Wilder, *American*, 13.

62. The rhythm of the refrain's first bar (and the nine echoes of that pattern in later measures) is of the type that Edward A. Berlin discusses as augmented syncopation, "a syncopated effect that is relatively weak," but nevertheless was "common in early rags" and cakewalk compositions; Edward A. Berlin, *Ragtime* (Berkeley: University of California Press, 1980), 83, 104. The lengthy mid-measure note can fit well with the high forward lift of the leg that is the core step of the cakewalk.

63. Wilder, *American*, 13.

64. An explanation of methodology: I collected a representative core sample of performances of each song, and from that core sample I tabulated information about performance practices. After the tabulations, I found more renditions, which were not integrated into the tabulation but which nevertheless seemed in line with the previous results. Resources grew during the writing process. The smallest core sample was thirty-three (for "Some of These Days"), the largest ninety-six ("You Made Me Love You"). Artists often repeatedly recorded a work. When appropriate, about some details I tabulated the number of *artists* who manifested a performance practice; at other times, I counted the number of *recordings*.

65. Banfield, "Sondheim," 155.

66. Banfield, "Sondheim," 156.

67. If each *recording* is counted as a separate instance, a slightly larger 66 percent use tags.

68. Steven Cornelius, *Music of the Civil War Era* (Westport, CT: Greenwood Press, 2004), 89.

69. Gioia, *Jazz*, 12, 91.

70. John Diamond, conversation with the author, late 1990s.

71. Furia, *Poets*, 29. Furia calls the images on the "Bill Bailey" sheet music cover "wooly-haired," but, indeed, in that image both heads are covered with headgear—the little we can see of Bill's hair is cut so short it is impossible to know whether his hair has been straightened (as would befit his overall dandified persona) or not.

72. L. M. Montgomery, *Rilla of Ingleside* (New York: Bantam Books, [1921] 1992), 98. The family's domestic retainer is shocked to learn about the lice in the trenches and, in a package to the eldest son, "slip[s] in a fine tooth comb" to help him, as he puts it, with "fighting the good fight against both Huns and cooties."

73. "Rousing" in Will Leonard, "Playboy's Action Faction Lives Up to Its Name," *Chicago Tribune*, February 21, 1971, E5; and in "Eddie Jackson, Sidekick to Durante, Dies of Stroke," *Chicago Tribune*, July 17, 1980, B15; "rowdy" in Will Leonard, "On the Town: Valiant Valkyrie," *Chicago Tribune*, January 31, 1954, F8; "playful, kick-up-your-heels" in Stephen Holden, "Cabaret: Joys and Sorrows of Life, From Funny to Personal," *New York Times*, March 12, 1996, C14.

74. The sheet music cover is one of the many contexts that define and redefine the meaning of each Tin Pan Alley song. The graphic artists were undoubtedly swayed and inspired, at times, by previous sheet music covers; the song's title, lyrics, and perceived subgenre; directives from the publisher; and shifting standards of design, beauty, and humor, in both the popular and high arts. Unfortunately, however, the specific influences on the graphic artist for any particular cover can only be conjectured. The extent that a specific cover is a response to the song that it encases is not known. Nevertheless, whatever the artist's and publisher's motivation and intention, to the person using the score the cover can function as a metatextual comment on the song.

75. For some listeners, Cooke's advice to "Bill Bailey" (at the Copa in 1964) may seem like an instance of supreme deadpan comic irony, but I feel certain details argue for an underlying attempt to approach the song seriously—details such as his choice of certain melodic variations, or of when to activate his slightly hoarse vocal texture, his struggle to alter the "comb" line in the second refrain, and his overall approach. This contrasts with his rendition of "Frankie and Johnny" on the same album, which features greater comic elaboration.

76. To summarize, about half of singers change the lyric to the first person: "I moan the whole day long." That includes more than 80 percent of female singers and a quarter of male singers.

77. The romantic conventions of Tin Pan Alley and its crooner tradition are ostensibly completely heterosexual, so the idea of a man sincerely wanting his lover, Bill, to come home would have been out of the question in the pop mainstream until very late in the twentieth century.

78. Patsy Cline also made an earlier radio transcription of "Bill Bailey," featuring in that instance two refrains both in fast tempo. It is that "live" version that Jessica Lange, as Cline, lip-synchs to in the 1985 biographical movie *Sweet Dreams*. As in other movies discussed below, in this biopic the song tellingly reflects the dramatic tensions of one phase of the singer's domestic life. This strictly up-tempo rendering is the one referenced in the popular Cline-based karaoke version.

79. Will Leonard, "On the Town: Talented Pros + Talented Kids = a Great Show," *Chicago Tribune*, February 18, 1968, G12.

80. For more on the "virility" aspect, see Krin Gabbard, *Jammin' at the Margins* (Chicago: University of Chicago Press, 1996), 82–89, 147–51.

81. Edgardo Vega Yunqué, *No Matter How Much You Promise to Cook or Pay the Rent You Blew It Cauze Bill Bailey Ain't Never Coming Home Again* (New York: Farrar, Straus and Giroux,

2003). The novel echoes situations in Vega's own life, including a broken marriage in which he was both father and stepfather.

82. Yunqué, *No Matter*, 633–34.

CHAPTER THREE: "I'M SORRY I MADE YOU CRY" AND "JAZZ HANDLING": THE STRANGE HISTORY OF THE AMERICAN WALTZ, PART ONE

1. Gardner, "Why," F3. The earliest reference to a torch waltz is from 1930, a blurb announcing that Vili Milli, Broadway ensemble member, had written "My Torch Song," "a waltz ballad," and had placed it with "a large Broadway house"; "Melody Mart Notes," *Billboard*, March 15, 1930, 27.

2. Edward Jablonski, LP liner notes, *All Alone*, performed by Frank Sinatra (Burbank, CA: Reprise Records, 1962). The original pressing included a double-fold sleeve containing a two-page essay that was shortened for later printings, but this passage is in both versions.

3. Jablonski, LP liner notes, *All Alone*.

4. John Diamond, "Jazz and Classical: Up on One and Three," unpublished lecture, September 3, 1998.

5. There is a montage of two concerts with Ellington teaching the audience about the offbeat, in *Jazz: A Film by Ken Burns* (Hollywood, CA: Paramount, PBS, 2001), episode 10, "A Masterpiece at Midnight." In *Swing!* "Two and Four" was written by jazz singer Ann Hampton Callaway, an original Broadway cast member.

6. Wilder, *American*, 219.

7. Kern, "Letter," 81.

8. Gershwin, *Lyrics*, 85, 101.

9. Oxford English Dictionary Online (accessed January 2, 2017).

10. "Amusement Machines: Here's a Tune Inspired by a Music Merchant," *Billboard*, July 22, 1939, 72.

11. O. M. Samuel, "New Orleans," *Variety*, March 10, 1916, 38.

12. Samuel, "New Orleans." The other local hits of 1916 New Orleans, now forgotten, were: "Don't You Leave Me Now, Daddy" (seemingly in the line that leads from "Bill Bailey, Won't You Please Come Home?" through "Some of These Days" to "Baby, Won't You Please Come Home" and beyond); "Who You For, Brown Skin?"; and a Latin-flavored number, "Tropical Girl."

13. There are no copyright records for "I'm Sorry I Made You Cry" in 1915 or 1916. Notice is first received from Triangle Music on February 8, 1917. Triangle's deposit copies followed ten months later, on December 8, at which point suddenly a copyright date is inexplicably asserted in the copyright record, giving January 1, 1916. This entry may have corrected an earlier clerical omission or (more likely) it may have been a retroactive claim—possibly an honest one, since by March 10, 1916, the tune's local popularity is already noted.

14. O. M. Samuel, "New Orleans," *Variety*, September 15, 1916, 47.

15. Advertisement for Bartlett Music, *Los Angeles Times*, August 28, 1917, 13.

16. Reported November 29: "Rosenbaum in Chicago," *Billboard*, December 8, 1917, 15.

17. A report dated March 9, "The Song World: Feist Absorbs Triangle," *Billboard*, March 16, 1918, 16.

18. Samuel, "New Orleans"—the March 10, 1916, blurb cited above.

19. "Lion and Serpent. Weighing One's Words," *Los Angeles Times*, September 24, 1917, II4.

20. "The Song World: This Week's Song of Songs," *Billboard*, June 15, 1918, 14.

21. The following year, 1919, the Original Dixieland Jazz Band would record the waltz "I'm Forever Blowing Bubbles," in a gentle version that plods at times but mostly achieves a jazzy roll, with a freewheeling clarinet filigree. This is another way of achieving "jazz handling," but whether some musicians used it with "I'm Sorry I Made You Cry" is not documented, while the duple-meter transformation of Clesi's tune is, via copyright records.

22. I was only able to locate Fuller's fourth waxing, on Edison, and Sweatman's medley; but I presume that Dabney's arrangement was also in duple meter; and that Fuller's other recordings were schematically similar.

23. Again, the copyright dates are ambiguous. Feist registered three relevant spring 1918 copyrights. First listed is an arrangement of May 25, with no specifications and thus presumably in waltz meter. Second is the "jazz fox-trot" arrangement, copyrighted June 12. Finally is "Same," copyrighted May 21. Unclear is why the earliest date is listed last and whether "Same" applies to the waltz or fox trot arrangements listed above it.

24. "The Song World: This Week's Song of Songs."

25. "German Women Weep at Going of Kind Yanks," *Chicago Daily Tribune*, May 22, 1919, 1.

26. "German Women Weep at Going of Kind Yanks."

27. W. E. Hill, "Bathroom Songsters," *Chicago Tribune*, October 9, 1927; W. E. Hill, "Old Fashioned Waltz," *Los Angeles Times*, December 1, 1935, I10.

28. "Woman's Kidnaper [*sic*] Forces Victim to Hear Him Croon," *Los Angeles Times*, December 29, 1934, 3.

CHAPTER FOUR: "KISS ME AGAIN" AND THE WISDOM OF WITMARK: THE STRANGE HISTORY OF THE AMERICAN WALTZ, PART TWO

1. Isidore Witmark and Isaac Goldberg, *From Ragtime to Swingtime: The Story of The House of Witmark* (New York: Lee Furman, 1939), 372–73.

2. Gardner, *Popular*, charts the rise of "Kiss Me Again" in 1906 and again in 1916. Whitburn, *Pop*, tracks it on singles in 1916 and 1919 and on LPs in 1960 and 1975. Vivienne Segal brought it to Broadway for a second hearing in the revue *Miss 1917*. A 1925 silent film of *Mlle. Modiste* had cinema accompanists pouring it forth again; and a 1931 sound version of the stage show made *Kiss Me Again* the title. The fourteen-year-old Susanna Foster precociously sang it in the biopic *The Great Victor Herbert* (1939).

3. Hill, "Old-Fashioned"; see also W. E. Hill, "Musical Americans," *Chicago Daily Tribune*, July 17, 1938, F9.

4. In 1898 Albéniz added "Córdoba" and one other piece to his 1892 suite *Chants d'Espagne* (*Cantos de España*). The resemblance of "Kiss Me Again" to "Córdoba" was noted by Witmark and Goldberg in 1939, but has been ignored in the scanty recent literature; Witmark and Goldberg, *From Ragtime*, 372–73. Journalist Frank Sullivan related "a pretty story, which one hopes is true," about Herbert creating the song; Frank Sullivan, "A Lament for the Grand Union Hotel," *New York Times*, August 24, 1952, X13. This doubtful, apocryphal tales goes: in the summer of (presumably) 1905, Herbert conducted the courtyard orchestra at the elite Grand Union Hotel in Saratoga Springs, New York. Resting one evening on a bench there, he heard a young woman whisper, "Kiss me again," and then rushed to the piano to write the melody. The anecdote does point to the fact that the title words do, indeed, fit the opening notes (i.e., Albéniz's motif), even though in the finished song that title is delayed until near the lyric's end.

5. Mezzrow and Wolfe, *Really*, 60.

CHAPTER FIVE: "I WONDER WHO'S KISSING HER NOW" AND WORK-FOR-HIRE: THE STRANGE HISTORY OF THE AMERICAN WALTZ, PART THREE

1. In 1931 Geller relayed a colorful story about the origin of the title. Hough and Adams threw a party at the latter's White Lake, Michigan, summer home. One young woman, thinking about an absent chum, "sighed 'I wonder who's kissing her now'"; Geller, *Famous*, 211. The lyricist pair wrote the phrase down and later fit it to one of the melodies supplied to them. As with all of Geller's stories, the veracity of this one is doubtful. Geller claims that Howard would furnish about forty

melodies for a new production, from which Hough and Adams would choose a dozen or so for setting lyrics; Geller, *Famous*, 212. Within such a routine, it is easy to comprehend why Howard might be eager to hire help in grinding out tunes—and that the lyricists may not have been aware of a second composer contributing.

2. Five Orlob compositions for *The Flirting Princess* can be viewed online at the Archive of Popular American Music of the University of California, Los Angeles.

3. Muir, "Before," 254–74.

4. Jasen, *Tin*, 213. Among Howard's questionable practices, seen in his file at the Library of Congress: he and lyricist Allen Lowe wrote "Who's Your Friend" in 1901 and sold it to Boston publisher G. W. Setchell. Two years later, he used pretty much the same melody for a similarly titled lyric by Raymond Peck, "Who's Your Lady Friend," and published it himself in Chicago.

5. Slide, *Encyclopedia of Vaudeville*, 252–53.

6. There is no detailed history of Chicago runs of this period. A schema of events can be gleaned from the *Chicago Daily Tribune*, *Billboard*, and *Variety*. In the *Tribune*, *The Prince of To-Night* is advertised at the Princess Theater until May 13. A subsequent tour can be assumed, particularly as Woodruff is mentioned in October as still singing in that show.

7. "The Chas. K. Harris Courier," advertisement, *Variety*, October 2, 1909, 21.

8. "The Chas. K. Harris Courier."

9. Whitburn, *Pop*, 634.

10. Silverman, "Fairman."

11. "Engage Western Composer," *Variety*, August 12, 1911, 9. Five years later, William Jerome, a multi-hit lyricist, writing in *Billboard*, also acknowledged Orlob (misspelled "Orloff") as a contributor to "I Wonder Who's Kissing Her Now"; William Jerome, "The Evolution of Song Writing," *Billboard*, December 16, 1916, 47.

12. E.E.S., "Alma Keller and Helene Dare," *Billboard*, May 21, 1927; the act contrasted hot jazz to "melodies of long ago," which included "I Wonder Who's Kissing Her Now." Community singing was a major appeal of the Oldtimers Orchestra; "Review of Records," *Billboard*, November 13, 1937, 18.

13. By "album," Edwards presumably means "folio"; Irene Thirer, "Cliff Edwards' Uke Placed on the Shelf Perhaps Forever," *New York Evening Post*, September 18, 1935, clippings file for Cliff Edwards, New York Public Library for the Performing Arts.

14. "I Wonder Who's Kissing Her Now" is dubbed a "revival hit" in England, starting with "Publishers' Song Notes" columns in *The Stage*, March 12, 1936, 11, and March 26, 6. Reports of performers using it steadily continue in that column until January 7, 1937.

15. The court case is documented in trade journals, starting with "Harris Estate, Marks, Vogel in Dispute On 'Kissing Her Now' Tune," *Variety*, September 14, 1938, 41; resolving with "E. B. Marks Loses Two Appeals on Song Suits Vs. Jerry Vogel, Vogel Loses One Against Marks," *Billboard*, February 5, 1944, 20.

16. "Music News: New York City," *Billboard*, April 10, 1937, 18; advertisement, *Variety* November 10, 1937, 43.

17. George Spelvin, "The Broadway Beat," *Billboard*, May 7, 1938, 5. ("George Spelvin" is the quintessential show-business pseudonym.)

18. "Chatter: Broadway," *Variety*, March 1, 1939, 53; Abel Green, "Second Takes," *Variety*, September 26, 1945, 57; Anderson, *Out*, 182.

19. "E. B. Marks Loses."

20. The revival into major hit status of old songs was a situation distinct from the sustained familiarity and currency of "standards," although the two phenomena overlapped.

21. "Joe Howard's Film Biog," *Variety*, May 23, 1945, 1.

22. "Clarke's [*sic*] N. Y. to L. A. Shuttle for Pix, Radio," *Variety*, June 19, 1946, 30. Clark was not acknowledged in the film's credits—an odd situation, because Clark, with his highly recognizable style, in the short interim had jumped to major star status.

23. "Gold in Them Thar Old Wax Sends Diskeries Stampeding to Re-Cuts, Even for Albums," *Billboard*, March 15, 1947, 15, 31.

24. Don Tyler, *Hit Parade* (New York: Quill, William Morrow, 1985), 131; Joseph Murrells, *Million Selling Records* (New York: Arco, 1984), 25.

25. "The Exhibitor Has His Say," *Boxoffice*, October 30, 1948, A3.

26. Musicians' union rules limited the number of records that could be played on the radio; but not all small stations could afford live musicians throughout their broadcast hours. Therefore, radio transcription services filled the gap with union-permitted prerecorded content.

27. "The *Billboard* Second Annual Music Record Poll," *Billboard*, January 3, 1948, 10–11.

28. When he was young, the future film-and-theatre historian Miles Kreuger knew Orlob and reports that even in the 1950s the composer still was irate about Howard's appropriation of "I Wonder Who's Kissing Her Now." Kreuger also saw Howard perform informally at the Friar's Club—but, probably significantly, he never saw the two showbiz veterans in the same room. Kreuger interviews with the author, summer 2015.

29. "Orlob Doesn't Want 'Kissing' Coin, Only Co-Authorship Credit," *Variety*, May 26, 1941, 35.

30. Craig, "House Review: Capitol, Wash.," *Variety*, September 11, 1940, 41.

31. The title was shortened in 1947 to "Honeymoon."

32. "New York Music Notes," *Billboard*, June 26, 1909, 9.

33. Mori Krushen, "Joe E. Howard, Troubador at 73, Has Been Around Show Biz Sixty Years," *Variety*, January 7, 1942, 156–57. By "interpolations" the journalist presumably means new, parodic lyrics or interjections between lines—or both.

34. Krushen, "Joe E. Howard"; and "Editorial Comment," *Billboard*, September 28, 1918, 28.

35. "Tokyo's 920 Club," *Broadcasting, Broadcast Advertising*, April 24, 1944, 70; "Variety Gossip: Welcome Home from Burma," *Stage*, June 15, 1944, 3.

36. Shan, "Talking Shorts: 'I Wonder Who's Kissing Her Now,'" *Variety*, December 8, 1931, 14.

37. I have not been able to examine the script for *The Prince of To-Night*. A plot summary is given in the review, "Chicago Amusements," *Billboard*, February 13, 1909, 7.

38. "Edward Abeles Retires from Cast," *Billboard*, January 22, 1910, 17.

39. Green, "Second Takes." Rose had some bias in claiming this, for he was the owner-producer of the Diamond Horseshoe nightclub, which was Joseph Howard's home base when he was not on tour.

40. Bill Halligan, "The Hotel Stakes," *Variety*, January 3, 1945, 149.

41. Cass Elliot was also featuring—and charting with—an occasional older standard in 1970, so perhaps John Randolph Marr was hoping for the same success.

42. Peter Marston, "Lost Treasures: John Randolph Marr," *Pop Geek Heaven*, Pop Geek Heaven, http://www.popgeekheaven.com/music-discovery/lost-treaures-john-randolph-marr (accessed July 13, 2017).

43. Other ponderings about what the absent beloved is doing are found in "Blue (And Broken-hearted)" (1922); "I Wonder Where My Sweetie Can Be" (1925); "Lonesome and Sorry" (1926); "Are You Thinking of Me Tonight" (1927); "I'd Do It All Over Again" (1927); "I Still Get a Thrill" (1930); "All Mine, Almost" (1934); "I've Got to Pass Your House (To Get to My House)" (1933); "Once in a While" (1937); "Is There Somebody Else" (1940); "Every Now and Then" (1945); "If You Could See Me Now" (1946); "I Could Have Told You" (1954); a batch of Irving Berlin ballads discussed in chapter 10; and let's not forget the parodic "I Wonder Who's Keeping Him Now" (1930).

CHAPTER SIX: "LET ME CALL YOU SWEETHEART" AND COMPETITION-AS-MUSE:
THE STRANGE HISTORY OF THE AMERICAN WALTZ, PART FOUR

1. In the summer of 2017, a database search in Ebsco Historical Newspapers for "Let Me Call You Sweetheart" with "Valentine's Day" turned up 290 results; with "wedding," 270 results; with "anniversary," 256 results; all with a span from about the late 1920s through 2017, with the majority of items being from recent decades.

2. Whitburn, *Pop*, 634. Whitburn estimates that "Let Me Call You Sweetheart" and "Down by the Old Mill Stream" each sold six million copies of sheet music. For "Sweetheart," this status is supported by vintage *Variety* articles: "Music Business Good and Normal: Plenty of Sellers, Pop and Show," March 10, 1926, 43; "'Sweetheart' Case Ended," April 6, 1938, 41; "'Alex' Clicks Again," August 31, 1938.

3. "A Line o' Type or Two," *Chicago Daily Tribune*, September 5, 1935, 16; *Chicago Daily Tribune*, September 11, 1935, 12.

4. "Music in the News," *Billboard*, April 17, 1943, 59.

5. "Brother Against Brother," *Variety*, August 13, 1910, 8. "In Publisher's Row: Brother-Against-Brother War of Will and Harold Rossiter Carried to Eastern Battleground with New Phase of Brotherly Hatred Seldom Encountered in History," *Billboard*, December 7, 1912, 16. The tale has been often relayed, for instance in David Ewen, *American Popular Songs* (New York: Random House, 1966), 221, 253.

6. "In Publisher's Row," *Billboard*, January 14, 1911, 13; "Leo Friedman Changes Quarters," *Billboard*, May 13, 1911, 19, 61; Gardner, *Popular*, 167–68; Ewen, *American*, 221, 253.

7. "In Publisher's Row: Brother-Against-Brother."

8. "In Publisher's Row: Harold Rossiter News," *Billboard*, October 14, 1911, 12.

9. William E. Studwell, *They Also Wrote* (Lanham, MD: Scarecrow Press, 2000), 71.

10. "Sweetheart Case."

11. Advertisement, *Variety*, October 29, 1924, 47.

12. Advertisement, *Variety*, October 29, 1924, 47. Also see "Music Business Good"; "Leo Friedman Dies," *Variety*, March 9, 1927, 46. In addition, see "Big Sellers in West," *Variety*, November 11, 1925, 45; Gardner, *Popular*, 353.

13. "'Whispering Pianist' to Sing from WCAP," *Washington Post*, October 28, 1925, 12.

14. Whitcomb *After*, 43. About Furry Lewis, more below.

15. Furia and Lasser, *America's*, 2.

16. Tawa, *Way*, 180–81.

17. Tawa, *Way*, 176–77.

18. Tawa, *Way*, 199, 161.

19. Tawa, *Way*, 119, 140.

20. Tawa, *Way*, 199.

21. This is implied by the chart given in Tawa, *Way*, 177. Of course, Henry Blossom had also done this for the pop version of "Kiss Me Again." But the original "If I Were on the Stage" context was gender-specific. It was only because of a request from publisher Witmark that Blossom altered it, penning a gender-neutral, first-person verse.

22. When I met Elisabeth Welch, she told me that her final album, *This Thing Called Love*, was entirely her personal favorites, the songs she most wanted to sing, which places "I Love You Truly" in noble company.

23. The other Carrie Jacobs-Bond standard is "A Perfect Day"—enigmatic (at least to me), beautiful, but probably not a love ballad.

24. Besides "I Love You Truly," there are other instances of duple meter songs being changed to triple meter. One will be discussed in chapter 8. Some such changes were either made officially

by the authors before first publication (as with "While We're Young"), some through performance tradition (as occasionally with "Ah! Sweet Mystery of Life").

25. "I Love You Truly" is sometimes printed as a waltz, for example, in the folio *Old-Fashioned Love Songs* (Milwaukee, WI: Hal Leonard, n.d.).

26. "Talking Shorts: Ruth Etting," *Variety*, October 27, 1931, 19.

27. An equally compelling rendition is on a Folkways album, *The Bahamas: Islands of Song*, on a track by Israel Forbes, who invents bluesy stanzas like, "You can leave me, / But, darlin', you don't know."

28. "(1345) Melissa Manchester & Zachary Scot Johnson Let Me Call You Sweetheart Cover thesongadayproject," YouTube, 2016. https://www.youtube.com/watch?v=w9ww3RSGHfo (accessed July 23, 2017).

29. "I Wonder Who's Kissing Her Now," YouTube, https://www.youtube.com/watch?v=g1hDn pecJhw (accessed July 11, 2017).

30. This passage draws on the ideas of Dr. John Diamond; conversations with the author, spring 2016.

CHAPTER SEVEN: "SOME OF THESE DAYS"

1. Critics emphasize the importance of "Some of These Days": Furia, *Poets*, 32–33; Furia and Lasser, *America's*, 1; David A. Jasen and Gene Jones, *Spreadin' Rhythm Around* (New York: Schirmer Books, 1998), 147; Wilder, *American*, 14. Other authors emphasize its importance by its praise-filled inclusion as the earliest song in a highly selective corpus: Morath, *NPR*, 181; Morris, "Selections," 31. Also of relevance is the analogous high evaluation of Sophie Tucker's 1911 recording of the song in David Wondrich, *Stomp and Swerve* (Chicago: Chicago Review Press, A Cappella, 2003), 155.

2. The complete piano-vocal score for Williams's "Some o' Dese Days" is transcribed in Michael G. Garber, "'Some of These Days' and the Study of the Great American Songbook," *Journal of the Society for American Music* 4, no. 2 (May 2010): 182–85.

3. Norton reports on Frank B. Williams in his entry for *The Policy Players*, in *Chronology*; and Gardner, *Popular*, charts the hit status of "Just One World of Consolation."

4. Norton reports on Frank H. Williams in his entry for *Bandanna Land*, in *Chronology*.

5. The sheet music of "My Dahomian Queen" lists Frank B. Williams as the lyricist (New York: Witmark, 1903); as does Norton in his entry for *In Dahomey*, in *Chronology*. The Internet Broadway Database, however, lists for *In Dahomey* "additional lyrics by Frank H. Williams." http://www.ibdb .com/production.php?id=414771 (accessed March 2013).

6. The Internet Broadway Database lists Frank H. Williams in the entry for *Rufus Rastus*. http://www.ibdb.com/production.php?id=414536 (accessed October 9, 2013). In Norton's entry for that show, in his *Chronology*, he lists just-plain-old Frank Williams, with no middle initial.

7. *Variety* states that the deceased is the Frank B. Williams "who wrote the words for 'Just One Word of Consolation,' of which the Bing Crosby recording is a big seller on the jukeboxes"; "Obituaries," *Variety*, February 11, 1942, 46. Although it is doubtful that, in 1942, Crosby's 1936 recording of the old-fashioned and sentimental "Just One Word" was still (if ever) a popular jukebox item, the song can be judged as continuing in prominence into the late 1930s simply because it was included in his recorded output.

8. As noted above, Norton gives just Frank Williams, while the Internet Broadway Database lists Frank H. Williams. Neither source lists Williams as part of the cast during the Broadway run, however.

9. "The Mid-Winter" (Chicago: Success Music, 1906) is found at the Library of Congress, in the same folder as those songs credited to Frank B. Williams and just-plain Frank Williams; there is no certain significance in this, however, for these files are arranged alphabetically by the author's name.

10. Errol G. Hill and James V. Hatch, *A History of African American Theatre* (Cambridge: Cambridge University Press, 2003), 247. See also Yvonne Robbins, "Shelton Brooks," in Vivian Robbins, *Musical Buxton* ([Buxton, Canada: Vivian Robbins, 1969]), 26–27. The latter is also cited by Raoul Abdul, another sometime Buxtonite, in "Musical Gems North of the Border," *New York Amsterdam News*, September 10–16, 2009, 25.

11. On young Brooks as an organist, see Jack Burton, *The Blue Book of Tin Pan Alley* (New York: Century House, Watkins Glen, 1951), 160. On his parents' musicality, see Michael Saffle, "Shelton Leroy Brooks," in *The International Dictionary of Black Composers*, ed. Samuel J. Floyd Jr. (Chicago: Fitzroy Dearborn, 1999), 174–76. This information is also found in Robbins, "Shelton Brooks," in *Musical Buxton*, 26–27. Robbins's volume reveals the rich African Canadian musical life in Buxton, where Reverend Brooks moved his family in 1892. Shelton's peers there would include Charles "Dave" Robbins, a singer with whom Shelton was a lifelong friend; Theolia Cromwell, who, with her family, was a choir member at Reverend Brooks's church and later became a choir director herself in Ann Arbor, Michigan; and Warren C. Lewis, whose family moved from Buxton to Detroit during the same years (coincidentally?) as did Shelton Brooks, and who became a trombonist-singer throughout the middle-western United States and Canada before returning to Buxton later in life. As so often, Brooks's brilliance was a manifestation of an inspired musical community.

12. Burns Mantle mentions that Brooks was lead comic at the Pekin in their original musical comedy, *Queen of the Jungles*; Burns Mantle, "News of the Theaters," *Chicago Daily Tribune*, February 24, 1908, 6. More generally, Bernard L. Peterson Jr. speaks of Brooks's involvement with the Pekin in *Profiles of African American Stage Performers and Theatre People, 1816–1960* (Westport, CT: Greenwood Press, 2001), 33. For information about the Pekin Theatre, see Hill and Hatch, *History*, 191–99.

13. Much later, in 1927 the blues singer-guitarist Charley Patton recorded a song "Some These Days" (sometimes given as "Some of These Days I'll Be Gone"), which bears no resemblance in music or overall structure to either Williams's or Brooks's song. Nevertheless, Patton does start his lyric with a phrase that resembles the first words in the refrains of both Williams and Brooks: "Some these days, you gonna miss me, honey / Some these days, you gonna be so lonely." Perhaps this was influenced by Brooks's song, which in 1927 was both well-remembered from the past and also newly repopularized. Or perhaps Patton's song drew on the same folk song material that possibly inspired both Williams and Brooks. At any rate, Patton's song has been recorded in recent years by the indie-folk-jazz musician Andrew Bird. An October 2013 search of iTunes for "Some of These Days" yielded many results, the majority clearly being Shelton Brooks's song, and yet iTunes offered Bird's rendition of Patton's song as the most highly ranked in terms of popularity.

14. For information about William H. Dorsey, see Eileen Southern, *The Music of Black Americans: A History* (New York: W. W. Norton, 1983), 347; Lynn Abbott and Doug Seroff, "'They Cert'ly Sound Good to Me': Sheet Music, Southern Vaudeville, and the Commercial Ascendancy of the Blues," *American Music* 14, no. 4 (winter 1996): 443–44.

15. "Everybody Makes Love to Someone, Why Don't You Make Love to Me?" (New York: Gotham-Attucks, 1912), music by Artie Matthews and lyrics by Paul Franzi; found in the file for Matthews's songs in the Library of Congress.

16. Wayne Shirley, conversation with the author, March 2011.

17. James J. Fuld, *The Book of World-Famous Music*, 5th ed. (1966; New York: Dover, 2000), 511–12.

18. Muir, *Long*, 200.

19. Jasen and Jones point to the resemblance of the standard boogie-woogie bass line to the main strain of Brooks's 1917 "The Darktown Strutters' Ball," but draw no conclusions about which came first; Jasen and Jones, *Spreadin'*, 148–49. Other possible precursors of boogie-woogie patterns appear about the same time. One is in Eubie Blake's 1917 piano roll of his composition "Charleston Rag," a.k.a. "Sounds of Africa," which Blake claimed he wrote in 1899; see Jasen and Jones, *Black*

Bottom Stomp: Eight Masters of Ragtime and Early Jazz (New York: Routledge, 2002), 37, 43. Others include Artie Matthews's "Weary Blues" (1915) and George W. Thomas's "New Orleans Hop Scop Blues" (1916); see Peter C. Muir, "Boogie-woogie (i)," *Grove Music Online*, 2013.

20. Burton, *Blue Book*, 160.

21. Burton, *Blue Book*.

22. Ian Whitcomb, "Shelton Brooks Is Alive and Strutting," *Los Angeles Times*, May 18, 1969, N12.

23. "Black Tin Pan Alley Composer Shelton Brooks Finally Gets Paid," *Jet*, November 29, 1951, Flickr, Yahoo, 2013, posted by vieilles annonces, October 15, 2012, http://www.flickr.com/photos/vieilles_annonces/8092148455/in/photostream/ (accessed February 23, 2013). *Jet* magazine may have gotten this information from Spaeth, who states "Some of These Days" "was first sung by Brooks himself and by Hedges Brothers and Jacobson, at Chicago's Majestic Theatre," leaving some doubt who performed it at the Majestic—Brooks, the other act, or both; Spaeth, *History*, 371.

24. June Provines quotes Tucker in her column "A Line o' Type or Two," *Chicago Daily Tribune*, May 12, 1938, 12.

25. Provines quotes Tucker.

26. Sophie Tucker with Dorothy Giles, *Some of These Days* (self-published, Sophie Tucker, 1945), 114.

27. Among those who relay the false tale I must, alas, include myself: Garber, "'Some of These Days' and the Study," 190. See also Jasen and Jones, *Spreadin'*, 146; Furia and Lasser, *America's*, 2; Jeffrey Melnick, *A Right to Sing the Blues* (Cambridge, MA: Harvard University Press, 1999), 57–58; Wondrich, *Stomp*, 155.

28. This according to Lloyd Ecker, Tucker researcher; conversations with the author, on the phone July 6, 2011, and, in person and with reproductions of Tucker's scrapbooks at hand, November 16, 2013.

29. Scrapbook photocopies, in the collection of Sue and Lloyd Ecker, of unidentified clippings, reveal Tucker performing in Edmonton, Ontario, on June 12, and in Calgary around the same time. Further clippings show her on the West Coast of the United States by June 20.

30. "Portland, Ore.," *Variety*, July 2, 1910, 148.

31. "Chicago Music Notes," *Billboard*, July 30, 1910, 41.

32. "Chicago Music Notes," *Billboard*, November 12, 1910, 17.

33. For the Chicago bill at the American Music Hall with Tucker (and also Carl McCullough, as mentioned below), see the advertisement in the *Chicago Tribune*, December 18, 1910, B2.

34. Advertisement for Sans Souci Park: "Free vaudeville . . . Last day for Sophie Tucker, the Mary Garden of Ragtime," *Chicago Daily Tribune*, June 24, 1911, 11.

35. *Variety* advertisements under "Representative Artists," January 21, 1911, 34; February 4, 1911, 34.

36. Armond Fields, *Sophie Tucker* (Jefferson, NC: McFarland, 2003), 42.

37. Fields, *Sophie Tucker*.

38. "Palace, Chicago, Reviewed Monday Matinee, November 15," *Billboard*, November 20, 1920, 9.

39. "In the Wake of the News," *Chicago Tribune*, December 20, 1920, 21. Note that the song "All Alone" mentioned is the Andrew Sterling–Harry Von Tilzer telephone-themed hit of 1911, not the better-remembered Irving Berlin waltz ballad of 1924 with the same title (see the discussion of these songs in chapter 1).

40. "Society and Entertainment: Society Cabaret to Spring One of Those Imported Dances" reveals Brooks as the only professional among "Chicago's smart set" performing in a benefit, *Chicago Herald Tribune*, June 28, 1919, 19. The ad for the Chateau bill is in the *Chicago Daily Tribune*, July 11, 1920, F2.

41. Rossiter got two plugs in *Variety* for the 1922 revival: "With the Music Men," July 21, 1922, 10; "Old Songs for New Disks," July 28, 1922, 7.

42. In the USA, the credit to Williams and Klickman does not appear on any of the later 1920s issuings of this arrangement, such as the ones heralding radio and motion picture usage of the song. I have seen it, however, prominently on the cover of a British edition, in the collection of Lloyd and Sue Ecker, the visual style of which indicates the period around 1922. In addition, the listing for a recording by Art Landry and His Call of the North Orchestra of "Some of These Days" also lists Klickman as a co-composer alongside Brooks; *Talking Machine World*, September 15, 1923, 188.

43. For Williams being Rossiter, see Goldberg, *Tin*, 104–5.

44. Fields, *Sophie*, 42. Tucker herself discusses the refashioning of her act in late 1921 and early 1922; Tucker, *Some*, 173–74.

45. "New Turns and Returns," *Billboard*, October 14, 1922, 119. The reviewer considered Tucker's adoption of religious singing technique to be "a decided affront." (See also the *Billboard* review of the whole bill, October 7, 1922, 14.) The same year, Tucker used this cantorial approach on a recording of "Blue Bird, Where Are You." The remarkable thing is how natural it sounds to our latter-day ears, because the vocal devices of traditional cantillation have since become interwoven into the fabric of popular singing.

46. Jasen and Jones, *Spreadin'*, 150; Robbins, "Shelton," 26.

47. Whitburn, *Pop*.

48. Stephen Banfield, *Sondheim's Broadway Musicals* (Ann Arbor: University of Michigan Press, 1993), 107, 114; Banfield, "Sondheim," 155.

49. See, for instance, Morath, *NPR*, 181; Morris, "Selections," 31; Wilder, *American*, 14.

50. In my own unpublished survey of 1908 songs I found that about one in fifteen refrains had a non-repeating melodic structure, which approximately correlates with the surveys of Tawa, *Way*, 179, 196.

51. The lack of any blackface semiotics in the Foster and Rossiter sheet music editions of "Some of These Days" did not prevent the first publicity blurb for the song in *Billboard* from referring to Brooks's piece as "Rossiter's new coon lament"; "Chicago Music Notes," July 30, 1910, 41. Thereafter, however, the work seems to have not been particularly linked to the coon song genre.

52. Wilder, *American*, 14.

53. Tawa, *Way*, 197.

54. Wondrich, *Stomp*, 155. Wondrich applies the descriptor "blackface" loosely; Tucker does not use blackface dialect in her recording and, by 1911, she had not used blackface for years.

55. Dr. John Diamond, conversation with the author, circa 2000.

56. Robert Dawidoff, *Making History Matter* (Philadelphia: Temple University Press, 2000), 130.

57. My thanks to Susan J. Carpenter for offering this interpretation of the song's emotional dynamics; conversation with the author, February 21, 2013.

58. For this, twenty singers, some in multiple renditions, were in the statistical sample.

59. Will Friedwald and Mitchell Zlokower, "Sinatra: Songs for Swingin' Singles: An Appreciation," CD liner notes, *The Complete Capitol Singles Collection*, performed by Frank Sinatra (Hollywood, CA: Capitol Records, 1996), 55.

60. For instance, in Rust, *Jazz Records*, there are over fifty entries indexed. Lord, *Jazz Discography*, indexes about 440 entries.

61. Muir, *Long Lost*, 65.

62. Muir points out a similar rearranging of "Twelfth Street Rag" (1912) adding dotted rhythms for the 1919 sheet music edition; *Long Lost*, 64.

63. Dawidoff, *Making*, 130.

64. June Sochen, "Fannie Brice and Sophie Tucker," in *From Hester Street to Hollywood*, edited by Sarah Blacher Cohen (Bloomington: Indiana University Press, 1983), 53.

65. To be precise, MacDonald at first picks up the "Some of These Days" sheet music, with Sophie Tucker's photo clearly visible, and then, confusingly, launches into "Dinah." I suspect that

this sequence was shot in such a way that the rendition of "Dinah" could be cut out to shorten the scene, if necessary. This 1920s "Radio's Big Hit" cover can be seen online at the site of the Lester S. Levy Sheet Music Collection.

66. Richard Howard, "A Foreword to *Nausea*," in Jean-Paul Sartre, *Nausea*, translated by Lloyd Alexander (New York: New Directions, 2007), vii. Howard says that he draws on "Contat and Ribalka, in their extensive annotated edition."

67. Sartre, *Nausea*, 21, 174.

68. Sartre, *Nausea*, 22.

69. Hayden Carruth, "Introduction," in Sartre, *Nausea*, xii. Carruth is quoted and seconded by Dawidoff, who states that "'Some of These Days' was not a blues or even a jazz song particularly"; *Making*, 131.

70. Sartre, *Nausea*, 21.

71. Sartre, *Nausea*, 21–22.

72. Sartre, *Nausea*, 173.

73. Sartre, *Nausea*, 177.

74. Sartre, *Nausea*, 177.

75. Sartre, *Nausea*, 178.

76. Sartre, *Nausea*, 173.

77. Sartre, *Nausea*, 177.

78. Sartre, *Nausea*, 177.

79. Diamond, *Music and Song*, 6, 97.

CHAPTER EIGHT: "THE SWEETHEART OF SIGMA CHI" AND THE POWER OF A SUBCULTURE: THE STRANGE HISTORY OF THE AMERICAN WALTZ, PART FIVE

1. Accounts differ whether the creation was in June or on October 4; Vernor graduated from Albion or not; they both were freshmen or Stokes was a junior and Vernor a sophomore. The longstanding sheet music credits indicate that Stokes was one year ahead of Vernor. Basics about the history of "The Sweetheart of Sigma Chi" can be cobbled together, despite contradictory reports, from early sheet music editions combined with retrospectives from later decades: Fuld, *Book*, 545; "Dudleigh Vernor, Composed 'Sweetheart of Sigma Chi,'" *New York Times*, April 25, 1974, 42; "'Sigma Chi' Songwriter F. D. Verner" [*sic*], *Washington Post*, April 25, 1974, B7; "'Sigma Chi' Song Writer Dies at 81," *Los Angeles Times*, April 24, 1974, 1; "Sigma Chi Sweetheart Marks 75th Birthday," *New York Times*, October 4, 1986, 6; "'The Girl of My Dreams' The Sweetheart of Sigma Chi," Sigma Chi at Sam Houston State, Epsilon Psi Chapter, 1999, https://www.shsu.edu/~eng_wpf/sweetheart.html (accessed February 3, 2019); "The Sweetheart of Sigma Chi Michigan Historical Marker," Albion, Michigan, website, 2017, http://www.albionmich.com/history/markers/amark08.htm (accessed August 2, 2017); Ken Wyatt, "Peek Through Time: Albion College's Sigma Chi fraternity's song 'The Sweetheart of Sigma Chi' Turns 100," MLive, 2017, http://www.mlive.com/living/jackson/index.ssf/2011/10/peek_through_time_albion_colle.html (accessed August 2, 2017); "Sweetheart of Sigma Chi," Sigma Chi Houston Alumni Chapter, 2017, http://houstonsigs.org/sweetheart-of-sigma-chi (accessed August 2, 2017).

2. The cover of "The Fellowship Song of Sigma Chi," found online at the site of Indiana University, indicates the piece was in its third edition in 1923. Stokes and Vernor also co-wrote a tribute to Sigma Chi soldiers in World War I, "I'm Glad I'm a Sigma Chi." For other compositions relating to Sigma Chi, from various hands, see "The Music of Sigma Chi," Sigma Chi at Sam Houston State, Epsilon Psi Chapter, 1999, https://www.shsu.edu/~eng_wpf/sigmachimusic.html (accessed January 15, 2019).

3. McCracken, *Real*, 131.

4. McCracken, *Real*, 131–32.

5. Owen Miller, "Whitey Kaufman's Original Pennsylvania Serenaders," Red Hot Jazz Archive, http://www.redhotjazz.com/kaufman.html (accessed August 13, 2018).

6. "Inside Stuff: Waring's Version of Sigma Chi," *Variety*, June 8, 1927, 46.

7. On the record label release pattern of dance version first, vocal version second: "Reviews of Recording Discs," *Variety*, April 21, 1922, 7.

8. McCracken, *Real*, 121.

9. As previously noted, this shift from duple to triple meter would soon also affect "I Love You Truly" and "Ah! Sweet Mystery of Life." In 1929 Rudy Vallee would insist on the publisher making this same change when reviving the 1916 "If You Were the Only Girl in the World"; Vallee, *Vagabond*, 150.

10. "Sweetheart of Sigma Chi," Sigma Chi Houston.

11. "Sweetheart of Sigma Chi," Sigma Chi Houston.

12. "Night Clubs: Torch Songs."

13. Also worth noting is the 1930 hit for Rudy Vallee and others, the similarly titled "Sweetheart of My Student Days"; however, the resemblance is diminished in its duple meter and focus on memory (rather than dreams).

14. David Shipman, *Judy Garland* (New York: Hyperion, 1992), 72.

CHAPTER NINE: "MY MELANCHOLY BABY"

1. The concluding chapter will address the further question: What led "My Melancholy Baby" to lose (partly) its status as the first and quintessential torch song?

2. According to the calculations of Whitburn, *Pop*, 633.

3. Watson's original unpublished lyric was found for me by librarian Karen Moses on July 18, 2011. It has the number E 276566 and was in the Music Division's Reserve Storage.

4. *Carousel of American Music: The Fabled 24 September 1940 San Francisco Concerts* (Berkeley, CA: Music and Arts Programs of America, 1997), CD-971, disc 2, track 21.

5. McNamara, *ASCAP*, 66.

6. From *Billboard*: "Medicine Show Notes," January 18, 1913, 21; "Cox Puts One Over," October 28, 1916, 12; "Cold Type Review," January 19, 1918, 14; "York and King Company Wants," October 16, 1920, 27; "Tabloids," January 1, 1921, 27. Tabloids, a.k.a. tab shows, were short musical comedies or revues, often truncated versions of longer productions; there are a string of such notices that place Burnett with the York and King Company in the Midwest. Also: "Ill and Injured," *Variety*, October 22, 1924, 5.

7. Jasen, *Tin*, 109.

8. To be fair, there are also some lyrics to Burnett tunes that I labeled "adequate," "competent," and, more positively, "cute" and "nice."

9. Hedda Hopper, "Screen: Hedda Hopper's Hollywood," *Los Angeles Times*, October 16, 1939, 9.

10. "Collides with a Schooner," *Urbana Courier*, July 23, 1907, 2.

11. The edition with the dedication to Maybelle Watson was printed by "Walton Process Chicago." The copy I examined is at the Lester S. Levy Digital Sheet Music Collection, and the cover features performer Jack O'Leary.

12. A stream of notices in *Variety* documents Maybelle E. Watson Bergmann's case, from "Inside Stuff—Music," November 23, 1938, through that same regular column on February 28, 1940.

13. "Archie Fletcher Assumes Some Troubles Along with Morris Music Co.," *Variety*, November 28, 1938, 39.

14. Hopper, "Screen."

15. "Old Song Paying Royalties to Matron," *Los Angeles Times*, February 18, 1940, 6.

16. Women in show business often retained their maiden name for their professional work; perhaps this explains the "Miss Maybelle" dedication. Nevertheless, at least parenthetical acknowledgment of her married name would seem likely.

17. "Old Song Paying."

18. Fuld supplies the exact publication date of October 25, 1912, for "Melancholy"; Fuld, *Book*, 384. He does not supply a citation. I have not been able to confirm that date, but this was Fuld's area of expertise. Bennett sent deposit copies for two other songs at this time; the Library of Congress received those music sheets on October 24 and the copyright registration forms the next day.

19. W. C. Handy, *Father of the Blues* (New York: Da Capo, [1941]), 106–11, with the dates given at 111.

20. Norton also had careers in journalism and advertising; McNamara, *ASCAP*, 373.

21. Norton shows up as collaborator on copyrights by Hal G. Nichols of Denver, in November 1911, and in one instance in mid-1913 by the Robert D. Sharpe company, Denver.

22. "New Music Firm Starts," *New York Clipper*, November 9, 1921, 18; "Norton in Arizona," *New York Clipper*, August 30, 1922, 18.

23. "Ben Light Dead, Songwriter, 72," *New York Times*, January 9, 1965, 25. Rex Strother places Light in Denver in 1911, and William Frawley there in 1912; Rex Strother, "Ben Light," Saxony Records, http://www.saxonyrecordcompany.com/ben-light.html (accessed March 3, 2018); Read Kendall, "Around and About in Hollywood," *Los Angeles Times*, January 9, 1937, A7.

24. Nevertheless, in 1919 Ben Light did copyright "Girl of My Dreams" (not the famous song by Sonny Clapp) and get published "You'll Want to Come Back"; later, in 1953 his "My Broken Heart Keeps Asking Why" was published, with words by Tom Adair, lyricist for a number of 1940s hits.

25. "Ben Light Dead."

26. Kendall, "Around."

27. Kendall, "Around." Don Tyler gives slightly different details (but with no citation information), stating that Frawley premiered "Melancholy Baby" at the Mozart Café in Denver, with Damon Runyon in the audience, in an act with pianist Franz Rath called "A Man, A Piano and Nut" (perhaps the "Nut" was brother Paul); *Music of the First World War* (Santa Barbara, CA: Greenwood, 2016), 132.

28. "TV-Radio Programming: Wheeling and Dealing," *Billboard*, March 31, 1958, 8.

29. The Dutch Mill, Denver, is mentioned as Bennett's home base on the cover of "That's What Makes a Wild Cat Wild" (by George A. Norton and Theron C. Bennett, 1918), found online in 2018 at the Charles Templeton Sheet Music Collection.

30. Edward C. Day, "Denver," *Variety*, May 16, 1919, 36.

31. William L. Simon, ed., *Reader's Digest Popular Songs That Will Live Forever* (Pleasantville, NY: Reader's Digest Association, 1982), 224.

32. Jasen, *Tin*, 109.

33. Patrick A. Warren, "Late Items from Chicago," *Billboard*, June 10, 1905, 11; "Chicago: Music Publisher's Notes," *Billboard*, November 18, 1906, 4.

34. Handy, *Father*, 107. Handy writes of Bennett pseudonymously as "Z." The earliest Theron C. Bennett publication I have found is the 1908 rag "All the Grapes," found online at the University of Colorado at Boulder Digitized Music Collections. Nevertheless, the Catalog of Copyright Entries shows that Bennett was still having his own compositions issued by Victor Kremer through November 1909.

35. Bennett's Long Beach Dutch Mill is mentioned frequently in *Variety*, onward from "Music: Bands and Orchestras," July 16, 1924, 33, 38. Obituaries: "The Final Curtain," *Billboard*, April 17, 1937, 35; "Theron C. Bennett," *Broadcasting*, April 13, 1937, 53.

36. As mentioned before, Burnett claimed to have written the 1911 lyric himself and falsely put Watson's name on it, presumably as a sentimental gesture. In fact, Burnett did in several cases write both words and music. Yet the pattern of late 1910, with three copyrights credits registered to the pair of Watson and Burnett, seems to support her claim that the spouses were in an ongoing collaborative partnership. Questions still remain, however: Was Watson with Burnett in Denver

when "Melancholy" was copyrighted? Or did they collaborate long distance, through the mail or telephone? Or was the ditty already a year old when Burnett sent it in for copyright?

37. If Ernie Burnett had himself commissioned the new lyric from Norton, the composer would probably have told about doing so in his late-1930s testimony.

38. The dedication to Maybelle Watson is on the first page of an early sheet music edition; it is also included along with the first eight measures of the refrain of "Melancholy" in the ad on the back cover of "Ain't It Funny," which, though never registered for copyright, bears a copyright notice of 1912. (Bennett was very arbitrary and inconsistent in sending in copyright registrations.)

39. I have examined copies featuring Jack O'Leary; Roy Schreiber; the Mozart Four (male guitar group); Rena Santos; a female trio (removed from the internet before I could take full notes); Fred Watson; Carrie McManus; and June Le Veay. In addition, Fuld reports the first printing featured Jas. E. Maloney; Fuld, *Book*, 384.

40. I base this estimate of months on the fact that a new address appears on the fresh edition. This location change was announced in the press seven months after the first printing; "Denver Too Small," *New York Clipper*, May 10, 1913, 12.

41. "Denver Too Small."

42. The printer for the first edition of "Melancholy" was Walton Process Chicago. Subsequent editions, the first of which seem to use the same plates as Walton, were done by P. J. Lawson. Bennett moved from 149 West 36th Street to 145 West 45th Street.

43. "Descriptive Review: Melancholy," *The Player*, June 6, 1913, 10; "Song Reviews: Melancholy," *Billboard*, July 12, 1913, 13. This practice of reviewing songs (in a manner similar to reviews of vaudeville acts, theatre, and, later, recordings) was unfortunately short-lived.

44. Handy reports on Bennett's sales claim for the instrumental version of "The Memphis Blues": *Father*, 109. Copyright records indicate when the new vocal version was registered.

45. Advertisement, Imperial Motion Pictures, *Variety*, June 5, 1914, 21; Billie Burr immediately used the "animated song" in Chicago vaudeville, "This Week's Chicago Vaudeville," *New York Clipper*, June 14, 1914, 9. These dates in June 1914 belie Fuld's claim that "the title was changed . . . on November 5, 1914"; Fuld, *Book*, 384.

46. Rick Altman has discussed both song-films and song-slides; Rick Altman, *Silent Film Sound* (New York: Columbia University Press, 2004), 106–15, 182–201. Such images often included the lyrics and were sometimes used to facilitate audience sing-alongs, though it is unsure whether those practices were used for "My Melancholy Baby."

47. Smith, *Bricktop*, 51–52. "Black-and-tan" was the era's designation for clubs that served both "colored" and "white" patrons.

48. Smith, *Bricktop*.

49. Lyman had "at times almost a boy tenor": "New Acts This Week: Tommy Lyman," *Variety*, April 22, 1921, 18. Also see Herb Graffis, "Last of the Minstrels," *Esquire*, May, 1946, 60.

50. In 1913 trade journals place Tommy Lyman in Chicago in January and Georgia in June. That he was in Nebraska by the fall is possible but not certain; "Pat Chat," *New York Clipper*, January 11, 1913, 12; "Correspondence," *Variety*, May 9, 1913, 31.

51. "Halligan Has to Quit Paris," *New York Clipper*, May 17, 1922, 7; "Unlucky Year for Halligan," *New York Clipper*, May 24, 1922, 6.

52. On "My Blue Heaven": "Inside Stuff," *Variety*, December 21, 1927, 53. On "Paper Doll": "Mills Brothers Breast the Changing Times," *Asbury Park Press*, September 28, 1975, 41.

53. Mezzrow and Wolfe, *Really*, 60.

54. Mezzrow's tearjerker set also included the 1909 "Ace in the Hole"—which offers another prime example of a song that was never a hit, yet continued as part of saloon culture beneath the radar of the mainstream and showbiz media, until the LP era brought it a series of recordings, such as by Jimmy Roselli, Maxine Sullivan, and Bobby Darin. To reiterate, this is not the Cole Porter song of 1941 with the same title.

55. Mezzrow and Wolfe, *Really*, 60.

56. Whitcomb, *After*, 70–71.

57. "New Songwriting Team," *Billboard*, February 26, 1916, 12. In 1922 the *New York Clipper*, in "Norton in Arizona," calls it "Melancholy." This is perhaps a good place to mention the mystery of the four other songs listed on the first and all subsequent Bennett editions of "Melancholy"/"My Melancholy Baby." First listed is "Sing Me a Song of the South," Norton's big hit of 1899. Two other songs listed were Burnett-Norton collaborations, but the chronology seems awry. "Tomorrow" was copyrighted as a publication by Buck and Lowney, St. Louis, in September 1914. "Let Me Really Live Tonight Sweetheart (And Tomorrow Let Me Die)" was issued by Theron C. Bennett, but not until 1915, and without being copyrighted. Why are these publications of 1914 and 1915 being blazoned on a cover printed in 1912? Perhaps Burnett and Norton collaborated on them in 1911 in Denver, and they optimistically bragged about them prior to placing them with a publisher. Finally, "That's Gratitude" was a 1907 hit for Norton and his frequent partner, Sheppard Camp, perhaps their biggest success together; "Season Good for Francis, Day and Hunter," *Billboard*, April 4, 1908, 17. Yet Burnett claimed "That's Gratitude" as one of his own compositions in the 1916 *Billboard* notice, above, and, decades later, in his ASCAP biography. Indeed (as with Joe Howard), Ernie, George, and Theron were none of them above a little dishonesty in their professional dealings. W. C. Handy's case against Theron's integrity is well known; *Father*, 106–12. Ernie was accused of stealing "At the Story Book Ball" and copyrighting it as his own; advertisement, Billie Montgomery and George Perry, *Variety*, October 27, 1916, 32. In 1943, when Ernie reissued that and another song from the 1910s, "My Kathleen," he omitted any mention of (and presumably any royalties to) the previously credited lyricists. Norton, too, recycled material without regard to copyright status with "I Just Can't Help from Liking You," copyrighted by Maynard in 1910 but unpublished; and "I Just Can't Keep from Liking You" with Sheppard Camp in 1912, published by Haviland. (Although, to give him the benefit of the doubt, Norton may have gotten Maynard's permission for this.)

58. "Reviews of Recording Discs," *Variety*, June 14, 1922, 19.

59. On one vintage sheet music cover of "Memphis Blues," Bennett heralds Morris as the "Sole Selling Agents" for the piece; accessible online at IN Harmony: Sheet Music from Indiana, Indiana University, http://webapp1.dlib.indiana.edu/inharmony/detail.do?action=detail&fullItemID=/lilly/devincent/LL-SDV-183001&queryNumber=2.

60. These dates are culled from various editions of later decades, plus: "H'wood Cavalcade-Minded: Old Songs Take on New Values," *Variety*, August 17, 1938, 1.

61. "H'wood Cavalcade-Minded." This article also claims: "My Melancholy Baby" was a "hit in 1914" (as discussed, its hit status was moderate); had resurgences of sheet music sales in 1919 (not mentioned in any other source) and 1927 (though actually it was in 1928); and that 1924 was when the copyright transferred from Bennett to Morris.

62. For the recording date, see the entry online at the Discography of American Historical Recordings, https://adp.library.ucsb.edu/index.php/matrix/detail/800013439/BVE-39177-My_melancholy_baby (accessed January 27, 2019).

63. Winchell, "Primer," 132.

64. "Recommended Disk Records," *Variety*, November 16, 1927, 42. "B.f." presumably is short for "boy friend," "g.f." for "girl friend."

65. E. M. Wickes, "New York Notes," *Billboard*, March 26, 1927, 23.

66. "My Blue Heaven" was Lyman's mid-twenties radio theme, according to Ewen, *All*, 226. Gardner is confident Lyman was singing "My Melancholy Baby" on radio; Gardner, *Popular*, 371.

67. Pitts and Hoffman, *Rise of the Crooners*, 61–62. One would think the success of Austin's disc of Lyman's radio theme, "My Blue Heaven," was the rationale behind Austin also being allowed to record the Lyman-associated "My Melancholy Baby." However, Austin waxed both tunes on the same day. Nevertheless, Paul Whiteman had already recorded "My Blue Heaven," in July, and that

song's growing success may have eased the way for Lyman's "Melancholy Baby" also to attract the interest of Austin and the Victor label.

68. The 1913 *Billboard* reviewer had critiqued this line, anyway (along with similar blame to the final refrain line), pointing out that it was "a trifle drawn out and devoid of contractions for a song line"; "Song Reviews: Melancholy." The 1927 alteration, "I'm in love with you," is less "drawn out" and features the contractions already favored in the 1910s by these professionals. As well, "lo-ve" chimes as a consonance with the closely following "ha-ve" and "sil-ve-r" in a manner more satisfying than Norton's alliteration of "s-trong" with "s-ilver," and the distantly following "s-un," and "s-mile."

69. Most of these renderings can be found on LP, CD, downloads, or YouTube. Only De Leath and Morgan deserve documentation, for their essayings of "My Melancholy Baby" were strictly on radio, respectively "Football and Symphonies on Air," *Los Angeles Times*, December 3, 1932, 12; "Radio Waves and Ripples," *Washington Post*, November 18, 1933, 10.

70. Joseph R. Fliesler, "Song Hits of 1936," *ASCAP Journal* 1, no. 2 (November 1937): 3. I accessed this at the New York Public Library for the Performing Arts. The most-often broadcast older composition was the Sousa instrumental march "Stars and Stripes Forever," with 24,802 performances; the top old pop song was "Star Dust" with 18,902 performances.

71. Whitburn, *Pop*, 440. As mentioned, in this volume Whitburn is unreliable, especially for the pre-1940 years for which evidence is scanty.

72. "Reviews and Ratings of New Albums," *Billboard*, January 12, 1957, 26.

73. See for instance, "A Line o' Type or Two: Bad Man," *Chicago Tribune*, February 24, 1964, 14. In this interview with frequent movie villain Jim Griffith, the actor says he often is attacked in bars by men who confuse his screen roles and real self, but "If you handle these things correctly, you soon have them purring 'Old pal, let's sing "Melancholy Baby"'!"

74. Smith, *Bricktop*, 51.

75. Hank O'Neal, CD liner notes, *Dave "Fingers" McKenna* (New York: SOS, Chiaroscuro, [1977] 2000). Pianist McKenna was born in 1930 and began his career in the mid-forties.

76. Hedda Hopper, "The Comeback Kid: Veteran Actor-Singer Tony Martin," *Chicago Daily Tribune*, April 24, 1955, H34; "First L. A. Date in 23 Years: Horn, Jazz Career, Classical Roots," *Los Angeles Times*, May 9, 1987, E3.

77. Mitch Albom, "Four a.m. Closing Time Won't Make Us Chic," *Detroit Free Press*, October 6, 2013, A15.

78. Ernie Santosuosso, "Shearing Busy as Ever," *Boston Globe*, March 7, 1986, 33.

79. Adam Gopnik, "The Outside Game," *New Yorker*, January 12, 2015, n.p.

80. David Bianculli, "Dr. John: A New Orleans Legend in the Hall of Fame," *Fresh Air*, NPR, [2011] 2018; Glenn Whipp, "It Is a Hell of a Thing," *Los Angeles Times*, December 4, 2014, S24.

81. So it is used (sardonically) by journalists and essayists: Liz Smith, "NBC Readies Its Executive Ax," *Chicago Tribune*, September 26, 1976, D2; George Miller, "Cool Climate," *Philadelphia Daily News*, June 4, 1992, 5; Nora Ephron, "Melancholy Babies," in *The Most of Nora Ephron* (New York: Alfred A. Knopf, 2013), 448–49.

82. To be more precise, I am referring of course to Felix Mendelssohn, *Lieder ohne Worte* (*Songs Without Words*), Opus 62, no. 6, "Frühlingslied" ("Spring Song"). Mendelssohn wrote this opus from 1842 to 1844.

83. "Modern words" is a phase on the cover of Remick's edition with O'Dea's lyrics. After "My Melancholy Baby," "Spring Song" kept going strong in 1910s popular culture and after; for example, a 1913 choral arrangement with lyrics by Julie M. Lippmann, from the Ditson company; the 1916 rag "Spring-Time Rag" by Paul Pratt, from Stark Music; and Judy Garland belting "Swing It, Mr. Mendelssohn," in *Everybody Sing* (1938). It was also mentioned in the lyric of the 1935 hit "Life Is a Song" and used extensively in movie underscoring during the 1930s (and probably was used as silent movie accompaniment before that), to indicate either springtime or a bucolic setting.

84. "Song Reviews: Melancholy."

85. "Descriptive Review: Melancholy."

86. "Song Reviews: Melancholy"; "Recommended Disc Records."

87. Furia, *Poets*, 33; Hamm, *Irving*, 169 et passant.

88. Using the verse of "My Melancholy Baby": Two-fifths of singers and one-fifth of instrumentals, plus a few early bands who feature a vocal refrain but the verse is only rendered instrumentally—averaging out to one-third of all the fifty-four renditions used for the tabulated portion of my survey.

89. Morris, "Selections," 42.

90. Wilder, *American*, 17.

91. Wilder, *American*.

92. There is also a vague resemblance between "My Melancholy Baby" and "Every Little Movement," a 1910 musical comedy hit composed by Karl Hoschna, which Burnett probably would have known. Overall, Hoschna's arching design also bears a faint kinship with Mendelssohn's "Spring Song"; and in Hoschna's first two refrain phrases, consisting of thirteen notes, five are shared with Burnett's ten-note refrain incipit.

93. Sheila K. Adams, *Melancholy Baby: A Comedy* (New York: Samuel French, [1978] 1981), 75.

94. Jimmy Rushing's 1960 recording was my first exposure to "My Melancholy Baby." He is among those who sounds like he is serenading a melon. Here, Rushing is oddly mated with the Dave Brubeck Quartet. The cool accompaniment and slightly slow tempo ill suits Rushing's (and the song's) potential for creating a party mood. I remember all too vividly being called on to demonstrate the tune so that others could learn it, and being at a loss for how the melody actually goes, because Rushing simply does not sing it.

95. Muir, *Long*, 18, augmented by a conversation with the author, December 2106.

96. I was not able to view *A Child Is Born* and reconstructed information about it from reviews, the Internet Movie Database, and the discussion of it in Jeanine Basinger, *A Woman's View* (Hanover, NH: Wesleyan University Press, University Press of New England, 1993), 417–18.

97. My gratitude to Ann Jennifer Mastrogiovanni for permitting me to use interview material gathered for her college coursework under Professor Susan J. Carpenter.

98. As previously mentioned, in Norton's original lyric the word "strong" is only weakly connected to other sounds. Perhaps that is one reason it was replaced by "love," which chimes with the various "l" sounds and the "v" sounds in the next line.

99. Meyerson and Harburg, *Who*, 181.

100. Although there are few lyrics that seem closely to parallel the combination of empathy, philosophy, and infantilization found in "Melancholy Baby," there are many lyrical consolations on parting: "Till We Meet Again" (1918), "Leave Me with a Smile" (1921), "We'll Meet Again" (1942), "We'll Be Together Again" (1945), "Think How It's Gonna Be" (1970), etc.

101. An interesting but obscure parallel is the song Claudette Colbert sings to her infant in the movie *Torch Singer* (1933), "Don't Be a Cry Baby," which paints a scenario of both comforting and gentle chiding somewhat similar to that of "My Melancholy Baby." Other songs that combine inquiry into the blue mood of the sweetheart with a comforting avowal of love are the 1938 Mary Lou Williams standard "What's Your Story, Morning Glory"; and the little-known 1944 "Sad Eyes," lyrics by Bonnie Lake and music by Jeanne Burns, that alludes both implicitly to "Morning Glory" and explicitly to "Melancholy Baby." Lake has her protagonist guess, with a hanging "maybe" similar to Norton's, that the love object is a "melancholy baby," asking if his eyes used to shine brightly for someone in his past, and desiring to kiss away his sadness—all factors that support the link of "Melancholy Baby" with lovelorn despondency and comforting.

102. In 1928 Victor Hall, on an Edison disc, was the second (and for decades, last) recording artist to use both verses. He also changes "tears" to "tear" to create a perfect rhyme for "cheer."

103. The plural "fancies" is found in sheet music: *Reader's Digest Popular Songs That Will Live Forever* (Pleasantville, NY: Reader's Digest Association, 1984, 1985), 224–27; *American Love Songs and Ballads* (Pacific, MO: Mel Bay, 1994), 103; and anthologized in Robert Gottlieb and Robert Kimball, eds., *Reading Lyrics* (New York: Pantheon Books, 2000), 621–22.

104. Further research might turn up earlier instances of the plural "fancies," but as of this writing the only instance before the mid-1930s is in a paraphrase in the 1913 review in *The Player*, "Descriptive Review: Melancholy."

105. "Vaudeville: Blossom Seeley Offered $3,000 by Club Alabam," *Variety*, September 21, 1927, 28.

106. A sign of this change is Fields's first club review, "Night Club Reviews," *Variety*, May 15, 1935, 48.

107. Two articles in the *Washington Post*, July 5, 1936: "Catchy Song Is Stars' Highway to Fame," AA3; "Down, Not Out," AA6.

108. "Night Club Reviews: Bowery Café, Detroit," *Variety*, July 13, 1940, 20; Moss Hart, "The Saga of Gertie," *New York Times*, March 2, 1941, X1.

109. "Music: Famous Names' Famous Songs," *Variety*, October 7, 1942, 72; both Fields and Lyman are listed as using "My Melancholy Baby" as their theme songs.

110. Jack Eigan, "Jack Eigan Speaking," *Chicago Daily Tribune*, August 22, 1959, S13.

111. Perhaps by coincidence, Tommy Lyman and Benny Fields are the only two performers who made "My Melancholy Baby" their theme song and the only two whom Ada "Bricktop" Smith praised in detail; Smith, *Bricktop*, 57–58.

112. In *Minstrel Man* (1944), Benny Fields sings "My Melancholy Baby" first in blackface, in the middle of the floor, physically distant from his nightclub audience. (It is the only instance I have encountered of "Melancholy Baby" being linked to blackface.) The second time, he is not in blackface, and he sits in close proximity to his listeners (see figure 9.6). This twin shift—away from blackface and toward the audience—is symbolic of the drift away from the racist stereotypes that were once associated with some vernacular ballads. For more on this, see chapter 11.

113. The original third-person verse of "Cuddle Up a Little Closer" was eventually superseded in some editions by a different melody with a first-person lyric—another instance of the performance tradition of personal lyrics and intimate song delivery influencing the print tradition, resulting in complicated authorship.

114. McCracken, *Real*, 304.

115. Raymond Bellour, "Segmenting/Analysing," in *Genre: The Musical—A Reader*, ed. Rick Altman (London: Routledge and Kegan Paul, British Film Institute, 1981), 110–11.

116. About jazz: Vassily Aksyonov, *In Search of Melancholy Baby*, translated by Michael Henry Hein and Antonina W. Bouis (New York: Random House, 1987); James A. Howard, *The Ego Mill: Five Case Studies in Clinical Psychology* (Chicago: Cowles Book, Henry Regnery, 1971); Coley Newman, "Melancholy Baby," in *Murder: Plain and Fanciful, with Some Milder Malefactions*, edited by James Sandoe (New York: Sheridan House, 1948), 545–51; John Sinclair, *It's All Good: A John Sinclair Reader* (London: Headpress, 2009); Baron Wormser, "Melancholy Baby," in *Blues for Bill: A Tribute to William Matthews*, ed. Kurt Brown et al. (Akron, OH: University of Akron Press, 2005), 80–81.

117. About depression, grief, self-pity, and hard luck (often hard drinking, as well), or offering consolation for those conditions: Jay Baglia, "Melancholy Baby: Time, Emplotment, and Other Notes on Our Miscarriage," in *Communicating Pregnancy Loss*, edited by Rachel E. Silverman and Jay Baglia (New York: Peter Lang, 2015), 225–38; Ephron, "Melancholy Babies"; Sue Gerhardt, *Why Love Matters: How Affection Shapes a Baby's Brain* (Hove, UK: Brunner-Routledge, 2004), chapter 5, "Melancholy Baby: How Early Experiences Can Alter Brain Chemistry, Leading to Adult Depression," 112–32; Howard, *Ego*; Kate Jennings, *Come to Me My Melancholy Baby* (Fitzroy, Victoria, Australia: Outback Press, 1975); Robert B. Parker, *Play Melancholy Baby* (New York: G. P. Putnam's Sons, 2004); Anthony Platipodis, "Tommy Bahama Plays 'Melancholy Baby,'" in *Disquiet*

Time, edited by Jennifer Grant and Cathleen Falsani (New York: Jericho Books, 2014), 305–21; Wormser, "Melancholy Baby."

118. About lost children or parents: Baglia, "Melancholy Baby"; Parker, *Play*; Pamela Winfield, *Melancholy Baby: The Unplanned Consequences of the G.I.s' Arrival in Europe for World War II* (Westport, CT: Bergin and Garvey, 2000). About caring for orphans: Adams, *Melancholy Baby: A Comedy*; Julia O'Faolain, *Melancholy Baby, and Other Stories* (Dublin: Poolbeg Press, 1978).

119. Aksyonov, *In Search*, 18. Aksyonov's biographical treatise is one of several works featuring "My Melancholy Baby" in the title or text that are explicitly about the narrativization of one's life. The other two: Baglia, "Melancholy Baby," and Platipodis, "Tommy Bahama." Perhaps also connected are the voiceover narrations featured in *The Roaring Twenties* and the "Born in a Trunk" sequence in *A Star Is Born*.

120. Aksyonov, *In Search*, 17, 21.

121. Aksyonov, *In Search*, 18.

122. Aksyonov, *In Search*, 29.

123. Aksyonov, *In Search*, 36, 90.

124. Aksyonov, *In Search*, 31.

125. Aksyonov, *In Search*, 203.

126. Aksyonov, *In Search*, 203.

127. Aksyonov, *In Search*, 205, see also 31.

128. Aksyonov, *In Search*, 21.

129. Aksyonov, *In Search*: clothes and hats, 38; smiles, 36; glowing faces, 126.

130. Aksyonov, *In Search*, 215.

131. Aksyonov, *In Search*, 220.

132. Parker, *Play*, no page; ellipses in original. The co-dedicatee is Richard Bissell, the popular novelist who wrote scripts for the Broadway musicals *The Pajama Game* and *Say, Darling*.

133. Parker, *Play*, 3.

134. Parker, *Play*, 91.

135. Parker, *Play*, 177.

136. Parker, *Play*, 93.

CHAPTER TEN: "WHEN I LOST YOU" AND THE MUSE OF FRIENDSHIP: THE STRANGE HISTORY OF THE AMERICAN WALTZ, PART SIX

1. On the bop waltz: Barry Kernfeld, "Beat," Grove Music Online, 201.

2. Most of the 1924 recordings of "What'll I Do" were as a waltz, but the Paul Specht band rendered it as a fox trot in March, the same month the sheet music was published.

3. Bergreen, *As Thousands*, 84.

4. Philip Furia, *Irving Berlin* (New York: Schirmer Books, 1998), 56.

5. Hamm, *Irving*, 152–72, especially 162–63.

6. E. Ray Goetz was the formal version of his name, but he was always called Ray.

7. There are a number of unidentified clippings that tell of the meeting of Dorothy Goetz and Berlin in the Irving Berlin Collection of scrapbooks at the Library of Congress, reel one, all undated but seemingly from late 1911, including "Berlin Humming Lohengrin Now."

8. Relayed by Michael Freedland, *Irving Berlin* (New York: Stein and Day, Scarborough, [1974] 1978), 38; he cites an undated interview of Berlin "years later" than 1912, by Eric Bennett in the *London Sunday Chronicle*.

9. "Irving Berlin Engaged," *Variety*, November 18, 1911, 3.

10. Alexander Woollcott, *The Story of Irving Berlin* (New York: G. P. Putnam's Sons, 1925), 103; Robert Kimball, and Linda Emmet, editors, *The Complete Lyrics of Irving Berlin* (New York: Alfred A. Knopf, 2001), xxi; "Mrs. Irving Berlin Dead," *Billboard*, July 27, 1912, 4.

11. Woollcott, *Story*, 103.

12. Woollcott, *Story*.

13. Woollcott, *Story*.

14. Kimball and Emmet, *Complete*, 59. Of course, Berlin may have delayed registering the copyright for "When I Lost You" (perhaps due to the personal nature of the song) until after he had registered the copyright of his other ballads and novelty pieces, but I have found no evidence for this time lag.

15. Woollcott, *Story*, 104.

16. Freedland, *As Thousands*, 42.

17. Kimball and Emmet claim Ray Goetz was his vacation companion in 1924; Kimball and Emmet, *Complete*, 225. But, in a discussion of "Lazy," Furia claims that Berlin's friends on this vacation were Dorothy Parker and others surrounding the Algonquin Round Table crowd; Furia, *Irving*, 95. If so, of course, Ray may well have been among them, perhaps along with his wife Irene Bordoni, who had just closed on January 26 in her Broadway star vehicle *Little Miss Bluebeard*. Berlin vacationed again in Palm Beach in early 1925, during which he wrote "Remember," and thus the pattern repeated itself; "Berlin-MacKay." An alternate origin tale exists for "What'll I Do," relayed by Max Wilk, *They're Playing Our Song* (New York: Atheneum, 1973), 279. Donald Ogden Stewart recounted that Berlin brought the start of "What'll I Do," and then completed writing it (though presumably just the refrain), at Stewart's birthday party in the fall of 1923. (Stewart was born on November 30.) If so, in Florida, Berlin may only have written the verse. However, an examination of Kimball and Emmet's *Complete Lyrics of Irving Berlin* reveal the songwriter did not register any songs with the copyright office between October 16, 1923 ("Maid of Mesh"), and January 16, 1924 ("The Happy New Year Blues"); his next two registrations after that were "What'll I Do" and "Lazy" on February 21. In light of that chronology, it seems unlikely Berlin finished even the chorus of "What'll I Do" as early as November 30, 1923, delaying copyright registration for nearly three months (though, of course, this is not impossible).

18. Mary Ellin Barrett, *Irving Berlin* (New York: Simon and Schuster, 1994), 300.

19. Hamm, *Irving*, 163; Bergreen, *As Thousands*, 85.

20. "Berlin-MacKay." Berlin would later add other personal songs to his list: "Oh, How I Hate to Get Up in the Morning" and "Count Your Blessings," both inspired by his difficulty sleeping; and "God Bless America," about his love of the United States.

21. Barrett, *Irving*, 20.

22. "Amusement Events of the Week in Big American Cities: Buffalo, N.Y.," *Billboard*, January 25, 1913, 52.

23. I looked at results for "megaphone" and "megafone" in *Variety* and *Billboard* for the period from 1900 to 1920. Most of the early instances of its use in music were by a sextet or an entire large ensemble. The low-pitched Madge Maitland and a male baritone were among the rare soloists who regularly used the megaphone—and among the fewer to get good reviews for doing so.

24. Jack Josephs, "San Francisco: Orpheum," *Variety*, July 4, 1919, 17.

25. Wynn, "Union Square," *Variety*, February 7, 1913, 22.

26. Wynn, "Union Square"; "Keith's Union Square," *Billboard*, February 15, 1913, 10.

27. "New Acts Next Week: Rene Parker," *Variety*, January 24, 1913, 19.

28. "Rene Parker Scores," *Variety*, February 21, 1913, 21; "London News Letter," *Billboard*, May 10, 1913, 17.

29. "When I Lost You" in London: being performed by Maude Lake, "London Review: Palace Theatre," *Billboard*, March 29, 1913, 13; and in pantomime, "London News Letter," *Billboard*, January 31, 1914, 19.

30. When Warner Brothers filmed *The Jazz Singer* in 1927, they planned to include "When I Lost You" in the score, according to a May 26 letter from Harry Warner to Al Jolson; but the

song was not used (although Berlin's "Blue Skies" was); James Fisher, *Al Jolson* (Westport, CT: Greenwood Press, 1994), 16.

31. Hamm discusses the unpublished lyric "That's Just Why I Love You," in relationship to "When I Lost You"; Hamm, *Irving*, 163. Kimball and Emmet do also—and add "They All Come with You"; *Complete*, 60.

32. For his very first waltz ballad, Berlin wrote the lyric for "Just Like a Rose" (1909) to a melody by tunesmith Al Piantadosi. The composer's refrain starts with an ascending gesture that might be seen as prefiguring later ones by Berlin. In 1912 Piantadosi's "That's How I Need You" was copyrighted three days after Berlin's "That's How I Love You," which may say something about the way Tin Pan Alley craftsmen were often similarly attuned to the market's flow.

33. Banfield, "Sondheim," 156.

34. Well, perhaps no one. A standard item advertised for sale in trade journals was parodies of current popular songs, but "parody" at the time meant new words. It did not necessarily mean making fun of the original, but perhaps making fun of some other subject merely fit to the hit's tune. Over a two-year period, there were such ads for parodies using "When I Lost You," among other tunes, in *Billboard* (three), *Variety* (two), and *The Stage* (four), starting with "Six Parodies," advertisement, *Billboard*, May 3, 1913, 34.

35. I highlight "Spring and Fall" in this discussion, although it is not a waltz, for two reasons: the images ally it to "When I Lost You"; and Berlin's apparent high-art musical aspirations in it relate closely to his slightly later "If All the Girls I Knew Were Like You," which is a waltz.

36. Furia and Lasser, *America's*, 10.

37. Muir, *Long Lost*, 40.

38. The critical comparison of "When I Lost You" to other early Berlin ballads could go on, pointing to the faults of disparate examples such as "You've Got Your Mother's Big Blue Eyes" (ambiguous emotional tonality in the lyric; phrases that are hard to articulate), "When I Leave the World Behind" (weak melody; overly complex structure), or "Smile and Show Your Dimple" (coy lyric; too short; unsatisfying in its asymmetry). Nevertheless, I have never heard a Berlin song that did not have some measure of allure.

39. Pease and Nelson had teamed for the 1920 hit "Pretty Kitty Kelly," followed the same year by the less successful "County Kerry Mary." Both lyrics allude to "My Wild Irish Rose" (1899). "Peggy O'Neil" instead features a "patter chorus" citing song heroines Annie Rooney, Molly-O, Rosie O'Grady, and Bedelia. It was the third (and most successful) entry in their intertextual Irish-maiden waltz cycle. In all three pieces, they draw on previous songs. Therefore, the melodic resemblance to "When I Lost You" fits into this pattern of borrowing.

40. "I'll Forget You" is not a song charted as a hit by either Gardner or Whitburn. Nevertheless, in the States, it appears once on the best-selling sheet music list in "January's Six Best Sellers," *Variety*, January 27, 1922, 3. Further, it is mentioned often in *The Stage* in 1922, indicating hit status in England. Alan Dean revived it on an MGM single in 1952, the flip of the hit "Luna Rossa." In 1953 it was sung by Doris Day, with some modern streamlining of the lyric, in the period movie musical *By the Light of the Silvery Moon*.

41. Willam G. Hyland, *The Song Is Ended* (New York: Oxford University Press, 1995), 98.

42. Berlin, "Song."

43. Berlin, "Song."

44. Wilfred Sheed, *The House That George Built* (New York: Random House, 2007), 18.

45. Bergreen, *As Thousands*, 118, drawing from an interview in the *Sunday News*, September 7, 1947. When Bergreen interviewed James T. Maher about a phone conversation that took place about 1971 between Berlin and Maher's collaborator Alec Wilder, Berlin reportedly again stated, "I only wrote six or eight songs. I just kept writing them over and over again"; Bergreen, *As Thousands*, 562–63. Berlin made this general claim about his "key songs" at various points. An undated

clipping in the Irving Berlin files at the Library of Congress, with a photo of the songwriter as he looked from about 1935 to 1950, says he had "only seven or eight really different tunes"; given by Sears in *Irving*, 8 (also 98n1), with information supplemented by Sears in an email exchange of August 12, 2017.

46. Berlin also demonstrates the probable influence on him of the lyric for "I Wonder Who's Kissing Her Now" in his obscure 1919 duple meter ballad "I Wonder."

47. The only mid-career Berlin waltz ballad refrain I surveyed that does not start with an ascending gesture is "I Can't Do Without You" (1928); even there, one could argue that the ascending gesture is simply delayed until the second phrase. Among his later waltzes, the main example of a descending incipit is "Just One Way to Say I Love You." (Note that Berlin's forgotten "Coquette" is a different song from the famous standard by Gus Kahn, Carmen Lombardo, and Johnny Green, also from 1928.)

48. Berlin specifically identified other key songs and their follow-ups. "Alexander's Ragtime Band" led to "Ragtime Violin," "Everybody's Doin' It," and "Syncopated Walk." "Everybody Step" led to "Pack Up Your Sins," "Puttin' on the Ritz," and "Top Hat, White Tie and Tails." "A Pretty Girl Is Like a Melody" led to "Say It with Music," "Lady of the Evening," "Crinoline Days," and "Soft Lights and Sweet Music." See Bergreen, *As Thousands*, 118, citing *Sunday News*, September 7, 1947. Other correspondence reveals that "Cheek to Cheek" inspired "I've Got My Love to Keep Me Warm"; Sears, *Irving*, 186.

49. "Berlin-MacKay."

50. Crosby and Martin, *Call*, 78. On the same page, Crosby also reports that, earlier in the 1920s, his bandmates would "take a waltz and make a fox trot out of it," but he conveys the impression that he later used the Berlin waltzes as a contrast to the up-tempo fox trot numbers.

51. When I conducted an informal multi-generational survey, fewer recognized the title of "When I Lost You" than any of the other songs in this book. It also had the least number of recordings available on Freegal and iTunes.

52. An instrumental, hurdy-gurdy version of "When I Lost You" inconspicuously underscores a scene in *This Is the Army* (1945)—Hollywood's version of Irving Berlin's 1942 all-soldier stage show. The scene is set in World War I, and the tune helps establish the period. In a working-class urban neighborhood, a Polish American mother tearfully bids her soldier son goodbye. Thus, despite the lively tempo of the rendition, the sentimental association of the song is drawn upon; and perhaps the usage vaguely echoes Berlin's claim that "When I Lost You" shares traits in common with the lullaby, the first song shared between a mother and child.

53. The story of the Berlin-Mackay romance and marriage is oft-told. The insider version is by their daughter; Barrett, *Irving*, 17–48.

54. "Night Clubs: Torch Songs."

55. "Vaudeville: Review of Recording Discs," *Variety*, May 19, 1922, 32.

56. "Faded Love Letters," *Billboard*, September 9, 1922, 41.

57. Advertisement for Waterson, Berlin and Snyder Co. products, *Variety*, February 22, 1923, 48. I examined this dual-meter edition at the University of Colorado, Boulder, Center for American Music. This twofer packaging soon ceased and starting in the 1930s publishers made customers buy separate triple- and duple-meter editions.

58. George T. Simon, *The Big Bands*, rev. and enlarged ed. (New York: Macmillan, 1974), 162–63; Peter J. Levinson, *Tommy Dorsey* (Cambridge, MA: Da Capo, Perseus Books, 2005), 88. Quotations are from Norman Pierre Gentieu's memory of the gig (in November 1937, unless Simon is off by one year in his attribution), and a report by Dorsey from June 1938, both originally in *Metronome*; and Jack Leonard's memories, quoted by Levinson.

59. Levinson, *Tommy*, 89.

60. Freedland, *Irving*, 132, 135; Barrett, *Irving*, 170.

61. Barrett, *Irving*, 170; Freedland, *Irving*, 135; Bergreen, *As Thousands*, 512.

62. On "You're the Only Star": Gene Autry and Mickey Herskowitz, *Back in the Saddle Again* (Garden City, NY: Doubleday, 1978), 59.

CHAPTER ELEVEN: "YOU MADE ME LOVE YOU"

1. The calculation was done by ASCAP; "ASCAP's No. 1 Love Songs," *Billboard*, February 26, 2000, 56.

2. Pearl Gregory as told to Walt Harrington, "When Life Was a Bicycle Built for Two," *Washington Post*, April 3, 1986, SM18–19, 21, 38.

3. Danny Aiello tells this story on *Danny Aiello Live from Atlantic City* (CD, Hopatcong, NJ: DreamMakers Music, 2008).

4. Phyllis Magida, "A Song for Your Sweetheart," *Chicago Tribune*, February 5, 1988, F16; Phil Vettel, "A Valentine's Day to Remember," *Chicago Tribune*, February 10, 1989, N3B. This program continued through 1991, always offering a choice of four songs; and "You Made Me Love You" was the only one retained all four years. It was also a staple in a similar Valentine's Day program in California: "Club Sweet on Singing Valentines," *Daily Report* [Los Angeles], February 6, 1997, T01.

5. Monaco info: Kinkle, *Complete*, 1456–57; McNamara, *ASCAP*, 354; Mark White, *"You Must Remember This"* (New York: Charles Scribner's Sons, 1985), 165–67.

6. McCarthy info: Kinkle, *Complete*, 1400–1401; McNamara, *ASCAP*, 318–19; Warren W. Vaché, *The Unsung Songwriters* (Lanham, MD: Scarecrow Press, 2000), 304–6. Also three from *Billboard*: "Music," January 22, 1910, 16; "Chicago Music Notes," February 5, 1910, 9; "Suratt in New Offering," February 4, 1911, 50.

7. "Will Von Tilzer Alone," *Variety*, February 14, 1913, 5.

8. "Notes of the Trade," *The Player*, April 25, 1913, 11. Along with Jolson, the other two acts were Miss Ray Samuels (who took the female lead opposite Jolson in the tour of *The Honeymoon Express*, discussed below), and the short musical playlet *The Trained Nurse*.

9. "Jimmy Monaco and Joe McCarthy Put Over a New One," *New York Clipper*, May 10, 1913, 12. The Knights of Honor supplied health insurance to mechanics and other workmen; it lasted from 1873 to 1916. Note, too, that this evidence proves false the claim of some historians that Jolson recorded "You Made Me Love You" before he performed it live; Kinkle, *Complete*, 1456–57; Vaché, *Unsung*, 304–5.

10. For the second edition: "Gaby's Party Sailing," *Variety*, April 25, 1913, 11.

11. *The New York Clipper* announced in their May 10 issue that Jolson had first included "You Made Me Love You" in his *Honeymoon Express* song set on Sunday "last week," which could mean April 27 (the last night Deslys and Pilcer played the show) or May 4 (one week after La Rue replaced Deslys in the cast); "Jimmy Monaco and Joe McCarthy." David Bret claims that Pilcer sang "You Made Me" in *Honeymoon Express* one night when Jolson was absent; *The Mistinguett Legend* (New York: St. Martin's Press, 1990), 76. The trade journals, however, prove that this would have been impossible. These details are only worth noting because, as related later in this chapter, Deslys, Pilcer, and La Rue continued to play roles in the history of "You Made Me Love You."

12. "Ray Samuels in *Express*," *Variety*, August 15, 1913, 11. Jolson kept "You Made Me Love You" in the tour of *Honeymoon Express*, as mentioned in a review given by Fisher, *Al Jolson*, 61; quoting Amy Leslie, "Garrick's Great Show," *Chicago Daily News*, January 5, 1914, 14. However, by mid-May perhaps Jolson drops it; it is not mentioned in the detailed song list of the *Seattle Post-Intelligence* reviewer, May 11, 1914; given by Fisher, *Al Jolson*, 62. Nevertheless, it is implied that Jolson was doing "You Made Me" as late as the 1917 tour of *Robinson Crusoe, Jr.*; Percy Hammond, "Mr. Jolson's Plea for American Songs," *Chicago Daily Tribune*, January 21, 1917, C1.

13. "Song Reviews: You Made Me Love You," *Billboard*, May 17, 1913, 9.

14. "White Rats Scamper," *Billboard*, June 7, 1913, 6. Among the seventeen acts that evening, Monaco and Jolson were only rivaled by the duo of Conroy and Lemaire.

15. "Correspondence: Chicago: Wilson," *Variety*, June 20, 1913, 20; "The Vogue of Songs," *Billboard*, August 9, 1913, 9.

16. "Protecting Songs for Week," *Billboard*, August 30, 1913, 16.

17. "Song Reviews: You Made Me."

18. "Fanny Brice," *Variety*, July 27, 1913, 20.

19. "Two Parodies," advertisement, *Billboard*, July 26, 1913, 58 (this is the same ad that mentions a parody of "When I Lost You"—unusual for the Berlin song, but common for the McCarthy-Monaco piece); "Great Northern Hippodrome," *Billboard*, August 30, 1913; "B. F. Keith's," *Billboard*, November 17, 1913, 11, 55.

20. "In Big Time Vaudeville Around New York," *New York Clipper*, November 7, 1913, 7.

21. "North American Cabaret," *Billboard*, September 7, 1913, 13.

22. "William Bence Co.," *Variety*, January 9, 1914, 20.

23. Heard on a live recording of Martin in Las Vegas; and mentioned in print, "In Person Contrasts: Perry Likes to Sing; Dean Has a Comedy Fling," *Billboard*, September 19, 1970, 50. In addition to those mentioned in this chapter, I collected eleven other examples of "You Made Me Love You" being used for comedy, for a total of nineteen. These hint at what are likely many additional undocumented instances.

24. "Songs Heard in New York Vaudevil [*sic*] Last Week," *Billboard*, October 11, 1913, 16.

25. "Chiswick Fire Matinee," *Stage*, September 18, 1913, 18.

26. "London Fails to Fall for Grace La Rue's Temperamental Spasm," *Chicago Daily Tribune*, December 14, 1913, G9, tells of how La Rue's conflict with Alfred Butt, manager of the Palace, led to her banishment from that field of triumph; she had been there, with only one break, for five months. She quickly bounced back by starring in her own musical comedy, *The Girl Who Didn't*; "Grace La Rue a Star in London," *Billboard*, December 27, 1913, 63.

27. "London Fails."

28. On England's ragtime craze, see the retrospective written by longtime Francis, Day and Hunter manager John Abbott, "Fifty Years of Tin Pan Alley: Close Anglo-U. S. Ties on Pop Tunes," *Variety*, January 3, 1951, 221. This tale is told perhaps most entertainingly by Ian Whitcomb, *Irving Berlin and Ragtime America* (New York: Limelight Editions, 1988), 153–68.

29. "Song Hits Abroad," *Billboard*, August 16, 1913, 9.

30. "Diary of the Week," *Observer*, September 7, 1913, 5.

31. *Hullo! Ragtime*: "Song Notes," *Stage*, October 23, 1913, 20; *Step This Way*: "Manchester," *Stage*, December 4, 1913, 29; *Keep Smiling*: "Song Notes," *Stage*, October 9, 1913, 26; *What About It?*: "Song Notes," *Stage*, October 16, 1913, 20; *Eightpence-a-Mile*: "Diary of the Week."

32. Advertisement for *I Love You*, *Observer*, September 28, 1913, 9; admittedly, the wording of the ad is a bit ambiguous—it is possible that the storyline of Yavorska's vehicle merely shed light on the song's subject matter. See also "Lydia Yavorska," *Dictionary of Women Worldwide: 25,000 Women Through the Ages*, edited by Anne Commire and Deborah Klezmer (Farmington Hills, MI: Thomson Gale, and Waterford, CT: Yorkin Publications, 2007).

33. "Song Notes," *Stage*, November 6, 1913, 18.

34. "Fragson Wants to Try," *Variety*, December 19, 1913, 23.

35. "The Good Samaritan Performance," *Stage*, October 16, 1913, 20.

36. Bret, *Mistinguett*, 19–20. "Fragson Shot," *Stage*, January 1, 1914, 35; "How Fragson Was Killed," *Manchester Guardian*, January 1, 1914, 7. Fragson's father died six weeks later, in prison awaiting trial; "Fragson's Father Dead," *New York Times*, February 18, 1914.

37. Peter Dempsey, CD liner notes, *Nuits de Paris*, performed by Mistinguett (London: Living Era, 2001).

38. Max Wilk, *Memory Lane* (New York: Ballantine, 1973), 23.

39. "G. B. S. on 'Mrs. Pat's' Phonetics," *New York Times*, May 10, 1914, X5.

40. "Variety Gossip," *Stage*, August 7, 1913, 14; "Playing with Gaby," *Variety*, August 29, 1913, 4.

41. Bret, *Mistinguett*, 76–89. Delys died after a throat operation trying to remove an infection caused by influenza; "Gaby Deslys Dies after Operation," *New York Times*, February 12, 1920, 11.

42. Bret, *Mistinguett*, 76–89. On Chevalier in London: "Variety Gossip: At the Palace," *Stage*, February 13, 1919, 12.

43. Bret, *Mistinguett*, 89.

44. "A Good Bill," *Billboard*, October 18, 1913, 13; "The Billboard's Song Hints," *Billboard*, July 25, 1914, 12; "The Song World: Hochberg and Company," *Billboard*, September 15, 1917, 14; "Kendis and Brockman," advertisement, *Variety*, December 28, 1917, 33; "Cold Type Review," *Variety*, February 2, 1918, 16; "Berlin and Snyder," advertisement, *Variety*, January 11, 1918, 29.

45. "Law Report: Song Copyright Case," *Observer*, October 18, 1914, 11; "English Song Decision," *Variety*, November 7, 1914, 6.

46. "I Hate to Lose You," advertisement, *Stage*, October 26, 1923, 5.

47. The 1926 "You Made Me Love You" is by Percy Venable. The 1929 title is sometimes given "(You Made Me Love You) Why Did You," and is by Carmen Lombardo and Mickey Kippel. To add to the confusion, there are also two disco-era songs titled "You Made Me Love You."

48. "Song Notes," *Stage*, November 17, 1927, 4. Beyond its existence, I have not discovered any facts about this British "You Made Me Love You" song.

49. "Plays on Broadway: Follies," *Variety*, July 7, 1931, 54.

50. Fisher, *Al Jolson*, 151, 153, 166. Jolson is also documented as performing "You Made Me Love You" on radio in early 1940 and on the Broadway stage in late 1940 (in a scene depicting a radio broadcast); Fisher, *Al Jolson*, 80, 167. After Jolson's career revival and James's "You Made Me" disc revival, Jolson waxed it again and broadcast it frequently; Fisher, *Al Jolson*, 144, 162, 169, 170. It is also possible Jolson sang "You Made Me" in 1931 during his Broadway run and subsequent tour of *Wonder Bar*. He started out sticking with the show's programmed score; Brooks Atkinson, "King of the Singing Fools," *New York Times*, March 18, 1931, 33. But, as it ended its run, "performances became virtually an Al Jolson concert": "*Wonder Bar* Closes, Too Much Work for Al," *Variety*, June 2, 1931, 53; see also Fisher, *Al Jolson*, 78. According to some sources, Jolson sings a brief unaccompanied excerpt of "You Made Me" in his 1930 movie *Mammy*; but the print released on VHS does not include this.

51. William Leonard, "Ethel Merman Returning, But to Empire Room," *Chicago Tribune*, February 25, 1968, F9.

52. Hugh Fordin, *The Movies' Greatest Musicals* (New York: Frederick Ungar, 1984), 357.

53. David Shipman, *Judy Garland* (New York: Hyperion, 1992), 38.

54. John Graham's version is relayed by Gerald Clarke, *Get Happy* (New York: Random House, 2000), 76–79, 433. Other versions that contribute: Shipman, *Judy*, 52, 64–66; Mickey Rooney, *Life Is Too Short* (New York: Willard Books, 1991), 102–6.

55. "Martha Raye, 'Newest Find,'" *Los Angeles Times*, July 28, 1936, 13.

56. Shipman, *Judy*, 64. Also, Jolson was doing "You Made Me Love You" on radio in 1936 on the October 1 special program *Sears: Then and Now*; Fisher, *Al Jolson*, 166. Perhaps Edens heard that broadcast, bringing the old standard to his attention.

57. Abel Green, "Broadway to Hollywood," *Variety*, February 15, 1956, 2.

58. "Timely Tune Topics," *Billboard*, December 12, 1914, 13.

59. "Timely Tune Topics."

60. Gerald G. Gross, "Singing Torch Song of Yesteryear, Judy Garland Scores Mightily in *Broadway Melody of 1938*," *Washington Post*, August 18, 1937, 16.

61. Gross, "Singing Torch"; Gerald G. Gross, "*Broadway Melody of 1938* Is Good, Gay and Tuneful," *Washington Post*, August 21, 1937, 22; Dave Vine, "As I See It," *Billboard*, November 20, 1937, 30; E. E. Krisler, "People in the Films," *Picturegoer*, January 8, 1938, 21; Shipman, *Judy*, 67, quoting the *Hollywood Reporter* and *Film Weekly*.

62. "Monaco-Burke's Crosby," *Variety*, September 1, 1937, 48.

63. McCarthy also had a bit of a fresh start at writing for movies, with "Ten Pins in the Sky" for Garland in *Listen, Darling*, but it only showed up for one week among the top radio plugs in *Variety* ("Network Plugs, 8 a.m. to 1 a.m.," October 12, 1938, 38) and *Billboard* ("'Partners' No. 1 for Second Week," October 15, 1938, 10).

64. Scott Schechter, *Judy Garland* (New York: Rowman and Littlefield, Cooper Square Press, 2002), 41.

65. Radio play for Garland's single: Peter J. Levinson, *Trumpet Blues* (Oxford: Oxford University Press, 1999), 95. When Clark Gable's wife, the beloved Carole Lombard, tragically died, Garland's "Dear Mr. Gable" was temporarily pulled off the air in Pennsylvania; "Star's Death Kills Disks," *Billboard*, February 7, 1942, 21.

66. "Vaudeville Reviews: Metropolitan, Providence," *Billboard*, January 11, 1941, 22–23.

67. "Vaudeville Reviews."

68. "Gray Rains Leads," *Variety*, June 10, 1942, 42. The arranger's name was sometimes spelled Rains and sometimes Raines.

69. Harold Humphrey, "Talent and Tunes on Music Machines: Release Prevues," *Billboard*, June 14, 1941, 71.

70. M. H. Orodenker, "On the Records," *Billboard*, August 30, 1941, 13.

71. "'Made Me Love You' Platterbug's Delight," *Variety*, February 18, 1942, 3. Radio play for "You Made Me Love You" in 1941 would also have been complicated by the famous ASCAP radio ban. Songs licensed for broadcast through ASCAP were off most stations from January through October.

72. "Strand, New York," *Variety*, December 31, 1941, 46.

73. "On the Stand," *Billboard*, June 20, 1942, 20.

74. Harold Humphrey, "Miller Three-Time Champ," *Billboard*, April 25, 1942, 3, 19, 21; "Harry James," *Billboard*, July 18, 1942: 4; Bill Henry, "By the Way," *Los Angeles Times*, May 19, 1942, A1; "Gray Rains Leads"; "James Started in Circus," *Billboard*, April 3, 1943, 63; "Credit for Records," *Billboard*, August 7, 1943, 72.

75. "Inside Stuff: Orchestras," *Variety*, June 16, 1943, 38, gives its sales as 1,063,000. In *Billboard*, the jukebox operator column, "Standard Tunes," lists James's disk through 1958.

76. "'Made Me Love You' Platterbug's Delight."

77. "'Made Me Love You' Platterbug's Delight."

78. Grable had helped introduce "I Can't Begin to Tell You" in *The Dolly Sisters* (1945), but was contractually forbidden to make records, so for her vocal on her husband's single she used the pseudonym Ruth Haag (her middle name plus his middle name).

79. "Waltz Big in Iowa Hills," *Variety*, April 15, 1942, 39.

80. "Waltz Big in Iowa Hills."

81. Donald R. Larrabee, "College Rhythm," *Variety*, December 24, 1941, 36.

82. Harold Humphrey, "Miller Three-Time Champ," *Billboard*, April 25, 1942, 3, 19, 21.

83. "Soldiers' Disk Favorites Varied, Calif. Survey Finds," *Billboard*, November 22, 1941, 61. See also: "Servicemen's Music Tastes Are Typical; James, Miller, Dorsey Favorites; Like Many Oldies, Too," *Billboard*, January 30, 1943, 60.

84. Lucy Greenbaum, "Shortage of Girls Big Worry of USO," *New York Times*, May 15, 1942, 10.

85. Abel Green, "Jolson Tees Off Big as One-Man Show on Tour of Army Camps," *Variety*, January 28, 1942, 3, 53.

86. "Judy Garland Draws Record 15,000 Patrons to Philly Dell Concert," *Variety*, July 7, 1943, 2.

87. Schechter, *Judy*, 100, 108.

88. Both *Variety* and *Billboard* published information about broadcast prevalence supplied by the John G. Peatman organization. Peatman was a sociology professor who got corralled into documenting popular song trends for Broadcast Music Incorporated (BMI); and then for slightly over ten years he helped figure out how big the audiences were who heard popular songs on radio

and television. This 1954 hit run starts with "Songs with Largest Radio Audience," *Variety*, February 3, 1954, 50, and ends with "Songs with Largest Radio Audience," *Variety*, March 31, 1954, 48.

89. Bob Manning did have a single out on Capitol, released in January 1954, with the plug tune the string-laden, lush "Venus de Milo," which charted for one week—and on the B side "You Made Me Love You," with Manning's mellifluous but somewhat unctuous vocal over an atmospheric Bobby Hackett–led, small-group jazz backing. Manning was doing a fair bit of radio and television work during those two months, but I looked closely to see if his broadcast activity might correspond to the way "You Made Me" was charting—it didn't.

90. On one of his radio broadcasts (with guest Dick Haymes) of the 1970s, Alex Wilder praised this pattern of a first phrase settling on a note not in the key, in relation to "Little White Lies."

91. Alan Lewens, *Popular Song* (New York: Billboard Books, 2001), 26. Readers will notice, comparing Lewens's entry for "You Made Me Love You" with this chapter, that I correct a number of his errors.

92. Isaac Goldberg relayed this story about Gershwin, regarding the "The Unofficial Spokesman" (in the 1927 and 1930 versions of *Strike Up the Band*); repeated in Deena Rosenberg, *Fascinating Rhythm* (New York: Penguin Books, Plume, 1991), 209–10. Similarly, Alec Wilder examines Bobby Troup's "Baby, Baby All the Time" (1946) and finds the "persistence" of "repeated measures" very American: "I try to look away but it's no use. . . . It may be monotonous, but it sure isn't Viennese"; Wilder, *American*, 515–16.

93. "Fanny Brice."

94. This sing-along phenomenon was noted as early as the September 24, 1940, Carousel of Music concert in San Francisco, as recounted by Handy, *Father*, 286. Unfortunately, Monaco's rendition of the song from that concert was not preserved.

95. "Song Reviews: You Made Me." This fleeting observation is one of the few musical analyses the tune has ever received.

96. Editor of *Musical Express*, "Songs, Sex and Susceptibility," *Accordion Times and Musical Express*, October 11, 1946, 2.

97. Furia, *Poets*, 34.

98. Furia and Lasser, *America's*, 11.

99. Furia, *Poets*, 34.

100. Horowitz, "Perils," 48.

101. Horowitz, "Perils."

102. Horowitz, "Perils."

103. The three-note ascent that underlies "I've been worried" and "Don't know if I'm" is followed by a repeated note motif that sets "I can't help just." This foreshadows a similar shift in the refrain, discussed previously.

104. "Song Reviews: You Made Me."

105. "Song Reviews: You Made Me."

106. Hammond, "Mr. Jolson's." In 1920 Hammond again printed this column, in a shortened version: "The Theaters," *Chicago Daily Tribune*, February 15, 1920, E1.

107. Robert Alton's staging in the 1934 movie musical *Strike Me Pink* creates exactly this mise-en-scène: Ethel Merman sings "First You Have Me High," a Lew Brown lyric in the lineage of McCarthy's "You Made Me Love You," in a field of darkness, with her pale, bare arms reaching up and out.

108. "Songs Heard."

109. "In Big Time Vaudeville Around Greater New York," *The Player*, September 26, 1913, 8.

110. "Songs Heard."

111. W. H. M., "Variety Theatres," *Manchester Guardian*, December 2, 1913, 18.

112. W. H. M., "Variety Theatres."

113. W. H. M., "Variety Theatres."

114. W. H. M., "Variety Theatres."

115. Edens's version for Garland uses, in its second ending (about "letting the whole world stop"), shorter notes that create a double-time feeling. This version has not appeared in print, however.

116. As I write this, the Garland biopic *Judy* is set to premiere, featuring "You Made Me Love You." It will undoubtedly further strengthen the association of this star and this song—and create interesting new wrinkles in the song's link to the phenomenon of star mythos.

117. Garland was fourteen when she recorded the movie soundtrack and fifteen when she did the studio waxing.

118. Joan Shaw later changed her professional name to Selena Jones.

119. I realize the irony in yoking this notoriously divorced pair.

120. Vachè, *Unsung*, 305.

121. Levinson, *Trumpet*, 94.

122. Levinson, *Trumpet*, 102, 113.

123. Gunther Schuller, *The Swing Era* (New York: Oxford University Press, 1989), 747.

124. Levinson, *Trumpet*, 95.

125. When I downloaded Miff Mole's version from Freegal, the track was mislabeled as "You Made My Love You (Why Did You)," which demonstrates why discographers may never disentangle the various songs by this title.

126. As with many usually fine singers, Bobby Darin and Connie Francis (in her studio rendering) disappoint when they engage with "You Made Me Love You": the tempos too slow, the arrangements bland and sappy. In contrast, Francis's live rendition at the Copa, with a "Dear Mr. Jolson" special arrangement, is compelling.

127. Lord in his *Jazz Discography* lists only six jazz recordings of the McCarthy-Monaco "You Made Me Love You," none of "You Made Me Love You (Why Did You)"—and two hundred of "You Made Me Love You (When I Saw You Cry)"! Since the recording of Monaco's tune by Miff Mole is wrongly being marketed with the subtitle "(Why Did You)," I am skeptical about the accuracy of these numbers. Nevertheless, my experience is that true-blue jazz instrumentals of Monaco's "You Made Me Love You" are scarce, far fewer than, for example, of "Bill Bailey" or "Melancholy Baby"; and this is probably due to James's version bringing on the scorn of many jazz advocates from the swing era to today.

128. In her years of fame, Hildegarde Sell went by her first name only.

129. Some claim that Jolson first used his trademark gesture of going down on one knee when he sang "Gimme, gimme" in "You Made Me Love You"; Max Cryer, *Love Me Tender* (London: Frances Lincoln, 2008), 120; Furia and Lasser, *America's*, 10. The notion may arise from Jolson's major biographer, Herbert G. Goldman, who first mentions the "one knee" technique in relation to "You Made Me"; Herbert G. Goldman, *Jolson* (New York: Oxford University Press, 1988), 76. Later historians ignore Goldman's context: describing the multiple manners in which Jolson interpreted the song *throughout* his career. Admittedly, Goldman also claims that Jolson got the "one knee" stance from Blossom Seeley when they briefly appeared together on Broadway in 1912, which hints that Jolson incorporated the action at about the same time as he adopted "You Made Me." Nevertheless, Goldman does not offer supporting sources for any of these claims, and I have not yet found any such contemporaneous evidence.

130. Sinatra sang "Dear Judy Garland": "Night Club Reviews: Desert Inn, Las Vegas," *Variety*, July 16, 1952, 117. Neither Sinatra nor Ella Fitzgerald ever recorded "You Made Me Love You," but both are reported as singing it at least once in clubs.

131. Horowitz, "Perils," 43.

132. Two British trade journal obituaries propagated the myth about Etting singing "You Made Me Love You": "Ruth Etting Dies at Eighty-One Following Long Illness," *Boxoffice*, October 9, 1978, 93; "Stateside: Ruth Etting," *Screen International*, October 7, 1978, 6. Cryer probably leans on them; Cryer, *Love*, 122.

133. Kelly's dance with Newton-John echoes particular routines of his past: "It Had to Be You," from *Living in a Big Way* (1946); and "Main Street," from *On the Town* (1950). According to the featurette on the DVD edition, the duet had to be added when preview audiences were disappointed that the two stars did not share a number together, perhaps a further demonstration of how Kelly's mythos and the audience's relationship to it shaped the film product right down to the final cut.

134. Dominic Johnson, *The Art of Living* (London: Palgrave Macmillan, 2015), 238.

135. Johnson, *Art*.

136. Johnson, *Art*.

137. Johnson, *Art*, 245.

138. Johnson, *Art*.

139. Starting with E. A. Montague, "Concerts Behind the Line," *Manchester Guardian*, December 2, 1939, 10, re: Dorothy Ward. Done in the United States by Dolly Dawn, starting with "House Review: Circle, Indpls," *Variety*, June 30, 1943, 46.

140. Starting with "Night Club Reviews: Bagatelle, London," *Variety*, June 25, 1958, 70, re: Julie Martin; and "New Acts: Betty Jo Baxter," *Variety*, May 13, 1959, 70.

141. "Night Club Reviews: Riviera, Las Vegas," *Variety*, February 16, 1983, 119.

142. Of note among the four romance novels is C. J. Carmichael, *You Made Me Love You* (Toronto: Harlequin, 2006). The plot concerns unraveling the mystery of the death of a famous singer-songwriter (of "torch songs") who *made* everyone love her, because of an "insatiable need to be adored by all who knew her" (271, 11, 77). One of them loves her to death—and kills her rather than not possess her. This is the natural, logical, albeit insane endpoint of the personalized, obsessive feelings of the fan toward the star that starts with Garland's "Dear Mr. Gable—You Made Me Love You." That song, however, is never mentioned in Carmichael's novel, though its ethos lurks around the story's edges.

143. Joanna Goodman, *You Made Me Love You* (New York: Penguin, New American Library, [2005] 2006). The interview is in a "conversation guide" packaged at the end of the volume, on unnumbered pages.

144. Goodman, *You Made Me*, 286.

145. Goodman, *You Made Me*, 42

146. Goodman, *You Made Me*, 105. Notice that Lilly (or Carmichael) identifies the song with Garland.

147. Goodman, *You Made Me*, 295.

148. Goodman, *You Made Me*, 373.

149. Goodman, *You Made Me*.

150. Shirley Cunningham, *Chasing God* (Scottsdale, AZ: Amoranita Publishing, 2002).

151. Cunningham, *Chasing God*, 212. The first ellipsis is mine; the second is in the original. This chapter that tells of Cunningham's second romance and marriage is entitled "You Made Me Love You." Notice that Cunningham identifies the song as being from the 1940s, and thus James's rendition is her implicit touchstone.

152. Cunningham, *Chasing God*, 272, 281, 298.

CHAPTER TWELVE: CONCLUSION—AUTHORS AND TORCH SONGS

1. Abel Green, "*Variety* All-Time Pop Standards," *Variety*, January 10, 1962, 185.

2. McCracken, *Real Men*, 322.

3. McCracken, *Real Men*.

4. Harvey Fierstein, *Torch Song Trilogy* (New York: Villard Books, 1983), 4. For the 1988 movie version, the songs that Fierstein and the filmmakers chose date from "S'Wonderful" (1927) to "Skylark" (1942). Only one is associated with Helen Morgan and Ruth Etting, "Body and Soul" (1929).

5. Fierstein, *Torch*.

6. Fierstein, *Torch*, 4, 19, 171.

7. Bill Smith, "Follow-Up Review: Bill Farrell," *Billboard*, September 16, 1950, 51. This review parallels and contrasts Farrell and Lyman.

8. Graffis, "Last," 60.

9. "Night Clubs: Torch Songs." Nine out of the thirty-two (28 percent) are depictions of happy, fulfilled love.

10. "Recommended Disk Records"; Hopper, "Screen"; Handy, *Father*, 285; Abel Green, "Vaude-Night-Clubs: Nitery Followup," *Variety*, October 11, 1939, 50; "Record Buying Guide: The Week's Best Releases," *Billboard*, August 14 1943, 66; "Music: Theme Songs and Song Cycles," *Variety*, January 4, 1956, 356. Similarly, in 1962, at the Copacabana, Tina Robin "cements the interest anew with a torch like 'Melancholy Baby'"; "Night Club Reviews: Copacabana, N.Y.," *Variety*, September 19, 1962, 58.

11. Wilder, *American*, 21; Loonis McGlohon, "Baby," in *Facts Behind the Songs*, 15.

12. Jones, "Torch"; Stacy Holman Jones, *Torch Singing* (Lanham, NJ: AltaMira, 2007); Moore, "'Hieroglyphics.'"

13. Moore, "'Hieroglyphics,'" 31; Jones, *Torch Singing*, 18.

14. Rick Altman, *Film/Genre* (London: British Film Institute, 1999), 101.

15. Altman, *Film/Genre*.

16. Jones, *Torch Singing*, 1; Moore, "'Hieroglyphics,'" 52.

17. Pickering, "Torch Singer," 110.

18. Altman, *Film/Genre*, 101.

19. Altman, *American*, 103.

20. Altman, *American*, supplemented by email correspondence of June 18, 2011.

BIBLIOGRAPHY

Abbott, Lynn, and Doug Seroff. "'They Cert'ly Sound Good to Me': Sheet Music, Southern Vaudeville, and the Commercial Ascendancy of the Blues." *American Music* 14, no. 4 (Winter 1996): 402–54.

Adams, Sheila K. *Melancholy Baby: A Comedy*. New York: Samuel French, [1978] 1981.

Aiello, Danny. *Danny Aiello Live from Atlantic City*. CD. Hopatcong, NJ: DreamMakers Music, 2008.

Aksyonov, Vassily. *In Search of Melancholy Baby*, translated by Michael Henry Hein and Antonina W. Bouis. New York: Random House, 1987.

Altman, Rick. *The American Film Musical*. Bloomington: Indiana University Press, 1987.

Altman, Rick. *Film/Genre*. London: British Film Institute, 1999.

Altman, Rick. *Silent Film Sound*. New York: Columbia University Press, 2004.

American Love Songs and Ballads. Pacific, MO: Mel Bay, 1994.

Anderson, John Murray. *Out Without with My Rubbers*. New York: Library Publishers, 1954.

Autry Gene, and Mickey Herskowitz. *Back in the Saddle Again*. Garden City, NY: Doubleday, 1978.

Baglia, Jay. "Melancholy Baby: Time, Emplotment, and Other Notes on Our Miscarriage." In *Communicating Pregnancy Loss: Narrative as a Method for Change* edited by Rachel E. Silverman and Jay Baglia, 225–38. New York: Peter Lang, 2015.

Banfield, Stephen. *Jerome Kern*. New Haven, CT: Yale University Press, 2006.

Banfield, Stephen. "Popular Song and Popular Music on Stage and Film." In *The Cambridge History of American Music*, edited by David Nicholls, 309–44. Cambridge: Cambridge University Press, 1998.

Banfield, Stephen. "Sondheim and the Art That Has No Name." In *Approaches to the American Musical*, ed. Robert Lawson-Peebles, 137–60. Exeter, UK: University of Exeter Press, 1996.

Banfield, Stephen. *Sondheim's Broadway Musicals*. Ann Arbor: University of Michigan Press, 1993.

Baral, Robert. *Revue: A Nostalgic Reprise of the Great Broadway Period*. New York: Fleet Publishing, 1962.

Barnet, Richard D., Bruce Nemerov, and Mayo R. Taylor. *The Story Behind the Song*. Westport, CT: Greenwood Press, 2004.

Barrett, Mary Ellin. *Irving Berlin: A Daughter's Memoir*. New York: Simon and Schuster, 1994.

Basinger, Jeanine. *A Woman's View: How Hollywood Spoke to Women 1930–1960*. Hanover, NH: Wesleyan University Press, University Press of New England, 1993.

Bellour, Raymond. "Segmenting/Analysing." In *Genre: The Musical—A Reader*, edited by Rick Altman, 102–33. London: Routledge and Kegan Paul, British Film Institute, 1981.

Bergreen, Lawrence. *As Thousands Cheer: The Life of Irving Berlin*. New York: Penguin, 1990.

Berlin, Edward A. *Ragtime: A Musical and Cultural History*. Berkeley: University of California Press, 1980.

Berlin, Irving. "Song and Sorrow Are Playmates." In *The Irving Berlin Reader*, edited by Benjamin Sears, 169–72. Oxford: Oxford University Press, 2012.

Bianculli, David. "Dr. John: A New Orleans Legend in the Hall of Fame." Transcript of interview, March 11, 2011. *Fresh Air.* NPR, 2018. https://www.npr.org/templates/transcript/transcript .php?storyId=134423135 (accessed July 4, 2018).

Biskind, Peter. *Easy Riders, Raging Bulls: How the Sex-Drugs-and-Rock-'n'-Roll Generation Saved Hollywood.* New York: Simon and Schuster, 1998.

Bleiel, Jeff. *That's All.* Ann Arbor, MI: Popular Culture Ink, 1993.

Bordman, Gerald. *American Musical Revue: From "The Passing Show" to "Sugar Babies."* New York: Oxford University Press, 1985.

Bowlly, Al. *Modern Style Singing ("Crooning").* London: Henri Selmber, [1934].

Bradley, Edwin M. *The First Hollywood Musicals: A Critical Filmography of 171 Features, 1927 through 1932.* Jefferson, NC: McFarland, 1996.

Bret, David. *The Mistinguett Legend.* New York: St. Martin's Press, 1990.

Brooks, Tim. "'Pop Memories,' Book Review." *ARSC Journal* 21, no. 1 (spring 1990): 134–41.

Burke, Patrick. *Come In and Hear the Truth: Jazz and Race on 52nd Street.* University of Chicago Press, 2008.

Burton, Jack. *The Blue Book of Tin Pan Alley.* New York: Century House, Watkins Glen, 1951.

Cahn, Sammy. *I Should Care: The Sammy Cahn Story.* New York: Arbor House, 1974.

Carmichael, C. J. *You Made Me Love You.* Toronto, Canada: Harlequin, 2006.

Carousel of American Music: The Fabled 24 September 1940 San Francisco Concerts. CD-971. Berkeley, CA: Music and Arts Programs of America, 1997.

Carruth, Hayden. "Introduction." In *Nausea,* by Jean-Paul Sartre, translated by Lloyd Alexander, ix–xiv. New York: New Directions, 1964.

Christakis Nicholas A., and James H Fowler. *Connected: The Surprising Power of Our Social Networks and How They Shape Our Lives.* New York: Little, Brown, 2009.

Cherney, Guy. *Everybody Sing.* LP. Mercury, 1956.

Citron, Stephen. *Noel and Cole: The Sophisticates.* New York: Oxford University Press, 1993.

Clarke, Gerald. *Get Happy: The Life of Judy Garland.* New York: Random House, 2000.

Collins, Randall. *The Sociology of Philosophies: A Global Theory of Intellectual Change.* Cambridge, MA: Belknap Press of Harvard University Press, 1998.

Cornelius, Steven. *Music of the Civil War Era.* Westport, CT: Greenwood Press, 2004.

Crawford, Richard, and Jeffrey Magee. *Jazz Standards on Record, 1900–1942: A Core Repertory.* Monographs, no. 4. Chicago: Center for Black Music Research, Columbia College Chicago, 1992.

Crosby, Bing, and Pete Martin. *Call Me Lucky.* New York: Simon and Schuster, 1953.

Cryer, Max. *Love Me Tender: The Stories Behind the World's Best-Loved Songs.* London: Frances Lincoln, 2008.

Cunningham, Shirley. *Chasing God: One Woman's Magnificent Journey of Spirit.* Scottsdale, AZ: Amoranita Publishing, 2002.

Dawidoff, Robert. *Making History Matter.* Philadelphia: Temple University Press, 2000.

Dempsey, Peter. CD liner notes. *Nuits de Paris,* by Mistinguett. London: Living Era, 2001.

Diamond, John. "Ballad Is Best." Audio. Unpublished lecture, August 27, 1992.

Diamond, John. "Composing: We Gotta Write Love Songs." Audio. Unpublished lecture, 1998.

Diamond, John. "Courtly Love, Wonderland and Marriage." *Diamond Report* 112 (June 1986).

Diamond, John. "Jazz and Classical: Up on One and Three." Audio. Unpublished lecture, September 3, 1998.

Diamond, John. *Life-Energy Analysis: A Way to Cantillation.* Valley Cottage, NY: Archaeus Press, 1988.

Diamond, John. *The Life Energy in Music, Vols. 1–3.* Valley Cottage, NY: Archaeus Press, 1981–86.

Diamond, John. *Life Energy: Using the Meridians to Unlock the Hidden Power of Your Emotions.* New York: Paragon House, 1985.

Diamond, John. *Music and Song, Mother and Love.* Bloomingdale, IL: Enhancement Books, 2001.

Diamond, John. "Songs and Intimacy." Audio. Unpublished lecture, February 12, 2004.

Discography of American Historical Recordings. Regents of the University of California, 2019. https://adp.library.ucsb.edu/index.php/matrix/search (accessed January 27, 2019).

Dixon, Robert M. W., John Godrich, and Howard Rye, compilers. *Blues and Gospel Records, 1890–1943,* 4th ed. Oxford, UK: Clarendon Press, 1997.

Engel, Lehman. *Their Words Are Music: The Great Theater Lyricists and Their Lyrics.* New York: Crown, 1975.

Engel, Lehman. *The Making of a Musical.* New York: Macmillan, 1977.

Ephron, Nora. "Melancholy Babies." In *The Most of Nora Ephron,* 448–49. New York: Alfred A. Knopf, 2013.

Erenberg, Lewis A. *Steppin' Out: New York Nightlife and the Transformation of American Culture, 1890–1930.* Westport, CT: Greenwood Press, 1981.

Ewen, David. *All the Years of American Popular Music: A Comprehensive History.* Englewood Cliffs, NJ: Prentice-Hall, 1977.

Ewen, David. *American Popular Songs: From the Revolutionary War to the Present.* New York: Random House, 1966.

Ewen, David. *The Life and Death of Tin Pan Alley: The Golden Age of American Popular Music.* New York: Funk and Wagnalls, 1964.

Fields, Armond. *Sophie Tucker: First Lady of Show Business.* Jefferson, NC: McFarland, 2003.

Fierstein, Harvey. *Torch Song Trilogy.* New York: Villard Books, 1983.

Fisher, James. *Al Jolson: A Bio-Bibliography.* Westport, CT: Greenwood Press, 1994.

Fletcher, Tom. *One Hundred Years of the Negro in Show Business.* New York: Da Capo Press, 1984.

Fordin, Hugh. *The Movies' Greatest Musicals: Produced in Hollywood USA by the Freed Unit.* New York: Frederick Ungar, 1984.

Forte, Allen. *The American Popular Ballad of the Golden Era, 1924–1950.* Princeton, NJ: Princeton University Press, 1995.

Forte, Allen. *Listening to Classic American Popular Songs.* New Haven, CT: Yale University Press, 2001.

Frank Sinatra Concert Collection. DVD. Los Angeles, CA: Shout! Factory, 2010.

Freedland, Michael. *Irving Berlin.* New York: Stein and Day, Scarborough, [1974] 1978.

Friedwald, Will. *Stardust Memories: A Biography of Twelve of America's Most Popular Songs.* New York: Pantheon Books, 2002.

Friedwald, Will, and Mitchell Zlokower. "Sinatra: Songs for Swingin' Singles: An Appreciation." CD liner notes. *The Complete Capitol Singles Collection,* by Frank Sinatra. Hollywood, CA: Capitol Records, 1996.

Fuld, James J. *The Book of World-Famous Music: Classical, Popular and Folk.* 5th ed. New York: Dover, [1966] 2000.

Furia, Philip. *Irving Berlin: A Life in Song.* New York: Schirmer Books, 1998.

Furia, Philip. *The Poets of Tin Pan Alley: A History of America's Great Lyricists.* New York: Oxford University Press, 1990.

Furia, Philip, and Michael Lasser. *America's Songs: The Stories Behind the Songs of Broadway, Hollywood, and Tin Pan Alley.* New York: Routledge, 2006.

Gabbard, Krin. *Jammin' at the Margins: Jazz and the American Cinema.* Chicago: University of Chicago Press, 1996.

Ganzl, Victor. *The Musical: A Concise History.* Boston: Northeastern University Press, 1997.

Gardner, Edward Foote. *Popular Songs of the Twentieth Century: Volume I; Chart Details and Encyclopedia, 1900–1949.* St. Paul, MN: Paragon House, 2000.

Garber, Michael G. "'Some of These Days' and the Study of the Great American Songbook." *Journal of the Society for American Music* 4, no. 2 (2010): 175–214.

Gavin, James. *Intimate Nights: The Golden Age of New York Cabaret*. New York: Grove Weidenfeld, 1991.

Geller, James J. *Famous Songs and Their Stories*. New York: Macaulay, 1931.

Gerhardt, Sue. *Why Love Matters: How Affection Shapes a Baby's Brain*. Hove, UK: Brunner-Routledge, 2004.

Gershwin, Ira. *Lyrics on Several Occasions*. 1959. Reprint, New York: Limelight Editions, 1997.

Gilbert, Douglas. *Lost Chords*. Garden City, NY: Doubleday, Doran, 1942.

"'The Girl of My Dreams' The Sweetheart of Sigma Chi." Sigma Chi at Sam Houston State, Epsilon Psi Chapter, 1999. https://www.shsu.edu/~eng_wpf/sweetheart.html (accessed February 3, 2019).

Gioia, Ted. *The Jazz Standards: A Guide to Repertoire*. Oxford: Oxford University Press, 2012.

Gladwell, Malcolm. "Group Think: What Does 'Saturday Night Live' Have in Common with German Philosophy?" *New Yorker*, December 2, 2002, 102–5.

Gladwell, Malcolm. *Outliers: The Story of Success*. New York: Little, Brown, 2008.

Goldberg, Isaac. *Tin Pan Alley: A Chronicle of American Popular Music*, introduction by George Gershwin; supplement, "From Swing and Sweet to Rock 'n' Roll," by Edward Jablonski. New York: Frederick Ungar, [1930] 1961.

Goldmark, Daniel. "Creating Desire on Tin Pan Alley." *Musical Quarterly* 90 (2008): 197–229.

Goodman, Joanna. *You Made Me Love You*. New York: Penguin, New American Library, [2005] 2006.

Gottlieb, Robert, and Robert Kimball, editors. *Reading Lyrics*. New York: Pantheon Books, 2000.

Hamm, Charles. *Irving Berlin: Songs from the Melting Pot—The Formative Years, 1907-1914*. New York: Oxford University Press, 1997.

Hamm, Charles. *Yesterdays: Popular Song in America*. New York: W. W. Norton, 1979.

Handy, W. C. *Father of the Blues: An Autobiography*. New York: Da Capo, [1941].

Hayakawa, S. I. "Popular Songs vs. the Facts of Life." In *Mass Culture: The Popular Arts in America*, edited by Bernard Rosenberg and David Manning White, 393–403. Glencoe, IL: Free Press, Falcon's Wing Press, 1957. Originally in *Etc.* 12 (1955): 83–95.

Hill, Errol G., and James V. Hatch. *A History of African American Theatre*. Cambridge: Cambridge University Press, 2003.

Horn, David. "Torch Singer." *Continuum Encyclopedia of Popular Music of the World, Volume II*. London: Continuum, 2003.

Horowitz, David A. "The Perils of Commodity Fetishism: Tin Pan Alley's Portrait of the Romantic Marketplace, 1920-1942." *Popular Music and Society* (summer 1985): 37–53.

Howard, James A. *The Ego Mill: Five Case Studies in Clinical Psychology*. Chicago: Cowles Book, Henry Regnery, 1971.

Howard, Richard. "A Foreword to *Nausea*." In *Nausea*, by Jean-Paul Sartre, translated by Lloyd Alexander, i–viii. New York: New Directions, 2007.

Hyland, William G. *The Song Is Ended: Songwriters and American Music, 1900-1950*. New York: Oxford University Press, 1995.

"I Wonder Who's Kissing Her Now." Sung by Michael Delaney. YouTube. https://www.youtube.com/watch?v=g1hDnpecJhw (accessed July 11, 2017).

Irwin, Kenneth, and Charles O. Lloyd. *Ruth Etting: America's Forgotten Sweetheart*. Lanham, MD: Scarecrow Press, 2010.

Jablonski, Edward. LP liner notes. *All Alone*, by Frank Sinatra. Burbank, CA: Reprise Records, 1962.

Jasen, David A. *Tin Pan Alley: The Composers, the Songs, the Performers and Their Times—The Golden Age of Popular Music from 1886 to 1956*. New York: Primus, Donald I. Fine, 1988.

Jasen, David A., and Gene Jones. *Black Bottom Stomp: Eight Masters of Ragtime and Early Jazz*. New York: Routledge, 2002.

Jasen, David A., and Gene Jones. *Spreadin' Rhythm Around: Black Popular Songwriters, 1880–1930*. New York: Schirmer, 1998.

Jazz: A Film by Ken Burns. DVD. Directed by Ken Burns. Hollywood, CA: Paramount, PBS, 2001.

Jenness, David, and Don Velsey. *Classic American Popular Song: The Second Half-Century, 1950–2000*. New York: Routledge, 2006.

Jennings, Kate. *Come to Me My Melancholy Baby*. Fitzroy, Victoria, Australia: Outback Press, 1975.

Johnson, Dominic. *The Art of Living: An Oral History of Performance Art*. London: Macmillan, Palgrave, 2015.

Jones, Stacy Holman. "Torch." *Qualitative Inquiry* 5, no. 2 (June 1999): 280–304.

Jones, Stacy Holman. *Torch Singing: Performing Resistance and Desire from Billie Holiday to Edith Piaf*. Lanham, NJ: AltaMira, 2007.

Kern, Jerome. "Letter from Jerome Kern to Alexander Woollcott from *The Story of Irving Berlin*." In *The Irving Berlin Reader*, edited by Benjamin Sears, 81–83. Oxford: Oxford University Press, 2012.

Kernfeld, Barry. "Beat." Grove Music Online, 2017. https://doi.org/10.1093/gmo/9781561592630.article.J033600.

Kimball, Robert, and Linda Emmet, editors. *The Complete Lyrics of Irving Berlin*. New York: Alfred A. Knopf, 2001.

Kiner, Larry F. *The Cliff Edwards Discography*. New York: Greenwood Press, 1987.

Kinkle, Roger D. *The Complete Encyclopedia of Popular Music and Jazz, 1900–1950*. 4 vols. New Rochelle, NY: Arlington House, 1974.

Knapp, Raymond. *The American Musical and the Formation of National Identity*. Princeton, NJ: Princeton University Press, 2005.

Kreuger, Miles. *Show Boat: The Story of a Classic American Musical*. New York: Oxford University Press, 1977.

Laird, Ross. *Moanin' Low: A Discography of Female Popular Vocal Recordings, 1920–1933*. Westport, CT: Greenwood Press, 1996.

Laurie, Joe, Jr. *Vaudeville: From the Honky-Tonks to the Palace*. New York: Henry Holt, 1953.

Lees, Gene. *Singers and the Song*. New York: Oxford University Press, 1987.

Leighton, Frank, and Bert Leighton. "Origin of 'Blues' (or Jazz)." In *Jazz in Print (1856–1929)*, edited by Karl Koenig, 164–66. Hillsdale, NY: Pendragon Press. Originally in *Variety*, January 6, 1922, 27.

Levinson, Peter J. *Tommy Dorsey: Livin' in a Great Big Way*. Cambridge, MA: Da Capo, Perseus Books, 2005.

Levinson, Peter J. *Trumpet Blues: The Life of Harry James*. Oxford: Oxford University Press, 1999.

Lewens, Alan. *Popular Song: Soundtrack of a Century*. New York: Watson-Guptill, Billboard Books, 2001.

Lord, Tom. *The Jazz Discography*. West Vancouver, Canada: Lord Music Reference, 1992.

Lott, Eric. "'Love and Theft' (2001)." In *The Cambridge Companion to Bob Dylan*, edited by Kevin J. H. Dettmar, 167–73. Cambridge: Cambridge University Press, 2009.

"Lydia Yavorska." In *Dictionary of Women Worldwide: 25,000 Women Through the Ages*, edited by Anne Commire and Deborah Klezmer. Farmington Hills, MI: Thomson Gale, and Waterford, CT: Yorkin Publications, 2007.

Magee, Jeffrey. *Irving Berlin's American Musical Theater*. Oxford: Oxford University Press, 2012.

Maher, James T. "Introduction." In Alec Wilder, *American Popular Song: The Great Innovators, 1900–1950*, xxiii–xxxix. London: Oxford University Press, 1972.

Marks, Edward B., as told to Abbott J. Liebling. *They All Sang: From Tony Pastor to Rudy Vallée*. New York: Viking Press, 1934.

Marston, Peter. "Lost Treasures: John Randolph Marr." Pop Geek Heaven, n.d. http://www.popgeekheaven.com/music-discovery/lost-treaures-john-randolph-marr (accessed July 13, 2017).

Mast, Gerald. *Can't Help Singin': The American Musical on Stage and Screen*. Woodstock, NY: Overlook Press, 1987.

McCracken, Alison. "'God's Gift to Us Girls': Crooning, Gender, and the Re-Creation of American Popular Song, 1928–1933." *American Music* 17, no. 1 (1999): 365–95.

McCracken, Alison. *Real Men Don't Sing: Crooning in American Culture*. Durham, NC: Duke University Press, 2015.

McGlohon, Loonis. "Baby" and "Torch Song." In *Facts Behind the Songs: A Handbook of American Popular Music from the Nineties to the '90s*, edited by Marvin E. Paymer. New York: Garland, 1993.

McLucas, Anne Dhu. *The Musical Ear: Oral Tradition in the USA*. Farnham, UK: Ashgate, 2010.

McNamara, Daniel I., editor. *The ASCAP Biographical Dictionary of Composers, Authors, and Publishers*. New York: Thomas Y. Crowell, 1952.

Melnick, Jeffrey. *A Right to Sing the Blues: African Americans, Jews, and American Popular Song*. Cambridge, MA: Harvard University Press, 1999.

Mercer, Johnny. *The Complete Lyrics of Johnny Mercer*, edited by Robert Kimball, Barry Day, Miles Kreuger, and Eric Davis. New York: Alfred A. Knopf, 2009.

Merman, Ethel. *Who Could Ask for Anything More?* Garden City, NY: Doubleday, 1955.

Meyerson, Harold, and Ernie Harburg. *Who Put the Rainbow in the Wizard of Oz? Yip Harburg, Lyricist*. Ann Arbor: University of Michigan Press, 1993.

Mezzrow, Milton "Mezz," and Bernard Wolfe. *Really the Blues*. New York: Random House, 1964.

Miller, Owen. "Whitey Kaufman's Original Pennsylvania Serenaders." Red Hot Jazz Archive. http://www.redhotjazz.com/kaufman.html (accessed August 13, 2018).

Montgomery, L. M. *Rilla of Ingleside*. New York: Bantam Books, [1921] 1992.

Moore, John. "'The Hieroglyphics of Love': The Torch Singers and Interpretation." *Popular Music* 8, no. 1 (1989): 31–58.

Morath, Max. *The NPR Curious Listener's Guide to Popular Standards*, with a foreword by Michael Feinstein. New York: Penguin Putnam, Berkley Publishing, Perigree, 2002.

Morris, James R. "The Selections." LP anthology booklet, 31–124. *American Popular Song*. New York: CBS Records, and Washington, DC: Smithsonian Collection of Recordings, 1984.

Muir, Peter C. "Before 'Crazy Blues': Commercial Blues in America, 1850–1920." Diss., City University of New York, 2004.

Muir, Peter C. "Boogie-woogie (i)." 2012. Grove Music Online, 2013. https://doi.org/10.1093/gmo/9781561592630.article.A2228520 (accessed January 21, 2015).

Muir, Peter C. *Long Lost Blues: Popular Blues in America, 1850–1920*. Urbana: University of Illinois Press, 2009.

Murrells, Joseph. *Million Selling Records: From the 1900s to the 1980s; An Illustrated Directory*. New York: Arco, 1984.

"The Music of Sigma Chi." Sigma Chi at Sam Houston State, Epsilon Psi Chapter, 1999. https://www.shsu.edu/~eng_wpf/sigmachimusic.html (accessed January 15, 2019).

National Child Welfare Association. *Music and Childhood*. New York: National Child Welfare Association, 1919.

Nesbit, Edith. *The Railway Children*. Harmondsworth, UK: Puffin, Penguin, [1906] 1974.

Newman, Coley. "Melancholy Baby." In *Murder: Plain and Fanciful, with Some Milder Malefactions*, edited by James Sandoe, 545–51. New York: Sheridan House, 1948.

Norton, Richard C. *A Chronology of American Musical Theater*, 3 vols. Oxford: Oxford University Press, 2002.

O'Faolain, Julia. *Melancholy Baby, and Other Stories*. Dublin: Poolbeg Press, 1978.

O'Neal, Hank. CD liner notes. *Dave "Fingers" McKenna*. Chiaroscuro CR 175. New York: SOS, Chiaroscuro, [1977] 2000.

Old-Fashioned Love Songs. Milwaukee, WI: Hal Leonard, n.d.

Pabst, Ralph M. *Gene Austin's Ol' Buddy*. Phoenix, AZ: Augury, 1984.

Parker, Robert. CD liner notes. *Torch Songs*. New Orleans: Louisiana Red Hot Records, 1997.

Parker, Robert B. *Play Melancholy Baby*. New York: G. P. Putnam's Sons, 2004.

Patinkin, Sheldon. *"No Legs, No Jokes, No Chance": A History of the American Musical Theater*. Evanston, IL: Northwestern University Press, 2008.

Peters, Richard, Ed O'Brien, and Scott P. Sayers. *The Frank Sinatra Scrapbook: His Life and Times in Words and Pictures*. New York: St. Martin's Press, 1982.

Peterson, Bernard L., Jr. *Profiles of African American Stage Performers and Theatre People, 1816–1960*. Westport, CT: Greenwood Press, 2001.

Pickering, Gregory F. "The Torch Singer: A Depth Psychology Study." Diss., Pacifica Graduate Institute, 1999.

Pinker, Steven. *The Better Angels of Our Nature: Why Violence Has Declined*. New York: Penguin, Viking, 2011.

Pitts, Michael R., and Frank Hoffman. *The Rise of the Crooners: Gene Austin, Russ Columbo, Bing Crosby, Nick Lucas, Johnny Marvin, and Rudy Vallee*, with the assistance of Dick Carty and Jim Bedoian, introduction by Ian Whitcomb. Studies and Documentation in the History of Popular Entertainment, No. 2. Lanham, MD: Scarecrow Press, 2002.

Platipodis, Anthony. "Tommy Bahama Plays 'Melancholy Baby.'" In *Disquiet Time: Rants and Reflections on the Good Book by the Skeptical, the Faithful, and a Few Scoundrels*, edited by Jennifer Grant and Cathleen Falsani, 305–21. New York: Jericho Books, 2014.

Pleasants, Henry. *The Agony of Modern Music*. New York: Simon and Schuster, 1955.

Pleasants, Henry. *Death of a Music? The Decline of the European Tradition and the Rise of Jazz*. London: Victor Gollancz, 1961.

Pleasants, Henry. *Serious Music—And All That Jazz! An Adventure in Music Criticism*. New York: Simon and Schuster, 1969.

Pool, Ithiel De Sola. *The Social Impact of the Telephone*. Cambridge, MA: MIT Press, 1977.

Potter, John. "The Singer, Not the Song: Women Singers as Composer-Poets." *Popular Music* 13, no. 2 (May 1994): 191–99.

Reader's Digest Popular Songs That Will Live Forever. Pleasantville, NY: Reader's Digest Association, [1984] 1985.

Robbins, Yvonne. "Shelton Brooks." In *Musical Buxton*, by Vivian Robbins, 26–27. Buxton, Canada: Vivian Robbins, 1969.

Rodgers, Richard. *Musical Stages: An Autobiography*. New York: Random House, 1975.

Rooney, Mickey. *Life Is Too Short*. New York: Willard Books, 1991.

Rosen, Jody. *White Christmas: The Story of an American Song*. New York: Scribner, 2002.

Rosenberg, Deena. *Fascinating Rhythm: The Collaboration of George and Ira Gershwin*. Penguin Books, Plume, 1991.

Russell, Tony. *Country Music Records: A Discography, 1921–1942*, with editorial research by Bob Pinson, assisted by the staff of the Country Music Hall of Fame and Museum. Oxford: Oxford University Press, [2004] 2008.

Rust, Brian. *Jazz Records, 1897–1942*, 4th rev. and enlarged ed. New Rochelle, NY: Arlington House, 1978.

Rust, Brian, with Allen G. Debus. *The Complete Entertainment Discography: From the Mid-1890s to 1942*. New Rochelle, NY: Arlington House, 1973.

Saffle, Michael. "Shelton Leroy Brooks." In *The International Dictionary of Black Composers*, edited by Samuel J. Floyd Jr., 174–76. Chicago: Fitzroy Dearborn, 1999.

Sanjek, Russell. *American Popular Music and Its Business: The First Four Hundred Years, Volume III: From 1900 to 1984*. New York: Oxford University Press, 1988.

Sartre, Jean-Paul. *Nausea*, translated by Lloyd Alexander. New York: New Directions, 2007.

Scarborough, Dorothy. *On the Trail of Negro Folk-Songs*. Cambridge, MA: Harvard University Press, [1925] 1963.

Schafer, R. Murray. *The Tuning of the World*. New York: Alfred A. Knopf, 1977.

Shaw, George Bernard. *Passion, Poison, and Petrification, or, The Fatal Gazogene*. In *Translations and Tomfooleries*. New York: Brentano's, 1926.

Schechter, Scott. *Judy Garland: The Day-by-Day Chronicle of a Legend*. New York: Rowman and Littlefield, Cooper Square Press, 2002.

Scheurer, Timothy E. "'Thou Witty': The Evolution and Triumph of Style in Lyric Writing, 1890–1950." In *American Popular Music: Readings from the Popular Press, Volume I: The Nineteenth Century and Tin Pan Alley*, edited by Timothy E. Scheurer, 104–19. Bowling Green, OH: Bowling Green State University Popular Press, 1989.

Schuller, Gunther. *The Swing Era: The Development of Jazz, 1930–1945*. New York: Oxford University Press, 1989.

Sears, Benjamin, editor. *The Irving Berlin Reader*. Oxford: Oxford University Press, 2012.

Shales, Tom, and James A Miller. *Live from New York: An Uncensored History of Saturday Night Live*. Boston: Little, Brown, 2002.

Sheed, Wilfrid. *The House that George Built, with a Little Help from Irving, Cole, and a Crew of about Fifty*. New York: Random House, 2007.

Shipman, David. *Judy Garland: The Secret Life of an American Legend*. New York: Hyperion, 1992.

Shirley, Wayne D. "The Coming of 'Deep River.'" *American Music* 15, no. 4 (winter 1997): 493–534.

Simon, George T. *The Big Bands*, rev. and enlarged ed. New York: Macmillan, 1974.

Simon, William L., editor. *Reader's Digest Popular Songs That Will Live Forever*. Pleasantville, NY: Reader's Digest Association, 1982.

Sinatra, Frank. *Everything Happens to Me*. CD 9 46116–2. Burbank, CA: Reprise Records, 1996.

Sinclair, John. *It's All Good: A John Sinclair Reader*. London: Headpress, 2009.

Singer, Barry. *Black and Blue: The Life and Lyrics of Andy Razaf*. New York: Schirmer, 1992.

Slide, Anthony. *The Encyclopedia of Vaudeville*. Westport, CT: Greenwood Press, 1994.

Smith, Ada "Bricktop," and James Haskins. *Bricktop*. New York: Atheneum, 1983.

Smith, Larry David. *Elvis Costello, Joni Mitchell, and the Torch Song Tradition*. Westport, CT: Praeger, 2004.

Sochen, June. "Fannie Brice and Sophie Tucker: Blending the Particular with the Universal." In *From Hester Street to Hollywood: The Jewish-American Stage and Screen*, edited by Sarah Blacher Cohen, 44–57. Bloomington: Indiana University Press, 1983.

Somewhere Over the Rainbow: Harold Arlen. DVD WHE73047. Directed by Don McGlynn. New York: Wellspring, 1999.

The Songwriters Collection. DVD LAN8041. New York: Wellspring Media, Lance Entertainment, 2004.

Southern, Eileen. *The Music of Black Americans: A History*. New York: W. W. Norton, 1983.

Spaeth, Sigmund. *The Facts of Life in Popular Song*. New York: Whittlesey House, McGraw-Hill, 1934.

Spaeth, Sigmund. *A History of Popular Music in America*. New York: Random House, 1948.

Strother, Rex. "Ben Light." Saxony Records. http://www.saxonyrecordcompany.com/ben-light.html (accessed March 3, 2018).

Studwell, William E. *They Also Wrote: Evaluative Essays on Lesser-Known Popular American Songwriters Prior to the Rock Era*. Lanham, MD: Scarecrow Press, 2000.

Subotnik, Rose Rosengard. "Shoddy Equipment for Living? Reconstructing the Tin Pan Alley Song." In *Musicological Identities: Essays in Honor of Susan McClary*, edited by Steven Baur, Raymond Knapp, and Jacqueline Warwick, 205–18. Aldershot, UK: Ashgate, 2008.

Surowiecki, James. *The Wisdom of Crowds: Why the Many Are Smarter than the Few and How Collective Wisdom Shapes Business, Economies, Societies, and Nations*. New York: Doubleday, 2004.

"Sweetheart of Sigma Chi." Sigma Chi Houston Alumni Chapter, 2017. http://houstonsigs.org/sweetheart-of-sigma-chi (accessed August 2, 2017).

"The Sweetheart of Sigma Chi Michigan Historical Marker." Albion, Michigan website, 2017. http://www.albionmich.com/history/markers/amark08.htm (accessed August 2, 2017).

Tawa, Nicholas E. *The Way to Tin Pan Alley: American Popular Song, 1866–1910*. New York: Schirmer Books, 1990.

Tomlin, Pinky. *The Object of My Affection*. Norman: University of Oklahoma Press, 1981.

"The Torch Song Sinatra." Sinatra Family Forum, 2004. http://sinatrafamily.com/forum/showthread.php/25356-The-Torch-Song-Sinatra (accessed July 8, 2015).

Tormé, Mel. *My Singing Teachers: Reflections on Singing Popular Music*. New York: Oxford University Press, 1994.

Tuchman, Barbara W. *A Distant Mirror: The Calamitous Fourteenth Century*. New York: Ballantine, 1978.

Tucker, Sophie. *Some of These Days*, with Dorothy Giles. Sophie Tucker (self-published), 1945.

Tyler, Don. *Hit Parade: An Encyclopedia of the Top Songs of the Jazz, Depression, Swing, and Sing Eras*. New York: Quill, William Morrow, 1985.

Tyler, Don. *Music of the First World War*. Santa Barbara, CA: Greenwood, 2016.

Uglow, Jennifer S. *The Lunar Men: Five Friends Whose Curiosity Changed the World*. New York: Farrar, Straus and Giroux, 2002.

Vachè, Warren W. *The Unsung Songwriters: America's Masters of Melody*. Lanham, MD: Scarecrow Press, 2000.

Vallee, Rudy. *Vagabond Dreams Come True*. New York: Grosset and Dunlap, 1930.

Van der Merwe, Peter. *Origins of the Popular Style: The Antecedents of Twentieth-Century Popular Music*. Oxford: Clarendon Press, [1989] 1992.

Waters, Ethel. *His Eye Is on the Sparrow*. New York: Jove/HBJ, [1950] 1978.

Whitburn, Joel. *Pop Memories, 1890–1954: The History of American Popular Music*. Menomonee Falls, WI: Record Research, 1986.

Whitcomb, Ian. *After the Ball: Pop Music from Rag to Rock*. New York: Proscenium, 1986, reprint of Penguin Press, 1972.

Whitcomb, Ian. "Introduction: The Coming of the Crooners." In *The Rise of the Crooners*, by Michael Pitts and Frank Hoffman, 1–50. Lanham, MD: Scarecrow Press, 2002.

Whitcomb, Ian. *Irving Berlin and Ragtime America*. New York: Limelight Editions, 1988.

White, Mark. *"You Must Remember This . . .": Popular Songwriters 1900–1980*, foreword by David Jacobs. New York: Charles Scribner's Sons, 1985.

Wilder, Alec. *American Popular Song: The Great Innovators, 1900–1950*. London: Oxford University Press, 1972.

Wilentz, Sean, and Greil Marcus, editors. *The Rose and the Briar: Death, Love and Liberty in the American Ballad*. New York: W. W. Norton, 2005.

Wilk, Max. *Memory Lane: The Golden Age of American Popular Music, 1890–1925*. New York: Ballantine, 1973.

Wilk, Max. *They're Playing Our Song*. New York: Atheneum, 1973.

Winer, Deborah Grace. *On the Sunny Side of the Street: The Life and Lyrics of Dorothy Fields*. New York: Schirmer Books, 1997.

Winfield, Pamela. *Melancholy Baby: The Unplanned Consequences of the G.I.s' Arrival in Europe for World War II*. Westport, CT: Bergin and Garvey, 2000.

Witmark, Isidore, and Isaac Goldberg. *From Ragtime to Swingtime: The Story of The House of Witmark*. New York: Lee Furman, 1939.

Wondrich, David. *Stomp and Swerve: American Music Gets Hot, 1843–1924*. Chicago: Chicago Review Press, A Cappella, 2003.

Woollcott, Alexander. *The Story of Irving Berlin*. New York: G. P. Putnam's Sons, 1925.

Wormser, Baron. "Melancholy Baby." In *Blues for Bill: A Tribute to William Matthews*, edited by Kurt Brown et al., 80–81. Akron, OH: University of Akron Press, 2005.

Wyatt, Ken. "Peek Through Time: Albion College's Sigma Chi fraternity's song 'The Sweetheart of Sigma Chi' Turns 100." MLive, 2017. http://www.mlive.com/living/jackson/index.ssf/2011/10/peek_through_time_albion_colle.html (accessed August 2, 2017).

Yanow, Scott. *Jazz on Record: The First Sixty Years*. San Francisco: Backbeat, 2003.

Yunqué, Edgardo Vega. *No Matter How Much You Promise to Cook or Pay the Rent You Blew It Cauze Bill Bailey Ain't Never Coming Home Again*. New York: Farrar, Straus and Giroux, 2003.

POPULAR PERIODICALS BIBLIOGRAPHY

Abbott, John. "Fifty Years of Tin Pan Alley: Close Anglo-U. S. Ties on Pop Tunes." *Variety*, January 3, 1951, 221.

Abdul, Raoul. "Musical Gems North of the Border." *New York Amsterdam News*, September 10–16, 2009, 25.

Advertisement, "Alabam's Sing-Copated Star." *New York Times*, March 9, 1926, 20.

Advertisement, American Music Hall. *Chicago Tribune*, December 18, 1910, B2.

Advertisement, Bartlett Music. *Los Angeles Times*, August 28, 1917, 13.

Advertisement, Berlin and Snyder. *Variety*, January 11, 1918, 29.

Advertisement, Billie Montgomery and George Perry. *Variety*, October 27, 1916, 32.

Advertisement, Campbell, Connelly Publishers. *Stage*, January 26, 1928, 7.

Advertisement, "The Chas. K. Harris Courier." *Variety*, October 2, 1909, 21.

Advertisement, The Chateau. *Chicago Daily Tribune*, July 11, 1920, F2.

Advertisement, DeSylva, Brown and Henderson Publishers. *Variety*, November 21, 1928, 33.

Advertisement, E. B. Marks Music. *Variety*, November 10, 1937, 43.

Advertisement, Eddie Leonard. *Variety*, March 19, 1910, 40.

Advertisement, "I Hate to Lose You." *Stage*, October 26, 1923, 5.

Advertisement, *I Love You*. *Observer*, September 28, 1913, 9.

Advertisement, Imperial Motion Pictures. *Variety*, June 5, 1914, 21.

Advertisement, Kendis and Brockman. *Variety*, December 28, 1917, 33.

Advertisement, "Lyon and Healy Draw Your Attention to These Victor Records." *Chicago Tribune*, January 6, 1919, 8.

Advertisement, "MGM List of Hits." *Billboard*, September 23, 1950, 22.

Advertisement, "Representative Artists." *Variety*, January 21, 1911, 34.

Advertisement, "Representative Artists." *Variety*, February 4, 1911, 34.

Advertisement, Sans Souci Park. *Chicago Daily Tribune*, June 24, 1911, 11.

Advertisement, "Six Parodies." *Billboard*, May 3, 1913, 34.

Advertisement, Victor Records. *Variety*, October 29, 1924, 47.

Advertisement, Waterson, Berlin and Snyder Co. *Variety*, February 22, 1923, 48.

Albom, Mitch. "Four a.m. Closing Time Won't Make Us Chic." *Detroit Free Press*, October 6, 2013, A15.

"'Alex' Clicks Again." *Variety*, August 31, 1938.

"Amusement Events of the Week in Big American Cities: Buffalo, N.Y." *Billboard*, January 25, 1913, 18, 52.

"Amusement Machines: Here's a Tune Inspired by a Music Merchant." *Billboard*, July 22, 1939, 72.

"Archie Fletcher Assumes Some Troubles Along with Morris Music Co." *Variety*, November 28, 1938, 39.

"Art Landry and His Call of the North Orchestra." *The Talking Machine World*, September 15, 1923, 188.

"ASCAP's No. 1 Love Songs." *Billboard*, February 26, 2000, 56.

Atkinson, Brooks. "King of the Singing Fools." *New York Times*, March 18, 1931, 33.

Babcock, Muriel. "'Torch Song' Defined: Text, Tunes May Differ—It Is Mood of Singer That Counts, Says Mayo Methol." *Los Angeles Times*, February 8, 1931, B11.

"Battle of the Hand Organs." *New York Times*, March 27, 1904, SM2.

"Beer Shower for a Singer." *Chicago Daily Tribune*, December 19, 1902, 2.

Bell, Nelson. "The New Week's Bills." *Washington Post*, April 29, 1929, 14.

"Ben Light Dead, Songwriter, 72." *New York Times*, January 9, 1965, 25.

"Berlin Humming Lohengrin Now." Unidentified, undated clipping [1911?]. Library of Congress, Irving Berlin Collection, reel one.

Berlin, Irving, and Justus Dickinson. "Love Interest as a Commodity." *Green Book Magazine* (April 1916). Quoted in Goldberg, *Tin Pan Alley*, 220.

"Berlin-Mackay Engagement Denied." *New York Times*, June 11, 1925, 14.

"B. F. Keith's." *Billboard*, November 17, 1913, 11, 55.

"Big Sellers in West." *Variety*, November 11, 1925, 45.

"The *Billboard* Second Annual Music Record Poll." *Billboard*, January 3, 1948, 10–11.

"The Billboard's Song Hints." *Billboard*, July 25, 1914, 12.

"Black Tin Pan Alley Composer Shelton Brooks Finally Gets Paid." *Jet*, November 29, 1951. Posted by vieilles annonces, Flickr, October 15, 2012. http://www.flickr.com/photos/vieilles_annonc es/8092148455/in/photostream/ (accessed February 23, 2013).

"Brother Against Brother." *Variety*, August 13, 1910, 8.

Budwin, Bud. "Times Square: Chatter—Spokane." *Variety*, April 12, 1932, 44.

Calhoun, Lucy. "Musical, Instead of Noise-Making, Toys Urged for Children." *Chicago Tribune*, September 4, 1919, 19.

"Catchy Song Is Stars' Highway to Fame." *Washington Post*, July 5, 1936, AA3.

"Chatter: Broadway." *Variety*, March 1, 1939, 53.

"Chicago Amusements." *Billboard*, February 13, 1909, 7.

"Chicago Music Notes." *Billboard*, February 5, 1910, 9.

"Chicago Music Notes." *Billboard*, July 30, 1910, 41.

"Chicago Music Notes." *Billboard*, November 12, 1910, 17.

"Chicago: Music Publisher's Notes." *Billboard*, November 18, 1906, 4.

"Chiswick Fire Matinee." *Stage*, September 18, 1913, 18.

"Clarke's N. Y. to L. A. Shuttle for Pix, Radio." *Variety*, June 19, 1946, 30.

Cobb, Will D. "The Business of Song Writing." *Variety*, December 16, 1905, 4.

"Cold Type Review." *Billboard*, January 19, 1918, 14.

"Cold Type Review." *Variety*, February 2, 1918, 16.

"Collides with a Schooner." *Urbana Courier*, July 23, 1907, 2.

"Color Camera Takes a Place Beside Talkies." *Chicago Daily Tribune*, September 15, 1929, G1.

"Coming Radio Events Cast Their Shadows." *New York Times*, October 11, 1925, XX18.

"Concerts Behind the Line." *Manchester Guardian*, December 2, 1939, 10.

Corb. "House Review: Keith's, Indpls." *Variety*, August 11, 1943, 23.

"Correspondence." *Variety*, May 9, 1913, 31.

"Correspondence: Chicago: Wilson." *Variety*, June 20, 1913, 20–21.

"Cox Puts One Over." *Billboard*, October 28, 1916, 12.

Craig. "House Review: Capitol, Wash." *Variety*, September 11, 1940, 41.

"Credit for Records." *Billboard*, August 7, 1943, 72.

Day, Edward C. "Denver." *Variety*, May 16, 1919, 36.

"Denver Too Small." *New York Clipper*, May 10, 1913, 12.

"Down, Not Out." *Washington Post*, July 5, 1936, AA6.

"Descriptive Review: Melancholy." *The Player*, June 6, 1913, 10.

"Diary of the Week." *Observer*, September 7, 1913, 5.

"Dudleigh Vernor, Composed 'Sweetheart of Sigma Chi.'" *New York Times*, April 25, 1974, 42.

"E. B. Marks Loses Two Appeals on Song Suits Vs. Jerry Vogel, Vogel Loses One Against Marks." *Billboard*, February 5, 1944, 20.

"Eddie Jackson, Sidekick to Durante, Dies of Stroke." *Chicago Tribune*, July 17, 1980, B15.

Editor of *Musical Express*. "Songs, Sex and Susceptibility." *Accordion Times and Musical Express*, October 11, 1946, 2.

"Editorial Comment." *Billboard*, September 28, 1918, 28.

"Edward Abeles Retires from Cast." *Billboard*, January 22, 1910, 17.

E. E. S. "Alma Keller and Helene Dare." *Billboard*, May 21, 1927.

Eigan, Jack. "Jack Eigan Speaking." *Chicago Daily Tribune*, August 22, 1959, S13.

"Engage Western Composer." *Variety*, August 12, 1911, 9.

"English Song Decision." *Variety*, November 7, 1914, 6.

"Every Dream Has Its Meaning." *New York Times*, May 12, 1912, MS3.

"The Exhibitor Has His Say." *Boxoffice*, October 30, 1948, A3.

"Faded Love Letters." *Billboard*, September 9, 1922, 41.

"Famous Stars Sing First Time by Radio to 6,000,000 People." *New York Times*, January 2, 1925, 1.

"Fanny Brice." *Variety*, July 27, 1913, 20.

"F. B. Haviland Dies; Music Publisher." *New York Times*, March 31, 1932, 21.

Feather, Leonard. "Month at Flamingo: B. B. King Opens in Vegas." *Los Angeles Times*, December 13, 1971, G23.

"The Final Curtain." *Billboard*, April 17, 1937, 35.

"First L. A. Date in 23 Years: Horn, Jazz Career, Classical Roots." *Los Angeles Times*, May 9, 1987, E3.

Fliesler, Joseph R. "Song Hits of 1936." *ASCAP Journal* 1, no. 2 (November 1937): 3.

"Football and Symphonies on Air." *Los Angeles Times*, December 3, 1932, 12.

"Fragson's Father Dead." *New York Times*, February 18, 1914.

"Fragson Wants to Try." *Variety*, December 19, 1913, 23.

"Fragson Shot." *Stage*, January 1, 1914, 35.

"Gaby Deslys Dies after Operation." *New York Times*, February 12, 1920, 11.

"Gaby's Party Sailing." *Variety*, April 25, 1913, 11.

Gardner, Bradford. "Why You Sing the Songs You Do." *Los Angeles Times*, March 12, 1933, F3, 20.

"G. B. S. on Mrs. Pat's Phonetics." *New York Times*, May 10, 1914, X5.

"German Women Weep at Going of Kind Yanks." *Chicago Daily Tribune*, May 22, 1919, 1.

"Gold in Them Thar Old Wax Sends Diskeries Stampeding to Re-Cuts, Even for Albums." *Billboard*, March 15, 1947, 15, 31.

"A Good Bill." *Billboard*, October 18, 1913, 13.

"The Good Samaritan Performance." *Stage*, October 16, 1913, 20.

Gopnick, Adam. "The Outside Game." *New Yorker*, January 12, 2015, n.p.

"Grace La Rue a Star in London." *Billboard*, December 27, 1913, 63.

Graffis, Herb. "Last of the Minstrels." *Esquire*, May 1946.

"Gray Rains Leads." *Variety*, June 10, 1942, 42.

"Great Northern Hippodrome." *Billboard*, August 30, 1913.

Green, Abel. "Broadway to Hollywood." *Variety*, February 15, 1956, 2.

Green, Abel. "Jolson Tees Off Big as One-Man Show on Tour of Army Camps." *Variety*, January 28, 1942, 3, 53.

Green, Abel. "Second Takes." *Variety*, September 26, 1945, 57.

Green, Abel. "*Variety* All-Time Pop Standards." *Variety*, January 10, 1962, 185.

Green, Abel. "Vaude-Night-Clubs: Nitery Followup." *Variety*, October 11, 1939, 50.

Greenbaum, Lucy. "Shortage of Girls Big Worry of USO." *New York Times*, May 15, 1942, 10.

Gregory, John. "How It Was During the Bill Bailey Era." *Los Angeles Times*, July 22, 1973, I1.

Gregory, Pearl, as told to Walt Harrington. "When Life Was a Bicycle Built for Two." *Washington Post*, April 3, 1986, SM18–19, 21, 38.

Gross, Gerald G. "*Broadway Melody of 1938* Is Good, Gay and Tuneful." *Washington Post*, August 21, 1937, 22.

Gross, Gerald G. "Singing Torch Song of Yesteryear, Judy Garland Scores Mightily in *Broadway Melody of 1938*." *Washington Post*, August 18, 1937, 16.

Haber, Joyce. "Eight Notes to Immortality." *Los Angeles Times*, August 18, 1974, O21.

Halligan, Bill. "The Hotel Stakes." *Variety*, January 3, 1945, 149.

"Halligan Has to Quit Paris." *New York Clipper*, May 17, 1922, 7.

Hammond, Percy. "Mr. Jolson's Plea for American Songs." *Chicago Daily Tribune*, January 21, 1917, C1.

Hammond, Percy. "The Theaters." *Chicago Daily Tribune*, February 15, 1920, E1.

"Harris Estate, Marks, Vogel in Dispute On 'Kissing Her Now' Tune." *Variety*, September 14, 1938, 41.

"Harry James." *Billboard*, July 18, 1942, 4.

Hart, Moss. "The Saga of Gertie." *New York Times*, March 2, 1941, X1.

Henry, Bill. "By the Way." *Los Angeles Times*, May 19, 1942, A1.

Henry, Bill. "A Window on Washington." *Los Angeles Times*, January 31, 1961, B1.

"'Here Comes the Bride'—Torch Singer Marries." *Washington Post*, November 16, 1940, 3.

Hill, W. E. "Bathroom Songsters." *Chicago Tribune*, October 9, 1927.

Hill, W. E. "Musical Americans." *Chicago Daily Tribune*, July 17, 1938, F9.

Hill, W. E. "Old Fashioned Waltz." *Los Angeles Times*, December 1, 1935, I10.

Holden, Stephen. "Cabaret: Joys and Sorrows of Life, From Funny to Personal." *New York Times*, March 12, 1996, C14.

Hopper, Hedda. "The Comeback Kid: Veteran Actor-Singer Tony Martin." *Chicago Daily Tribune*, April 24, 1955, H34.

Hopper, Hedda. "Screen: Hedda Hopper's Hollywood." *Los Angeles Times*, October 16, 1939, 9.

"House Review: Circle, Indpls." *Variety*, June 30, 1943, 46.

"How Fragson Was Killed." *Manchester Guardian*, January 1, 1914, 7.

Howard, Maude Nooks. "Black Mammy's Apotheosis." *New York Times*, January 28, 1923, XX6.

Hume, Paul. "New York Report: From Pengo to Ella to 'Ariadne,' Too." *Washington Post, Times Herald*, February 10, 1963, G1.

Humphrey, Harold. "Talent and Tunes on Music Machines: Release Prevues." *Billboard*, June 14, 1941, 71.

Humphrey, Harold. "Miller Three-Time Champ." *Billboard*, April 25, 1942, 3, 19, 21.

"H'wood Cavalcade-Minded: Old Songs Take on New Values." *Variety*, August 17, 1938, 1.

"Ill and Injured." *Variety*, October 22, 1924, 5.

"In Big Time Vaudeville Around Greater New York." *The Player*, September 26, 1913, 8.

"In Big Time Vaudeville Around New York." *New York Clipper*, November 7, 1913, 7.

"Influence of Mind on Body." *Washington Post*, March 5, 1911, MS3.

"In Person Contrasts: Perry Likes to Sing; Dean Has a Comedy Fling." *Billboard*, September 19, 1970, 50.

"In Publisher's Row." *Billboard*, January 14, 1911, 13.

"In Publisher's Row: Brother-Against-Brother War of Will and Harold Rossiter Carried to Eastern Battleground with New Phase of Brotherly Hatred Seldom Encountered in History." *Billboard*, December 7, 1912, 16.

"In Publisher's Row: Harold Rossiter News." *Billboard*, October 14, 1911, 12.

"Inside Stuff." *Variety*, December 21, 1927, 53.

"Inside Stuff—Music." *Variety*, November 23, 1938, 38.

"Inside Stuff—Music." *Variety*, February 28, 1940, 32.

"Inside Stuff: Orchestras." *Variety*, June 16, 1943, 38.

"Inside Stuff: Waring's Version of Sigma Chi." *Variety*, June 8, 1927, 46.

"In the Wake of the News—Do You Remember 'Way Back When.'" *Chicago Tribune*, December 20, 1920, 21.

"Irving Berlin and Modern Ragtime." For "the *Mirror*," ca. December 1913. Unidentified, undated clipping. Irving Berlin Collection, Library of Congress, reel one.

"Irving Berlin Engaged." *Variety*, November 18, 1911, 3.

"Is an Only Son a Menace to Society? This Doctor Says He Is." *New York Times*, September 8, 1912, SM12.

"James Started in Circus." *Billboard*, April 3, 1943, 63.

"January's Six Best Sellers." *Variety*, January 27, 1922, 3.

Jerome, William. "The Evolution of Song Writing." *Billboard*, December 16, 1916, 46–47, 168.

"Jimmy Monaco and Joe McCarthy Put Over a New One." *New York Clipper*, May 10, 1913, 12.

"Joe Howard's Film Biog." *Variety*, May 23, 1945, 1.

Josephs, Jack. "San Francisco: Orpheum." *Variety*, July 4, 1919, 17.

"Judy Garland Draws Record 15,000 Patrons to Philly Dell Concert." *Variety*, July 7, 1943, 2.

"Juvenile Operetta at Gonzaga Hall." *Washington Post*, November 26, 1902, 10.

"Keith's Union Square." *Billboard*, February 15, 1913, 10.

Kendall, Read. "Around and About in Hollywood." *Los Angeles Times*, January 9, 1937, A7.

Kingsley, Grace. "Personal Grief and Dramatic Talent Blend in Portrayal of Actress in 'Copperhead.'" *Los Angeles Times*, March 21, 1926, 23.

Krisler, E. E. "People in the Films." *Picturegoer*, January 8, 1938, 21–22.

Krushen, Mori. "Joe E. Howard, Troubador at 73, Has Been Around Show Biz Sixty Years." *Variety*, January 7, 1942, 156–57.

Larrabee, Donald R. "College Rhythm." *Variety*, December 24, 1941, 36.

"Law Report: Song Copyright Case." *Observer*, October 18, 1914, 11.

Leighton, Frank, and Bert Leighton. "Origin of 'Blues' (or Jazz)." *Variety*, January 6, 1922, 27.

"Leo Friedman Changes Quarters." *Billboard*, May 13, 1911, 19, 61.

"Leo Friedman Dies." *Variety*, March 9, 1927, 46.

Leonard, Will. "On the Town: Improved Haymes-Jeffries Act." *Chicago Daily Tribune*, December 3, 1961, D14.

Leonard, Will. "On the Town: Talented Pros + Talented Kids = a Great Show." *Chicago Tribune*, February 18, 1968, G12.

Leonard, Will. "On the Town: Valiant Valkyrie." *Chicago Tribune*, January 31, 1954, F8.

Leonard, Will. "Playboy's Action Faction Lives Up to Its Name." *Chicago Tribune*, February 21, 1971, E5.

Leonard, William. "Ethel Merman Returning, But to Empire Room." *Chicago Tribune*, February 25, 1968, F9.

"A Line o' Type or Two." *Chicago Daily Tribune*, September 5, 1935, 16.

"A Line o' Type or Two." *Chicago Daily Tribune*, September 11, 1935, 12.

"A Line o' Type or Two: Bad Man." *Chicago Tribune*, February 24, 1964, 14.

"Lion and Serpent. Weighing One's Words." *Los Angeles Times*, September 24, 1917, II4.

Litwak, Leo E. "A Fantasy That Paid Off." *New York Times*, June 27, 1965, SM22.

"London Fails to Fall for Grace La Rue's Temperamental Spasm." *Chicago Daily Tribune*, December 14, 1913, G9.

"London News Letter." *Billboard*, May 10, 1913, 17.

"London News Letter." *Billboard*, January 31, 1914, 19.

"London Review: Palace Theatre." *Billboard*, March 29, 1913, 13, 60.

"'Made Me Love You' Platterbug's Delight." *Variety*, February 18, 1942, 3.

Magida, Phyllis. "A Song for Your Sweetheart." *Chicago Tribune*, February 5, 1988, F16.

"Man Is Divine, Says Rector in Sermon." *Washington Post*, August 14, 1922, 5.

"Manchester." *Stage*, December 4, 1913, 29.

Mantle, Burns. "News of the Theaters." *Chicago Daily Tribune*, February 24, 1908, 6.

"Marilyn Chandler of Monroeville Recreates the Past and Writes About." *Pittsburgh Post-Gazette*, August 1, 1996, VN-4.

"Martha Raye, 'Newest Find.'" *Los Angeles Times*, July 28, 1936, 13.

"Medicine Show Notes." *Billboard*, January 18, 1913, 21.

"Melody Mart Notes." *Billboard*, March 15, 1930, 27.

Miller, George. "Cool Climate." *Philadelphia Daily News*, June 4, 1992, 5.

"Mills Brothers Breast the Changing Times." *Asbury Park Press*, September 28, 1975, 41.

Milstein, Gilbert. "Jazz Temple on Times Square." *New York Times*, November 29, 1953, SM25.

"Monaco-Burke's Crosby." *Variety*, September 1, 1937, 48.

Morris, Ruth. "Uncommon Chatter." *Variety*, November 10, 1931, 48.

"Mothers of Married Sons." *New York Times*, August 14, 1911, 6.

"Mrs. Irving Berlin Dead." *Billboard*, July 27, 1912, 4.

Murray, Jim. "A Place to Ponder." *Los Angeles Times*, July 12, 1962, B1.

"Music." *Billboard*, January 22, 1910, 16.

"Music." *Chicago Daily Tribune*, December 22, 1872, 7.

"Music: Bands and Orchestras." *Variety*, July 16, 1924, 33, 38.

"Music Business Good and Normal: Plenty of Sellers, Pop and Show." *Variety*, March 10, 1926, 43.

"Music: Famous Names' Famous Songs." *Variety*, October 7, 1942, 72.

"Music in the News." *Billboard*, April 17, 1943, 59.

"Music News: New York City." *Billboard*, April 10, 1937, 18.

"Music: Theme Songs and Song Cycles." *Variety*, January 4, 1956, 356.

"Network Plugs, 8 a.m. to 1 a.m." *Variety*, October 12, 1938, 38.

"New Acts: Betty Jo Baxter." *Variety*, May 13, 1959, 70.

"New Acts Next Week: Rene Parker." *Variety*, January 24, 1913, 19.

"New Acts This Week: Tommy Lyman." *Variety*, April 22, 1921, 18.

"New Girl Trio to Make Debut on Steelmakers." *Chicago Daily Tribune*, May 25, 1941, NW4.

"New Music Firm Starts." *New York Clipper*, November 9, 1921, 18.

"New Songwriting Team." *Billboard*, February 26, 1916, 12.

"New Turns and Returns." *Billboard*, October 14, 1922, 119.

"New York Music Notes." *Billboard*, June 26, 1909, 9.

"Night Club Reviews." *Variety*, May 15, 1935, 48.

"Night Club Reviews: 500 Club, Atlantic City." *Variety*, August 31, 1955, 53.

"Night Club Reviews: Bagatelle, London." *Variety*, June 25, 1958, 70.

"Night Club Reviews: Bowery Café, Detroit." *Variety*, July 13, 1940, 20.

"Night Club Reviews: Copacabana, N.Y." *Variety*, September 19, 1962, 58.

"Night Club Reviews: Desert Inn, Las Vegas." *Variety*, July 16, 1952, 117.

"Night Club Reviews: Fire Station House, Garden Grove, Cal." *Variety*, August 23, 1967, 81.

"Night Club Reviews: New Frontier, Las Vegas." *Variety*, June 29, 1955, 53.

"Night Club Reviews: New Frontier, Las Vegas." *Variety*, August 29, 1956, 53.

"Night Club Reviews: Olympic Hotel, Seattle (Georgian Room)." *Variety*, April 25, 1951, 54.

"Night Club Reviews: Riviera, Las Vegas." *Variety*, February 16, 1983, 119.

"Night Clubs: Torch Songs." *Variety*, September 25, 1934, 48.

"North American Cabaret." *Billboard*, September 7, 1913, 13.

"Norton in Arizona." *New York Clipper*, August 30, 1922, 18.

"Notes of the Trade." *The Player*, April 25, 1913, 11.

Nye, Carroll. "Ruth Etting Scorns 'Dance Band Cuties.'" *Los Angeles Times*, September 22, 1935, A6.

Nye, Myra. "Society of Cinemaland." *Los Angeles Times*, January 27, 1929, C27.

"Obituaries." *Variety*, February 11, 1942, 46.

O'Brien, Richard B. "Crooners in the Spotlight as Year Nears an End." *New York Times*, December 6, 1931, XX29.

"Old Song Paying Royalties to Matron." *Los Angeles Times*, February 18, 1940, 6.

"Old Songs for New Disks." *Variety*, July 28, 1922, 1, 7.

"On the Stand." *Billboard*, June 20, 1942, 20.

"Orlob Doesn't Want 'Kissing' Coin, Only Co-Authorship Credit." *Variety*, May 26, 1941, 35.

Orodenker, M. H. "Music Reviews: On the Records." *Billboard*, November 29, 1941, 10.

Orodenker, M. H. "On the Records." *Billboard*, August 30, 1941, 13.

"Palace, Chicago, Reviewed Monday Matinee, November 15." *Billboard*, November 20, 1920, 9.

"Palace, New York." *Billboard*, October 7, 1922, 14.

Parrott, Jennings. "Apron Strings Entangled in Red Tape." *Los Angeles Times*, April 12, 1976, B2.

"'Partners' No. 1 for Second Week." October 15, 1938, 10.

"Pat Chat." *New York Clipper*, January 11, 1913, 12.

"Playing with Gaby." *Variety*, August 29, 1913, 4.

"Plays on Broadway: Follies." *Variety*, July 7, 1931, 54.

"Portland, Ore." *Variety*, July 2, 1910, 148.

"Protecting Songs for Week." *Billboard*, August 30, 1913, 16.

Provines, June. "A Line o' Type or Two." *Chicago Daily Tribune*, May 12, 1938, 12.

"Publishers' Song Notes." *Stage*, March 12, 1936, 11.

"Publishers' Song Notes." *Stage*, March 26, 1936, 6.

"Publishers' Song Notes." *Stage*, January 7, 1937, 6.

"Radio Waves and Ripples." *Washington Post*, November 18, 1933, 10.

"Ray Samuels in *Express*." *Variety*, August 15, 1913, 11.

"Recommended Disk Records." *Variety*, November 16, 1927, 42.

"Record Buying Guide: The Week's Best Releases." *Billboard*, August 14, 1943, 66.

"Record Reviews." *Billboard*, January 7, 1950, 80.

"Rene Parker Scores." *Variety*, February 21, 1913, 21.

Revell, Nellie. "Remarks at Random." *Variety*, April 25, 1928, 49.

"Review of Records." *Billboard*, November 13, 1937, 18.

"Reviews and Ratings of New Albums." *Billboard*, April 7, 1956, 24.

"Reviews and Ratings of New Albums." *Billboard*, January 12, 1957, 26.

"Reviews of Recording Discs." *Variety*, April 21, 1922, 7, 28.

Rich, Frank. "Revue: *Tintypes* Scrapbook of Nostalgia." *New York Times*, October 24, 1980, C3.

Robbins, Richard. "'Bill Bailey, Won't You Please' . . . Composer's Star Twinkled a Century Ago." *Tribune-Review*, May 13, 2001, Focus section 2–3, 10.

"Rosenbaum in Chicago." *Billboard*, December 8, 1917, 15.

"Ruth Etting Dies at Eighty-One Following Long Illness." *Boxoffice*, October 9, 1978, 93.

Samuel, O. M. "New Orleans." *Variety*, March 10, 1916, 38.

Samuel, O. M. "New Orleans." *Variety*, September 15, 1916, 47.

Santosuosso, Ernie. "Shearing Busy as Ever." *Boston Globe*, March 7, 1986, 33.

"Science Discovers Reality of Dreams." *New York Times*, May 8, 1910, SM14.

Scott, Helen Frances. "Berceuse." *Los Angeles Times*, May 21, 1924, A4.

"Season Good for Francis, Day and Hunter." *Billboard*, April 4, 1908, 17.

"Servicemen's Music Tastes Are Typical; James, Miller, Dorsey Favorites; Like Many Oldies, Too." *Billboard*, January 30, 1943, 60.

Shan. "Talking Shorts: 'I Wonder Who's Kissing Her Now.'" *Variety*, December 8, 1931, 14.

"'Sigma Chi' Song Writer Dies at 81." *Los Angeles Times*, April 24, 1974, 1.

"'Sigma Chi' Songwriter F. D. Verner" [*sic*]. *Washington Post*, April 25, 1974, B7.

"Sigma Chi Sweetheart Marks 75th Birthday." *New York Times*, October 4, 1986, 6.

Silverman, Sime. "Fairman and Manion." *Variety*, November 25, 1911, 18.

Silverman, Sime. "Ruth Etting." *Variety*, June 15, 1927, 26.

Smith, Bill. "Follow-Up Review: Bill Farrell." *Billboard*, September 16, 1950, 51.

Smith, Liz. "NBC Readies Its Executive A." *Chicago Tribune*, September 26, 1976, D2.

"Society and Entertainment: Society Cabaret to Spring One of Those Imported Dances." *Chicago Herald Tribune*, June 28, 1919, 19.

"Soldiers' Disk Favorites Varied, Calif. Survey Finds." *Billboard*, November 22, 1941, 61.

"Song Heals Marital Rift." *Los Angeles Times*, June 27, 1924, A19.

"Song Hits Abroad." *Billboard*, August 16, 1913, 9.

"Song Notes." *Stage*, October 9, 1913, 26.

"Song Notes." *Stage*, October 16, 1913, 20.

"Song Notes." *Stage*, October 23, 1913, 20.

"Song Notes." *Stage*, November 6, 1913, 18.

"Song Notes." *Stage*, November 17, 1927, 4.

"Song Reviews: Melancholy." *Billboard*, July 12, 1913, 13.

"Song Reviews: You Made Me Love You." *Billboard*, May 17, 1913, 9.

"Songs Heard in New York Vaudevil [*sic*] Last Week." *Billboard*, October 11, 1913, 16.

"Songs with Largest Radio Audience." *Variety*, February 3, 1954, 50.

"Songs with Largest Radio Audience." *Variety*, March 31, 1954, 48.

"The Song World: Feist Absorbs Triangle." *Billboard*, March 16, 1918, 16.

"The Song World: Hochberg and Company." *Billboard*, September 15, 1917, 14.

"The Song World: This Week's Song of Songs." *Billboard*, June 15, 1918, 14.

"Soul Analysis and Nerves." *Washington Post*, July 18, 1911, 6.

Spelvin, George. "The Broadway Beat." *Billboard*, May 7, 1938, 5.

"Sporting Sidelights." *Washington Post*, March 26, 1908, 9.

"Star's Death Kills Disks." *Billboard*, February 7, 1942, 21.

"Stateside: Ruth Etting." *Screen International*, October 7, 1978, 6.

"Strand, New York." *Variety*, December 31, 1941, 46.

Sullivan, Dan. "*Tintypes*: Nostalgia Songbook." *Los Angeles Times*, March 20, 1981, H1.

"Suratt in New Offering." *Billboard*, February 4, 1911, 10, 50.

"'Sweetheart' Case Ended." *Variety*, April 6, 1938, 41.

"Tabloids." *Billboard*, January 1, 1921, 27.

Taylor, Bert Leston. "A Line o' Type or Two: After Life's Fitful Fever." *Chicago Daily Tribune*, October 14, 1941, 12.

"Ted Healy Returns with His 'Racketeers.'" *New York Times*, September 15, 1930, 33.

"Telecasts This Week." *New York Times*, December 31, 1939, 94.

Thayer, Mary V. R. "Sen. Kennedy Gets Two More Supporters—by Mistake." *Washington Post*, July 11, 1960, B3.

"Theron C. Bennett." *Broadcasting*, April 13, 1937, 53.

Thirer, Irene. "Cliff Edwards' Uke Placed on the Shelf Perhaps Forever." *New York Evening Post*, September 18, 1935. Clippings file for Cliff Edwards, New York Public Library for the Performing Arts.

"This Week's Chicago Vaudeville." *New York Clipper*, June 14, 1914, 9.

"Timely Tune Topics." *Billboard*, December 12, 1914, 13.

"Today's Radio Programs." *Washington Post*, August 8, 1923, 11.

"To Diplomatic Corps: First State Reception of the Season at the White House." *Washington Post*, January 9, 1903, 3.

"Tokyo's 920 Club." *Broadcasting, Broadcast Advertising*, April 24, 1944, 70.

Trumbull, Robert. "Bill Bailey Isn't Budging." *New York Times*, September 1, 1962, 5.

"TV-Radio Programming: Wheeling and Dealing." *Billboard*, March 31, 1958, 8.

"Unlucky Year for Halligan." *New York Clipper*, May 24, 1922, 6.

"Variety Gossip." *Stage*, August 7, 1913, 14–15.

"Variety Gossip: At the Palace." *Stage*, February 13, 1919, 12.

"Variety Gossip: Welcome Home from Burma." *Stage*, June 15, 1944, 3.

"Vaudeville: Blossom Seeley Offered $3,000 by Club Alabam." *Variety*, September 21, 1927, 28.

"Vaudeville: Review of Recording Discs." *Variety*, May 19, 1922, 9, 32.

"Vaudeville Reviews: Metropolitan, Providence." *Billboard*, January 11, 1941, 22–23.

"Vaughn De Leath, Radio 'First Lady.'" *New York Times*, May 29, 1943, 13.

Vettel, Phil. "A Valentine's Day to Remember." *Chicago Tribune*, February 10, 1989, N3B.

Vine, Dave. "As I See It." *Billboard*, November 20, 1937, 30.

"The Vogue of Songs." *Billboard*, August 9, 1913, 9.

"Waltz Big in Iowa Hills." *Variety*, April 15, 1942, 39.

Warren, Patrick A. "Late Items from Chicago." *Billboard*, June 10, 1905, 11.

Whipp, Glenn. "It Is a Hell of a Thing." *Los Angeles Times*, December 4, 2014, S24.

"'Whispering Pianist' to Sing from WCAP." *Washington Post*, October 28, 1925, 12.

Whitcomb, Ian. "Shelton Brooks Is Alive and Strutting." *Los Angeles Times*, May 18, 1969, N12.

"White Rats Scamper." *Billboard*, June 7, 1913, 6.

W. H. M. "Variety Theatres." *Manchester Guardian*, December 2, 1913, 18.

"Why One Man Likes Housecleaning." *Chicago Tribune*, September 13, 1903, 42.

Wickes, E. M. "New York Notes." *Billboard*, March 26, 1927, 23.

"Will Von Tilzer Alone." *Variety*, February 14, 1913, 5.

"William Bence Co." *Variety*, January 9, 1914, 20.

Willig, John M. "*Follies* a Homecoming for Ethel Shutta." *New York Times*, November 14, 1971, D32.

Winchell, Walter. "A Primer of Broadway Slang." *Vanity Fair*, November 1927: 67, 132, 134.

"With the Music Men." *Variety*, July 21, 1922, 10.

Wolf, Rennold. "The Boy Who Revived Rag-time." *Green Book Magazine* (August 1913), 201–9. Library of Congress Irving Berlin Collection Scrapbooks, microfilm 92/20013, reel one.

Wolters, Larry. "Eighty Voice Choir to Sing 'St. Louis Blues.'" *Chicago Daily Tribune*, July 17, 1932, F4.

"*Wonder Bar* Closes, Too Much Work for Al." *Variety*, June 2, 1931, 53.

"Woman's Kidnaper [*sic*] Forces Victim to Hear Him Croon." *Los Angeles Times*, December 29, 1934, 3.

"Women Song Writers." *Chicago Daily Tribune*, November 17, 1907, G8.

"Writing of Songs Declared Great Fun by Crooner." *Los Angeles Times*, December 4, 1927, C32.

Wynn. "Union Square." *Variety*, February 7, 1913, 22.

"York and King Company Wants." *Billboard*, October 16, 1920, 27.

GENERAL INDEX

Page numbers in *italics* indicate an illustration.

SONG INDEX

ABOUT THE AUTHOR

Photo by Susan J. Carpenter

Michael G. Garber is an interdisciplinary scholar and artist of theatre, film, music, dance, media, communication, and literature. He teaches in those fields, as well as in anthropology and education, at universities throughout the New York City metropolitan area. Using his training in the Diamond Method, he leads music-making groups with people of all ages. He is a Visiting Research Fellow of both the University of London, Goldsmiths, Pinter Centre for Research in Performance and Creative Writing and the University of Winchester Department of Performing Arts; and an International Visiting Scholar Affiliate of the University of Kansas Department of Theater and Dance.

He can be contacted through his website: www.michaelggarber.com.

Supporting materials for this book can be found at www.michaelggarber .com/firstballadsofthegreatamericansongbook and the YouTube channel The First Ballads of the Great American Songbook.